SOLIDARITY ECONOMY: BUILDING ALTERNATIVES FOR PEOPLE AND PLANET

PAPERS AND REPORTS FROM THE U.S. SOCIAL FORUM 2007

Edited by Jenna Allard, Carl Davidson, and Julie Matthaei

ChangeMaker Publications
Chicago IL USA

ORDERING INFORMATION

For individual copies, order online from ChangeMaker Publications, Chicago IL USA, www.lulu.com/changemaker

For bulk orders, special discounts may be available. Contact Germai Medhanie at Guramylay: Growing the Green Economy, germai@growingthegreeneconomy.org, 617-868-6133.

For college textbook orders, or orders by U.S. trade bookstores and wholesalers contact Germai Medhanie at Guramylay: Growing the Green Economy, germai@growingthegreeneconomy.org, 617-868-6133.

Printed in the United States of America

ISBN 978-0-6151-9489-9

Globe Cover Graphic:
Tiffany Sankary, www.movementbuilding.org/tiffany
Cover Design: Carl Davidson

To Father Jose Maria Arizmendi (1915-1976)
who thought deeply, put human solidarity first,
made tools our servants rather than the reverse,
and together with his students,
brought the Mondragon cooperatives into this world,
to blaze a path forward

To Alice Lovelace
and the other organizers of the U.S. Social Forum 2007
for making this all possible

To the U.S. Solidarity Economy Network,
may it thrive and grow

And to the second superpower
the millions of people around the globe
who are bringing about a better world for us all

About Our Editors

Jenna Allard is an editor of TransformationCentral.org, and works for Guramylay: Growing the Green Economy. She is also part of the Coordinating Committee for the U.S. Solidarity Economy Network. She graduated from Wellesley College with a B.A. in Political Science and Peace and Justice Studies. She was excited to be part of the first U.S. Social Forum, and spent most of her time there behind the single eye of a camera lens, recording workshops in the solidarity economy track and the caucuses. She has been passionate about studying and experiencing the solidarity economy ever since she traveled to Brazil and visited a small women's handicraft cooperative in an informal community on the outskirts of Rio de Janeiro.

Carl Davidson writes on the social theory of globalization–*CyberRadicalism: A New Left for a Global Age'* with Jerry Harris. He is publisher and editor of Changemaker Publications, and a founder of the Global Studies Association, North America. Carl is also an IT consultant and webmaster for the U.S. Solidarity Economy Network and SolidarityEconomy.net, as well as a national steering committee member of United for Peace and Justice and a national committee member of the Committees of Correspondence for Democracy and Socialism. He was a writer and news editor for many years for *The Guardian* newsweekly, New York City. Carl is also prominent in the community technology movement—as a founding national board member of the Community Technology Center Network (CTCNet), as a technical skills trainer for ex-offenders with the Prison Action Committee, and as school technology specialist for the Small Schools Workshop. He was on the design team for Austin Polytechnical Academy, a new high school in Chicago. In the 1960s, he was a national secretary of Students for a Democratic Society, a freedom marcher in Mississippi, and a national leader of the Vietnam-era antiwar movement. His academic work in the 1960s was in philosophy, which he studied and taught at Penn State University and the University of Nebraska.

Julie Matthaei is an economist who has spent over thirty years studying U.S. economic history and the current forces for positive economic transformation. Active in the anti-Vietnam-war, ecology, and feminist movements while an undergraduate at Stanford, Julie went on to study economics at Yale University, receiving her Ph.D. in Economics in 1978. A professor of economics at Wellesley College, she is the author of *An Economic History of Women in America* (1982); of *Race, Gender and Work: A Multicultural Economic History of Women in the U.S.* (1991 and 1996), with Teresa Amott; and of articles in *The Review of Radical Political Economics, Feminist Economics,* and other progressive journals and collections. For the last ten years, Julie has shifted her research focus to the present economic historical conjuncture and possible ways forward, and is writing a book with Barbara Brandt on *The Transformative Moment.* A big fan of (and participant in) the Social Forum movement, she was a member of the Working Group for the US Social Forum which planned the caucuses and sessions which are documented in this book. She is currently Co-Director of Guramylay: Growing the Green Economy, and a member of the US Solidarity Economy Network Coordinating Committee.

Contents

III. BUILDING THE SOLIDARITY ECONOMY THROUGH SOCIAL MOVEMENTS

IV. BUILDING THE SOLIDARITY ECONOMY THROUGH COOPERATIVES AND SOCIALLY RESPONSIBLE BUSINESS

Acknowledgments

Solidarity Economy represents the combined creative energies of many, many committed, co-creative, progressive people, groups, and movements. In a way it is a remarkable example of the solidarity economy in action.

First, this book represents the energies, process, and "Another World is Possible" vision of the vibrant World Social Forum movement, as expressed by the organizers of the US Social Forum 2007. This dedicated group, most of them volunteers -- led by Alice Lovelace, an amazing woman in all respects -- made the US Social Forum, and hence this book, happen. They circulated the following call for participation:

> The US Social Forum is more than a conference, more than a networking bonanza, more than a reaction to war and repression. The USSF will provide space to build relationships, learn from each other's experiences, share our analysis of the problems our communities face, and bring renewed insight and inspiration. It will help develop leadership and develop consciousness, vision, and strategy needed to realize another world.
>
> The USSF sends a message to other people's movements around the world that there is an active movement in the US opposing US policies at home and abroad.
>
> We must declare what we want our world to look like and begin planning the path to get there. A global movement is rising. The USSF is our opportunity to demonstrate to the world Another World is Possible!
>
> People world-wide know that another world is needed. The Social Forum movement believes that is possible. At the US Social Forum, people from all over the country gathered to think about what kind of world is needed and how we can get there.
>
> The US Social Forum is a very special kind of gathering: one that has never taken place in this country up to now. It isn't a conference with an agenda and a program of events; it's a gathering whose participants produce our own agenda and our own programs.

The mere process of planning, thinking, talking and preliminary organizing will move you, the people you're working with and the rest of us forward. The moment you think of an idea, you are already participating in the Social Forum.

In the end, an estimated 15,000 people attended the US Social Forum 2007, participating in 1,200 workshops.

This leads us to acknowledge and thank the members of the Solidarity Economy Working Group for the US Social Forum 2007, and the organizations which they represent. The Working Group planned the "Building Economic Alternatives and the Social/Solidarity Economy" events at the USSF2007 which are documented in this book; it was comprised of Emily Kawano, Center for Popular Economics; Julie Matthaei, Guramylay: Growing the Green Economy and Wellesley College; Ethan Miller, Grassroots Economic Organizing and Data Commons Project; Dan Swinney, Center for Labor and Community Research; Melissa Hoover, U.S. Federation of Worker Cooperatives; Jessica Gordon Nembhard, Democracy Collaborative; Heather Schoonover, Institute for Agriculture and Trade Policy; Yvon Poirier, Groupe Economie Solidaire Quebec and Canadian Community Economic Development Network; and Michael Menser, Professional Staff Congress, American Federation of Teachers, and Brooklyn College, City University of New York. As the USSF2007 call predicted, the prospect of an all-US Social Forum piqued their imaginations, and inspired them to dream big about bringing diverse groups together from all over the U.S. to share their experiences and building an ongoing solidarity economy network.

This book would not exist without all of its contributors – who planned, moderated, and presented in the Solidarity Economy track of workshops, and wrote their presentations up for us. We thank them for their wonderful writings. They made this book a pleasure to put together. We also thank the many others who participated in the caucus meetings, or spoke in the sessions, whose insightful questions and comments are also included in this volume. They illustrate the fact that the project of building knowledge about the solidarity economy is truly a grassroots effort.

We also want to acknowledge and express our gratitude to the organizations represented in the Solidarity Economy Working Group for the USSF 2007 for their support of this effort, especially Guramylay: Growing the Green Economy, Wellesley College, the Center for Popular Economics, Grassroots Economic Organizing, and the Center for Community and Labor Research. Guramylay funded Jenna Allard's work as the Managing Editor, without which the book would never have happened. It also supported Julie Matthaei's part-time leave to work on the project in the spring of 2007, and the video documentation of the caucus and many of the workshops. Germai Medhanie, Guramylay's Co-Director, provided invaluable administrative, planning, and logistical support for the preparatory work for the forum, at the forum, and, since then, for this book.

Wellesley College has been a huge resource for this project. In addition to Julie Matthaei's salary, the Wellesley College Economics Department provided generous administrative assistance from staff and students, detailed below. The Dean's Office funded Julie Matthaei's semester sabbatical leave in the fall of 2006 during which the ideas for the track incubated, and the Economics Department and Dean's Office funded two student summer interns who worked on the project. Staff at Wellesley were an endless wellspring of help, especially Pat Sjostedt and Cynthia Garratt of the Economics Department, who provided administrative support; Heather Woods and Susan Hand of the Knapp Center for Media and Technology who helped us with video equipment and website development; and Veronica Brandstrader.

A group of wonderfully energetic and creative Wellesley students was indispensable to this project. Julie met Jenna in the spring of 2007 through Wellesley, where Jenna was a graduating senior with a passionate interest in the solidarity economy, and hired her to work for Guramylay. Julie's summer interns, Alexis Frank, Hiywete Solomon, and Nimmi Ariaratne, prepared posters to publicize the track of sessions, and helped develop TransformationCentral.org as a site for posting the materials and program; then Alexis and Hiywete attended the forum and, along with Jenna, videotaped as many workshops as they could, and returned to Wellesley to process them and post them on the website. From there, Maria Lisiakova, Jessica Planos, and Tina Tam carefully transcribed many of the videos, along with Jenna. Loren Nelson, Beth Schaaf, Ari Roche, Elizabeth Shirey, Clarice Gan, Ley Muller, Jennifer Kim, Maura Atwater, Diane Seol, Teju Velayudhan, and Jessica Underwood helped with the manuscript, from editing footnotes to proofreading.

The Center for Popular Economics (CPE) played a key role in the creation of this book, especially through its Executive Director, Emily Kawano. Emily and CPE had the idea for a track of workshops at the USSF, as an alternative to their regular week-long Summer Institute. CPE's ongoing connections with progressive groups enabled it to bring key players into the Working Group, which it convened. Emily chaired Working Group meetings and provided overall coordination. CPE staffers Heidi Garrett-Peltier and Shaun Lamoury provided outreach and administrative assistance. CPE staff economists – Heidi Garrett-Peltier, Helen Scharber, Tom Masterson, Hector Saez, Anita Dancs, Matt Riddle, Kiaran Honderich, Suresh Naidu, Geert Dhondt and Emily -- presented or participated in the solidarity economy track of workshops, and many of them wrote for this book. CPE interns Stephanie Gimenez and Elizabeth Kelly put in long hours transcribing the videotapes of conference sessions.

Since the USSF, Emily has taken on the responsibilities of serving as Director of the U.S. Solidarity Economy Network (U.S. SEN), -- while retaining her position with CPE. In this capacity, Emily has convened and chaired U.S. SEN Coordinating Committee meetings which oversaw the development of this book. We thank Emily for her wise, steadfast, and visionary leadership; her bold intellect, critical thinking, and ability to listen and learn from others; and her incredible capacity to create and nurture collaboration. We also gratefully acknowledge the Solidago Foundation for their generous support of this book, through U.S. SEN.

Another important support for the book has been Grassroots Economic Organizing (GEO), which has been documenting the existence of solidarity economy initiatives, especially in the U.S. and Canada, for over fifteen years. Ethan Miller, GEO boardmember, played a key role with his knowledge of and writing about the solidarity economy. Ethan's experience putting together the program for the Boston Social Forum of 2004 was invaluable to the Working Group as it conceptualized the track of workshops for the USSF.

Further, Ethan put together the program (Appendix A), and wrote the first draft of the "Think Paper" (Chapter 27) which provided a concrete vision for the discussion of a U.S. solidarity economy network at the second caucus meeting. Ethan represented the younger generation on the Working Group, and his total dedication to living the values of the solidarity economy in every aspect of his life, from his collective farm to his writing to his dumpster-diving, has been an inspiration. Jessica Gordon Nemblard, GEO boardmember and treasurer, also brought valuable expertise to the Working Group.

Another final organization which has been key to the creation of this book is The Center for Community and Labor Research (CCLR). Its founder and director, Dan Swinney, has provided invaluable expertise on framing a vision of the solidarity economy for the U.S. in a way that connects to all potential constituents. As cofounder and boardmember of the North American Network for the Solidarity Economy (NANSE), he connected the Working Group's efforts to the larger North American Network, especially the Canadian Networks, and involved Canadian, Mexican, and South American representatives in the events at the forum. Dan was also invaluable because he involved his daughter, Erica Swinney, and coworker, Matt Hancock, in presenting workshops and attending the caucus meetings. Last but certainly not least, he connected Carl Davidson to the USSF events, and Julie and Jenna met Carl at the caucus meetings, where he proposed (and promised to publish) this book!

Jenna would like to acknowledge her friends and family, for their smoothies and their support: her mom, Steph, Jon, and Kayvan. She would like to thank Germai, who provided many meals that kept the writing and editing process going, and on one fateful night, even lent his computer. Finally, she would like to thank all of the contributors for making this book a pleasure to put together, and for their wonderful writings and careful revisions.

Carl thanks several people for their support, both material and intellectual: David Schweickart, who, along with his keen insights, opened a number of doors; Dan Swinney and the CLCR staff, along with Ivan Handler, Jerry Harris, Ra Chaka and all the other comrades in the Third Wave Study Group, who offered new ideas and critical feedback on the solidarity economy over more than a decade; and Alynne Romo, his partner, who shares a vision, both personal and political, which, together with her critical judgment and practical good sense, helped put this project on the road.

Julie is full of gratitude for all the love, support, teaching, and inspiration she has received from a host of people over many years, all of which have led to her cocreation of this book. In particular, Julie's family has been a continual resource: her father and mother, Fred and Malora; her siblings, Carl, Marcella, Maru, Bill, Amy, and Morgan; and her co-parent, Wec. Heartfelt thanks to Ella, who has been a wonderful daughter and teacher, and to her partner, Germai Medhanie, for his amazing, unending, and multifaceted love, companionship, and support. Julie also wants to thank Janice Goldman, Maureen Brodoff, and Emine Kiray for their enduring friendship; Dan Cherry, David Anick, Claudia Scully, Joan

Corr, Tracy McNab, Susan McNab, and Eckhart Tolle for their contributions to her healing and growth; and Andy Shennan, Andrea Levitt, and Susan Skeath for their support and understanding during a difficult time. Barbara Brandt has been a wonderful coauthor and friend, as well as editor. Julie's cohousing community, Cornerstone, as well as three professional groups -- Marxist-Feminist I (MF), the Union for Radical Political Economics (URPE), and the International Association for Feminist Economics (IAFFE) – have been educational, inspiring, challenging, and supportive for many years.

Finally, we thank the millions of people and thousands of organized groups around the world who are transforming economic life into more democratic, egalitarian, cooperative, and sustainable forms. It is a very great pleasure and honor for us to be able to share the news of the worldwide solidarity economy movement with you.

Introduction

The economy we have been waiting for is here! It has been growing up in our midst, pushing out of the cracks in our dysfunctional economic practices and institutions, and immigrating here via people, practices, and places once thought too marginal, too utopian, or too "underdeveloped" to matter. In this book, we share with you a wealth of new economic alternatives springing up in our country and around the world, and we invite you to become part of this courageous, creative, and diverse global movement to build a solidarity economy.

Our country's emerging solidarity economy embodies wisdom earned through countless manifestos, meetings, demonstrations, and experiments with change. It is led by our country's vibrant social movements – worker and anti-class, civil rights and anti-racist, feminist, welfare rights and anti-poverty, ecology, lesbian and gay liberation, disability, and peace movements – in connection and interaction with movements abroad. These movements have engaged millions of Americans in processes of individual and social transformation. They have taught us to recognize and overcome our prejudices; to become more whole and balanced; and to honor our bodies and the Earth. They have taught us to question the competitive consumerist "American dream" which denies us the well-being it promises, while destroying our planet. They have pointed out, each from their own lens, the many ways in which our economic practices and institutions must change if they are to truly embody the American ideals of equality, democracy, and freedom. In this way, our social movements have laid the groundwork for an epochal shift in our country, out of a paradigm based on polarization, hierarchy, competition, and domination, to one based instead on equality, democracy, freedom, and solidarity.

The turn of the millennium saw these social movements, which had cross-fertilized one another for decades in the U.S. and in the world, begin to come together in a global "movement of movements." The first expressions of this movement of movements came together globally to express a resounding "no" to the current reigning neoliberal economic agenda. This agenda, driven by corporate greed – and epitomized in "free trade," privatization, and the destruction of social safety nets – had been wreaking havoc on communities across the globe and on our planet itself (see Chapter 1). What Dr. King called the "fierce urgency of now" was further intensified by the impending climate change crisis. The Seattle 1999 demonstration against the World Trade Organization (WTO) – and the many similar demonstrations since then, at gatherings of the world economic powers – represent a dynamic convergence of social movements around this opposition to neoliberalism and corporate-run globalization.

Two years later in 2001, the first World Social Forum (WSF) was organized in Porto Alegre, Brazil. Its goal was to bring people and movements together, based on a shared Charter of Principles, to share visions and solutions, under the motto, "Another World is Possible." The principles which unify the WSF include opposition to neoliberalism, commitment to nonviolence, and:

> .... respect for Human Rights, the practices of real democracy, participatory democracy, peaceful relations, in equality and solidarity, among people, ethnicities, genders and peoples, and condemns all forms of domination and all subjection of one person by another. [1]

Unity around a shared commitment to these basic principles is accompanied by a commitment to valuing diversity. In conscious contrast with traditional leftist discourse, the WSF was organized according to the Zapatista saying, "Un solo no, un million de si" (One no, and a million yeses) – that is, to invite and showcase a diversity of opinions and strategies, and create conversations and linkages among them.[2]

Anyone who agrees with the Social Forum principles and belongs to a social change group is welcome to attend, and the program is largely "self-organizing," that is, created by the participants, who propose workshops via the Internet. The WSF was created to encourage civil society organizations around the world to introduce into the world dialogue "the change-inducing practices they are experimenting [with], in building a new world in solidarity."[3]

The first forum drew an astounding 20,000 people from all over the world. Since then, World Social Forum meetings have been held almost annually, in Porto Alegre, Mumbai, Nairobi, and Caracas, drawing up to 155,000 people at a time. Other Social Forums, based in cities, regions, countries, or even in particular issues, have also sprung up like mushrooms – for example, there were 2,560 Social Forum activities in the world in 2005.[4]

These Social Forums reflect the flowering of a new form of consciousness on a grass-roots level – and they, in turn, help educate, develop, and direct this new consciousness. It is a consciousness which stands in solidarity with all struggles for equality, democracy, sustainability, freedom, and justice, and seeks to inject these values into every aspect of our lives, including our economic lives. It is a consciousness which is locally rooted, but globally connected, involving what the WSF Charter calls "planetary citizenship." It is a consciousness, a set of values, which has the power to transform our economy and society from the bottom up. This new consciousness is the heart and soul of the solidarity economy.

History and Definitions of the Solidarity Economy

The Growth of the Solidarity Economy Movement

The solidarity economy is a global movement. Yet until now, the term has been virtually unknown in the U.S. Like elsewhere in the world, the spread of the solidarity economy framework is closely connected to the Social Forum movement, and for good reason. Both the solidarity economy and the Social Forum movement share characteristics and yearnings. They both desire to synthesize the experiences, values, and visions of progressive social movements, while at the same time respecting their diversity. They both search for a plurality of answers to neoliberal globalization through participatory learning and reflection on our organizing and goals. If not for the "privileged space" of the World Social Forums, solidarity economy organizing would still be a regional phenomenon. And even locally, the Social Forum movement can fuel the growth of the solidarity economy. Illustrating this in their report on the organizing experience of the solidarity economy movement in Brazil, the Brazilian Forum on the Solidarity Economy states:

> In our country, the growth of the Solidarity Economy as a movement – going beyond isolated, independent actions, and organizing itself towards a common association, networks configuration and struggle – takes a significant leap with the World Social Forums, a privileged space where different actors, organizations, initiatives and solidarity economy enterprises were able to develop an integrated work that resulted in a demand presented to newly elected president Lula to create a Solidarity Economy National Secretariat (SENAES). Together with the creation of this Secretariat, the Brazilian Forum of Solidarity Economy was created during the III Solidarity Economy National Plenary that represents this movement in Brazil. We can say that these two organizations, plus the World Social Forum, led the Solidarity Economy in Brazil to a significant growth and structuring.[5]

The term "solidarity economy" may not have spread without the aid of truly global networking, but we see economic activity that embodies progressive social values in every corner of the globe, even if these initiatives do not consciously identify as members of the movement. Paul Singer, National Secretary of the Solidarity Economy in Brazil, argues in an interview that: "Under the form of cooperativism, solidarity economy has already existed for 200 years in practically all countries of the world." [6] Currently, there are economic actors on every continent that identify as solidarity economy initiatives, and they are forming and strengthening networks to support and learn from each other.

Solidarity Economy Organizing Around the World

Latin America has one of the oldest and most vibrant solidarity economy movements. It is also the place where the term itself was coined, adapted from the work of Luis Razeto, a Chilean professor of philosophy.[7] Razeto writes about the solidarity market, and about creating economic enterprises that embody 'Factor C' – cooperation, co-responsibility, communication and community.[8] By the 1990s, solidarity economy organizing and networking was already starting to flourish in Latin America, largely in reaction to the harsh neoliberal policies implemented by authoritarian governments in the previous decade. Activists and academics in Latin America realized that the neoliberal model of development was not working, particularly for the poor. As Marcos Arruda, a prominent Brazilian researcher of the solidarity economy, writes:

> Solidarity Economy recognizes humankind, both the individual and social being, not only as creators and producers of economic wealth but also as co-owners of material wealth, co-users of natural resources, and co-responsible for the conservation of Nature. The dominant system leads to the concentration of wealth among the few and the disenfranchisement of the many. Solidarity Economy strives towards producing and sharing enough material wealth among all in order to generate sustainable conditions for self-managed development of each and every member of societies, the peoples and the planet.[9]

The solidarity economy took shape as a way to provide the most excluded and vulnerable members of the community with work and welfare services. Today, it is a mass movement with a strong and critical sense of social justice. Besides many local, national, and regional networks, some left-leaning governments have also begun to champion the movement, creating public sector offices and programs to promote the solidarity economy.

Elsewhere in the Global South, in Africa and Asia, solidarity economy organizing, at least by this name, is new but growing rapidly through the creation of forums and networks. Again, sustainable development and wealth redistribution is of critical importance in these places. Africa hosted the Third International Meeting on the Globalization of Solidarity in 2005, and the headquarters for the Intercontinental Network for the Promotion of the Social Solidarity Economy (RIPESS) is currently located in Dakar.[10] The first Asian Forum for Solidarity Economy was held in Manila, in October 2007.[11] Out of this was created a banking facility that links socially responsible investors to socially responsible enterprises, the Bayanihan Banking Window (BBW). (Bayanihan is a Filipino word meaning community solidarity and cooperation.) These early Asian examples of the solidarity economy are focusing on micro-credit organizations, from the Inner City Development Initiative in the Philippines, to the Grameen Bank in Bangladesh. Japan has also started its own Solidarity Economy Forum in March 2007, which is composed of academics and activists. They identify the solidarity economy in Japan as composed primarily of producer and consumer cooperatives.[12]

In Europe, there has also been a long-standing movement, mostly centered on the concept of the social economy – taken from the French term *économie sociale*. Members of the traditional social economy are located within the 'third sector' (as opposed to the private profit-oriented sector and the public redistributive sector), and they generally include worker and consumer cooperatives, and non-profit associations and foundations. The 'third sector' in Europe has played a major role in providing public services, and also in challenging the boundaries of the other sectors. Evers and Laville, two leading researchers on the social economy and the third sector in Europe, argue that these social economy movements are linked to: "a range of political and economic ideas to create mechanisms for the production of wealth and welfare other than market exchange or state protection. They represent a wide spectrum of collective actions coming from civil society, based on various forms of solidarity."[13] These expressions of solidarity have grown to include ethical businesses and ethical consumption activities. In addition, the cooperative movement originated in Europe, and today, in the Basque region of Spain, the Mondragon Cooperative Corporation is one of the largest cooperatives in the world, and an important and inspiring example of a large-scale solidarity economy. Europeans, particularly the French, have played a leading role in funding research and networking for the social and solidarity economy globally.

Another vibrant example of solidarity economy organizing in the global North is in Canada, and some of this organizing is represented in this volume (see Chapter 15). Much of their initial organizing grew out of the Community Economic Development movement, and used the language of the social economy. Today, there are "networks of networks" across Canada that are organizing cross-sectorally, and are mobilizing support for regional and national solidarity economy policy initiatives.

Defining the Solidarity Economy: From Practice to Framework

Defining the solidarity economy can be quite difficult, especially when those most involved in it, those doing work at the grassroots, often do not have access to the Internet, or the multi-linguistic ability to network with other international initiatives. They certainly do not have the time. We are just now starting to conceptualize the solidarity economy by analyzing, learning from, and connecting these grassroots practices. Globally, the most commonly used definition of the solidarity economy is provided by Alliance 21, the group which convened the Workgroup on the Solidarity Socioeconomy:

> Solidarity economy designates all production, distribution and consumption activities that contribute to the democratization of the economy based on citizen commitments both at a local and global level. It is carried out in various forms, in all continents. It covers different forms of organization that the population uses to create its own means of work or to have access to qualitative goods and services, in a dynamics of reciprocity and solidarity which links individual interests to the collective interest. In this sense, solidarity economy is not a sector of the economy, but an overall approach that includes initiatives in most sectors of the economy.[14]

Even this definition leaves a lot of room for the diversity of practices contained within the solidarity economy, but it makes it clear that this economy should be centered on human needs rather than an insatiable drive for profit. Solidarity economy initiatives can also be loosely defined as practices and institutions on all levels and in all sectors of the economy that embody certain values and priorities: cooperation, sustainability, equality, democracy, justice, diversity, and local control.

Because the solidarity economy denotes a multiplicity of practices rather than a unified theory, universal definitions can be difficult to pin down (as you will soon see in this book). Yet this desire not to squelch diversity in order to achieve a comfortable and homogenous uniformity, but rather to consciously pursue a bottom-up approach, is part of the very ethic of the solidarity economy. It is a framework of practices held together by values, in contrast to the abstract theoretical models of socialist alternatives to capitalism that describe egalitarian, oppression-free utopias. These utopias always seem disappointingly out of reach, but the solidarity economy framework has evolved to describe and make visible the plethora of actually existing economic alternatives that are growing up all around us, in the midst of neoliberal capitalism.[15] The solidarity economy framework allows for and values diversity, and honors local knowledge. It provides a messy, loose description of what is already going on, other ways of being and acting to which our dominant, capitalist system has tried to blind us, or that we missed because our noses were stuck in books, reading theory. This imprecision makes the more academically minded cringe, but when we look closely, we can detect a higher organization emerging out of this multitude of authentic, grassroots transformative economic efforts. As Ethan Miller writes:

> Solidarity Economics begins here, with the realization that alternative economies already exist; that we as creative and skilled people have already created different kinds of economic relationships in the very belly of the capitalist system. We have our own forms of wealth and value that are not defined by money. Instead of prioritizing competition and profit-making, these economies place human needs and relationships at the center. They are the already-planted seeds of a new economy, an economy of cooperation, equality, diversity, and self-determination: a "solidarity economy."[16]

The Solidarity Economy at the U.S. Social Forum

The United States, the "belly of the beast" as it were, has trailed the rest of the world both in its participation in the Social Forum movement, and in its development of solidarity economy practices and networks. Nevertheless, regional social forums were held in the Midwest (Wisconsin, yearly since 2003), Northeast (Boston, 2004), the Northwest (Seattle, 2004), the Southeast (North Carolina, 2006), and Southwest (2006). This momentum built towards the first-ever all-U.S. Social Forum in the summer of 2007.

This book documents the "Building Economic Alternatives and the Social/Solidarity Economy" workshop track and caucus meetings which took place at this historic first U.S. Social Forum. These events were organized by the "Solidarity Economy Working Group for the USSF 2007." A group of economists and economic activists came together under the leadership of Emily Kawano, Director of the Center for Popular Economics (CPE), a nonprofit collective of over sixty economists that works to promote economic justice and sustainability through economic education. Realizing that the USSF was a great organizing opportunity, CPE had decided to focus on organizing a workshop track at the U.S. Social Forum, in lieu of holding its annual summer institute. Emily organized the first meeting of the Solidarity Economy Working Group in January of 2007, at which the group decided to sponsor a track of sessions focused on economic alternatives and the social/solidarity economy. Within a few meetings, a core group had formed: Emily Kawano of the Center for Popular Economics; Julie Matthaei of Guramylay, TransformationCentral.org, and Wellesley College; Ethan Miller of Grassroots Economic Organizing and the Data Commons Project; and Dan Swinney of the Center for Labor and Community Research and the North American Network for a Solidarity Economy (NANSE). Also part of the Working Group, and participating in much of the planning, were Melissa Hoover of the U.S. Federation of Worker Cooperatives; Jessica Gordon Nembhard of the Democracy Collaborative; Heather Schoonover of the Institute for Agriculture and Trade Policy; Yvon Poirier of the Solidarity Economy Quebec; and Michael Menser of American Federation of Teachers and Brooklyn College.

Members of the Solidarity Economy Working Group had attended, and in some cases helped organize, other Social Forums, and were aware of the ongoing critique of the Social Forum movement – that it brings people and groups together for an inspiring event, but that the energy often dissipates afterwards, with little or no permanent effect. We were determined to use the USSF 2007 as an opportunity to bring together economic activists from all over the country to build an ongoing organization focused on growing the solidarity economy. For this reason, we planned both a set of workshops on the solidarity economy, and two caucus meetings, before and after the main workshop days, to use to try to form an ongoing solidarity economy network. Through bi-weekly conference call meetings, we developed a list of groups which were active in the emerging U.S. solidarity economy, from different sectors of the economy and civil society. We contacted them about presenting in our bloc of workshops and participating in our caucus meetings.

In the end, we organized twenty-seven workshops on the theme of "Building Economic Alternatives and the Social/Solidarity Economy," and two Solidarity Economy Caucus meetings. We also studied the Forum program on the web, and asked groups holding sessions on related topics whether we could add them to our program as allied events (we listed 53 in our program; see Appendix A). Jenna Allard videoed both caucuses and many of the sessions for Guramylay: Growing the Green Economy, with the plan of making them available on the Internet (see www.TransformationCentral.org and www.ussen.org) and in written form. Finally, we organized a Solidarity Economy Tent, with daily introductions to the solidarity economy, and workshops on political song-writing and using the Internet for economic and social transformation.

Organization and Overview of the Book

Our goal in this book was to record the events of the Solidarity Economy Track at the first-ever U.S. Social Forum. Although this book contains many vibrant and dynamic chapters that capture the essence of many of the workshops and much of the track, we were not able to obtain write-ups for all the sessions we wished to document. Further, the track of workshops itself was not meant to be a fully coherent or comprehensive representation of solidarity economy initiatives in the U.S. In a sense, both the track and the book evolved organically, much like a solidarity economy project, and they tell the story of the solidarity economy through a diversity of voices and through a diversity of projects.

Creating the sections of this book was in some ways like creating a taxonomy of the solidarity economy: it provides a window into one way of conceptualizing the movement. It also provides a window into some of the unique features of the solidarity economy in the U.S. Each chapter embodies the multidimensional values of the solidarity economy framework – e.g. anti-racist, feminist, ecological, pro-worker values – and describes practices that have both local and global aspects. We focus the sections of the book on the different ways that the solidarity economy is being built and defined in the U.S. It is being defined through visions, through models, and through principles. It is being built through social movements, through cooperatives and socially responsible businesses, through networking and community organizing, through public policy, and through daily practice. Like any categorization, it can and should be rethought and rearranged as other, new minds write and think about these practices.

I. New Visions and Models

Part I begins the project of defining the solidarity economy in a conceptual manner. In order to do this, we must remember that the solidarity economy is a framework, as opposed to an economic model or system with a specific set of assumptions about how things work and a specific set of structures that are most likely to make things go smoothly. The solidarity economy does not, as neoliberal capitalist theory does, try to enumerate certain critical, universal characteristics of human nature – namely self-interest – or advocate for a particular set of economic interactions, namely competition. If anything, the solidarity economy is trying to subvert neoliberal capitalism's theoretically and oftentimes physically violent colonization of economic space. It is a project of diversification; a project of making space for other practices and relationships. And so, because the solidarity economy's refusal to be rigidly classified can be best understood by first understanding neoliberalism's rigid dogma, we start with what we are against in Chapter 1: *Why We Need Another World: Introduction to Neoliberalism*. In this piece, the authors introduce the Shrink-Shift-Shaft framework to explain some of the effects of neoliberal ideology.

Chapter 2: *Social Economy and Solidarity Economy: Transformative Concepts for Unprecedented Times*? conceptually distinguishes solidarity economy organizing from social economy organizing. The authors employ a three-sector conception of the economy, with the private profit-oriented logic of neoliberal capitalism making up the first sector, but attempting to encroach upon and shrink both the public and the social sector. The authors argue that solidarity economy organizing is cross-sectoral, and must contend in all sectors, even though the third sector is currently its primary site of organizing. This chapter includes three visual representations of the social and solidarity economy which were presented in the first caucus meeting and informed much of the discussion about the solidarity economy in the workshops.

A good point of balance to any conceptual vision of the solidarity economy is provided by Chapter 3, *Between Global and Local: Alternatives to Globalization*. Opposition to neoliberal globalization has mobilized the solidarity economy all over the world, and this piece features a conversation about trade and local self-sufficiency among four activists with different concerns and constituencies.

Chapter 4: *There is an Alternative: Economic Democracy and Participatory Economics*, and Chapter 5: *Introduction to the Economics of Liberation: An Overview of PROUTt* present three economic models that embody solidarity economy values. Chapter 4 records a debate between Michael Albert and David Schweickart, two important thinkers in the economic alternatives movement. Chapter 5 provides a short outline of the PROUTist economic system, first proposed by Indian philosopher, Shrii Prabhat Ranjan Sarkar.

II. Defining the Solidarity Economy through Diverse Practices

Part II focuses on the incredible breadth of solidarity economy grassroots initiatives. All the chapters in this section showcase the diversity of organizing in the U.S. that can be counted as the solidarity economy. Chapter 6: *Building a Solidarity Economy Through Real World Practices* is based on a participatory exercise developed by Emily Kawano and Ethan Miller to illustrate the solidarity economy. Instead of creating practices to fit principle, they instead create principles to fit practice, and it is both inspiring for the participants to see that the solidarity economy exists and works, and for the organizers to realize that the principles of the solidarity economy are so infallibly intuitive. Chapter 7: *Beyond Reform or Revolution: Economic Transformation in the U.S.* is a roundtable discussion featuring many of the prominent solidarity economy organizers in the U.S., discussing their work, the challenges they face, and their hopes for the future of the solidarity economy movement.

Chapter 8: *Building Community Economies Any Time Any Place* is a collection of pieces by the Community Economies Collective, a research group located in Western Massachusetts, and founded by J.K. Gibson-Graham. They focus on changing our relationship to the economy, so that instead of assuming that we are passive subjects who have to trust the economist "experts," we can realize that we are active, creative participants in the economies and communities around us. After an introduction and summary by Stephen Healy, Janelle Cornwall helps us see how many non-capitalist relationships and transactions exist in our lives, just below the surface, in the Iceberg Exercise. Then, Ted White sees a new type of relationship between producer and consumer, an "economy of trust," in small-scale, local farmstands, and Karen Werner describes how monetary systems work on a conceptual level, and then describes her experience starting one of her own, in the form of a local time bank.

III. Building the Solidarity Economy through Social Movements

Part III is the first of the series of sections which focuses on how the solidarity economy is being built from the grassroots, not on how it is being defined (not that there is always a difference). This section is featured front and center because social movements play an important and unique role in creating the values upon which the solidarity economy is based, and in challenging particular initiatives to live up to them. We want the solidarity economy in the U.S. to be, as Michael Albert describes his own organizing project: "An alliance which gets its gender definition from the feminist movement, gets its anti-racist definition from the movements around race, gets its labor definition from the labor movement, and gets its ecology from the ecological."[17] Many activists in these social movements are drawn to the solidarity economy because they want to address the structural, economic roots of injustice, and are incorporating an analysis of neoliberal globalization into their work on issues and campaigns.

The social movements represented in this volume are the feminist movement in Chapter 9, the immigrants' rights movement in Chapter 10, and the movement of women of the African Diaspora in Chapter 11. Although they are not represented in this volume, the Solidarity Economy Track at the U.S. Social Forum included workshops on the Poor People's Economic Human Rights Campaign, and a UNITE workshop was listed in our Allied Events, while the environmental movement was represented in our caucuses by the Environmental Health Coalition. Absent from both this volume and the Solidarity Economy Track, however, is the gay, lesbian, bi-sexual, and transgender movement; we hope to connect with and support their struggles in the future.

IV. Building the Solidarity Economy through Cooperatives and Socially Responsible Business

Part IV discusses the role of cooperatives and socially responsible businesses in building the solidarity economy. Throughout the world, worker cooperatives have always been a cornerstone of the solidarity economy. And while many leftists dismiss the corporate world as intrinsically exploitative and destructive, Dan Swinney, a member of the Solidarity Economy Working Group and co-creator of NANSE, suggests that a key task of solidarity economy organizing is to pressure and support privately held capitalist firms to take what he calls the "high road":

> There's a definite low road sector of capital—a portion of the 13,000 publicly traded companies that are larger and can typically roam the world to solve their production problems—at the expense of local communities. But there are 8 million privately held, usually locally-owned companies that represent a large section of the business community that can and will be won to our side." [18]

In the U.S., locally-owned small businesses are also becoming an important part of the burgeoning solidarity economy, especial through "buy local" and "local first" campaigns, which often form the starting point for more radical economic transformation.

In the first chapter in this section, Chapter 12: *Growing Transformative Businesses*, Jessica Gordon Nembhard offers a framework for thinking about how community-owned cooperatives are formed; Ann Bartz, representing the Business Alliance for Local Living Economies, talks about the transformative impact of localization campaigns; and Adam Trott presents a personal account of being a worker-owner at Collective Copies. Chapter 13: *Competing by Cooperating in Italy* explores the particular conditions in a certain district in Italy that have allowed cooperatives – and their workers – to thrive in an increasingly globalized economy. Chapter 14: *Another Workplace is Possible: Co-ops and Workplace Democracy* offers a nuts and bolts approach to the organization of co-ops, how the movement in the U.S. has progressed, and how we can continue to build it.

V. Building the Solidarity Economy through Networking and Community Organizing

Part V features exciting cross-sectoral work – building alliances among different types of solidarity economy initiatives, and in different sectors of the economy. The first chapter in the section, Chapter 15: *Solidarity Economy as a Strategy for Changing the Economy*, offers the experience of our international allies to the north and south, who were present at the Forum to support and encourage solidarity economy networking in the U.S. Ethel Cote and Nancy Neamtan describe the solidarity economy movement in Canada, where networks of networks have been able to engage the public sector and receive government funding for their initiatives. Then Nedda Angulo Villareal outlines the different characteristics of the solidarity economy in Peru: how it specifically addresses the problem of poverty, incorporates indigenous forms of economic activity into its practices, and responds directly to the devastation caused by neoliberal policies. Throught networking, the Peruvian solidarity economy has also been able to pressure the government into providing funding for programs that help the poorest and most vulnerable. In Chapter 16: *High Road Community Development, Public Schools, and the Solidarity Economy*, Dan Swinney describes a grassroots partnership between a solidarity economy organization and the state – in this case to create a school. This local organizing in Chicago includes an impressive array of actors and stakeholders, and is informed by a transformative vision of social change. Our friends in other countries inspire us in the U.S. to think about the power for change we could generate with regional and national networking, while Swinney's piece shows a powerful example of something which is already happening here.

VI: Building the Solidarity Economy through Public Policy

Part VI showcases policy initiatives and democratic processes that embody solidarity economy values – the kind of initiatives and processes that a solidarity economy network could effectively advocate for and build coalitions around. The first chapter in the section, Chapter 17: *Participatory Budgeting: From Porto Alegre, Brazil to the U.S.*, first profoundly questions the elitist assumptions of traditional democratic theory, and then discusses actual participatory budgeting practices abroad and in the United States. It also talks about a new participatory budgeting network which was formed at the U.S. Social Forum to help support and grow these initiatives. In the other chapters, progressive economists advocate specific policy initiatives that express solidarity economy values. Chapter 18: *The Sky as a Common Resource* proposes a Cap and Dividend Approach to dealing with greenhouse gas emissions, a measure which preserves the idea of the sky as a commons, and recognizes the disproportionate contribution that the richer countries have made to the global warming problem, and the disproportionate effects it will have on the poorer countries. Chapter 19: *U.S Economic Inequality and What We Can Do About It* addresses two questions: how do we measure inequality (through the Levy Institute Measure of Economic Well-Being), and how do we redress it (through the Basic Income Grant)? Chapter 20: *You Are What You Eat* talks about the U.S. food system, and how we can organize to make it reflect our own values.

VII. Building the Solidarity Economy through Daily Practice

Part VII brings the solidarity economy to the individual level, to where transformative changes start to take place in our own lives. As Heather Schoonover, a member of the Solidarity Economy Working Group for the USSF 2007, commented in the second caucus, "The one question and point that came up in almost every workshop by an attendee was: 'This is great! I support this! What can I personally do on my own, in my house, today?' People liked the idea of big changes, but really wanted to know what they could do to bring them about."[19] We wanted to end the book with the workshops which answered this question; workshops which challenge us to re-evaluate our consumption, work, and investment through the lens of our priorities and values.

The first chapter in the section, Chapter 21: *Live Your Power: Socially Responsible Consumption, Work, and Investment*, includes both a presentation by Julie Matthaei and comments from the workshop audience that describe the ways that they live their deeply anti-authoritarian, anti-consumerist, and communitarian values in their daily economic practices. Chapter 22: *Household Economic Justice Strategies* is a short outline of resources for analyzing your own consumption and making it congruent with your values. The section ends with Chapter 23: *Spirituality and Economic Transformation*, which includes three essays about the relationship between spirituality and the growth of the solidarity economy, and how progressive faith groups are uniting for transformative change.

VIII. The Birth of the U.S. Solidarity Economy Network

Part VIII begins with summaries of the two Solidarity Economy Caucus meetings, Chapters 24 and 25. The Solidarity Economy Working Group for USSF 2007 used the first caucus meeting, which took place before the workshops started, to introduce the solidarity economy framework to participants, present reports from experienced organizers in Canada and Peru, and discuss some of the challenges faced by the movement. This provided an excellent foundation for the Working Group's track of workshops. On the evening of the third and last day of workshops, the second caucus meeting was held, which focused on creating a structure to build on the networking that had occurred, and move forward solidarity economy organizing after the USSF. The benefits of forming a U.S. solidarity economy network, and the various functions such a network could play, were discussed. It was here that Carl Davidson, our co-editor and publisher, first urged the group to publish the conference proceedings, and the idea for this book was born. The caucus ended with a unanimous approval of the Working Group's proposal to create a U.S. Solidarity Economy Network, with Emily Kawano as Director. Chapters 26: *The Emerging Solidarity Economy: Some Common Themes*, and 27: *Solidarity Economy Organization in the U.S. Context: A Think-Paper Towards First Steps* were hand-outs provided to caucus members in preparation for the meetings; the first, to familiarize them with basic information about the solidarity economy framework, and the second, to raise key issues relevant to the formation of a solidarity economy network.

*   *   *

As we write this, seven months after those historic meetings, the U.S. Solidarity Economy Network (U.S. SEN) has taken its first baby-steps as a new organization: creating a structure, applying for and receiving funding, beginning to develop a membership, establishing a website (ussen.org), and planning a first conference for the fall of 2008. As members of U.S. SEN's Coordinating Committee, and editors of this collection, we are excited to herald the creation of this new movement, and we are continually inspired by the grassroots economic initiatives and actors who are not new at all, but have been working to transform our economic system in wonderfully radical ways right under our noses. We hope our book can show you that the solidarity economy is already well underway in the U.S. – it only needs you to join it.[20] Another Economy is Possible!

NOTES

[1] *The World Social Forum Charter of Principles*, Principle 11. http://www.forumsocialmundial.org.br/main.php?id_menu=4&cd_language=2, accessed Feb. 20, 2008.
[2] Chico Whitaker. (March, 2006). Speech presented at Left Forum, New York City, NY.
[3] *WSF Charter*, Principle 14.

[4] Data is from World Social Forum Secretariat. *An X-Ray of Participation in the 2005 Forum: Elements for Debate* and Speech by Chico Whitaker, above. For more on the WSF movement, see William F. Fisher and Thomas Ponniah, Eds. *Another World is Possible: Popular Alternatives to Globalization at the World Social Forum.* New York: Zed Books, 2003.

[5] Brazilian Forum of Solidarity Economy. (2006, January) "The Management and Organization Experience of the Solidarity Economy Movement in Brazil", 4.

[6] Gomes, Christiane. (2005, March 27) "A Brazilian Alternative to Neoliberalism: Solidarity" Brazzil Magazine.http://www.brazzil.com/content/view/8972/79/

[7] Arruda, Macros. (2005, November). "Annex: Different Names and Practices that are Complementary to Each Other." in *Solidarity Socioeconomy as an Integral New System: Global Vision.* Dakar: Workshop on a Global Vision of Solidarity Socioeconomy, 55.

[8] Gadotti, Moacir. (1996). "ICEA-Brazil: A Brief History." São Paulo: International Community Education Association / Instituto Paulo Freire. For more on Razeto's concept of "Factor C", also see Razeto, Luis. (1997). "'Factor C': la solidaridad convertida en fuerza productiva y en el factor económico," in Globalización de la solidaridad: un reto para todos, Lima: CEP.

9 Arruda, Macros. (2005, November). "A Global Vision of a Solidarity Socioeconomy: Reflections for Discussion" in Solidarity Socioeconomy as an Integral New System: Global Vision. Dakar: Workshop on a Global Vision of Solidarity Socioeconomy, 2.

[10] To read the Final Declaration of the Third International Meeting on the Globalization of Solidarity, go to: http://www.ripess.net/docs/declaration_dakar_en.pdf

[11] For more information, visit the website: http://www.asianforum2007.net/

[12] Kitazawa, Yoko. (2007, April). "Forum on Solidarity was Launched in Japan" Workgroup on Solidarity Socioeconomy.

[13] Evers, Adalbert and Jean-Louis Laville. (2004). "Defining the Third Sector in Europe" in Evers, Adalbert and Jean-Louis Laville (Ed.). The Third Sector in Europe (pp. 11-42). Cheltenham: Edward Elgar Publishing, 36.

[14] Workgroup on the Solidarity Socioeconomy. (2001, May). "Proposal Paper on the Solidarity Economy" Alliance 21.

[15] J.K. Gibson-Graham, *The End of Capitalism (as we knew it): A Feminist Critique of Political Economy.* Cambridge, MA: Blackwell Publishers, 1996) made this point in 1996; subsequent research by the Community Economies group, whose work is featured in Chapter 8, also takes this stance.

[16] Miller, 6.

[17] This volume, Albert, p74.

[18] This volume, Swinney, p293.

[19] Schoonover, Heather qtd. in Transformation Central. (2008, January 4). "Caucus II: Workshop Feedback" [video file].

[20] Thanks to J.K.Gibson-Graham for these words, contributed for our book cover.

SECTION I:

NEW VISIONS
AND
MODELS

1

Why We Need Another World: Introduction to Neoliberalism

Heidi Garrett-Peltier and Helen Scharber

Heidi Garrett-Peltier is a PhD candidate in Economics at the University of Massachusetts, Amherst and has been a CPE Staff Economist since 2005. Heidi has taught various workshops as well at the CPE Summer Institute. She is currently researching the employment effects of expanding renewable energy and energy efficiency. Other recent research includes the employment effects of military spending versus other types of public spending.

Helen Scharber is a PhD candidate in Economics at the University of Massachusetts and a Staff Economist with CPE since 2005. Helen studied environmental politics prior to beginning her economics degree and she looks forward to living in a world where people and the environment are both more important than neoliberal economic ideals.

Why a Session on Neoliberalism?

The U.S. Social Forum, like the World Social Forums before it, sprouted from an opposition to the current neoliberal economic regime. The economic policies enacted in the past few decades have clearly had some devastating effects. But the underlying justification for those policies, the "neoliberal paradigm" from which they arose, are still unfamiliar to many people. Participants at the USSF attended this workshop in order to get a better understanding of the term neoliberalism, which is used much more regularly in the rest of the world than it is in the U.S., and to understand its causes and consequences. Through this workshop, participants learned that neoliberalism is an attack on government services, on social solidarity, on equality, and on human rights. It is a belief that markets are king and that they alone can provide the best outcomes for the world's population. However, all around us we see rising inequality, increasing poverty, shrinking public services, and the rich getting richer. So who is being served by neoliberalism? And how we can move beyond it to an economic system which satisfies human needs, rather than fattening the pocketbooks of the rich?

The session started with an introduction of the Center for Popular Economics (CPE) and the staff economists who were leading the session. CPE is a collective of political economists based in Amherst, Massachusetts. It was founded in 1978 and is primarily an organization that teaches economic literacy to activists.

CPE works for social and economic justice by demystifying the economy and bridging the gap between academics and grassroots activists. We provide educational materials and participatory training that examine root causes of economic inequality and injustice including systems of oppression based on race, class, gender, nation and ethnicity. We create space where networking and movement-building is strengthened.

Since the group was large in size, we broke into subgroups so that participants could meet each other and briefly introduce the issues they are working on. We also introduced the pedagogy of CPE, the goal of which is to engage workshop participants and learn about economic issues through their own experiences and through participatory activities.

Shrink-Shift-Shaft

The Shrink-Shift-Shaft (S-S-S) framework was jointly developed by the Labor Center at the University of Massachusetts, along with United for a Fair Economy.

We employed the S-S-S framework because it is visual and allows us to understand the ideology of neoliberalism through the strategies and tactics employed by the global elite and others who seek to benefit from neoliberal practices and policies.

What we are seeing in our communities and workplaces is an all-out attack on gains of the past. It is not random, but rather flows from an *ideology* which informs *strategies* and *tactics*. That *ideology* is *neoliberalism*.

THE RIGHT WING AGENDA:

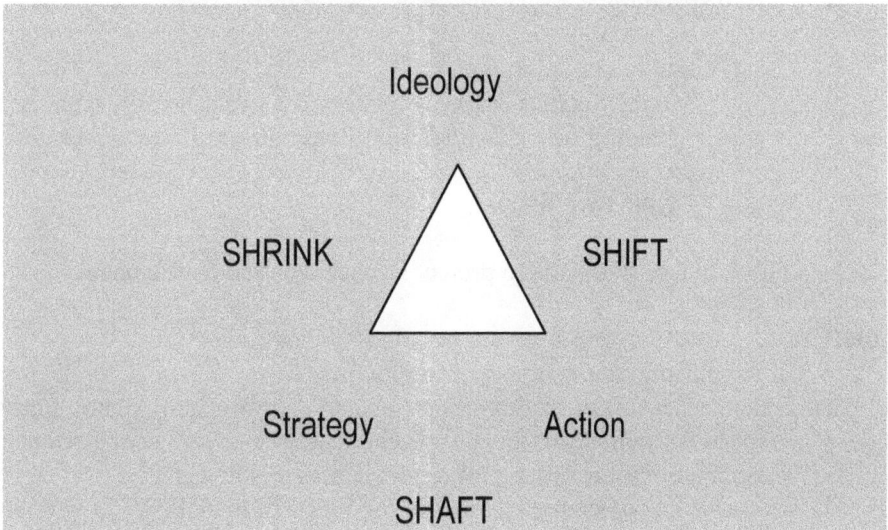

Ideology

SHRINK   SHIFT

Strategy   Action

SHAFT

Ideology: a political dogma or coherent philosophy rooted in a specific political and economic system that evolved over time (neoliberalism)

Strategy: with concrete goals and timetables, with its own cultural, economic, and political institutions and organizations (i.e., media, think-tanks, lobby groups, networks of supporters, etc.)

Action: specific acts, events, and decisions manifested through executive orders, judicial appointments, legislation, and budgetary plans.

SHRINK
- The size of government
- Social spending:

    o Safety net programs
    o Money to cities & towns for services (water, roads, schools)
    o Spending on infrastructure – commuter rail, roads, bridges, etc.
    o Health care, etc.

- Government standards to protect workers and the environment

SHIFT
- Jobs (outsourcing, temporary employment)
- Tax burden (away from corporations and toward individuals; from wealthy individuals to the middle class and low-income populations)
- Responsibility for social programs to cities and towns
- Control and ownership of wealth from PUBLIC to PRIVATE (privatization) and from LOCAL GOVERNMENT/COMMUNITY to TRANSNATIONAL CORPORATIONS (globalization)

SHAFT
- Unions and workers rights decimated
- Civil and human rights under attack
- Democratic institutions
- Working folks

What is Neoliberalism and What are its Institutions?

Definition of Neoliberalism
In brief, neoliberalism is a strategy to remove all barriers to the free market. In neoliberalism, the market is king. Prices and quantities determine how people exchange goods and services. Government is seen as an impediment to the market. Letting the free market reign means removing government protections and scaling back government as much as possible.

History of Neoliberalism
The term neoliberalism means "new liberalism." Here, this refers to economic liberalism, which is very different from political liberalism. In fact, they are extreme opposites. Political liberalism, in the U.S., has come to mean strong social protection and a large role for government. Economic liberalism, however, is born from the work of Adam Smith, who wrote *The Wealth of Nations* in the late 1700s. Smith was rebelling against mercantilism, a strategy by which governments hoarded gold and silver. Smith sought to "liberate" the markets from excessive government intervention; whence came the term liberalism. Economic liberalism implied scaling back the government and letting competition play the major role in deciding how goods and services are allocated and distributed. It is a Darwinian system, whereby the strongest in the market survive. Equality, solidarity, community are all left out of the picture, as competition over goods and services (and thus market power and political power) are at the forefront.

While a little healthy competition might be good for science and progress, the Great Depression taught us what happens if markets are left unregulated. Bank failures, severe unemployment, and famine made some economists realize that free markets were not the best way to organize economic activity. The work of John Maynard Keynes, a British economist, focused on the role that government can play to regulate economic activity and mitigate the instability that is inherent in capitalism. Government intervention could soften the effects of a recession and possibly prevent a depression. It could also lead to higher employment, better conditions for workers, lower poverty, and many other socially-minded outcomes. Keynes's work ushered in a new era of economic policymaking, including the New Deal in the U.S., which gave a large role to government. In the early 1930s, President Franklin D. Roosevelt instituted a series of programs which included environmental conservation, building up public infrastructure (such as schools, bridges, dams, parks, and hospitals), strengthening unions and setting minimum wages. FDR's New Deal, in the Keynesian tradition, sought to end cut-throat competition and ensure that people were employed and earning decent wages.

As a result, in the '50s and '60s (the 'Golden Age'), we saw high levels of social services, high worker productivity, high rates of unionism, and high wages (the real minimum wage peaked in 1968) in the United States. This era showed the benefits to workers and more generally, the population, of having strong social programs and a large role for government. Why did this era come to an end? The more powerful and better-paid workers threatened business profits and made the global elite uncomfortable. (It is important to note that business profits were actually quite high, and thus it was not the falling profits that made business owners uncomfortable, but rather the fact that workers were gaining an increased share of the profits through high unionization and high employment rates.) In reaction to their perceived loss of power, the global elite developed a strategy to attack the gains made by workers and to reinforce their own power. The neoliberal ideology of free markets and small government was promoted by economists (mainly through Milton Friedman and the "Chicago School" of economics) and adopted through policy in the U.S. and abroad in order to make big businesses powerful again. Unions were busted, taxes on businesses and large wealthholders were lowered, and financial flows between countries were liberalized. Now, businesses in the U.S. have levels of freedom and power not witnessed since before the Great Depression, while workers' power has declined and economic inequality has increased.

In particular, countries—especially developing ones—have been encouraged by wealthy nations and international financial institutions like the World Bank and the International Monetary Fund to make "structural adjustments" to attract foreign investment. These lending institutions make their loans conditional on Structural Adjustment Programs (SAPs). The SAPs are designed to reduce the size of government and open markets to foreigners. For example, these adjustments include allowing currency to "float" to make exports more competitive, liberating financial institutions to provide high interest rates to investors, and liberating financial flows to allow foreign investment to flow freely to projects and businesses with the highest yields. While these policies may sound okay in theory, they have been devastating in practice. They have created a bias toward high interest rate policies that hurt exports and jobs, caused instability when investors suddenly pull out, and exacerbated economic inequality by redirecting income from workers to the already wealthy. Furthermore, developing countries are encouraged to lower tax rates on business, which results in eroding the tax base and thus government revenues and finally restricts the ability of developing-country governments to provide social services to their population. Neoliberal policies—spread to the developing world through the institutions of the World Bank and the IMF —serve to shrink the size of developing countries' governments, shift power over economic institutions to multinational corporations and outside governments, and shaft the populations of those countries that these lending institutions are allegedly helping.

What are the policies of neoliberalism?

- Privatization (of schools, roads, transportation, resources, etc.)
- Scaling back government (services, regulations, jobs)
Free flow of money and goods (and free flow of people in theory but not in practice)
- Fighting inflation rather than unemployment (in the Golden Age, the government sought to fight both inflation and unemployment; in the neoliberal era, unemployment is no longer a concern and instead there is excessive attention to fighting inflation, which affects owners more than workers)

What are the effects?

- Loss of worker protection, both in developed and developing countries (threat effects, informalization of labor, lower wages and benefits, lower rates of unionization)
- Reduced services (such as healthcare, education, eldercare, housing assistance)
- Loss of public sector jobs
- Increased unemployment in the 'primary sector' of the U.S
- Increased frustration and insecurity, which leads to increased domestic violence and crime
- Environmental degradation
- Increased income inequality

Group Work on Relating Participants' Issues to S-S-S

After discussing the history and policies of neoliberalism, we broke into small groups and participants discussed how the issues they work on fit into the shrift-shift-shaft framework. Often the issues within a group were quite different, so groups chose one or two issues to discuss.
They tried to answer the following questions:

- How do your issues fit into this framework?
- Does understanding neoliberalism help to understand the causes of and possible responses to your issues?

Participants were then asked to write their issues on sticky notes and post them on the triangle where they seemed to fit. After a number of people described and posted their issues, we discussed common threads and noticed that many activist issues have been affected by the shrink, shift *and* shaft of neoliberalism.

Group Work: How Neoliberalism Affects Different Groups of People

Finally, we assigned each group an "identity," so that they could discuss how neoliberalism affected one segment of the population. Some identities included workers, owners, people of color, immigrants, and women. The participants discussed how people might be affected by neoliberalism. Some examples included:

- Less health insurance, more expensive healthcare
- Less food assistance
- Forced to work because partner is unemployed
- Inability to find a job, higher risk of unemployment
- Lower wages
- Increased frustration and insecurity

Take-Home Lessons

Neoliberal policies affect us all. And for those of us who are not part of the global elite, they can have devastating consequences. Through this workshop at the USSF, we learned that what we are seeing in our communities – whether it be shrinking funding for public education, collapsing bridges and pot-holed roads, or inadequate healthcare coverage – is all part of a systematic plan to consolidate power in the hands of a few while eroding the communities and opportunities of the many.

This system is not sustainable. It is failing us environmentally, politically, socially and economically. The USSF was a first step toward both realizing the problems with the neoliberal regime as well as devising strategies toward making change. There can be a better way to organize economic activity – a way that serves human needs, not corporate needs. Rather than accepting the neoliberal values of individualism, competition, and profits, we can work towards a system which prioritizes values such as community, health, solidarity, equality, sustainability and democracy.

Resources

Harvey, David. (2006). *A Brief History of Neoliberalism*. London; New York: Oxford University Press.

Pollin, Robert. (2005). *Contours of Descent: U.S. Economic Fractures and the Landscape of Global Austerity.* London; New York: Verso.

Econ-Atrocities published by the Center for Popular Economics: Visit www.populareconomics.org to subscribe or view the Econ-Atrocity blog at http://www.fguide.org/?cat=3

2

Social Economy & Solidarity Economy:
Transformative Concepts
for Unprecedented Times?

Michael Lewis and Dan Swinney[1]

*Mike Lewis is editor of Making Waves magazine, Executive
Director of the Centre for Community Enterprise, and past
chair of the National Policy Council of the Canadian CED
Network. Contact him at 250-723-1139 or
ccelewis@island.net.*

*Dan Swinney is the executive director and founder of the Center
for Labor and Community Research (CLCR) and has 35 years
of community and labor organizing as well as community-
development experience. After graduating with a B.A. in history
from the University of Wisconsin, Madison, Dan worked for 13
years as a machinist in the Chicago area. He organized Steelworker Local 8787 at G+W Taylor Forge in Cicero, Illinois,
and served as Vice President. He is a Board member of the
Leadership Greater Chicago Fellows Association. He has written articles appearing in Economic Development America, Social Policy, Business Ethics, New Labor Forum, Working USA,
the South Africa Labour Bulletin, Yes!, and other publications.
He is part of the coordinating committee for the U.S. Solidarity
Economy Network.*

"Community economic development," "economic democracy," "worker ownership," "co-operative economy," "fair trade," "sustainable community development," "social economy" — a range of movements currently challenges the way
North America lives and works.

In addition to a tremendous body of talent and practice, they share a range of
concepts, accumulated experience and, to a lesser extent, related research. All
seek to reinsert social goals into the heart of our economic life, an agenda contrary to the economic model of the last four decades. Many have roots in the 19th
century struggles of people relegated to the margins by the industrial revolution.
Others have grown out of the modern "margins," where the failures of "free

market" orthodoxy have created enclaves in which people have few options other than to invent economic alternatives.

"Social economy" and "solidarity economy" are two frameworks for understanding the economic alternatives springing up around the globe. In parts of western Europe, Latin America, and Africa, these terms are commonly applied to a range of socio-economic-cultural development strategies, activities, and structures, ranging from the small and local to the large and global. They are less familiar in North America, outside Québec. To some their meaning is uncertain. To others, it is unimportant. Are they not just two more additions to our "alphabet soup" of terminology?

We don't think so. Both frameworks deserve close consideration, especially by those working in the field. Murky conceptualization will not serve us well, particularly given the major trends that are cutting a swath across all segments of human society (Peak Oil and climate change most prominently). They present us with unprecedented demands for thoughtful, energetic, and broad-based societal action. One has to wonder if these rapidly shifting realities are outstripping many of the conceptual formulations we use to guide and explain our work. It is with this concern in mind that we explore the conceptual boundaries we live within, challenging their probity and relevance to the risks we and our planet face in the decades ahead.

Exploring the Conceptual Terrain

The social economy can be understood to lie within what John Pearce calls the "third system" of the economy, as opposed to the "first" (private/profit-oriented) and "second" systems (public service/planned provision). This third system also includes the voluntary sector, a range of associations, and the family economy. They share an orientation to self-help, to reciprocity, and to realizing social purpose through various types of organization and association. (See Diagram 1, "Three Systems," next page)[2]

Diagram 1: Three Systems of the Economy

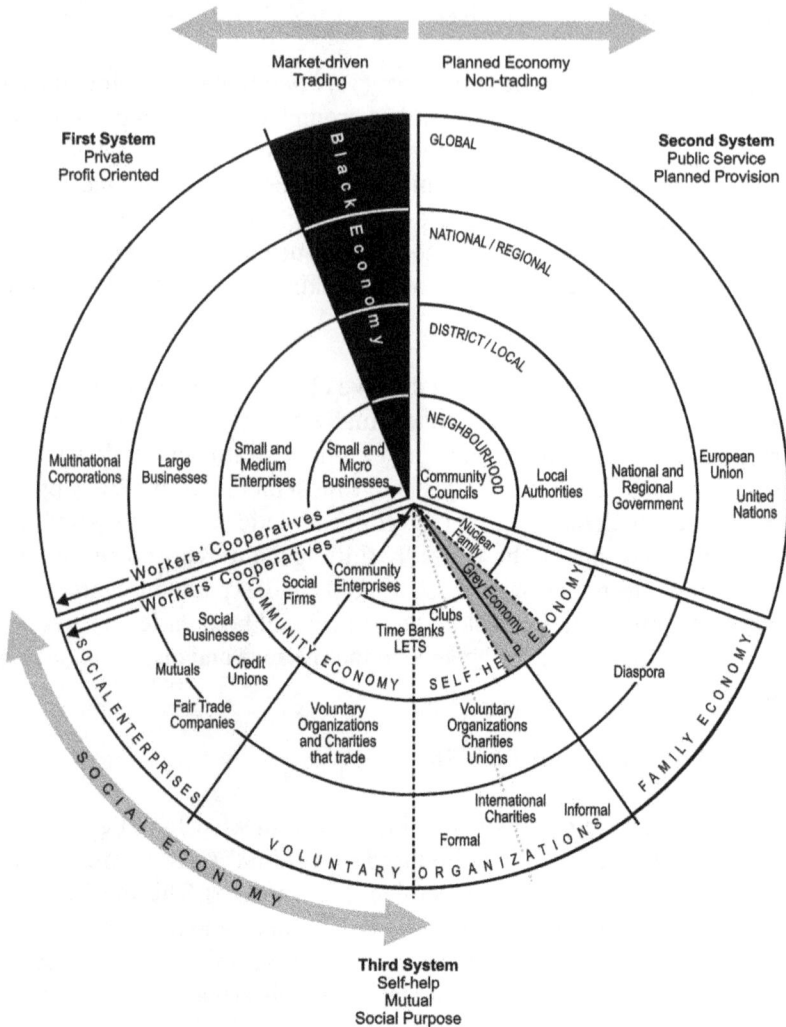

Market-driven
Trading

Planned Economy
Non-trading

First System
Private
Profit Oriented

Black Economy

GLOBAL

NATIONAL / REGIONAL

DISTRICT / LOCAL

NEIGHBOURHOOD

Second System
Public Service
Planned Provision

Multinational
Corporations

Large
Businesses

Small and
Medium
Enterprises

Small and
Micro
Businesses

Community
Councils

Local
Authorities

National and
Regional
Government

European
Union

United
Nations

Workers' Cooperatives

Workers' Cooperatives

Social
Firms

Community
Enterprises

Nuclear
Family

Grey Economy

Social
Businesses

Clubs
Time Banks
LETS

Mutuals

Credit
Unions

SELF-HELP

Diaspora

Fair Trade
Companies

Voluntary
Organizations
and Charities
that trade

Voluntary
Organizations
Charities
Unions

COMMUNITY ECONOMY

SOCIAL ENTERPRISES

International
Charities

Informal

Formal

FAMILY ECONOMY

VOLUNTARY ORGANIZATIONS

SOCIAL ECONOMY

Third System
Self-help
Mutual
Social Purpose

In this context, the social economy involves the use of market-based trading activities to meet social goals. It represents a broad social consciousness within civil society where the interests of poor, immigrant, worker, and women's groups are explicitly recognized and integrated into production settings through various types of social enterprise, including co-ops.

There are different perspectives on the role of the social economy in social change. Reformists generally focus attention on securing resources to better support marginalized constituencies. Radicals, however, look upon the social economy as a means for transformation. It is a construction site for building strategies, tools, and institutions that can challenge neoliberal hegemony in the market and the state.

Pearce draws firm boundaries between the private, the public, and the third sector. John Restakis argues that the private, public, and social economy sectors are animated by distinct economic principles. While the boundaries between them may be permeable to some degree, there is no changing the logic that animates each of them.[3]

The focus within the private sector is the exchange of goods and services for commercial gain. Ownership is determined by the private control of capital. The primary purpose is to maximize returns on investment to shareholders. Capital controls labor. The key aim of the commercial exchange is the economic principle of *efficiency*. The operations of the public sector focus on the redistribution of wealth and the provision of public goods for the purpose of promoting the economic principle of *equality*.

The economic principle that animates the social economy is *reciprocity*. The primary purpose of social economy organizations is the promotion of mutual collective benefit. The aim of reciprocity is human bonding or *solidarity*. In contrast to the private sector, reciprocity puts labor, citizens, or consumers in control of capital.

In Restakis' view, the social economy includes all co-operatives and credit unions, nonprofit and volunteer organizations, charities and foundations, service associations, community enterprises, and social enterprises that use market mechanisms to pursue explicit social objectives. It includes only those collectively-owned for-profit enterprises whose surpluses are shared by members, and no government or private businesses of any kind.

How useful are these definitions of social economy? When applied to the real world of community revitalization, do they clarify or obscure? Profiles of two prominent social economy organizations, one in Montreal and the other in Chicago, may shed some light here.

RÉSO: Revitalizing Southwest Montreal

Southwest Montréal suffered industrial decline from the 1960s through the early 1990s. By 1984, 40-50% of the residents of the formerly solid working class neighborhoods lived below the poverty line. That was the year organizations in the neighborhood of Point St. Charles began to mobilize in opposition to deindustrialization and gentrification. In 1989, these efforts culminated in the formation of RÉSO (Regroupement pour la relance économique et sociale du sud-ouest de Montréal), a unique partnership committed to the economic and social renewal of Point St. Charles and four other poor neighborhoods.

RÉSO evolved into a membership-based organization. Its board comprises elected representatives from five member categories: the community movement (four directors), trade unions (two), big business (one), small business (one), and individual members (one). Today, RÉSO has 300 organizational members and 1500 individual members.

Owing to the comprehensive nature of its mandate, RÉSO has taken action on a vast range of issues relating to human resource development, business retention and development, land use, infrastructure, and local promotion. It directly provides and brokers training and job development services for up to 1500 people each year. It also has assisted hundreds of training businesses over the years to customize their investments to the needs of local business and the capabilities of residents. An early warning system alerts RÉSO to the potential closure of local businesses.

The synergy created by this approach is illustrated by the actions of the largest manufacturer in southwest Montreal, CAD Railway Industries. A RÉSO board member, CAD's CEO became convinced that the company had to re-orient its business to contribute more significantly to neighborhood revitalization. It maximized local purchases in the company's $70 million annual procurement budget. Another more dramatic example is that of a Spanish supplier who opened a business in the area in order to keep the $5-6 million annual supply contract it had enjoyed for several years. The result was 65 new jobs to local people referred by RÉSO.

In the mid-'90s, RÉSO launched a community venture capital fund in partnership with the Québec Solidarity Fund, and with support from the federal and provincial governments. By means of this $5 million fund, RÉSO can directly invest as a business owner to create jobs and diversify its financial base.

By the mid-1990s, Statistics Canada reported that the decline in manufacturing in southwest Montreal had stopped. Between 1998 and 2003, RÉSO helped some 40 social enterprises come into being, creating close to 500 local jobs.

To what does RÉSO owe its success? "The ability of RÉSO to bring all these diverse people together has been remarkable," asserts Fausto Levy of CAD. "It provides a forum for everyone to discuss issues that are important to them and allows for understanding to begin. As a result, we've been able to solve many problems with everyone being very satisfied."

This is echoed by Gaston Lemieux, President of the local Aluminum, Brick, and Glass Workers Union, who thinks of RÉSO as a key ally. "RÉSO is a tool that's very useful to the private, public, and commercial sectors as well as to the unions and the community," says Lemieux. "It gathers all the forces of all the sectors to conserve jobs. All sectors are interconnected. RÉSO is the forum where everyone can get together and make things work again."

CMRC: Revitalizing Chicago's Manufacturing Sector

Austin, a large neighborhood on Chicago's West Side, has experienced an industrial and social implosion over the last 25 years. It lost roughly 20,000 industrial jobs; 30% of residents live below the poverty line; nearly a third of households receive public assistance; drug trafficking and gang activity are at alarming levels.

In 2001, an analysis conducted by the Center for Labor and Community Research (CLCR) and the Chicago Federation of Labor indicated that one factor in the decline of neighborhoods like Austin is the failure of the public education system to graduate students with the skills needed by local manufacturing companies. The report outlined a 20-year corrective strategy that included the creation of small high schools linked to the manufacturing sector. The Illinois Manufacturer's Association (IMA) took an interest in the report. More than 85% of its members are small, privately-held companies with limited resources. Unable to relocate their premises, these companies face a loss of 40% of their workforce over the next ten years.

Under contract to the IMA, the CLCR completed a study of Illinois manufacturing. The study recommended that IMA form a partnership with labor, government, and community groups in order to compete in the high value-added segment of manufacturing complex products. With products that command top dollar on the marketplace, employers could pay higher wages and provide good benefits while still making a solid return. This type of production requires a world-class education system, as well as a world-class social, physical, and technological infrastructure. Investment by both the public and private sectors coupled with a strong role for civil society and community were fundamental to achieving the goal.

This report became the basis for the founding of a unique public-private-community partnership in July 2005, the Chicago Manufacturing Renaissance

Council. CMRC brings together all the stakeholders to help manufacturing companies

- Become more innovative in production.
- Reinvest in equipment and in their workforce.
- Improve the educational institutions that produce the next generation of workers.
- Ensure that government and labor support the sustainability and growth of manufacturing companies.

To CMRC, three principles are crucial:

- Genuine social partnership of labor, business, community, and government.
- Participation of each partner in the design and implementation of every initiative.
- Development that is economically, socially, and environmentally sustainable.

These linkages are unmistakable in the CMRC's first major investment: a manufacturing-centered public high school in Austin. Austin Polytechnical Academy opened in September 2007 with a freshman class of 140 students. It will add a class per year to reach a size of 550 students.
So far, 24 companies have partnered with the school to provide general support, work experience, internships, and summer jobs, as well as prospects for full-time employment upon graduation. Companies as well as teachers, community members, parents, and students are represented on the school's governing body.

Unlike the typical vocational educational experience, which often mimics the racial discrimination of the larger society, Austin Polytech will promote career paths into skilled production positions, as well as into the management and ownership of companies. More specifically, the school is anchored in a development agenda that aims to realize a mixed economy with a vibrant high-performance manufacturing sector at its core, returning Chicago manufacturing to the top ranks of global innovation while revitalizing some of the city's most devastated neighborhoods.

Exploring the Profiles

The two profiles provide a rich basis for exploring Pearce's and Restakis' understanding of social economy. By their respective definitions, both RÉSO and CMRC are social economy organizations. However, their governance structures, their constituencies, their partners, their clients, and their funders include significant private and public sector engagement.

RÉSO provides a wide range of services and supports that benefit locally-based private business as well as a range of social enterprises. Similarly, CMRC is a "3-system" initiative with "mutual economic and social goals" embedded in its mandate. Key players from each "system" are involved financially, strategically, and operationally. A number of actors have decided to create another social economy organization, Austin Polytech, to link the rebuilding of the manufacturing sector to high-quality education, poverty reduction, and neighborhood revitalization.

Do not these experiences reflect a level of relationship, social purpose, mutual aid, and reciprocity that challenges the boundaries of social economy depicted by Pearce and Restakis? In both cases, does not mutuality in fact extend across and among all three systems? Are not social goals embedded in the economic decision-making and strategy? If RÉSO or CMRC had confined their strategic targets, partnerships, and alliances to "third system" actors, and excluded the private and public sectors, could they have achieved the same level of innovation and socio-economic impact? It seems unlikely.

This evidence undermines the notion that the principle of reciprocity is confined to the social economy and its actors. While RÉSO and CMRC are representatives of the "social economy," they are doing more than social economy. They have entered the realm of the *solidarity economy.*

A Cross-Cutting Concept

Conceptually, the social economy occupies the societal space between the public and private sectors. In contrast, the solidarity economy is located at the intersection of all three.

In Diagram 2, "Reframing the Debate" (next page), the solidarity economy appears as a small circle cutting across the boundaries of all three systems. However, its aim is large: to compete against the dominant Low Road development paradigm, expanding the reach and scale of High Road strategies across all of society. (See Textbox, "Roads High and Low.")

Diagram 2: Reframing the Debate

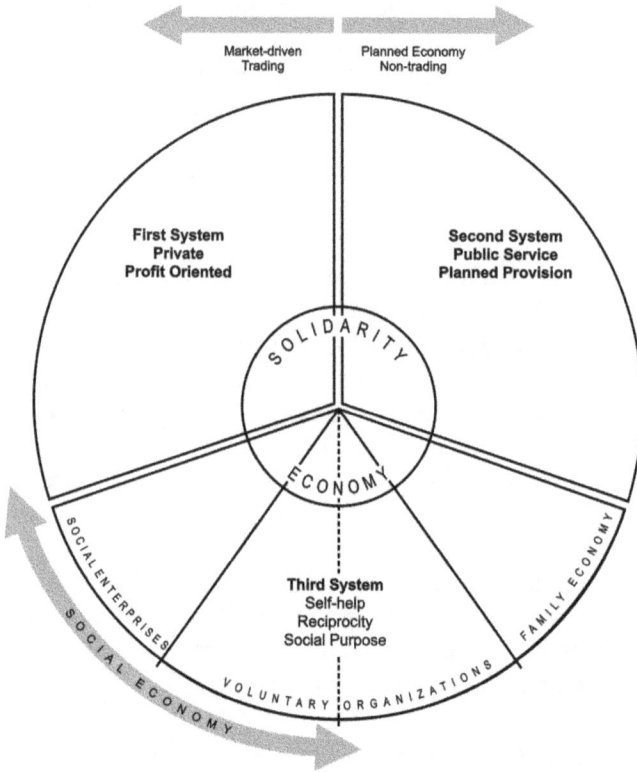

Market-driven
Trading

Planned Economy
Non-trading

First System
Private
Profit Oriented

Second System
Public Service
Planned Provision

SOLIDARITY

ECONOMY

SOCIAL ENTERPRISES

SOCIAL ECONOMY

FAMILY ECONOMY

Third System
Self-help
Reciprocity
Social Purpose

VOLUNTARY ORGANIZATIONS

Roads High and Low

Distinguishing the High Road from the Low is not science but a judgment. Typically, the practices of companies, organizations, and agencies are a mix of both. In both the private and public sectors, the High Road seeks a strong return on investment by:

- Being smarter and investing in innovation in the more competitive environment.
- Making a commitment to the continual enhancement of employees' skills.
- Being more efficient and cutting waste.
- Having a long-term vision and commitment.
- Providing strong material incentives for high performance, as well as providing decent wages, benefits, and security.
- Promoting useful partnerships with stakeholders in the firm, in the sector, and in the community.
- Being transparent, straightforward, and fair.

At the very heart of a High Road strategy is a commitment to innovation, such as developing new niches and markets, adding value to existing products, investing in research and development, expanding market share, and improving the efficiency of the productive process and the productivity of employees. Some would see this as the way manufacturing was generally done in the past; it is not a particularly new concept.

In contrast, the Low Road in business seeks a strong return on investment by:

- Emphasizing short-term gains, even if they mean postponing or sacrificing improvements in the productive capacity of the company or sector.
- Keeping wages and benefits at the lowest possible levels.
- Managing by intimidation, undermining employee initiative, and discouraging the exercise of employee rights.
- Ignoring the needs and concerns of others apart from the most powerful (and short-sighted) shareholders, investors, and/or managers.

Public sector organizations or agencies follow the Low Road when they give their own rewards and benefit such a high priority that they are willing to damage their partners or the broader economy. For example:

- *In government:* holding on to bureaucratic strength and privilege no matter what the consequence for the public.
- *In labor:* excessive demands from a high road employer that, in the pursuit of short-term benefits for union members, place the community fundamentally at risk.
- *In community:* nursing a "community benefits agreement for a specific constituency with a company (e.g., Wal-Mart) whose business plan will devastate the regional economy.

The scope of this agenda parallels the radical view of the social economy as a transformative strategy. The conceptual cloth of the solidarity economy is cut quite differently, however. While connecting to all three systems, the solidarity economy requires that we reconsider their boundaries for strategic purposes. From the vantage point of strategy, one's location within one or another of the three systems is not so important as one's commitments and actions. Do they reflect the "life-damaging, growth-addicted features of Low Road capitalism"? Or do they manifest "the values of justice, inclusion, balance, diversity, ecological sustainability, and financial viability" characteristic of the High Road?

The solidarity economy, which admittedly is more a "strategy" than it is a "system," explicitly contends for High Road values and practices in all three "economic systems," and in this way is complementary to the social economy. On the one hand, one may argue that the social economy is the only system where social goals are central to the development equation. On the other hand, the solidarity economy significantly expands the legitimate terrain of engagement for social economy practitioners; it challenges the claim that social purpose and reciprocity cannot become manifestly central to exchange within the private and public sectors. In short, the agenda is to maximize the space occupied by the values of the High Road across the society.

This assertion has profound implications for the scope, targets, and criteria that guide alliance-building among those committed to transformative change. Actors within any of the three systems — community, labor, business, government, finance, and educators — may follow either a High Road or a Low Road strategy. Values, priorities, policy, and performance are the distinguishing features.

Without denying the distinctive qualities of each system, the solidarity economy challenges "system" smugness on the part of actors in all of them. It explicitly encourages collaboration between systems in order to enlarge the space within which reciprocity can be re-woven into the fabric of the community.

In addition to expanding the domain of action, the concept of the solidarity economy elevates the importance of leadership on the part of organizations rooted in the values, principles, and goals that animate the "third system." It commits them to advance their key aims and principles into both the private and the public sectors. Thus, bridges are built and reinforced across old divides; whole new realms open up for strategic thinking and engagement.

It is fascinating to consider the contexts out of which innovations in the social economy, CED, economic democracy, co-operatives, and social enterprise have emerged. How many gated communities have established a social enterprise or a CED organization to realize social change? None that we know of. Where key social innovations have emerged and continue to emerge is among people, places, and sectors that markets have failed.

Many of these innovations were responses to the consequences of the exclusion and oppression instigated by the wealthy and powerful. Building the co-operative economy, mobilizing citizens to reciprocally share resources, organizing workers to defend their interests against unregulated capitalists — all were part of addressing the concrete circumstances of the day.

Today, there are global trends still more powerful and expansive than those that shaped the context of the 19th and early 20th centuries.

First, communication is global, immediate, and cheap. Animation, education, and organization are possible in ways unimaginable even 25 years ago. Second, the human- and planet-threatening consequences of a consumption-led economic "free-for-all" are recognized by only a very small portion of the world's population. Climate change and Peak Oil, food and water security, and the increasing number of human beings suffering exclusion and poverty — all these are issues that we cannot effectively address within "system" silos.

In this unprecedented and bewildering situation, the cross-cutting strategy embedded in the concept of the solidarity economy appears a better meta-framework from which to chart the terrain in the 21st century.

This need not lead "social economy" actors to ignore their own domain. Quite the opposite, in fact. The solutions we so desperately need to invent in the 21st century will require us to practice the economic principle of reciprocity more rigorously, creatively, and broadly. Social economy organizations must become more effective agents in creating the societal space within which solidarity can grow. This requires understanding the larger system and continuously scanning for opportunities to extend and expand life-supporting innovations.

Diagram 3 (next page) depicts where we are at present. The circle of solidarity is small, evident more in the "third system" than in the other two. The boundaries are open within the circle, still divided beyond it. Within the circle, there is a conscious striving to journey on the High Road. Beyond the circle there is much less consciousness. The actions of those within the circle — their capacity to ruminate, agitate, animate, educate, communicate, advocate, and consummate innovations that reach beyond the "inner circle" — are fundamental to facilitating positive social and economic change.

Diagram 3: Where are we starting from?

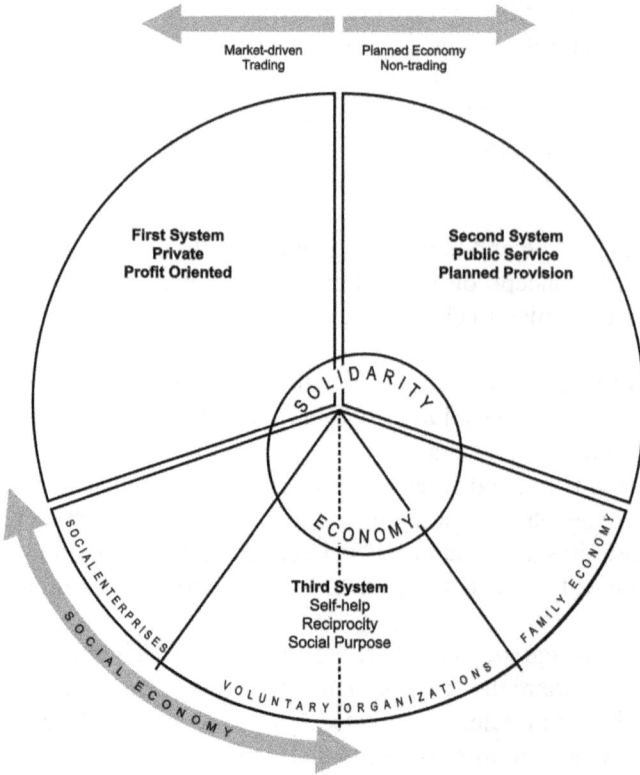

In summary, the solidarity economy demands we explicitly contend for "third system" values (justice, inclusion, balance, ecological sustainability, and economic viability) and the economic principle of reciprocity in both the marketplace and in the state. As solidarity grows, space and relationships are created in which to incubate innovation and scale up success, thus expanding the circle, thus constructing and extending the High Road as we travel.

Viewed thus, solidarity becomes more than a result, more than a strategy; it is a vital resource, a source of energy and perspective that helps us move beyond the pedantic and the pedestrian, and compels us to act out of a deeper, moral consciousness. The solidarity economy can inject energy, creativity, and organizing capacity into the most compelling and difficult transition human beings may ever have the opportunity to make.

This article is an abridgement of the authors' paper "Social Economy? Exploring the Implications of Conceptual Nuance for Acting in a Volatile World" (BC-

Alberta Social Economy Research Alliance Working Paper Series, September 2007 ,17 pp.

References

Pearce, John. (2003). *Social Enterprise in Any Town*. London: Calouste Gulben-
    kian Foundation.
Restakis, John. (2005). "Defining the Social Economy: The BC Context."
    British Columbia Co-operative Association. January 2006. Accessed
    30 September 2007 from:
    http://www.bcca.coop/pdfs/Defining_Social_Economy.pdf.

Notes

[1] This article was originally published in *Making Waves: Canada's Community Economic Development Magazine*, 18,4 (Winter 2007), 9-15. Reprinted by permission of the Canadian Centre for Community Renewal, Port Alberni, B.C.

[2] Revised from John Pearce. (2003). Social Enterprise in Any Town. London: Calouste Gulbenkian Foundation.

[3] John Restakis. (2005). "Defining the Social Economy: The BC Context". British Columbia Co-operative Association. January 2006. Accessed 30 September 2007 from http://www.bcca.coop/pdfs/Defining_Social_Economy.pdf.

3
Between Local and Global: Alternatives to Globalization

Sally Kohn

> *Sally Kohn is the Director and Founder of the Movement Vision Lab at the Center for Community Change, supporting grass-roots leaders and activists to share and debate new, visionary ideas for the future. She regularly convenes discussions with grassroots activists and other thinkers about the most pressing issues our society is facing, including the future of the economy in the face of globalization and other transformations. Kohn previously worked with the Ford Foundation, the Social Justice Infrastructure Funders, the Urban Justice Center, the Third Wave Foundation and the National Gay and Lesbian Task Force, among other organizations. She holds a BA from George Washington University and a joint MPA/JD from New York University, where she received a Root Tilden scholarship. She is a regular contributor to the Huffington Post, AlterNet, Common Dreams and Tom Paine, among other news and opinion sources.*

In some debates, the questions are more important than the answers. By today's standards, even questioning the inevitability of economic globalization in its current form is a radical act. The answers, then, are potentially revolutionary.

On June 29, 2007, a group of economists and grassroots community organizers participated in a discussion at the first United States Social Forum in Atlanta, Georgia. Entitled "Challenging the myth of free trade: What is the alternative?," the discussion grew out of a recognition that while we know economic globalization and free trade in their current forms aren't working for the vast majority of Americans nor communities around the globe, we're not exactly overwhelmed with plausible alternatives. The alternatives we do explore tend to focus on making economic globalization as-is more humane and more fair. But we spend woefully little time as a global justice movement unpacking the deep assumptions and structures of global capitalism in its current form and debating our vision for the global economy's future.

The panel, convened by the Movement Vision Lab at the Center for Community Change and the Center for Popular Economics, featured a mock debate between two economists (Hector Saez from the University of Vermont and Corrina Steward from Grassroots International) and responses from two grassroots leaders (Alyce Gowdy-Wright from South Florida Jobs with Justice in Miami, Florida, and Omar Freilla from Green Worker Cooperatives in the Bronx, New York). The interactive format between panelists and audience participants surfaced a much more complex picture of global trade's benefits and pitfalls as well as other models and how they interrelate.

In its current form, economic globalization produces big wins for big corporations and big losses for most everyone else. Natural resources are robbed from the global South for the gain of the global North. Low-wage workers, too, are exploited in the global South for corporate titans based in the North. In turn, local producers — from furniture makers to farmers — are driven out of business across the global South due to the flood of cheap goods and crops from the North. In Mexico alone, over two million family farms were put out of business by NAFTA. But the pain is felt in the North as well, with factory workers and family farmers from South Dakota to South Carolina reeling as jobs move overseas and subsidized crops grown at a global scale flood local markets. Under the current rules of the game for global capitalism, all the points go to big business while families and workers across the globe increasingly find themselves on the sidelines.

Fair Trade as an Alternative to Neoliberal Globalization

Thus the idea evolved from social justice circles to humanize economic globalization and make it work for families and workers across the globe. The idea of "fair trade" emerged as the primary, progressive alternative to the existing hegemony. Fair trade argues that trade is a good thing as long as the playing field is leveled — creating uniform, global standards around worker rights and the environment, setting fair base prices, ensuring profits accrue to producers and not just corporate intermediaries, etc. Local producers in the global South can't compete with large corporations in the North that benefit from agricultural subsidies or government tax breaks for building new factories. Imagine the behemoth Wal-Mart competing with a local clothing store in Panama City when on top of the advantages of its size, advertising budget and more, Wal-Mart is getting over $1 billion in tax breaks and other subsidies in the United States that help it keep costs artificially low. Wal-Mart wins and U.S. taxpayers and Panamanian business owners are set up to lose. That's not fair. That's cheating.It's also not fair when U.S. corporations move their factories overseas to exploit poor workers in the global South for greater profits and drive down wages and worker standards in the U.S. and everywhere. Workers across the globe are played against each other and, again, they all lose while big business rakes in the bucks. A robust fair trade agenda mandates equitable labor standards across the globe, no matter where a company does its business, as well as environmental and human rights standards that ensure a floor that we don't let any company sink below, anywhere in the world.

All of which makes economic globalization a lot better. And, as Hector Saez argued, this allows the benefits of economic globalization to shine. After all, there's something to the efficiency principles that undergird modern capitalism. Saez says, "It's hard to argue against the theory of comparative advantage. We have to argue against the institutions that surround it." Fair trade arguably allows different regions of the world to produce what they're best at, at the best price point, and trade with others to everyone's advantage. Theoretically, especially if environmental costs of shipping or local crop diversity and security aren't factors, it makes sense for Chile to grow strawberries and Washington State to grow applies because of their climates, and then the US exports applies South while Chile sends strawberries north. A further benefit is that through trade, we also export social norms — and not only through labor and environmental standards we can write into trade pacts. Many (though not most) of the Hollywood films we export to Russia, Afghanistan and Indonesia introduce the idea of equality for women in powerful and potentially revolutionary ways (in addition to some less desirable cultural messages that we also export...). Fair trade standards on worker justice and the environment have the potential to spread positive norms as well, with the added benefit of economic incentives for such awareness and practice.

Local Economies as an Alternative to Neoliberal Globalization

Yet the problem with trade-driven economies, argues Corrina Steward, is that local economies become oriented around meeting external needs as opposed to internal ones. People feed the market first, then themselves. But from the preservation of local culture and variety, to the practicalities of local self-sufficiency in the event of global shortages or disasters, to the environmental wastefulness that comes from shipping resources and goods around the world, there are strong arguments against any trade whatsoever. And obviously, given the fact that throughout history, trade has most often played out as resources and wealth trading hands from the poor to the rich worldwide, disenchantment with trade is understandable. Steward cites, as examples of the localization movement, communities in Latin America such as the landless peasants' movement (MST) in Brazil engaged in take back the land movements, creating seed banks of indigenous crops, relying on locally grown food and restoring local markets as social and cultural spaces and not just economic. Such movements dovetail with the environmental critiques of trade as ruining local crop diversity and security and wasting gas and pollution on shipping, as well as with cultural critiques of global trade as devastating to local cultural uniqueness and variety.

But the "back to the land, off the grid, unplug and go entirely local" vision has some problems, too. Politically, we have come to measure success and progress in terms of economic growth and a purely self-sufficient local economy produces no new wealth. Through increased productivity, the community can increase its wellbeing. And through individual productivity or lack thereof, an individual can have more or fewer resources. But the total economic pie of the unit — whether a family, a community or a nation — won't grow since growth is a relative concept. Geopolitically, gross domestic product (GDP) is the benchmark for national accomplishment — but GDP is meaningless without trade. So to the extent that economists and politicians alike promote economic growth as the singular ambition of the world's nations and people's, completely localized and self-sufficient economies would seem politically unlikely.

A Call for Balance

Moreover, Alyce Gowdy-Wright points out a pragmatic obstacle to localization. The movement of capital across countries has led to a movement of people as well. Officially sanctioned or undocumented, people have shifted across the globe as local economic opportunities in their home countries evaporated. Speaking of the community she lives and organizes in, Gowdy-Wright talks about Miami, Florida, where more than half of the population is foreign born. America's immigrant communities expanded in the wake of economic globalization and are evolving and enriching the story of our country. Certainly none of us who share community values and value inclusion want to send immigrants home, but how much does the immigration we champion and defend depend on the form of economic globalization we critique? Plus, while many immigrants would prefer to return to their home countries if meaningful opportunities existed there, for those who stay, immigration — new and old — realistically creates demands for goods and foods from around the world, which demands trade. Thinking about the United States alone, could we really produce everything for a multicultural nation within our own borders? Gowdy-Wright's points suggested that while localization may have once made sense, and might still idealistically, the pendulum may have swung too far in the global direction to swing entirely back.

All of which calls for a balance — the diversity and creativity of trade blended with the equity and sustainability of local economies. Perhaps the vision isn't just humanizing trade nor reviving local self-sufficiency but finding a new hybrid for a new era.

Omar Freilla posits that a key component of making global *and* local economies work for everyone worldwide is the issue of ownership. Freilla, who runs a worker-owned cooperative in the South Bronx of New York, explains that whereas most global trade today is dominated by large, multi-national corporations headquartered in the global North, it's not a huge improvement when corporations from the global South enter the trade game, dominated by elites from those countries. The challenge, then, is ensuring that small coffee growers in Central America can compete equally with large factory enterprises. And that means changing the scale on the retail end beyond just improving the rules of trade. Small growers can't make it with Wal-Mart, which will only deal with large bulk producers, but locally-owned grocery stores and coffee shops can deal with smaller-scale producers. And what's arguably lost in "efficiency" is gained in variety, not to mention a more fair and just distribution of money and opportunity to everyone worldwide.

In other words, whether the rules of trade are fair or not — providing fair profits and opportunities to small, local providers in every corner of the globe as well as environmental and labor safeguards and standards — that doesn't mean that the distribution of the goods of trade will necessarily be fair. Freilla's argument is that the Wal-Mart model of multi-national, wealthy investor-owned corporations which pay their workers a pittance, provide few benefits and destroy local economies in their wake will never be part of a fair economy, even if their stock comes from so-called "fair trade." For the entire economy to be fair, justice and equity must also be considered at the final leg of the consumer chain, offering incentives to small, worker-owned local businesses where that helps ensure market profits are spread as widely as possible.

Aristotle said, "Everything in moderation," which is an ironic quote to arrive at after claiming to explore radical questions and revolutionary answers. But perhaps the most revolutionary response to economic globalization which has invaded every space of our society and every pore of our being is to put it in its place, not with a reactionary swing in the complete opposite direction but by balancing the opportunities of globalization with the needs of communities. For communities that want to provide for themselves but also share their goods and resources on a regional or even global scale, ensuring fair prices, worker rights and environmental sustainability, we must build an economy for the future that works best for the whole while also working for every part.

4

There is an Alternative: Economic Democracy & Participatory Economics

A Debate Between David Schweickart and Michael Albert

David Schweickart is Professor of Philosophy at Loyola University Chicago. He holds PhD's in mathematics and philosophy. He is the author of three books and coauthor of one, his latest being <u>After Capitalism</u> (2002), as well as numerous articles in social and political philosophy. Professor Schweickart is a long-time member of the Radical Philosophy Association and has served on the editorial board of the Review of Radical Political Economics. He was a founding member of Loyola University's Amnesty International Chapter, the Loyola Organization in Solidarity with the People of El Salvador, and the Committee on Racism at Loyola.

Michael Albert is the founder and a current staff member of Z Magazine and ZNet. He has written many books and articles, including <u>Remembering Tomorrow: From SDS to Life After Capitalism</u> (2007), and <u>Parecon: Life After Capitalism</u> (2004). He is a public speaker, organizer, media worker, and he is also co-author of the economic model called participatory economics.

David Schweickart's Presentation

Let me begin by saying what Michael Albert and I agree about. We agree that:

- Capitalism is a deeply flawed economic system that needs to be replaced by a more humane social order. Capitalism gives rise to obscene inequalities; it is ecologically destructive; it is undemocratic.

- The Soviet model of central planning is not the answer. Even if democratized, the system would not be desirable. The model itself, as an economic model, is fundamentally flawed.

- We need to be able to articulate an alternative model to both capitalism and centrally-planned socialism that is economically viable and ethically desirable. Critique is not enough. Perhaps it once was, but no longer. The Left has to be able to answer the question, "What is your alternative?" We've got to be able to respond to the sort of remark Winston Churchill made with respect to democracy: capitalism is the worst of all systems–except for all the alternatives. We need to be concrete here, and not just offer pious generalities. We have to be able to specify institutions that can withstand critical scrutiny by both professional economists and committed activists.

- Participatory democracy should be a fundamental value of the new social order: people should have the right to participate in the decisions that affect them–in the workplace as well as in society at large.

We agree on a lot–and yet we disagree fundamentally on a number of key issues, the *most* fundamental being our assessment of "the market" as mechanism for allocating resources and distributing goods and services.

In my view, "the market" is not in fact a unitary mechanism, but should be regarded as three quite distinct markets: a market for goods and services, a labor market and a capital market. In my view, it is those latter two markets–the labor and capital markets–that do the most damage under capitalism. We need to stop treating labor as just another commodity to bought and sold; we need to get rid of those financial markets. We do *not* need to get rid of that first market. In my view, a competitive market for goods and services, while not wholly benign, is vastly preferable to alternative mechanisms for handling day-to-day decisions about production and consumption, whether these alternative mechanisms be centralized planning as in the Soviet Union, or the decentralized participatory planning of ParEcon.

Michael wants all markets abolished: "Markets aren't a little bad, or even just very bad in some contexts. Instead, in all contexts, markets instill anti-social motivations in buyers and sellers, misprice items that are exchanged, misdirect aims regarding what to produce in what quantities and by what means, misremunerates producers, introduces class divisions and class rule, and embody an imperial logic that spreads itself throughout economic life."[1]
I'll return briefly to our disagreement at the end of this talk. What I want to concentrate on here are the basic institutional structures of a model that I believe would address the most fundamental evils of capitalism. This model, I believe, is now on the horizon. It is eminently defensible both to professional economists and to lay people. It represents the natural extension of the democratic impulse, which has been developing now for several centuries, from the political realm

into key areas hitherto regarded as off limits to democracy: the workplace and investment decisions. I call it "Economic Democracy."[2] The basic model has three fundamental features.

1) Enterprises are governed democratically by their workers. Ultimate authority rests with the workforce, one person, one vote. Workers elect a worker council, which selects and monitors management.

   Workplace democracy is the replacement for the capitalist labor market. Labor is no longer a commodity, to be bought and sold. When you join an enterprise, you join a community, with full voting rights.

2) Enterprises compete for customers in a relatively free market. That is to say, the market for goods and services is carried over from capitalism.

3) Capital markets are replaced by what I call "social control of investment." Funds for investment are generated from a capital-assets tax, a flat rate tax imposed on all enterprises–not from the private savings of wealthy individuals. (This tax may be regarded as a "leasing fee" paid by the enterprise for the use of a portion of society's collective capital.")

   These funds are allocated to regions on a per-capita basis–that is to say, if a region contains X% of the nation's population, it gets X% of the nation's investment money–and then to public investment banks in the regions. These banks then give out these funds to

   a) Existing enterprises wanting to expand production or upgrade their technology,

   b) Individuals wanting to start up new enterprises, and

   c) Local governments wanting to upgrade infrastructure, build more schools and parks, etc.

In essence, "capital" under ED is *public money*, generated by a business tax, which flows to where the people are. This contrasts with capitalism, which generates its capital from the private savings of private individuals, who are free to invest wherever they choose, thus compelling people to go to where the capital is flowing.

Let me point out that this model did not spring out of thin air. It synthesizes trends that have been going on for some time. Humanity has long been searching for an alternative to capitalism–one that preserves the undeniable dynamic strengths of capitalism while eliminating its destructive effects. Consider the two basic aspects of the model.

First of all, workplace democracy: As capitalism came to dominate the European economies, it destroyed the livelihoods of millions, turning independent peasants and artisans into wage laborers, individuals having nothing to sell but themselves, their capacity to labor. Working people found themselves "alienated," having no control whatsoever over their conditions of work, no say whatsoever as to what they were producing or how it was to be produced.

In reaction, producer cooperatives came into being. Experiments with democratic workplaces date back to the early nineteenth century. Thousands of worker cooperatives exist today, some of them quite large. The Mondragon Cooperative Corporation in the Basque region of Spain is by far the dominant economic enterprise in that region and is now the third largest employer in all of Spain. The network of worker cooperatives in the Emilia-Romagna region of Italy's has been for years one of Italy's most vibrant industrial sectors. In the U.S. today there are some 2,500 businesses that are majority worker-owned.[3]

Democratic Workplaces

Democratic enterprises have been studied extensively. And the conclusion of virtually every study is the same: democratic workplaces work! They are almost always as efficient as their capitalist counterparts, and often more so. This is not so surprising. Everyone is motivated to work efficiently, since everyone's income is tied directly to how well the enterprise does. Moreover, workers usually better positioned than distant owners to see when managers are incompetent. In a democratic firm they can act on this knowledge before things spiral out of control.

Consider now, social control of investment: Once capitalism began to surge forth in Europe, increasing prosperity but also wreaking havoc, society fought back, attempting to counter its most destructive features. It's no accident that state has grown ever larger as capitalism has advanced–providing funds for infrastructure, education, basic research, social security, environmental protection, etc. It is now obvious that the state can generate investment funds via taxation, and can allocate them using criteria other than sheer profit maximization.

Of course the capitalist class has set the basic priorities of the state so as to promote their own interests, but even capitalists realize that relying on financial markets alone to channel investment is a recipe for chaos.

Moreover, many local initiatives have developed to direct the flow of at least some capital into areas where it is most needed: Community Development Credit Unions, legislation to require banks to reinvest a part of their holdings into the communities from which their savings have come, etc.

Of course, at present, these institutions control only a tiny fraction of the nation's investment funds, but they point to a radical conclusion. If there were no "capitalist class" functioning to generate and allocate capital, if these roles were absorbed into the democratic process, then rational development that accords with the real needs of the population would become possible.

These are the three basic features of Economic Democracy: workplace democracy, a competitive market for goods and services and social control of investment. I've proposed several other features in what I call, in my most recent book, the "expanded model" of Economic Democracy. Let me mention them briefly, to give you a fuller picture. Economic Democracy would also include

- The government acting as employer-of-last-resort: if you cannot find employment elsewhere a government agency will employ you (at a low but living wage) to do socially-necessary work.

  It is important to understand that we *cannot have* full employment under capitalism. The threat of unemployment is the disciplinary stick that keeps the workforce in line. Not only is unemployment necessary, but the condition of the unemployed must be humiliating enough and miserable enough for the threat to be credible.

  Under Economic Democracy this disciplinary stick is not required, since workers' basic motivation is positive. Everyone's income is a share of the firm's profits, so everyone is motivated to work effectively–and to encourage co-workers to do likewise. Of course irresponsible or incompetent people can be discharged, but the whole workforce does not have to be kept in line by fear.

- A quasi-capitalist sector comprised of small businesses and perhaps a sector of entrepreneurial capitalist firms.

It is important to distinguish between the "entrepreneurial capitalist" and the capitalist *qua* capitalist. Entrepreneurs remain important under Economic Democracy, be they capitalist entrepreneurs or socialist entrepreneurs. But the people whose social function it is to "supply capital"–these are the people we *don't* need. To rely on private individuals with far more money than they can spend to provide the investment funds that will shape the future for all of us is historically explicable, but no longer makes sense. A tax on capital assets is a far more transparent and effective mechanism for generating investment funds.

- A policy of "socialist protectionism" that blocks low-wage competition from poor countries but rebates the tariff proceeds to those countries.

  Economic Democracy does not object to competition per se. Indeed, it regards some forms of competition healthy. But it does not regard as healthy competition that forces workers to compete with each other to see who will work for the lowest wage, or countries to compete to see which has the least stringent environmental or labor legislation. These forms of competition will be blocked.

  At the same time Economic Democracy recognizes an obligation to help nations in need of developmental assistance. Hence the tariffs imposed to block unfair competition will be rebated to the poor country on whose products the tariff was imposed, either to the government, if it is progressive, or to labor and environmental groups in the country.

I have argued at length elsewhere that such an economic structure would be at least as efficient as capitalism, more rational in its growth, more egalitarian, better able to cope with the ecological challenges we face, and vastly more democratic. Let me note briefly a couple of the arguments.

We can have full employment under Economic Democracy. Since the incentive for efficient production is positive, not negative–everyone's income is a share of the firm's profits–the threat of unemployment is no longer needed to keep the workforce in line. This means a huge increase in economic security for almost everyone, and a huge increase in self-respect. Remember, when a person cannot find a job, society is, in effect, saying to that person: "There is nothing you can do that we need. You are useless, a parasite. We may give you a little something so that you don't riot or starve, but basically, you are worthless." (Is it any wonder that unemployment breeds pathological behavior?)

Subtle but Important Difference

Firms under Economic Democracy compete, but not as intensely as do firms under capitalism–for they tend to maximize profit per worker, not overall profits.
Firms compete for market share, but they do not try to drive their competitors out
of business. The subtle difference has far-reaching consequences.

- Monopolies are less likely to develop under ED than under capitalism.
  Competition is more like athletic competition, not Darwinian survival-of-
  the-fittest competition. There's an incentive to "win," but losers don't lose
  everything. They rarely go bankrupt.

- Firms do not need to "grow or die." A democratic market economy is fully
  compatible with ecological sanity. A capitalist market economy is not.

- Social control of investment allows us far more pro-active control over development than we have under capitalism. In particular, funds under democratic control are available to begin redesigning our communities, our regions
  and our nation so that we might live more lightly on the earth–and hence
  preserve our planet for posterity.

A final note on Economic Democracy: it's not so difficult to imagine a transition
from what we have now to Economic Democracy –at least not in theory. It's important to understand that not all that much need to change–in order for everything to change. Let me tell a story. This isn't a prediction, but it represents a
real possibility.

Suppose we had a stock market collapse. There would be an enormous clamor
from below for the government to do something–for the pensions of millions are
at stake. Suppose a progressive government is swept into office. It then buys up
the stock of the publicly traded companies for almost nothing and turns these
companies over to the workers, to be run democratically. (Notice, the capitalist
class has been mostly eliminated, since their paper assets have become nearly
worthless. The expropriators have been expropriated, not by an angry proletariat
but by the irrationality of their own financial markets.) The government then in-
stitutes a capital-assets tax. It then nationalizes the banks–which are also in deep
trouble–and apportions the capital-asset tax to them.

There you have it– Economic Democracy. For most people, at first, very little
would have changed. And yet, soon enough it would become apparent–a capitalist economy had been replaced by something very different–a democratic order
genuinely responsive to human needs.

In the meantime, there's work to be done. The model also suggests economic reforms for which we should be struggling now. Four come immediately to mind. There are others.

- More worker cooperatives
- More technical and financial support for worker cooperatives
- A capital-assets tax on corporations to fund community development
- More job security and some participation rights for workers in capitalist firms
- Fair trade, not free trade (socialist protectionism)

Let us now turn briefly to ParEcon. This model can also be characterized by three basic features:

1) All job-complexes are to be equally empowering, both within enterprises and across the economy as a whole.

2) Remuneration is to be based on effort only, not on one's contribution to society, for the latter includes such morally irrelevant factors as talent, training, job assignment, tools and luck.

3) All elements of production and consumption—labor, resources, consumer goods—are to be allocated by participatory planning, *not* the market.

I think this model is fundamentally flawed. I think the vision Michael advocates is excessively, I'd even say obsessively, egalitarian.

I understand the underlying impulse. We want to live in a society where *everyone* has meaningful work, and we want to live in a society that rewards labor *fairly*. But Michael wants more than that. He wants mechanisms in place that would equalize job-empowerment across the nation, and insure that only effort is rewarded. I don't think the mechanisms he proposes to accomplish these goals are viable. Moreover, if implemented, they would have serious negative consequences.

It should be noted that much of what ParEcon aspires to in this regard could be accomplished under Economic Democracy, *if* workers find these reforms desirable. In a democratic workplace, workers have the power to redesign jobs so as to make them more satisfying. Indeed, I would expect a democratic workforce to do just that–perhaps not going so far as ParEcon requires, but certainly in the direction of enhancing job satisfaction for all. The ability to do this is one of the many virtues of workplace democracy.

A Parconista contingent within a democratic firm might also persuade their fellow workers to have their incomes based solely on effort. Of course they would have to come up with some way of measuring effort and figure out who is to do the monitoring and measuring. They would also have to persuade their peers that this would not lead to a loss of efficiency–and hence a loss of income. Frankly, I doubt that could persuade their comrades to make such changes, but there is nothing in the structure of Economic Democracy that precludes such an attempt.

Allocation under ParEcon

My fundamental objection to ParEcon is to its allocational mechanism–the set of procedures and institutions that replace the market. In ParEcon, enterprises do not compete for customers. Decentralized, participatory planning is supposed to replace market competition in determining what gets produced in society. Critics of central planning point to two fundamental kinds of problems inherent in the system.

1) There's the *information* problem–how are producers to know what to produce? One solution is to let a central authority play "father knows best" and tell people what they're going to get. If this solution is deemed unacceptable (as it is to almost everyone, including Michael), then producers need to know, in detail, what items people want and in what quantities. The market solves this problem by letting consumers choose. Producers must respond to consumer demand, producing more of what people want the most (judged by their willingness to pay), cutting back on things that are less in demand. This adjustment of supply and demand takes place automatically, without any central authority deciding the quantity and quality of what should be produced (the Soviet model). It takes place without individuals having to specify in advance what they want to consume during the course of the year, without any consumer councils weighing alternative possibilities, without voters having to vote on the aggregated production plans (as they must do under ParEcon). Instead, people shop. Producers see what people are buying. They respond.

2) There's the *incentive* problem–or rather incentive *problems*.

   • How do we motivate producers *to care* about what people want? How do we motivate them to produce more of the items in demand and cut back on those that aren't?

- How do we motive enterprises to upgrade their products, to refine them to make them more functional or more appealing?

- How do we motivate them to produce efficiently, to use the resources at their disposal in an effective manner, and not squander them?

- How do we motivate the workers themselves to work conscientiously?
- How do we motivate enterprises to innovate, to introduce new products or new technologies?

In a market economy, all of these questions are answered with one word: competition. Those enterprises that are concerned to find out what their customers want, to marshal their labor and non-labor resources efficiently and to innovate make more money than those that don't or work shorter hours. If we give up market competition, what is to replace this crude–but effective–motivator?

Michael is aware of these problems. He tries to address them. I don't think he succeeds. I won't say any more at this point. I'll let you be the judge.

Michael Albert's Presentation

It is tempting to start by replying to some of David's assertions about my views, but I won't. That wasn't the assignment. I'll try to present a case for an alternative economy called participatory economics. Ordinarily, the way I would do that is to start with four values: self-management, diversity, equity, and solidarity, and I would also talk about meeting needs and developing potentials without waste – which is efficiency. But I'm not going to do that either, because this panel is sponsored by the solidarity economy people. So I'm going to start with one value, solidarity, and see where we can get just with that.

It seems to me that if we want solidarity now, then we try to win related reforms. We fight for better trade relations. We fight for firms to pay attention to the plight of those who must breathe dirty air. We fight for changes which will cause economics to be motivated more by the effects on human communities than individual advancement. We probably all agree on that. But if we want a truly solidarity economy, that means we want to change the economy in such a way that its institutions literally produce, rather than destroy, solidarity. The economy's institutions should enhance people's mutual concerns and understanding of each other's situations and inclination to relate to one another positively rather than generating a rat-race in which you try to get ahead, and if others suffer, well that's the way the cookie crumbles, because the economy makes that the only viable form of behavior.

So, if we want a solidarity economy, one thing that we certainly have to do is have the economy not create constituencies of people, classes who have opposed interests. If we create constituencies that have opposed interests then we don't have solidarity. What we have, instead, is those constituencies competing and struggling with one another for the advancement of one group to the disadvantage of the other. So the first thing that you need, and that I imagine David and I agree about, is that you can't have a sector of people who own the means of production and the economy, and who advance themselves by way of their profit at the expense of people working for them. If we want a solidarity improvement, we could retain that situation, and ameliorate some of the suffering that it causes. But if we want an economy that literally produces solidarity, then it can't produce that class division, so we have to get rid of private ownership.

I am not going to dwell on that. But something that Participatory Economics says, which may or may not be correct, but that ParEcon believes deeply, is that getting rid of private ownership of productive assets isn't the end of the class issue. There is another class issue. There is another division among the population that can be produced by an economy. This additional division is not based on a monopoly of property – that's what capitalists have, a monopoly of productive property. It's based instead on a different monopoly, a monopoly that has to do with the division of labor – a monopoly over empowering work.

If one set of people, typically about 20% of the population, does all the work that conveys information, skills, confidence, even personal initiative and energy, essential in participation in deciding what's going to be done in the economy, and another sector of people, typically roughly 80%, is involved in labor that not only does not convey those attributes, but that squashes those attributes of out people's lives, because it's rote, it's redundant, it's repetitive, it's tedious, it's debilitating, it's exhausting – then the former group, the 20%, will dominate the latter group, the 80% and will have an interest in maintaining the monopoly on empowering work that gives them their greater status, their greater influence, their greater power, their greater income. The other sector, the 80%, will be essentially struggling against that dominant constituency or class. I would call the first group the coordinator class, and the second group the working class.

Solidarity Economy Must Be Classless

So, since it seems to me that we have to have a classless economy if we want a solidarity economy, then not only do we have to get rid of the system that puts the capitalists on top, but we also have to fix the division of labor to eliminate this division of people into two classes, the coordinator class and the working class.

Another kind of fundamental change that is necessary to have a solidarity economy is that the economy shouldn't give people a set of incentives which causes them to essentially be anti-social. The economy should not cause people to seek only their own well-being regardless of the situation and the implications for others. This has to do mostly with allocation. If an allocation system provides neither the information that we would need to have solidarity, nor the incentives, nor the environment, nor the conditions that we would need to have solidarity, than it's not a solidarity allocation system. This is the market system. To the extent it even works, it propels us into being anti-social. It creates a context where, as a famous baseball manager used to say, "nice guys finish last." He was right. As a description of the way the economy in the United States works, nice people finish last, it's true. If you pay attention to the well-being of others you are hampered in the fight to climb in a market system.

Suppose we move now to trying to envision another economy, a truly solidarity economy – I think we'll see that participatory economics is truly a solidarity economy – we have to try and address these issues. So how do we solve the division of labor question? Well, suppose we visited another country and we looked at its workplaces, and we saw that 20% of the people in the workplaces earned way more than the other 80%. And not only that, we saw that the 20% made all the decisions, dominated all the outcomes. In meetings, even in a workplace setting that was formally democratic, 20% set the agenda, 20% have all the information at their disposal, 20% have the social skills, the confidence, and the circumstances to determine outcomes, and 80% were basically spectators, and not mostly not even showing up.

And suppose we looked, and it turned out that the 20% each day came to work and started the day eating a chocolate bar. The 80% didn't. The 20% got all the chocolate, and the 80% had none of it. It may sound a bit silly, but bear with me for a minute. So the 20% has all the chocolate, and the 80% has none, and then we discover also that eating chocolate in the workplace gives you skills, confidence, information, energy, and that the absence of chocolate exhausts and debilitates you.

Fair Share, No Monopolies

Well, if that was the situation, it wouldn't take a genius to realize that we would have to get rid of the chocolate distinction if we wanted to get rid of the class division. Between the 20% and the 80%, we'd have to redistribute the chocolate. We'd have to create a situation in which people have a fair share of chocolate, rather than some people having a monopoly on the chocolate.

If you arrive at that conclusion for this odd example – and I would be very surprised if any of us wouldn't – and therefore you believe that conditions which produce elevated participation, skill, knowledge, and confidence for some, and reduced participation, skill, knowledge, and confidence for others are critical, then we can translate the analogy over and look at American work, and actually look all over the world in workplaces, and we see that same division. And more, now we realize that what creates the difference for people, isn't genetics or desire, it's a monopoly not on chocolate, but on empowering work. And if that's the case, if we accept that, if we believe that having empowering work does in our economies what having chocolate did in the analogy, then what we would have to do to eliminate the 20/80 class division is to redistribute the empowering work. We would have to adopt what participatory economics calls balanced job complexes.

That is, we'd have to change the division of labor so that each person, in the workplace and across the economy, has a mix of responsibilities and tasks that compose what they do each day, which is balanced for empowerment effects – a balanced job complex. Everybody by virtue of their position in the economy is comparably prepared and empowered to participate in self-managed decision-making, which I think we would all agree is an important value. So to eliminate this class division, and to have real participation and real self-management and not merely that everyone gets a vote but only 20% matter – only 20% have the means, the circumstances, the confidence, and the skills, by virtue of their situation in the economy, to participate economically.

If we want to have real participation, and we want to have real self-management, then we have to create the conditions that are conducive to it, and that propel it. That, I would say, requires that we alter the division of labor, and so one of the components of the system of participatory economics is the balanced job complex to try and deal with this class division.

Market Abolitionism

The second component bearing particularly on these concerns is, as mentioned, an allocation system. And it's true, as David noted earlier, that I am what you might call a market abolitionist. I actually think that in fifty or a hundred years, or even less, one hopes, people will look back and will find markets to have been the single most horrendous and destructive creation of humanity in all history. So, I'm a market abolitionist, but I do realize that we have markets, we can't act as though they don't exist, and I know they're not going to disappear tomorrow. Nonetheless, we can think about an allocation system that would operate differently. So Participatory Economics makes a proposal there too, for what's called participatory planning. It's a system by which workers, now organized into self-managing workers councils, and consumers, now organized into self-managing consumer councils, have to arrive at what they are going to do and what the economic tasks, and outcomes will be. That's the so-called plan, the so-called aims for an economy. And the way they do that is by a kind of cooperative negotiation. It's by a planning process that has no center, it has no top, but which engages in a back-and-forth process which molds and alters the people's agendas in accord with preferences, and I think in accord also with true social costs and benefits.

We don't have a lot of time. I can't give a full presentation on participatory planning, I think, in the time that's available. But what's going on in participatory planning is basically straight forward. We want to eliminate the authoritarianism of central planning. We want to eliminate the anti-social competitive dynamic of market competition. We also want to eliminate another dynamic which is within markets, even without private ownership. Profit is gone because there's not an owner to profit, and that's good. But there's still surplus and surplus in a market system, even one that's post-capitalist, will be distributed among the workforce. This provides various motivations and incentives, and it also provides, I think, very deleterious, very harmful effects having to do with the way markets operate, including the way they don't take into account ecological effects, the way they don't take into account social effects beyond the buyer and seller, and the way the cause the buyer and seller to confront each other as adversaries in the exact opposite of solidarity. So, again I don't want to go into too much detail.

Participatory Economics is not just a solidarity economy, I think it's also a self-managing economy. What does that mean? It means it's not democracy. Democracy is like a tactic, just like consensus is a tactic. By democracy I mean one person, one vote, and majority rule. By consensus I mean, probably everyone here is familiar with it, a process by which there's a discussion, and a debate, and a negotiation, with the possibility of blocking and of resolving. And in addition you can also easily imagine, different kinds of votes, two-thirds are required, you could imagine more or less time going into the discussion, more or less time going into assessing the results of the discussion and so on. These are all tactics. What do they aim to accomplish? Well, from my point of view, what they should aim to accomplish is self-management, meaning that people should have a say in decisions in proportion to the degree they are affected by them. I think Participatory Economics can convey that, not to the tenth decimal place, but as a broad social project, it can convey that, not only – and this is a claim that nobody should buy based on what I'm saying here – but not only in the sense that if this group of us here is a workplace, we can all participate in the decisions inside this workplace in a self-managing way, but even over the economy as a whole, over what's produced and consumed, and in kind of investment happens, and so on.

I think Participatory Economics is also an equitable economy. What does that mean? Equity is a term meant to address how much people get. There's a social product, but how much do people get from the social product. What's our share? We can receive a share based on the property we own and the productivity of that property, profits, but I'm ruling that out completely, and David rules it out at some levels but not at others. I rule it out completely, because I think there's nothing ethical or moral about it. It's in my mind a kind of a barbaric notion, morally, but I also think it has no economic value. It accomplishes things that can be accomplished in better ways without the by-products of markets that are harmful.

What's the next possibility for remuneration? Well, we can have an economy in which you take what you can get, which is basically the kind of economy that Al Capone or the graduates of the Harvard Business School advocate. Really, that's their mantra. They like an economy in which bargaining power determines the shares you are able to take. And that's what a market system does. It enables you, or in fact it tells you, to levy prices and to levy the amount of quality or non-quality that's going into your goods in such a way as to increase your income. Income is a function of bargaining power. It's a thuggish economy. Whether or not that's what one believes markets do, I think we can all agree that we don't want a thug's economy in which power determines what you get.

The next option, an option typically advocated by many socialists, is that we should get in accord with the output we ourselves contribute to the social product. By my labor, I do some production, and it yields some output, and the question is, should I get more than that? If I do, I would be getting what someone else produced. Should I get less? Then somebody else would be getting some of what I produced. So the idea is, and it sounds plausible, that we should get back basically what we produce.

However, I think like remunerating for property and power, this is also a bad idea. I think it's ethically bad, and also economically bad. When Michael Jordan was earning $20 million a year for playing basketball with the Chicago Bulls, how many of you think he was overpaid? Hands up. It is unanimous. Okay, that's your values speaking. But by this standard of remunerating people for the value of their output, Jordan was way underpaid. Leftists might not want to hear that, but the value of watching Michael Jordan play basketball was vastly higher than the amount of income he received. The owners of Nike, and the owners of the Chicago Bulls, and other people had enough bargaining power to take a lot of that, but the actual value to people seeing Michael run up and down the court, was much, much higher than the $20 million or whatever it was that he got.

I don't think we should remunerate essentially inborn talents and skills, genetic endowment, as one of our criteria for how much income people should get. But I also don't think we should remunerate people who happen to be using better tools than other people, who happen to be doing something that's more highly valued than other people, who happen to be working with others who are more productive than other people. I don't think those are the norms that we should use to determine incomes. What I think we should do for remuneration, and Participatory Economics has developed a system that I believe accomplishes this, is that we should remunerate for how long people work, for how hard people work, and for the onerousness of the conditions in which they work. So that's equitable remuneration, I think, and it turns upside-down the norms of income we're familiar with. Balanced job complexes turn upside-down the division of labor we're familiar with. Participatory planning turns upside-down the allocation system we're familiar with. So while I commiserate with the difficulty David mentioned of presenting something that's almost like capitalism in thirty minutes, imagine trying to present something that is entirely and fundamentally different in all aspects, ParEcon, in thirty minutes.

We Need an Ecological Economy

I think we should also ask of an economy that it be an ecological economy. Leftists have this value of sustainability; it drives me crazy. If the best that we can ask for is that the human race is not suicidal, we're in deep trouble. Sustainability is not a very big request, really. I'm not sure what value we should have for the ecology, but we all know what we mean. An economy should take into account the ecological as well as the social implications of actions. It should allow consumers and producers to make decisions about their activities that are solidaritous but also ecologically sound. You can't do that if your prices, your indicators of value, are way off. If your indicator of values says that a gallon of gasoline should cost $3, but the truth is that it should cost $15 or $20, because of the damage that it is doing to the ecology, then using the mis-assessed prices you can't make a solidaritous or ecologically sound judgment. All you can do is try to advance your own circumstances in light of mispriced gasoline prices.

But markets misprice everything. They do it worse in some cases than in others. So I think we could use an ecological economy, a solidaritous economy, a self-managing economy, an equitable economy, a diverse economy, and that's what I think Participatory Economics provides.

Let me just say, who cares?

I think it's a serious question. Many people, even on the left, don't care. That is, many people on the left feel like, "What difference does it make? We'll get around to this later. We're not going to get economic democracy, we're not going to get market socialism, we're not going to get centrally planned socialism, and we're certainly not going to get Participatory Economics tomorrow. Tomorrow we might be able to fight for something that we want right now. Why does any of this vision stuff matter?"

I think it matters for two reasons, or more than two, but two that I want to address. It matters partly to provide hope, and to provide incentive, and to overcome the idea of TINA, that "There Is No Alternative." I believe, perhaps idiosyncratically, that lack of hope has become the main obstacle to developing social movements. Our underlying doubt about the possibility of anything better, and our underlying doubt about the possibility of obtaining anything better, severely restricts out commitment and energy. I don't think it's the case, as it was when I got started, back in the 1960s, that what prevents people from dissenting is confusion about whether or not poverty hurts or exists, or confusion about whether or not racism hurts or exists, or sexism hurts or exists, or confusion about whether those things are unjust, criminal, and horrible. I think people understand all that now. What people don't have is the feeling that there's an alternative.

If I said come join me in a movement against aging, come join me in a social movement against aging, I think most of you would sort of digest it for a few seconds, and then laugh at me. You know, you would think, "what?" But aging kills more people than poverty. It diminishes our lives more than cancer does. It restricts everything about what we can do as we get older. It afflicts basically everybody who is lucky enough to get to be older. So why the hell shouldn't we form a social movement against it? Answer: because that's insane.

But why is it insane? It's insane because aging is not a function of the institutions around us. And it's insane because we can't affect aging by forming a social movement against it, because fighting against aging is like blowing in to the wind, or organizing against gravity. It makes no sense.

But consider the broad public. When we talk to them, we keep saying poverty is horrendous. They know that. We keep saying war kills and it's horrendous. They know that. What we don't say is what the alternative is, and why winning something in the short-term can contribute to winning the alternative in the long-term, and why their activity would make a difference. We don't overcome the obstacle which is the same obstacle that prevents people fighting aging. They don't think poverty and suffering are good, they just think they are a fact of life. Detailing how bad they are is no more relevant to them than detailing how bad aging is, In fact, it is only annoying.

When people say to us, "Go get a life. Grow up. Face reality," that's exactly what I would say to someone who said to me, "Let's go organize against aging." And I think people say those things to us for the same reason. They see poverty like we see aging. They see it as just a fact of life, and until we have the abilty to convey in an inspiring way the possibility of something better, and the possibility of attaining it, that obstacle remains to forming movements. Alright, so that's one reason for vision.

Vision is Important

The second reason why I think vision –whether we're talking about economics in this panel, or about kinship, or culture, or politics, or whatever – is important is because what we want to attain, where we want to arrive, has implications for what we do to get there. If we do things just based on hatred of capitalism, we can wind up with something that is not much better than what we left behind and that certainly isn't in tune with out fullest values.

It seems to me that, for instance, Participatory Economics, says to us that our organizations, our institutions that we create as vehicles for our power to influence society, should be organized in such a way that they melt into the type of future society we desire. We shouldn't organize in such a way that what we build presents an obstacle to arriving where we want to go. If Participatory Economics is, as it turns out, what people decide they like and they desire, and that it became what motivated people and informed what they see and want, then it would imply, for example, that our movements should have balanced job complexes. Our movements should not look like corporations. They should not have donors or fundraisers who know them dominating outcomes. They should not have some people in corner offices making all the decisions and other people doing all the work. They should embody the structures that we're trying to work toward, partly to learn about those structures, partly because it's exemplary, and partly to avoid the catastrophe of being motivated by a desire for classlessness, but winding up, nonetheless, with a society, like the Soviet Union, Yugoslavia, and so on, with a new economy that's not capitalist, but that still embodies the class division and has a new ruling class above the workers, in this case the coordinator class.

Secondly, take something like participatory budgeting, or any other project that we might embark on. Again, it seems to me that if we have an understanding of where we're going – not just what we don't like, but what we want, and we need that to be inspiring, where we're going – then the way we do things would differ. We would talk about even short term programmatic aims in a way that tends to raise consciousness and to develop desires and commitments aiming toward this future that we're seeking. We wouldn't fight for gains now in a way that's dead end-ish, or that's leading someplace other than where we seek to go in the long run.

So, you can do a participatory budget with a mindset that over time self-managing democratic control should extend to the whole economy, not just, we probably agree on this, not just to government budgets. It changes our words. There was a battle at Harvard University just recently about the wages of campus police, students there were supporting the campus guards at Harvard, who were fighting for higher wages, and one of the students them came up to me and said, "you know, I know we should do this. We're going to do a hunger strike in support." They won, by the way. "But really, what does this have to do with 'An-

other World Is Possible'? How does a dollar extra per hour for these campus police move us toward that, when we just win the dollar, and that's the end of it?"

And I said, well, you're right, but why not fight for it, not just because you have
to but because it's right. People who work hard do deserve more. People do deserve a good income. But you can fight for the limited change in different ways.
So, suppose you said, "we support these demands, we'll hunger strike to win
these demands, but we'd also like to open a new discussion on the campus at
Harvard. We want to know – why do the professors earn more than the guards?
Why do the professors earn more than the people who are cooking in the dorms?
Why do the professors earn more than the people who are cleaning their offices?" Suppose you added: "We don't think it is morally or economically justified. The guards and the cooks work harder, longer, and under worse conditions.
We think it's a function of a monopoly over information, skills, and circumstances, that has nothing to do with an economic need of society per say and that
has nothing to do with anything moral."
  That kind of fight about a dollar an hour could have led to turmoil on the campus of Harvard, because everything about Harvard, the whole identity, everything, would be called into question by that debate. So that's what I'm saying.
Where we're going, what we want, can inform how we talk about what we're
seeing and doing in the present. So our fight for a modest gain becomes part of a
process, part of a trajectory, that's actually leading forward instead of just being
an event unto itself.

The Case of Argentina

I was in Argentina, recently, sitting in a room. I was there talking to people who
had occupied factories about their experiences. There were about fifty people
from various factories, and they wanted me to speak, and instead we started by
going around the room and having people report on their experiences in these occupied factories, and then I would try to speak. By the time we got through about
fifteen people, there were tears all over the room.

And by the time we got all the way around, people were just – it's hard to describe. What was going on was people were saying, "We took over the factory.
We were hell-bent on democracy. We were hell-bent on real justice and equity,
and on paying attention to reality, and on serving people's needs. And damned if
over time, our workplace, which at first we re-constructed and were proud of,
didn't start looking exactly like it looked before we did anything. And over time
it began to feel exactly the way it felt before." And they actually said things like,
"you know, I know what I want, but I'm afraid my old boss was right – there is

no alternative. I'm afraid there's something about humans that yields these hier-archies; that yields these differential powers among us leading to different in-comes; that yields our workplace losing its concern for the well-being of people who are consuming what we produce, and instead just being concerned about gathering funds." And they went around the room. Some people cried. Some were saying that it was their life's work, their life's dream, and yet they were do-ing the experiment and feeling like it was hopeless, and feeling like it lasted a while, but it's unraveling.

When I spoke, I tried to suggest, what later exploring the experience with people revealed was the case, that while they tried to make incomes equitable in the workplace, and while they tried to replace the people who left, the owners and the managers and so on, they didn't re-construct the workplace with a new divi-sion of labor. They kept the old division of labor but under them, initially popu-lated with workers as managers, with workers filling in the slots of engineers. You go into the occupied workplace, and you talk to a woman in the workplace, and you ask, "what are you doing?" and she says, "the finances, I am the chief financial officer. " And you ask, "Well, that was probably pretty difficult over the past six months, to make the change. What were you doing before?" "I was working with the glass at the furnaces, all day, sweltering doing the same thing over and over."

"Well, what was the hardest part of being able to do the finances? She said, "It was learning to read." This is not the United States. The hardest part was learn-ing to read. "What about dealing with the finance books and the difficulties of that?" I asked. She said, "That was a snap, you know, once I could read, once I could do that stuff, the rest of it wasn't particularly difficult. It took me a while to learn, but it wasn't that hard." So much for the idea that workers doing rote and repetitive tasks aren't fit for other responsibilities.

But what the workforce did, on taking over the factory, was that they put work-ers doing all the same tasks that were being done before by managers and engi-neers and so on. At first, doing the elite job, it's a worker, they came from the as-sembly line, who has the same consciousness as everybody else, the same desires that we talked about. But over time, the position in the workplace, the position in the economy – like imagine yourselves as a prison guard, for a graphic example – the position in the economy distorts the values, slowly but surely, of the person doing the work.

So we talked about the taking over of the plant needed to go further than it did because it didn't talk about the division of labor. Keeping the old division of labor subverted their other accomplishments causing the workplace to revert to its old character.

Markets as Anti-Social

And then we talked about the implications of markets for what they were doing. Even if they did have a new division of labor, the market would still push inexorably, horrendously powerfully, toward an anti-social attitude, motivation, an logic, and it would also push toward the emergence of a class division. It would be a longer discussion, but let me try to say briefly: this is the Yugoslav workplace we are talking about, in fact, or the Argentinean.

We've taken over as workers, and we're all in charge of the workplace, working on the market. We are working in a market system. We are trying to meet needs based on how a market functions. We have to compete. If we don't compete, we go out of business. We'll get out-competed. So we compete, but what does that mean? We have to reduce our costs. You all know what reducing costs means. It means we have to make decisions which increase the output at less cost. We have to cut back on the welfare features, the daycare center that we wanted to put in, or maybe we did put in, but to compete, we to cut it, it's too expensive. Some other firm doesn't have that, so they have more revenues to invest in advertising and infrastructure. We want to clean up our own pollution, because we care about the community, but we can't do that anymore, either, because some other firm doesn't do it, and if we do it, we won't have the funds to compete with them. We wanted to have a sensible workday, but we can't have that anymore. We have to speed up.

So, are we going to be able to make those decisions to cut those costs? Think of us as a workforce in our own firm. We have new norms of remuneration, a workers council, real self management. But, in the market, is any of us going to be able to make the cut back decisions? This is a longer discussion, but here's what happened in Yugoslavia. They went to the Wharton School in Pennsylvania, or to the Harvard Business School, or to Oxford, or to comparable schools in Yugoslavia, and they found people who by their education, and by their disposition, and by their training, were perfectly happy making decisions that would hurt others and not themselves. The people they sought out had developed a capacity to do that, and were well-armed and well-trained to be able to do that. They moved into the workplace, and the workers didn't give them a balance job complex, they didn't pay them like everybody else, because then they would have been subject to the effects of the cost-cutting decisions too, and they would no longer have been good at them.

So instead the workers put these new cost cutters they hire, these new managers, in air-conditioned offices. We give them a guaranteed situation, and then we say, "Okay, cut costs, screw us. Make the decisions that will cut our costs so we can compete in the market." So the reason these Argentine workers in occupied factories were experiencing a kind of roll back of their circumstances and even values was that old divisions of labor and old market practices, unaddressed, were subverting their many innovations. Again, knowing what we want can inform how we understand our current actions and choices.

The key point is that our attempt to eliminate the class division between coordinators and workers will be subverted, not only if we retain an old division of labor, but even if we overcome the old division of labor, but retain the market. So what Participatory Economics says is, look, if we're serious in the long haul about having a classless economy, about having an equitable economy, about an economy where people have a say in decisions in proportion to the degree which they are affected, and if we are concerned about an ecological economy, not just sustainability, but ecological wisdom, then it seems to me we need a new set of institutions that foster, and promote, and make viable those values. And the case in Participatory Economics is that it does that, that its basic institutions, it's not a blueprint, but it's basic institutions: workers and consumer self-managing councils, balanced job complexes, equitable remuneration, meaning remuneration for how long, and how hard, and how onerous our socially valuable work is, and participatory planning, can deliver on these values of classless economy, solidarity economy, etc. And not only that, it can help us to see how we can fight now in ways that will relate to working people's true aspirations but lead where we want to go. We tend to produce movements, structures, behavior patterns, and cultures, on the left, that are actually quite hostile to working people. They are quite imbued with the values of the coordinator class, the working person's worst nightmare. They are imbued with the values and the denigration of that which is worker-identified, and it comes from lawyers and doctors and engineers. It's not hard to see why, but I do think it has a great deal to do with why and we're having a hard time progressing. So I think ParEcon can help us both envision and make strategy.

First Round of Audience Questions

1. In the system of Economic Democracy, if entrepreneurial capitalist enterprises were welcomed into this system, how would it prove any different from our current system?
2. In discussing the implementation of these models, what is a scenario in which Participatory Economics could come into fruition within the next 50 years?
3. In these models, how do you synthesize centralized and decentralized planning, and ensure that the society moves forward on certain social, economic, and political priorities? How do you regulate economic development to serve certain overriding societal goals and directions?

David Schweickart's Response:

Okay, how do you avoid the entrepreneurial capitalist becoming the regular capitalist that we have today? That's a good question, but I think it has a straightforward answer. There's a structural solution to the problem you pose. As long as the individual entrepreneur is active in the enterprise, that's fine. But when he retires, or decides to move on, then the entrepreneur sells the business to the state. The state takes over the enterprise, and it's turned over to the workers. This mechanism encourages entrepreneurship, without having entrepreneurs evolve into a dominant class like we have today. The key point is this: a person can make money, even a lot of money, so long as he or she is actively engaged in a business, but that person cannot make money from ownership alone. There are no stocks or bonds in Economic Democracy that pay dividends and interest forever.

The question about the relationship between Economic Democracy and such things as racism or the destruction of our natural environment is an important one. When I talk about the structure of Economic Democracy, I am fully aware that economic structure is not the whole story. The quality of a democracy depends on the consciousness of the people, on their values, on what they see as priorities. That's why social movements focusing on such things as racism or sexism or homophobia or ecology are so important. Economic democracy makes it *possible* to have a society without racism, but democracy itself does not eliminate racism. Nor does it eliminate consumerism. If people want to consume ever more things, and disregard the ecological consequences of their behavior, then democratic control over investment priorities, in and of itself, won't prevent environmental catastrophe. So we need an environmental movement that will change those priorities. Such a movement cannot succeed under capitalism. Capitalism requires ever-expanding consumption. If consumption slows, we get a recession

– or worse. A democratic economy, by contrast, does not have to grow to remain stable and vibrant. Ecological sanity is possible under Economic Democracy as it is not under capitalism. But we need a strong environmental movement to ensure that this possibility becomes a reality.

Michael Albert's Response:

I'm going to set aside the entrepreneurial capitalism issue, but mention something else. The economy is a very entwined system, inexorably so. So, imagine that we have the wrong price of pencils, just pencils, or anything else you might want to think about. If we have the wrong price of something, then that price is used in calculating the prices of everything else. Any wrong price – what do I mean by "wrong price?" I mean a price which inaccurately reflects true social costs and benefits – ecological, social, personal, etc. If there's a wrong price, it contributes to other wrong prices. That's why the wrong price of gasoline is much more important than just being the wrong price of gasoline. It throws off everything. So, the idea here is that there is a tendency for certain features to grow, and I would agree with the questioner that there are tendencies for the feature of private ownership to extend itself and expand over time; you can see it historically.

The scenario of implementation – I don't know how long it's going to take. I certainly hope it will take less time than more time. It's easy to view the Participatory Economic project, if you will, alongside a feminist project, and an anti-racist project, and an inter-communal project, which isn't trying to disappear cultural differences, but is trying to provide integrity and space and so on, and an ecological project, and politically, an anti-authoritarian participatory democracy project. An economic project alongside all that is a process that looks maybe something like this: it contains many broad social movements, but the social movements are entwined; they're in a part of something larger. Not a coalition, a least common denominator thing, "we're all against the war, so we all work together against the war, and hate each other on everything else… or at least we ignore everything else." Not that, but something that's the greatest sum of all its parts. An alliance which gets its gender definition from the feminist movement, gets its anti-racist definition from the movements around race, gets its labor definition from the labor movement, and gets its ecology from the ecological. Each component of the broad overarching project understands that their success depends upon the development of the whole project and therefore the whole alliance. Each constituency therefore accepts the leadership of the constituencies that are most effected by each realm. And so the program of the whole thing is all its parts summed up. That doesn't mean there are no differences; there's continuing difference and debate, but also solidarity.

We want to produce a new society; a society isn't a lock-step homogenous thing. We ought to be able to have movements inside a good society that have dis-agreement and difference, but that yet unify in the broad. So that's what we build to reach the new society, to build it, win it, melt into it, something like that.

Alongside that big overarching movement of movements, workers councils form in workplaces, consumer councils form in neighborhoods, and also perhaps have besides them assemblies that are political institutions. We can also imagine workplaces that that are created new, or occupied, in the short-run, and that are made ParEcon-ish, let's say, or whatever it is.

And so, we have an unfolding process in which we're winning reforms and we're improving people's lives now but it doesn't end, it continues to grow and ad-vance. Anybody in here who thinks that a reform is a bad thing, I should perhaps point out, needs to think again. Reforms improve people's lives. If the Left is critical of, or rejects, reforms, it means we are callous and uncaring in the short-term. That should not be the case. But, we aren't reformists, so we fight for re-forms with those apparatuses mentioned above as part of a process that talks about the immediate gains, and organizes for them, and develops movements for them but in a way that leads forward.

We don't go to New Hampshire in an electoral campaign and count votes to see whether we're succeeding. We don't go to Seattle, and look to see whether peo-ple get in the building or not, to see whether we're succeeding. We look at whether or not consciousness is changing, whether or not commitment is grow-ing, whether or not more people are deeply embedded in our project and in our movements, and are getting their lives improved by our movements and continu-ing to fight for a larger vision. With that kind of a project, with a project that deals with class the way we've dealt with race and gender, and we still need to go further on those fronts, but we understand the need for the movement not to be a repository of Jim Crow racism, which it was once. We need the movement not to be a white club or a male locker-room, which it was, once. We understand that it won't incorporate women, and it won't incorporate people or color if it has those features. We need to do the same thing around class. We need to under-stand if the movement really reflects and manifests coordinator consciousness, coordinator values, coordinator will – that means managers, lawyers, doctors, engineers – their way of looking at the world – it won't empower, inspire, in-volve, be led by working people. We've overcome some of those problems, and I think we're well on the way. I don't think it takes forever. I think history shows it doesn't take forever. It's remarkable that we've accomplished what we have with what we had.

Desirable Outcomes

The last question is a fundamental question. You're right that it isn't only a question of participation; it isn't only a question of self-management. There's also a question of desirable outcomes. What you're suggesting by the question, I think, is that there are some issues in which desirable outcomes will be enhanced by a degree of central deliberation and instruction, so to speak. And, this is a difference we have. I think what you suggest is true if there's a repository of wisdom that everyone else is excluded from, then the people with that wisdom can yield better outcomes than everyone else can. But if we have a society in which that monopolization of knowledge and information has been undone, we still have experts, of course, who know more about this or that, but they share their projects so we can all use them in deciding our preferences, then what we need is an economy that meets people's preferences. We don't need an economy that proceeds by simply obeying what a central planner says it should do. We need an economy that develops, that invests in, that pursues channels that are in accord with people's freely expressed and appropriately weighted preferences and desires. That's not only self-management, a good in itself, but it will also yield better results, because the definition of a good result is a result that meets people's needs, and it's people who know their needs best; people who know their preferences best.

One last thing. You asked about racism in the economy. Well, it's very important. ParEcon does a lot to affect racism, like giving people balanced job complexes, giving people equitable incomes. It's simply impossible to have a racial, or any other kind of unjust hierarchy or power differential inside the economy, but you can still have racism, and that's why you need anti-racist movements. That's why you need movements around culture and around gender, to attain sought goals around those things too. A good society isn't just a good economy, but also gender, race, politics, ecology, etc.

Second Round of Questions

1. In the system of Participatory Economics, what scale is appropriate for the participatory planning process? Also, is community supported agriculture could be a positive step toward Participatory Economics and participatory planning?
2. The system of Economic Democracy can provide examples with scale, like the Mondragon Cooperatives, for instance. How can Participatory Economics also work towards real-life initiatives on a larger scale, and that can contend with capitalist forces?

3. Can either model prove effective at both the local, and regional scale, and also grow to prove effective at a larger scale?

Michael Albert's Response:

Yes, to community-based agriculture, yes to almost anything else that people fight for, with a caveat. If we fight for these things in a way which makes them an end in themselves, which makes them an island of sanity in a sea of horror, then that is not so great. If we fight for them in a way that produces institutions of our own, and movements of our own, but that aren't going forward, that aren't continuing on, then no, that is not so great. So, it depends very much how we do it. If we do it in a way that is talking about the deep need for participation, for self-management, for participatory planning on a grand scale as well as locally, if we do it in a way that connects what we're doing now with what's going on broadly, and with what we seek in the future, then yes, very much so.

ParEcon doesn't work on a small scale better than a large scale; it actually works better on a large scale than on a small scale. If you have a small workplace – as but one example, and this is going to sound a little bit silly but it's true – if you have a small workplace, and you change it over to ParEcon, everyone is right on top of everybody else, and if two people don't like each other it can be a disaster for the whole group. If you have a larger workplace you simply separate people who don't get along. That might sound trivial, but actually in the experience of many collectives, it becomes a real problem for people. The larger scale also lets you develop balanced job complexes far more simply. The larger scale facilitates participatory planning rather than making it more difficult, but that's a more technical argument. But in any case, ParEcon is not a model or a system that only works on a small scale – I mean it for the United States and all over the world, same as anybody else that proposes an economic vision.

Can you do it on a small scale in the short-run? Sure, to a degree. You can create a participatory economic institution right now: a publishing house, a café, a dentist's office, an organization that does travel stuff, and on and on. They exist. I mean, these are real ones that I'm talking about. And what you do is you incorporate balanced job complexes, you incorporate equitable remuneration, and you incorporate self-management, and you struggle against the market, which is pushing against what you're doing. Sure, you can do it that way, and the result will be better or worse depending upon our values, depending on how they are talked about, and how they are pursued: Is it a trajectory that leads forward or does it fall apart. That's the critical thing with everything we fight for or build, not the intrinsic character of the demand, or of the project in some sense, but the way it contributes to the overall project of building a new society.

To get people on board is critical, I think, and I think that the issue is how to appeal to constituencies. Suppose we are trying to get people on board in the anti-war movement in 1969, in which women sitting in the anti-war movement are less comfortable than they are in the society outside. It isn't whether or not the movement has a good demand to end the war; it isn't whether or not the movement is courageous or energetic that undermines reaching women, it is that the movement despite good aims around war, and good energy, is sexist. It's that the movement's internal characteristics are disempowering, even repellant, to various sectors of the population. What I'm suggesting is that a movement which doesn't address in a forthright and very upfront and aggressive fashion, the issue of the difference between the 20% who monopolize empowering work and the 80% who are left with only disempowering tasks, the issue of the class difference between the working class and the coordinator class, will not be inspiring to, and will not galvanize and incorporate in leadership – which is necessary if it's going to be a valuable and effective movement – working people. And we've seen it for decades.

So I agree with the need to have a process, and a movement, and a project, and a vision that's inspiring and that gets people involved, but I think that's precisely what a ParEcon movement has a possibility of contributing around this critical issue of working class involvement, and working class leadership, and working class participation, because it really does seek a classless economy, not a new class rule economy, not out with the old boss in with the new.

David Schweickart's Response:

As for community supported agriculture, I happen to think that's really a good idea, one which would be more feasible under Economic Democracy than under capitalism. In Economic Democracy investment funds come to communities every year. People have to make decisions as to investment priorities. So if the communities decide that they would like to invest in community supported agriculture, the funds are there to do so.

As for contending forces: When you start talking about workplace democracy, this resonates with lots of people. Ask anyone: Would you rather have the ability to vote for your boss or not? You say, "Hey, look, you can vote for your mayor, your congressmen, even your president–who can send you off to war to kill or die. Why can't you vote for you boss?" Then you add, "Don't tell me it won't work. There are lots of statistics that show that workplace democracy *does* work, that enterprises that are structured democratically are usually *more* productive than comparable capitalist firms." The fact of the matter is, capitalist forces

work hard to keep this question off the political agenda. If we had public, tele-
vised debates on workplace democracy, you'd see a lot of support, as well as
support for the proposition that corporations are out of control and that we need
to do something to rein them in.

As for the state/local level question–things can be done at these levels: Cooperatives can be set up. Local governments can be pressured to support such endeavors, perhaps providing loans and technical assistance. They can also give tax-
breaks to companies that offer their employees more participation-rights and
greater job security, rights that are central to our vision of full Economic Democracy. We can't have full Economic Democracy at just the state or local level, but
experiments and reforms are possible there that prefigure the larger vision.

Third Round of Questions

1. At what point do we start to dismantle the life that we know now, and
    when can these models begin? More specifically, how does either of
    these models apply to higher education processes, or to the transition
    from the university to the workplace?
2. How do the crises and contradictions inherent in capitalism help to bring
    about either of these models? Also, in either of these models, how do we
    democratically decide which types of consumption in an economic sys-
    tem are unnecessary or harmful?
3. The Santi Asok Buddhist movement in Thailand can possibly provide an
    example of a market that is non-isolating. This is a socially engaged,
    back-to-the-basics community of monks that make almost everything
    they use, and they sell the surplus in their stores and vegan restaurants at
    or below cost. They follow a system of merit-based economics, and be-
    lieve that if you make a profit, you lose the same amount of merit. How
    can these examples of "good markets" be accommodated in the Partici-
    patory Economics system?

David Schweickart's Response:

The question of higher education has been raised. Do university professors make
too much, compared to staff, for example? It is often suggested that we are privileged because we have tenure. To start with the latter issue: I think everyone
should have "tenure." Democratic firms tend to offer this–not explicitly, but the
fact is, democratic firms rarely expel members, not without serious cause. When
demand slackens, everyone works less, takes home less money. You don't vote

to lay off colleagues so that your own income won't suffer. This is almost never done.

As far as redesigning the university's salary structure, this could be done if the university were run democratically. I think there would be more equality than there is currently if everyone, faculty and staff alike, were able to determine salary scales. At the same time, I don't think the issue of intra-firm inequality is the major issue at the present time. Yes, many CEOs and other top administrators make obscene amounts of money. But such inequality is not the *major* problem with capitalism. One of the insights to economic democracy is that it isn't the fact that rich people are consuming too much that's the problem; it's what they are doing with what they don't consume. It's *investment*, not consumption, that's the problem, the fact that the control over where and how the social surplus gets invested–which determines the quality of our collective life–is not in our hands.

I think it's a mistake to overemphasize income inequality. It's okay to denounce those CEO salaries, but it's a mistake to suggest that what we want is income equality across the board, or something approximating that. I happen to think that such relative equality would tend to come to pass, over time, in a democratic economy, since intra-firm inequalities would have to be justified to the workers in the enterprise. But we have to think about what should be emphasized in building a movement. It's a question of transition. If we're going to build a serious movement for social change, we can't be telling huge numbers of people– people whose skills and expertise we need–that we're going to cut their salaries way back, come the new order. That threat needlessly polarizes, and pushes the upper middle class to support the ultra-rich.

If we are able to usher in a democratic economy, we will need to scale back consumption for most people, not just the wealthy, for ecological reasons. As things now stand, consumption is ridiculous and out of control, but it can't be brought down overnight. It can't be brought down under capitalism *at all*, at least not without a major recession–which of course, hits the most vulnerable the hardest.

People need an alternative to ever-increasing consumption. This is where democratic workplaces are important. What is the alternative to consuming more? Working less. That is not an option under capitalism, but in a democratic workplace, it is. We don't want a movement telling people that all their stuff is junk, and so we'll be taking it away. We need a movement that persuades people that consumption is not the royal road to happiness, and convinces them that there is a viable alternative. We have to think of the transition from consumption to leisure as more gradual. Workplace democracy is crucial.

Let me conclude with a brief remark on that fundamental difference between Michael and me, our assessment of the market. The question of community-supported agriculture was raised earlier. Let's think about a farmers' market. People bring produce to market. The fact that customers can choose which farmers to buy from keeps prices in line. So there's competition–but individual farmers are not trying to drive their competitors out of business. Neither producers nor consumers are being exploited by *these* markets.

The point is, markets are not inherently evil. Competition is not always bad. It's true that markets don't always get the prices right, but what's the alternative? ParEcon offers one–we'll sit at our computers and make lists of our annual needs; we'll get feedback; we'll revise our lists; the process will go back and forth for several iterations; ultimately society will vote. Will *this* procedure get the prices right? Is such a procedure preferable to letting democratic producers and economically-secure consumers interact freely? You decide.

Michael Albert's Response:

For me, regarding the first question, the education question, the issue with education is if you have a society in which, again, 20% are monopolizing the empowering work, and 80% are doing the route work, then you need an educational system which does what? For 80%, it must teach you how to endure boredom and take orders. If you remember being in school, watching the clock, praying for the end of the day, but sitting there waiting, you're enduring boredom and you're obeying orders. But if you're in the fancy track, the 20%, you're excited about what's going on. You are getting ready to rule. The horrible stunting of most people occurs because it's necessary to rob most people of their capacities. Education is not about fulfilling capacities, it's literally about damping down capacities.

Fifty years ago, there were few women doctors. It wasn't because they were genetically incapable of doing it, which is what most people claimed – it was because the educational system had them in the 80%, almost entirely, so it robbed them. So the first thing about ParEcon and the implications for the educational system is that it requires that the educational system graduates people into society who are prepared to participate, and who have fully developed their capacities. In other words ParEcon promotes good education, not stifling capacities.

After the 1960s, the U.S. government sponsored something called the Carnegie Commission to investigate what went wrong in the 60's. The Carnegie Commission investigated, and they came up with an answer. They decided that the population was being overeducated; that people were graduating and they actually expected to have a life; they actually expected to have some say in what happened to them; and then they became the workers, or saw that they were about it, and of course had no say, and got angry. Now, that wasn't the whole of what happened in the 60's, but there was truth to it, and as a result, the policies that emerged were to raise costs of education, cut back the resources for schools in which the constituency in the schools isn't going to be in the 20%, and so on. It's capitalism – or coordinatorism – are work.

There was a question about crisis. I don't believe in building movements that are founded on the idea that we're going to resurrect society on the basis of a crisis. First of all, I don't think it's in the cards. But second of all, I don't think that kind of movement is likely to arrive where we want to go. If we have a crisis in the United States on the scale the questioner raises, we are far more likely to get fascism than we are economic democracy or Participatory Economics, unless we have a massive movement that is already striving not on the basis of crisis, but on the basis of positive vision and positive aspirations for a new alternative that people understand, and that has become a part of their life, and part of their desires. I hope we don't have crises, unlike some people on the Left. It's not going to help us unless we are already helping ourselves quite a lot, and it would cause horrific pain.

.

Markets: the system tries to trick us about lots of things. For instance, efficiency, efficiency is a good word. Efficiency just means accomplishing what you desire without wasting things that you care about. That's what efficiency means. But most of us get nauseous when we hear the word efficiency, on the Left, because it means accomplishing what the owners desire without wasting what the owners care about, and so it's contrary to our interests. So efficiency actually winds up hurting us when it's corporate efficiency, and capitalist efficiency, even though efficiency per se is a good thing – efficiency at meeting needs and developing potentials.

The way markets are talked about is similar. The popular discussion makes us think that stores are markets, that exchange is markets, that prices are markets. But that's not markets. All that is present in any economy. Markets are a system in which buyers and sellers compete; each tries to fleece the other. It's a broad system, it's a societal system. What you described in Thailand, well that is what I would call people taking markets and adapting them, bending them, having in mind exactly the kinds of values and desires that I'm talking about, and trying to move toward an allocation system which embodies those values. It is a bit like if you live under a dictatorship and impose constraints on it that are more consistent with democracy. They are good, but that doesn't mean dictatorship is good.

When Chavez in Venezuela says to the Bolivians, "Let's exchange," and the Bolivians say, "Okay, the market price is x," and Chavez says back, "I don't give a damn what the market price is. Let's exchange in a cooperative way that is beneficial. We're richer, you're poorer. We have more resources, you have less. We have the oil, so let's set a rate that gives you more of the benefits." So he's bending markets, and he's bending them in precisely the way I'm talking about, and that's part of fighting for Participatory Economics, so I don't have any problem with doing things like that at all, particularly if they are part of a larger on-going project. I think it's great. But it is best if it's imbued with a consciousness that it's ultimately calling for something utterly different, not just for the old ways refine, but for a whole new society.

You're right. I didn't offer details about participatory planning, partly because there's not enough time. Usually when I talk it's an hour and a half or two hours, and three hours of discussion. It's very hard to discuss a whole new system quickly. But there is a book, *ParEcon: Life After Capitalism*, that does run into all these issues, and it does raise the complaints and the concerns that people have, including ones that people don't often raise that I think up, and it tries to addresses them. I agree, it would be wrong for anybody, based on this talk, to say, "Okay, I like Participatory Economics." The most I want to try and get across is the idea that we should try for classlessness, we should try in our vision and understanding of what it means, to win real classlessness. We should try to understand what the implications are for our work.

And if we want that, then we see, here's this guy who's saying this model of Participatory Economics can deliver that. He doesn't seem to be insane or incoherent. Lots of people are starting to agree. So it's probably worth looking into, but looking into it means seriously looking at it, thinking about it, and addressing it. Luckily books about ParEcon are not written like *Empire*, say. They are not obscure. They are not designed to make people feel ignorant. They are plain and straightforward, and you have to and can judge for yourself, I agree.

My last little point, almost a joke, is that I agree that we have to put economic democracy, self-management, and participation on the table, but to me that's not eliminating the bosses. Imagine this is a prison, and a couple of officers are running for warden and everyone can vote. Some people will vote, some people will feel like they don't want to be a part of choosing a person who governs me, rules me, and creates the environment that I find abhorrent. Can we see that any place else? Does it only apply in the prison? Of course not. It is, instead, typical of all votes in the U.S.

How about if we have a poll and ask the American population whether they would like to vote for their boss, the president. 50% already say no. Of the 50% that say yes, about 30%, I would guess, maybe a little bit more, vote based on whether or not they like the person's personality. I actually think that's not a bad idea. The person's going to be around for four years, totally visible, creating an environment, a mood, and since everything else they say is a lie, why not judge based on what we can actually have knowledge of, their personality. It's only we leftists who simultaneously develop the capacity to say, "They lie – listen to them. They lie – judge what they say." It's a peculiar stance that the Left has. We got the first half right, they lie. Not only do they lie, but we know what their real interests are, we know what their real desires are. We have an analysis that says that it's inconceivable that any of the candidates who might win are interested in getting out of Iraq, unless the population forces them too, and then we say "Let's listen to what they have to say about Iraq." I think the people who say, "Let's vote for the one who dresses nicer, and who looks friendlier," are actually more rational, and the most rational are the ones who don't vote.

On the other hand, suppose God comes down and says, "We're going to have an election. We're going to run, I don't know, it doesn't matter, Bush against Chomsky. We're going to have six months of discussion, and during the six months of discussion, I, God, am going to oversee every exchange. If a candidate lies even just once, I strike them into dust. Not only that, if they mislead, or say anything other than what they actually intend to do – they are dust. And the discussion is going to be pervasive throughout the whole society. Everybody is going to be able to hear everything that is going on, and so the candidates' plans will be clear. Not only that, whoever wins in this free election from the American population, whoever gets more votes and becomes president, I, God, am going to make sure that they carry through the program that they have discussed, and that nothing impedes doing that."

How many people would vote in that election? 120% of the population would vote. Every single person in the United States, and a whole lot of people that nobody knows exists would vote. Why? Because something's at stake. If there's truth, there's real difference, and there's real issues. But if we're voting for a boss, we're voting for one of two people who is a boss, it's not so exciting and really not very rational.

Resources

Albert, Michael. (2004). *Parecon: Life After Capitalism*. New York: Verso Books.
Albert, Michael and Robin Hahnel. (1991). *Looking Forward: Participatory Economics for the Twenty First Century*. Boston: South End Press.

Schweickart, David. (1993). *Against Capitalism.* Cambridge: Cambridge University Press.
Schweickart, David. (2002). *After Capitalism.* Lanhan: Rowman and Littlefield

Notes

[1] Stated in: Albert, Michael, interview by Barbara Ehrenreich. (2004, April 26). "ParEcon? Ehrenreich interviews Albert". Znet.
<http://www.zmag.org/content/showarticle.cfm?SectionID=41&ItemID=5403>
[2] This model is elaborated and defended in: Schweickart, David. (1993). *Against Capitalism.* Cambridge: Cambridge University Press., and (less technically) in: Schweickart, David. (2002). *After Capitalism.* Lanhan: Rowman and Littlefield
[3] Logue, John and Jacquelyn Yates. (2001). *The Real World of Employee Ownership.* Ithaca: IRL Press, p. 18.

5

Introduction to the Economics of Liberation: An Overview of PROUT

Nada Khader

Nada Khader has been working on social justice issues since September 1995. Her personal experience with community organizing in the United States around issues of social, economic and racial justice has revealed the various obstacles in the path to becoming a serious, powerful, unstoppable force for progressive social change. She believes that it is difficult for our voices to obtain meaningful mainstream media coverage in ways that give us space to articulate our full analysis of current events, and that the 501c3 proliferation has also weakened our ability to engage in substantial political work that needs to happen in order for progressive candidates to be elected and given adequate exposure. She also realizes that a decreasing quality of life and a decline in real wages since the 1970s have made ordinary folk more concerned about meeting their family's needs as opposed to attending community meetings and events, and that our capitalist framework has also atomized people where we feel compelled to behave primarily as individual consumers as opposed to a surge of powerful collective catalysts of progressive change. Nada remains optimistic that we will find the strength and wisdom within ourselves to work collaboratively on meeting the pressing issues of our time, and that we will start with a fundamental re-examination of our economic system as the starting point needed in order to move forward into a brighter future.

Introduction to the Workshop

I attended the first ever US Social Forum in Atlanta, Georgia, in June 2007 to be with thousands of others who believe that serious progressive social and economic change is necessary in the very short term in order to help heal our planet and ourselves from decades of environmental destruction, harmful exploitation and abuse of our natural resources. I presented a workshop at the forum on PROUT, an alternative economic model that is based on worker-owned cooperatives, economic decentralization, regional self-sufficiency and a functioning world government in which to address international conflict and tension.

In my workshop, I showed a 28 minute video entitled "The Economics of PROUT" that was produced by Paul Narada Alister from Australia. I then facilitated a discussion about what we can all do now to move towards a more cooperative model of organizing human economic activity, including shopping from cooperatives, community gardening, supporting the co-housing or housing cooperative movement, buying locally grown produce as much as possible, setting up a bartering system to meet real human needs and so forth. It is with pleasure here that I present a synopsis of PROUT developed by the PROUT Institute of Australia (http://pia.org.au) with input from Dr. Sohail Inayatullah, Jayanta Kumar and Acarya Shambushivananda.

Introduction to PROUT

PROUT (an acronym for **Pro**gressive **U**tilization **T**heory) is a social and economic system first proposed by the eminent Indian philosopher, Shrii Prabhat Ranjan Sarkar (1921-1990). It is arguably the only socio-economic theory to emerge out of the developing world that has direct applicability to the developed world.
1. PROUT draws on environmental, social and spiritual wisdom accumulated as a result of thousands of years of human struggle and experimentation.
2. A PROUTist economy is based on the *cooperative system*. It is community based, decentralized and promotes an economic voice for women. PROUT satisfies human needs by promoting the utilization and rational distribution of all resources, physical, mental and spiritual.
3. PROUT also has a program for globalization based on the concept of *political centralization* and *economic decentralization*.
4. PROUT has a theory of class and a historical analysis based on the concept of *collective psychology*.

Building Communities

The primary goal of PROUT is to build healthy communities which, like living systems, need to be nurtured and cultivated. An economic system cannot be divorced from the people, the community and the bioregion in which it is embedded. Therefore PROUT opposes the neoliberal agenda of deregulation, privatization and free trade. These policies bleed wealth from local communities and the already impoverished 'third world' into a comparatively few centers of global economic dominance.

PROUT advocates a constitutional guarantee that all persons have the right to obtain their minimum requirements of life, in particular food, education, health care, clothing and housing. After that, surplus wealth can be distributed as determined by the community values of the day. PROUT also promotes a system of cooperative community budgets to determine the shares of annual aggregate income going to households, government and business.

New Definitions of Economic Progress

Per capita GDP is a defective measure of economic progress. It counts every new nuclear missile, tourist casino and cigarette sale as positive growth – as contributing to prosperity. It ignores tremendous disparities in wealth between rich and poor.

PROUT recognizes that human beings are not just *Homo economicus*. We have intellectual, emotional, cultural, social and spiritual needs in addition to the economically obvious physical needs. To satisfy these needs requires the management of many kinds of 'subtle' capital in addition to physical and financial capital. Satisfying these diverse needs underlies our productive activity and our community life. A healthy community with a healthy economy requires ...

- **An expanded definition of economic resources:** Future economic theory and practice will have to come to terms with a much broader definition of economic resources to satisfy the spectrum of human needs. Sarkar's second PROUT principle states that "There should be maximum utilization and rational distribution of all mundane, supramundane and spiritual potentialities of the universe." Australian PROUTist Jayanta Kumar explains that this principle begins the process of defining resources and capacities as wider than the purely physical. An equal footing is established for comparing subtle and economic values. For instance, the aesthetic value of a forest is no less important than its economic value as woodchips. In fact, Sarkar's fourth fundamental principle establishes the subtle value as more important.

  Kumar further explains that maximum utilization is not the same as indiscriminate use or exploitation. Utilization means proper use and implies the opposite of abuse and non-utilization or resources stagnation. When people are starving, the production of materials for war is clearly misutilization. In similar circumstances, the hoarding of produce for trade advantages is criminal non-utilization. Maximum utilization of physical resources provides the means of properly generating the basic social requirements and amenities. Economic growth, properly directed, is not a goal but a necessary condition for a society expanding through improvements in the quality and span of human life. Economic development implies proper balance and distribution in this growth process, and maximum utilization of subtle resources implies full consideration of peoples' development and expression in the midst of this economic development.

Rational distribution refers to access to subtle resources as well as an equitable and constantly adjusted income policy. Minimum requirements must first be guaranteed to all and then the surplus can be distributed to merit, provided that the differential gap is progressively closed and the minimum level adjusted upwards. Some socialist countries succeeded in cutting the tails of income distribution – the extreme highs and lows – but failed to maintain constant adjustment and so disparity has grown again. It should be noted that this principle extends to include the requirements of the animal and plant worlds; their requirements as independent life forms and not simply as functions of human existence. This principle thus includes the existential value of all living creatures.[1] Under a PROUT economy, with the development of technology for the general welfare of all as opposed to profit-maximization, people will be able to work fewer and fewer hours a day in order to support themselves and their families. They will have more time to pursue sports, poetry, hobbies, personal development as well as more time to spend with families and friends.

- **Multi-bottom line accounting:** PROUT supports the introduction of triple- and multi-bottom-line accounting to ensure efficient management of the full spectrum of resources, in that we must take into consideration the impact of our economic activity on people, the planet and the economy. Furthermore, PROUT is based on Neo-Humanism which is a system of ideas that does not see humans as the center of our ecosystem; rather PROUT is aligned with Indigenous traditions from around the world where we see ourselves as part of a web of life where animals and plants and other inanimate entities have as much right as we do to flourish in good health and prosperity. Both capitalism and communism are based on a materialistic outlook and do not necessarily support the notion that plants and animals have existential value separate from any utility value that we may ascribe to them.

- **New economic indicators:** To measure social and economic progress, PROUT embraces alternative economic indicators such as those developed by the Calvert-Henderson group and others. The Calvert-Henderson Quality of Life Indicators, first published in 2000, are the result of a six-year study by a multi-disciplinary group of scholars from government agencies, for-profit firms, and nonprofit organizations who see the need for more practical and sophisticated metrics of societal conditions.[2]

- **Resource taxation:** PROUT supports shifting the tax base by gradually replacing personal income tax with a rational system of taxes on finite natural resources.

Economic Democracy

Economic democracy in PROUT is achieved through 1. Economic decentralization; 2. A cooperative based economy; and 3. A significant voice for women in economic planning and decision making. Local communities can solve local economic problems more easily because they are closer to the source of the problem and by definition the problems are on a smaller scale. Economic decentralization also decentralizes population and so contributes to sustainable population centers.

Sarkar argues for five principles of economic decentralization:
1. Local people should have control of local resources.
2. Production should be guided by local consumption needs and not the profit motive.
3. Production and distribution should be organized through the cooperative system.
4. Local people should have employment priority in local industry.
5. A community should not import what can be produced locally.

Three Tiers of Enterprise

PROUT divides the industrial system into three sectors:
1. Most businesses, especially those producing the essential requirements of life, are best operated as cooperatives. For example, the agricultural and housing sectors fall into this category.
2. Businesses too small for cooperative management and producing non-essential goods are private enterprises.
3. Very large-scale industries and key/strategic industries are public utilities. Key industries operate on a no-profit, no-loss basis.

PROUT advocates a monetary system managed by a central bank run as a public utility with numerous cooperative banks providing ordinary people with their banking needs.

PROUT supports the development of a *balanced economy*, in which the agricultural sector, agro- and agrico-industries, manufacturing and the service sectors all develop in balanced proportion. The agricultural and manufacturing sectors of so-called developed countries are being decimated by free trade. This is a worrying trend.

A cooperative economy will encourage a large not-for-profit sector which contributes to the accumulation of social capital. It would also recognise the productive role played by mothers and caregivers not employed within the formal economy.

Globalization

In the long term, PROUT envisages the establishment of a system of tiered communities from the local to the global level. The lowest level would be the *block*, a bioregion having about 100,000 inhabitants. At the global level, a world government is essential to solve pressing problems such as global warming and human rights abuses. However a world government cannot be imposed from the top. When local communities around the world have economic security, they will naturally see the advantages of a world administration. PROUT promotes the concept of *political centralization* and *economic decentralization*. It is very important to mention that PROUT is not a rigid ideology that is to be implemented the same way all over the world but is rather a set of principles that will vary considerably in its implementation according to time, place and person. Local cultural expressions and traditions, as long as they do not violate human rights as defined by the Universal Declaration of Human Rights are to be respected and encouraged. Schooling should always be in the indigenous language and all the languages of the world should be encouraged and promoted as part of our collective human patrimony. This approach can make the notion of globalization work for all, a world where human beings are free to live, work and develop their potential wherever they choose to do so, as they merge their economic interests with the overall interests of the local area (allowing no scope for a group of people to come into an area, exploit the resources and local people, and siphon the profits outside the area).

How will it happen?

The contemporary world is threatened by three main sources of instability. First, *economic instability* arises from gross concentration of wealth which generates speculative bubbles, most obvious today in the equities, futures and foreign exchange markets. All speculative bubbles inevitably burst. The flip side of wealth concentration is *institutionalized poverty* encouraged by policies of the World Bank, IMF and the World Trade Organisation. So the second source of instability is *social instability*, which in the worst case is expressed as violence and war. A third source of instability comes from *environmental degradation* and *climate change*. Given these sources of instability, each of them potentially catastrophic, it is hard to imagine how 'business as usual' can continue much longer.

According to Prout, societies transform themselves through dialectical struggle. The existing order (the *thesis*) in decay is gradually or rapidly replaced by progressive ideas (the *antithesis*). The antithesis to capitalism is already emerging. Civil society including communities, women, workers, indigenous people, artists and green organizations all over the world are setting the agenda where large business corporations and governments have failed.

Personal Change

An important lesson learned by political and social activists in recent decades, and arising in particular from women's experience of social struggle, is that social change requires personal change. Outer change must be accompanied by inner change. Keeping this in mind, PROUT encourages three kinds of personal transformation:

- **Universal outlook:** the struggle to accept all women and men, regardless of social status, economic class, cultural or ethnic background, as equal members of one universal family. PROUT is the application of family spirit in the social and economic arena.

- **Ethical lifestyle:**   Personal ethics underpin all political and economic practice. A limited vision of ethics is contributing to the disintegration of contemporary society. To build a healthy society, PROUT promotes the acceptance of cardinal human values, defined by Sarkar to mean the spirit of benevolence, a sense of aesthetics, rational thinking, dynamicity and equipoise[3]

- **Spirituality:** This is the constant endeavor to maintain one's connection with Spirit, the well-spring of hope and the source of all that is sweet and subtle in human life. Many people consider the regular practice of meditation or contemplation to be helpful in this regard.

To conclude, PROUT offers an alternative set of principles to both capitalism and communism that can help us move towards this "other world" that so many of us are aspiring for. PROUT takes into account the various dimensions of human existence and does not neglect the rights of plants, animals and other inanimate entities. Today, there are PROUT conferences and workshops held all over the world, in Australia, India, Taiwan, Philippines or Maharlika, Europe, North, Central and South America. There is a PROUT Institute of Australia as well as a PROUT Research Institute in Caracas, Venezuela, (www.priven.org) that is helping to document some of the issues facing the thousands of worker owned cooperatives that have sprouted up since the Bolivarian Revolution has taken hold in Venezuela. We face an exciting moment in human history where immense change must happen in a short amount of time; we must all work together to help our planet regain the balance and dignity that has been so long denied us. Let us boldly take the first steps into this new era.

References

Kumar, Jayanta. (1987). *New aspects of Prout.* Denmark: Proutist Universal Publications

Notes

[1] Kumar, Jayanta. (1987). *New aspects of Prout.* Denmark: Proutist Universal Publications.

[2] Please see http://www.calvert-henderson.com/overview.htm for more details.

[3] Please see http://www.gurukul.edu/pubs_journal_cardinalvalues.php for more details

SECTION II:

DEFINING THE SOLIDARITY ECONOMY THROUGH DIVERSE PRACTICES

6
Building a Solidarity Economy from Real World Practices

Emily Kawano and Ethan Miller

Emily Kawano is an economist and the Director of the Center for Popular Economics and the U.S. Solidarity Economy Network. She taught economics at Smith College, worked in the national office of the American Friends Service Committee, and has been involved in popular economics work for over 18 years. While working in North Ireland, she served on the N.I. Social Economy Network Working Group and worked with two Belfast Community Development Agencies to develop and deliver a social economy training program for community groups seeking to start up social enterprises.

Ethan Miller is a writer, organizer, musician and independent researcher whose work focuses on cultivating a democratic culture and economy of solidarity, dignity and justice. Author of a number of articles on solidarity economics, he is a founder and current coordinating committee member of the U.S. Solidarity Economy Network (www.ussen.org), as well as a website editor for Grassroots Economic Organizing Online (www.geo.coop) and the coordinator of the Data Commons Project, a national data-sharing cooperative working to create a public directory of solidarity economy initiatives (http://dcp.usworker.coop). Ethan lives, works and tends the local orchard at the JED Community Land Trust (www.jedcollective.org), an intentional community and cooperative subsistence farm in Greene, Maine.

Neoliberal Globalization and Why We Need a Solidarity Economy

This workshop began with a warm-up exercise in which people formed a 'human sculpture' to express the impact of *neoliberalism*, currently the dominant economic model in the world. If neoliberalism had a slogan, it would be something like "markets good, state bad." It's about freeing up markets in ways that empower big business, by pushing through favorable rules in trade and investment, and lowering corporate taxes. It means attacking government through privatization (e.g. water, schools, social security, Medicare), deregulation (e.g. health, safety, and environmental protections), and downsizing government.

The exercise provided a bit of grounding as to why we need an alternative to neoliberalism. Through an interactive physical exercise, participants used their bodies to represent their feelings and ideas about neoliberalism. They expressed sentiments of anger, losing control, and feeling choked, and a sense of things being taken away; they highlighted the term "race to the bottom."

Following up from this exercise, we had a discussion of the term 'neoliberalism,' which seemed confusing to some in the group, given the other meanings–contradictory to the conservative meaning of neoliberalism–that many associate with the term liberalism. We suggested that the 'neo' in neoliberalism means 'new,' and the 'liberalism' of the term harkens back to its original meaning of the freedom of individuals from the divine rule of kings or an absolutist state. So this 'new liberalism' argues for individual, and particularly corporate, rights to be free from interference from the state.

We on the Left have a great critique of neoliberalism, but there's less clarity about what should take its place. Fortunately there is a wealth of material upon which to build. Alternative economic practices and policies have always existed, but there's been an upsurge throughout the world as of late, in part due to the ravages of neoliberal globalization. The 'solidarity economy' is a framework that pulls these practices and policies together into a more coherent and powerful system.

In this workshop, our goal was not to propose a specific definition of the solidarity economy, as much as to facilitate a process through which participant would define it themselves. We supplied some of the puzzle-pieces (in the "Stepping Stones" exercise) and the group identified a set of shared ethical principles that link diverse initiatives together.

Stepping Stones to a Solidarity Economy

In this participatory exercise, people learned about and discussed a wide range of existing economic alternatives that we can use as stepping-stones to build a solidarity economy. We broke into small groups and distributed stacks of cards, each of which gave a short description of a solidarity economy initiative. The groups read over and discussed the cards, then chose their favorite three or four. We then came back together and each group took turns sharing and discussing their favorite cards.

This is a list of all the stepping stone cards at the time of this writing, however, the cards are a work in progress, continually open to changes and additions.

Stepping Stones Toward 'Another World'

What is it Called?
Worker Center/ Worker Justice Centers.

What is its Aim?
To organize workers where traditional unionization drives are almost impossible: informal sector, transient workers, undocumented workers, sweatshop workers.

How Does it Work?
-Brings together workers and others by providing education, literacy training, advocacy, social service advice, legal aid.
-Builds upon this social/community nexus in order to organize for worker rights.

Successes:
-Garment Worker Center shortened work day and helped 7 workers from Forever 21 to receive $100,000 in back pay.
-Coalition for Humane Immigrant Rights of L.A. improved working conditions for day laborers at Home Depot and obtained a city-funded center in the parking lot of a Home Depot.
-Coalition of Immokalee Workers staged a 4yr boycott on Taco Bell and won penny-per-pound pass through which nearly doubled the worker's paychecks.

The categorization is meant to group similar initiatives, but there are many examples where cards could be listed under additional categories.

Stepping Stones Toward 'Another World'

What is it Called?
Zapatista Autonomous Communities

What is its Aim?
-To be independent of the Mexican government's neoliberal policies and military oppression.

How Does it Work?

Following the 1994 uprising, many communities in Zapatista-controlled territories have declared themselves autonomous from the government. They run their communities in a participatory and democratic manner. They have shoe-making, weaving, and health clinic cooperatives. They are dependent on the international and activist community to buy products, contribute money, and create enough visibility to prevent the Mexican government from attacking them.

Successes:
They have continued for 11 years. Even though they are probably not economically sustainable, the community feels empowered and people have much more dignity and self-respect.

Wikipedia Article: http://en.wikipedia.org/wiki/EZLN
EZLN website: http://www.ezln.org.mx/

Finally, this is not meant to be an exhaustive nor authoritative list of elements of the solidarity economy. Some may be disputed. Many more could and should be added. We hope that you will help by contributing to the Stepping Stone cards which are available on our website: www.ussen.org

Supporting local, democratic communities
- Co-housing
- Gaviotas
- Zapatistas autonomous communities
- Community schools
- Regional tax-base sharing

Redistribution
- Progressive taxation
- Basic income grants

Property rights & Commons
- Common property management
- Creative commons
- Slum dwellers international
- MST - Movement of landless workers, Brazil
- Community Concession agreements
- Community land trusts

Environmental sustainability
- Organic agriculture

- Brownfield development
- Conservation easements
- Living machines
- Biomimicry

Finance & investment
- Democratizing the Fed
- Tobin tax
- Local currency
- Micro-lending
- Economically targeted investment
- Participatory budgeting

Consumption & distribution
- Fair trade
- Alonovo

Work, Labor & Production
- Worker centers
- Factory take-overs, Argentina
- Living wage
- Corporate social responsibility
- Cooperative movement
- Social economy
- Father quotas in parental leave
- Community-supported agriculture
- Community gardens

Measurement
- Alternative economic indices

In the discussions that followed our sharing of the Stepping Stone cards, the group talked about the recent surge of cooperative development in Venezuela. In 2000 there were less than 100 co-ops in Venezuela, and now there are thousands. This is a good example of an alternative to the market economy within Venezuela. Yet this rapid growth of a cooperative sector also presents great challenges: many of the cooperatives are struggling because the model is being implemented without the necessary process of education for participatory democracy. Cooperatives without a culture of cooperation are less likely to succeed. Some participants also mentioned the village of Gaviotas in Colombia as an important example of an inspiring solidarity economy initiative not mentioned in our Stepping Stones. Gaviotas is a self-sustaining and socially-egalitarian community amidst a landscape otherwise riddled with violent conflict between leftist guerilas and the paramilitaries. They have developed innovative water purification systems, biofuel production, and have reforested and changed the local climate. It is an example worth learning more about.

Building a Solidarity Economy Framework

Drawing on the real world examples provided in the Stepping Stones exercise, we talked about the importance of a framework–the solidarity economy–that can link these inspiring but often isolated initiatives and projects together. How do we put all these elements into a larger context, where they can be more successfully linked together in a spirit of movement building?

The "Values for a Solidarity Economy" exercise mimics what has happened around the world with the concept of the solidarity economy. Instead of a few people coming up with a big model about how the economy should work, the solidarity economy framework has emerged from people looking around them, seeing alternatives that are bubbling up, and trying to make sense of this diverse set of creative efforts.

This approach is very different than that often taken in the past by the Left in regard to alternative economics: develop a big model, debate the model, and then split it into 400 different factions based on disputes about little details. The solidarity economy approach is more of a dialog to bring people together to find common ground from which to organize and build movements. The detailed debates are still encouraged and fostered, but they happen in the context of a movement that we all can share, because the movement is being built through our creativity, and though our collective problem solving.

In small groups, we discussed: "what are the basic values and principles that the Stepping Stones share? What values do they hold in common?" Each group was asked to come up with five values that summarize the connections between these different stepping-stones. The small group report-backs were remarkably similar. The core values and principles that were consistently mentioned were:

- stewardship of the environment/sustainability
- cooperation
- shared well-being (with an emphasis on the importance of diversity)
- equality
- exploring and promoting non-monetary and non-traditional forms of wealth
- democracy and participation

This set of principles is completely consistent with those that have been articulated around the world as characterizing the solidarity economy. Shared values, of course, don't automatically translate into collective organizing. These values may be articulated differently by different groups; they may be only partly and imperfectly realized in actual practice; there may be varying commitments to these values by diverse participants in a given organization; and, in some cases, a particular economic structure might generate effects that are in line with the values while not consciously articulating them as an organization.

Building a solidarity economy, then, is not a matter of simply identifying shared values; it is a process of organizing around those shared values to build a shared story of economic possibility. The common values form the fertile ground in which new relationships between diverse groups and actors can be built.

With more time, the next step for the group might have been to identify concrete forms of linkage and alliance between some of the diverse Stepping Stones. How can these shared values translate into concrete, shared action? What kinds of examples of solidarity economy movement-building can we identify or imagine? How can we work to build this nascent movement in our daily lives and work? We hope that these are some of the questions that participants carried home with them.

7
Beyond Reform vs. Revolution: Economic Transformation in the U.S

A Roundtable Discussion with Stephen Healy, Emily Kawano, David Korten, Julie Matthaei, Germai Medhanie, and Dan Swinney

Moderator's Introduction

Julie Matthaei:
My name is Julie Matthaei, and I will be the moderator for this session. I am a professor of economics at Wellesley College, and have recently started an organization called Guramylay: Growing the Green Economy. Last summer, Guramylay created a website, www.TransformationCentral.org, and we are always looking for people to submit material on economic transformation and positive economic alternatives. I am also a member of the Solidarity Economy Working Group for the U.S. Social Forum; we put together this track of social and solidarity economy related workshops.

I have been writing about economic history for over thirty years, trying to understand the forces for positive transformation in the United States at the present moment. Right now I feel that the US is at an incredible historical conjuncture, a time which is bursting with potential for radical economic transformation. In my writing with Barbara Brandt, we call this time "the Transformative Moment," because we have been able to document a deep-seated and multifaceted transformative response to the imbalances, inequalities, and lack of freedom created by the reigning "hierarchical polarization" paradigm.[1] This paradigm of social life, which has ruled Western societies for thousands of years, undergirds our current unequal and exploitative economic system. It is based on hierarchy and polarization by class, race, gender, sexuality, ability-disability, nation, and so on.

For the last half century, social movements have been organizing in the U.S. against these different hierarchical polarities, such as the worker, Civil Rights, feminist, ecology, and gay rights movements. Each of these movements has undergone a process of maturation, as well as of interaction and integration with the other movements, through coalition politics and the efforts of members who experience multiple types of oppression. At the present time, these social movements are beginning to come together, especially through the worldwide Social

Forum movement, around a shared opposition to oppression and exploitation in any form. There is a growing commitment both to systematic change, as expressed in the Social Forum slogan, "Another World is Possible," as well as to a diversity of ways forward, as expressed in the Zapatista slogan, "Un solo no, un million de si" (Only one no, and a million yeses).

This historic first U.S. Social Forum is part of the Social Forum movement, and represents this coming together of movements to create a new country and a new world. The organizers of this track of sessions are hoping to use this forum as an opportunity to organize and energize economic alternatives in the U.S. through the creation of a solidarity economy network, similar to those which exist in Latin America, Europe, Africa, and Canada.

Today we have a fabulous panel here to talk with us on the subject of "Beyond Reform or Revolution: Economic Transformation in the U.S." I organized this panel because I believe that it is crucial for advocates of economic transformation to transcend this polarizing dichotomy.

I was part of the New Left of the 1960s, what we could call the "old New Left," since the many of us who are still active are now in our fifties and sixties, old compared to the new generation of leftist activists. As advocates for deep-seated economic and social change, we used to argue incessantly about what was truly revolutionary as versus what was "just a reform." Reforms were not only *not* revolutionary – they were considered to be counterrevolutionary since they eased the plight of workers and postponed the needed revolution. Deeply influenced by Marx, we saw class struggle – and worker organizing – as the most important type of political organizing. Anything which did not work towards socialist revolution and getting rid of markets altogether was denigrated as being "reformist." As a socialist in my early twenties, I joined the feminist movement to try to win women into the revolutionary struggle. I ended becoming a socialist feminist, however, and organized around a range of women's issues. For this, I was attacked by leftists, mostly white men, for reformist organizing for rights for women rather than working for the socialist revolution, which was supposed to solve the problem of women's oppression altogether.

Much of the reform versus revolution debate has died down since then, in large part because of the vibrancy of purportedly reformist, non-class-centered, non-socialist social movements – such as the Civil Rights, feminist, and ecology movements – and also due to the comparative stagnation of revolutionary labor organizing.[2] However, the reform-revolution distinction still lives on in the U.S. left – especially in discussions of radical economic transformation. I hope that this panel will help put it to rest once and for all, especially as a critique of the current transformative economic practices and institutions which we will discuss here today, and at various other panels throughout this conference.

The basic assumption underlying this panel is that the reform vs. revolution dichotomy is not helpful. There are many different kinds of economic transformation happening now, and none of them are perfect, but they are all bringing change. Trying to exclude some from our movement on the basis that they are "reformist" is not useful. At the same time, I want to argue that we can learn a good deal from constructive criticism within and across movements. For instance, the cooperative movement has done some fabulous things, but it does not explicitly include other progressive values; it is not inherently anti-racist, feminist, or environmentalist.

Cooperatives and Social Movements

To help guard against single-issue organizing, Canadian activists have organized social economy networks which include social movements as well as cooperatives, community development organizations and the like, so that they can take advantage of social movements' critiques of their work. This helps create a multi-faceted multidimensional approach to economic transformation. I would like to set up that kind of dialogue here, where people talk about the different types of economic transformation they are involved in, and we can engage in constructive criticism of one another. Not a "this is the right thing and I'm going to convince you" approach, like we had in the 60's and 70's, but an inclusive dialogue where everyone can examine how they are – or are not – incorporating progressive values into their life and their work.

I have invited five speakers to our roundtable: David Korten, Emily Kawano, Dan Swinney, Stephen Healy, and Germai Medhanie. I have prepared three questions which you all will have a chance to answer. Then we will open the floor up for questions from the audience, and for discussion.

Introduce yourself and your organization, and talk about how your organization is involved in economic transformation.

David Korten:
I have three significant organizational affiliations. I am board chair of *Yes* magazine, which is helping to define a new mainstream grounded in principles of justice and sustainability. I'm a board member of the *Business Alliance for Local Living Economies (BALLE)*, which is rebuilding local economies around these principles. And I'm a founding member and active participant in the *Interna-*

tional Forum on Globalization, which exposes the truth of corporate-led global-ization as a power grab by global corporations and financial institutions of the old economy we must now put behind us.

I am also the author of *When Corporations Rule the World* (1995 and 2001) and *The Great Turning: From Empire to Earth Community* (2006), among others. My work draws on the experience and lessons of twenty-one years living over-seas working on economic development. I began with a mainstream perspective, but gradually came to recognize that economic development by the conventional model is a process by which the rich expropriate the assets of the poor and turn them into garbage at an accelerating rate, in order to make money for people who already have more than they need. Economic mismanagement has immersed the human species in a potentially terminal crisis of environmental and social devas-tation that threatens our very survival. We now face the imperative to rethink the nature and purpose of economic life in the most fundamental way. We must move beyond the growth model, reallocate resources from rich to poor and from harmful to useful applications, and invest in the regeneration of human, social, and natural capital.

Of the three organizations in which I have a major role, I want to focus here on the Business Alliance for Local Living Economies (BALLE). It was launched in 2002 by the *Social Ventures Network (SVN)*, which is a business responsibility group distinguished by two characteristics. First, its members are entrepreneurs who own their own businesses, which give them the freedom to bring their val-ues into their businesses. They are distinguished from members of other business responsibility groups by the fact that they have a fire-in-the-belly commitment to the idea that business should serve society, not the reverse. Discussions in SVN led to a conclusion that the deep changes we need cannot just come out of indi-vidual responsible enterprises. They require building a new economy comprised of responsible, locally-rooted businesses that function within a framework of community values and accountability.

Because we identified absentee ownership as a source of serious economic pa-thology, we absolutely bar participation by publicly traded corporations on the ground that they represent the most extreme and pernicious form of absentee ownership.

BALLE now has 52 chapters around the United States and Canada with roughly 15,000 business members. The networks generally form around "Local First" campaigns devoted to building public awareness of the distinction between pa-tronizing local businesses to keep your money in the community, and patronizing box stores such as Wal-Mart. As the business members participate and get more involved, there is a gradual opening and expanding of perspective to embrace the other environmental and social values. Our premise is that as local living economies grow in size and strength, they give people more choices as to where they work, shop, and invest. This allows us all to withdraw more of our life energy from what we call the global suicide economy and transfer it to the new local living economies. We believe that business is not simply about financial profit. When you are operating your business within a community context, part of your return comes from living in a healthy community and a healthy environment.

Emily Kawano:

My name is Emily Kawano, and I'm the director of the Center for Popular Economics. We are a collective of some 60 economists that works to promote economic justice through organizing and demystifying the economy. We work with community groups and activists engaged in a wide range of issues. We believe that the economy is deliberately mystified and obfuscated, which leads people to think, "Oh, this is beyond what I can understand – I'll just leave it to the experts." We believe that the economy is much too important to leave in the hands of the so-called experts. The economy is made up of all of us – we live and experience it every day of our lives, and therefore we all have a stake in how it's structured and run. We should all have some say, some input, into shaping economic decisions, policies, and institutions.

That's the core of our work – trying to help people understand how the economic system works and strengthening their engagement in making it better. We do trainings and produce publications and other resources. We use participatory methodology in our trainings because economics can be so scary and off-putting to many people. We start by connecting the economy to people's own experiences. We build from there to help people understand issues such as: why would the Federal Reserve create a recession (as it did in the early '80s), why has inequality increased, why is Wall Street happy when unemployment goes up, what is neoliberalism and what are its main policies, what is monetary and fiscal policy?

CPE does a bang-up job of helping people understand the workings of capitalism in general and specifically the critique of neoliberal capitalism, a particularly cut-throat model of capitalism (there are many different models of capitalism). The problem is that the critique and analysis of global capitalism can leave people feeling disempowered and discouraged. So it's really important to show and discuss what alternatives are out there. What is going on right now that we can bring together, build on and make coherent. How can we create a systemic vision of what the alternative would be? The framework of the solidarity economy pro-

vides such a unifying vision, one that is built on real world examples and experiences. There are a serious cracks in neoliberalism and an historic opportunity to
create change.

Dan Swinney:

I'm Dan Swinney. I founded and direct the *Center for Labor and Community Research (CLCR)* in Chicago. Our work is focused in building the solidarity economy in what is called the traditional market and traditional state, and we have
been working in the field for twenty-five years. I came out of the labor and plant
closings movement, and after all the work we've done in manufacturing, I'm
convinced that 80% of the 200,000 jobs and 4,000 factories lost in Chicago in the
1980s and 1990s could have been saved. If we had been proactive and focused
on the details of how companies really operate, embraced what we call capital
strategies[3], and broadened our alliances to include sections of the business community, we could have done a great deal to prevent the kind of deep poverty that
we see in urban as well as rural communities. At CLCR, we work to develop
and modernize our manufacturing base because we think it should really be at the
heart of a dynamic and progressive modern society, and because we see this kind
of development as a way to end poverty. We think that the best way to oppose
low road globalization strategies is a positive alternative that meets the practical
needs of people, is embraced by a broad section of the society, including a significant section of the business community, and reflects our social vision.

The two projects I want to discuss are the *Chicago Manufacturing Renaissance
Council* (CMRC) and Austin Polytechnical Academy(APA). I'm the Executive
Director for CMRC, which represents top labor, business, government, educational, and community leadership around the development strategy of leading the
race to the top in global high-performance high-value-added manufacturing. The
CMRC is founded on the explicit social partnership of labor, business, community, and government; and it promotes development that is economically, socially, and environmentally sustainable and restorative.

The CMRC is doing a variety of projects, and one I want to tell you about is the
launch of *Austin Polytechnic Academy*–a public high-school. We opened with
145 students in the freshman class in September 2007. It's a union school, not a
non-union charter school, and it is profoundly linked to the modern manufacturing economy. APA is premised on the fact that 40% of the small privately-held
companies in manufacturing are going to lose their labor force in the next 10
years, which means that if they don't solve the problem of the labor market,
they're out of business. These are companies that are now competing in the
global economy, paying anywhere from fifteen to fifty dollars an hour for production jobs. We're not just talking about a "living wage," we're talking about

three times that. So, in this situation, there is an opportunity for us to intervene on behalf of the public sector in production. Austin Polytech is located in an African-American community that was devastated by deindustrialization. Our program will prepare kids for three tracks in manufacturing: high-skilled technical positions, management, and ownership. It's exactly the same model of a school that started Mondragon in 1942. That's how Mondragon started. They created a polytechnical school that gave their students the technical competence, and the social values to then intervene in production, and lead in its development with the values of the broader community at the core of the initiative.

APA has a pre-engineering program, a top-rate principal and teaching staff, and twenty-five manufacturing companies that are our partners. Our company partners are pledging internships and summer jobs. They are invested in our project because they need a next generation of workers to lead in production, as well as to aspire to become owners of these companies, as many are without an obvious successor. In this way, our school is now preparing young people in Austin to have the competence and aspirations to develop, manage, and own production in their community. We have already been told that we will probably do five or six other schools throughout Chicago.

Stephen Healy:
My name is Stephen Healy. I am about to start teaching this fall at Worcester State, a teaching college in western Massachusetts. I've been involved since 1996 with a group called the *Community Economies Collective*, which is an academic research-based organization operating in both the United States and Australia. I am actually here to speak on behalf of J.K. Gibson-Graham, who published the *End of Capitalism* and *A Post-Capitalist Politics*. Julie Graham, who is the U.S. half of the J.K. Gibson-Graham writing partnership, is recovering from an extended illness, and was unable to be here today, so I am going to do my best to try and summarize the work that has been inspired by their writings. There are actually several members of the *Community Economies Collective* here, graduate students that have been working with Julie, trying to think about how, from an academic location, we can do socially-engaged research at a local or regional level that rethinks the process of economic development. Our goal here is to disseminate a vision of the economy that isn't something organized in relation to an over-arching set of imperatives or a logic, nor simply reflective of the interests of the so-called capitalist class, but is instead a heterogeneous space. In the same way that we have racial diversity, ethnic diversity, sexual diversity, or a diversity of social concerns, the economy is actually composed of many different relations of production, different types of exchange and compensation, and different forms of owning property. Someone mentioned open-source, which is just one example.

If you produce this different representation of the economy, where every facet of it is up for grabs, you can then teach people that they are part of this existing widely dispersed set of practices that span not only into their working life, but also their homes, their community relations, and their relations with their neighbors. If they feel a part of that, they can take responsibility for these relations, and they can engage in the process of development in a different sort of way. Most people know that Mondragon Cooperatives, for instance, was preceded by a polytechnical institute, but actually Jose Maria Arizmendi started that school over dinner conversations with about five people. It was initially an idea that took off. That is the power of trying to think differently. It is the precursor to imagining a different world.

There has been a longstanding historical tension between academic groups and community groups – a suspicion of the academy. I think largely because Julie has lived in the Pioneer Valley for thirty years, and was part of the women's movement there, she was able to create a model that allows us to think about how we can just sit down and have a conversation with groups like the Alliance to Develop Power or Collective Copies, in order to think about the way in which we could direct our academic research in the service of a different practice of local economic development. Just to give an example, we've been talking with Caroline Murray from the Anti-Displacement Project for about ten years or more. That group initially started as an organization that was trying to retain affordable housing in an area where there was a lot of development pressure to go market rate, because of all the college students. Through sheer force of will, the ADP has been able to retain a significant amount of affordable housing. They have around $30 million in housing assets that is owned and controlled by the low-income residents living there. But they didn't stop there, they actually went on to form a worker cooperative that deals with landscape and maintenance. That was an expansion of their mission, and it was a way of providing employment for their members, and also supporting their organization. More recently, in collaboration with local unions, they have founded an alternative hiring hall and labor education center, and have gotten really involved with immigrant rights groups and so forth. What is so interesting here is that really there's a link here between the efforts of the volunteer-based economy, the ADP, a different way of engaging with unions and other community organizations, and the market economy as a whole. This labor center potentially fundamentally transforms people who would otherwise have to go to a temp agency like Slave Ready – I mean Labor Ready – in order to find employment. They also got the district attorney at the state level involved in investigating, among other things, Labor Ready's pay-docking and transportation fee practices.

I guess on some level I have always felt self-conscious about the "localness" of our efforts because I came out of the sectarian Marxist movement, saying to myself "what are you doing being involved in these local reformist efforts?" But as a geographer, what I've learned is to say to myself, "wait a minute, things can jump scales." Experiments such as those conducted by the ADP can go from the local to the regional to the national to the global. In the same way that experiments in the natural sciences require replication in order to gain validity, social experiments conducted by the ADP also require replication. The role that scholar-activists can play in this process is to encourage the replication of these experiments simply by talking about them in the classroom and other settings. The idea that conversation plays a critical role in constituting social reality—what Judith Butler calls the performative effect of discourse—is not new. Where did feminism start from? On some level, as Julie has said many times, feminism was a bunch of ideas, conversations at different locations, that eventually became the basis for thinking about gender in a fundamentally different way.

Some of the economic experiments being conducted in our home region of the Pioneer Valley are attempting to propagate themselves in precisely this way. One local example is Collective Copies, which was born out of a capitalist organization, a strike where the capitalists left the area. The community provided the loans for the workers to buy out the owners and start this business, which has been running for twenty-three years. Today they have $1.4 million in sales and three locations, and because the workers are in control of the surplus, they are able to give back to the community, and they donate to everything from the Dakin Animal Shelter, to the UMASS GLBT organization, to environmental groups. So, there is a link there between the cooperative movement and every other type of concern. Just a thought, more than that, an *example*. Collective Copies is interested and actively involved both in promoting cooperatives as an economic model as well as spreading the idea that worker-owned businesses can be powerfully connected to local social movements and the democratic process.

Germai Medhanie:

My name is Germai Medhanie. Because my organization is very new, I don't have much to report, but I would still like to talk a little bit about what we would like to do. The organization is called Guramylay: Growing the Green Economy, and our website is www.TransformationCentral.org. With the website, we are trying to tell people about the positive things that are happening within our movement. These are stories about ordinary people who are starting transformative initiatives, whether it's creating jobs, working with the land and growing organic products, or informing children about global warming. That is power, and it inspires others.

The other thing that I want to talk about in Transformation Central is about immigrants' experiences. I'm an immigrant, and I really want to bring immigrants to tell their stories, stories that have not been told because they have never had the invitation or opportunity to share them. Right now, conditions in the U.S. are hostile to immigrants, and they may feel it is too risky to expose themselves. In addition, there is often a language barrier.

I want these immigrants to tell stories about the good and the bad things about living in the United States. It could be their first experience as car-washers or dish-washers, and the ups and downs of living here as an immigrant. True stories will help other new immigrants who come to this country learn what life had been for those who came before them, and can help guide them to make better choices.

As I see it, for many immigrants, in particular for immigrants of color, it is harder to succeed now than at the time that I came, twenty-eight years ago. At that time, we were able to work part-time at minimum-wage jobs, and also able to go to school part-time. Now, with the high cost of education, housing, and transportation, it is difficult to survive on a minimum wage income. It is almost impossible to both work and go to school. When the economy is bad, anti-immigrant sentiments get intensified, and it is a bad time to be a new immigrant. One way to help is to have recent immigrants who are US citizens tell their stories, describe how they succeeded, and be vocal for immigrants' rights. This could be a healing process for both the new and old immigrants to assess the myth that "America is the land of opportunity" because there many Americans who live in the shadow of that myth.

Also, at Guramylay we are interested in promoting a greener economy. We want to create an alternative market in the Cambridge area using public space. We want to bring producers or inventors who are creating green products to an outdoor market, an alternative to a mall. We want to connect the people who want to consume green products that are made in a socially and environmentally sustainable ways with people who are producing these types of products and services. These markets could serve as an educational vehicle as well as be an outlet for small green businesses to introduce their products to the public and also to sell them.

Talk about the biggest challenges you have encountered in your own work, and how your group has been working to solve them.

David Korten:
First of all, as in so many progressive efforts, and in this room, the racial composition of the *Business Alliance for Local Living Economies* is very white, which is a serious issue across the progressive movement. It is very clear to us that the depth of change that needs to happen cannot happen unless we build solidarity across racial lines. We need to find and ally with groups in communities of color that are working on parallel kinds of economic initiatives.

We became very conscious in the Social Ventures Network (SVN) of another important challenge. SVN was the meeting place of many of the iconic socially responsible businesses like Ben & Jerry's, Odwalla, and so forth. At the time we founded BALLE, many SVN members were becoming conscious that these companies, one by one, were going public, selling public shares, to raise money for expansion. Once their shares were in play, the values-driven owners were ultimately driven out as the shares were bought up by bigger corporations that did not hold the same values. At first the responsible businesses claimed victory, in the belief that they were infiltrating the dominant system in order to transform it. Gradually, however, they woke up to the reality that being bought out was the beginning of the end. Their companies and products were absorbed, but the social mission was not. This remains a serious problem. There has to be a transition at some point in any business to a new set of owners as the original owners age and retire. We have not solved the problem of how you do that in a way that maintains the independence and the values of the business.

Third, there is the huge issue of how investment funds can be channeled to local businesses without stripping the original owners of control. Many investors are interested in supporting this process. The whole economy and financial system, however, are geared towards demanding maximum financial returns to their investments, which means maximizing returns to the richest people around. If we're going to move towards greater equity in the economy, we actually have to reverse that process so that money from people of wealth is moving into community investments that actually transfer ownership equitably to people who are not previously owners. This creates a huge dilemma. How can we manage the financial process to move in the direction of greater equity in ownership and income, instead of inexorably increasing the concentration of wealth as the existing system is designed to do?

Emily Kawano:
One of the biggest problems that we face is the "TINA syndrome." For those of

you who don't know this phrase made famous by former British Prime Minister Margaret Thatcher – TINA stands for "There Is No Alternative," meaning there is no alternative to the reigning model of capitalist globalization, the neoliberal model. It does, at first glance appear to be invincible, but I agree that this is a transformative moment. There are lots of cracks in that model. People in the U.S. might be the least likely to perceive these cracks, but all throughout the world there is a huge upsurge and opposition to neoliberalism. The global institutions, the IMF, the World Bank, the World Trade Organization, are all under siege. The failures of this model to deliver economically, as well as in terms of equity and sustainability are really glaring and inescapable.

It is a challenge, to get past the TINA syndrome, particularly in the United States where many people are resigned to this model of neoliberal globalization. A common attitude is that it's here to stay and we have to make the best of it. Piecemeal reforms become an end unto themselves, instead of being seen as part of a transition towards transformation of the system. We need to understand that the neoliberal model is seriously flawed. There's growing resistance to it and I believe that it is coming down. Look at all the left-leaning governments in Latin America that have ridden to power on a platform of anti-neoliberalism – Brazil, Venezuela, Uruguay, Bolivia, Chile, and Argentina.

We should help people understand what neoliberalism means. If it were to have a simple slogan, it would be "Markets good, State bad." Neoliberal policies aim to 'liberate' markets by removing controls on trade, corporate investment and international finance – all of which is good for big corporations. At the same time neoliberals want to cut taxes and roll back the state: weakening environmental or worker safety regulations, privatizing schools and water services, and cutting back social welfare programs. Neoliberals have been waging a war on the public good – our public institutions, our environment, our social solidarity, our sense that we should take care of one another. More and more, markets rule our lives and everything is valued in terms of price and profit.

Some people argue that we shouldn't use don't the term neoliberalism because it's alienating economistic jargon. But neoliberalism is a term that is worth getting into popular circulation because it is so widely used throughout the world and it has such clarity, especially in comparison to the terribly mushy term of globalization. I think it's paternalistic to think that regular folks can't learn a new term.

Another big challenge that we see in our work is that of fragmentation due to a single issue approach and identity politics. It's time to come together, to work together to create systemic change, rather than piecemeal solutions. Again, the solidarity economy has the potential of unifying a lot of single issue organizing efforts.

Dan Swinney:

CLCR is a very small organization, but we're now engaged in very big projects. I think one of our biggest challenges is managing growth. This is something that we all need to address if we really are about fundamental change, as opposed to being comfortable opponents in a failing system. We must anticipate success, which means going to a larger scale, and contending to define the development agenda for society, not just carving out some little niche for ourselves. For better or for worse, that is what we are trying to do in Chicago.

We have a partnership that includes key leading mainstream organizations in Chicago: the Chicago Federation of Labor (not just a local union or two), the Illinois Manufacturers Association which represents 4,000 manufacturers, the CEO of Chicago Public Schools, and so on and so forth. It is often challenging to maintain and manage these relationships, but this is a challenge we are forced to confront if we aren't to be marginalized in this process. You can have a lofty idea and then blow it because of your inability to manage or cope with the details, and then it is much harder to even get back in the game.

One challenge we have in this context is remaining true to our vision as we grapple with the details of change. As I said before, we think that manufacturing is central to our modern society. There are complicated questions associated with manufacturing. What will it look like in 20 years? What is its role in terms of the environment? How do we change its products and the processes to restore the planet? We need to stay focused on some of the key larger issues as we grapple with the details. To fail to be successful in maintaining that tension could undercut everything that we are doing. The same is true with language. An essential part of our program is our partnership with the labor movement. But much of the labor movement is comfortable with an anti-corporate mantra. In our view, we're not anti-corporate. We're against the Low Road in corporate America, and in favor of the High Road. CLCR is a corporation and so are many of the organizations in this room   The corporate enemy is typically a subset of the 13,000 publicly traded companies that are Low Road, predatory, and do real damage to our society by their total focus on short-term financial gain no matter what the consequence to our local or global society. On the other hand, there are eight million privately-held companies that are locally-owned and that often have owners whose values are similar are to our own. These businesses are potentially really important allies. So if we have a language that, by virtue of their legal structure, excludes them from our discussion, we have more opponents rather than more friends.

Competency. One of our major partners is government, yet one of the major problems is the incompetence of government. We are a defender of the public sector yet we can't become apologists for public sector failures. In the CMRC, we have been actively engaged in the candid critique of major systems like Community Colleges, but always offered a positive agenda for transformation and a determination to see that agenda implemented and a real competency-based system established.

We're in a constant battle to show how the public sector can intervene in areas that are normally reserved for the private sector and to do so in a way that demonstrates competence. There are a lot of people, even our friends, who are really hesitant to be critical of the public sector in light of the character of the political debate in our country. So finding our space within that has been a challenge.

And then finally–maintaining an adequate revenue base is a challenge. We were a not for-profit and when we started; we relied on foundation support. Now some foundations don't support our work. They like to help poor people but they don't understand initiatives that could really end poverty. So 50-60% of our income comes from fee-for-service. We ourselves have had to know how to generate our own revenues to maintain the scale of our work, as a business focused on social goals.

Stephen Healy:
I didn't realize I was going to have to talk about the difficult part of things…. I find teaching to be a really big challenge. I just came off a two-year stint – I mean job – at Miami University teaching students who came from households with an average income of $120,000 a year, so I was kind of out of my element as a working class kid. My intellectual and political commitments constantly came through in my teaching, and I found that, for the most part, the students who wanted to get into business school were also anxious about being able to reproduce the material privilege they had grown up with. My fundamental conclusion was that they were not closed to ethical ideas, or to having different values, but that they were too afraid to take those concepts seriously. Even the well-to-do feel this kind of anxiety or unease. What I ended up wondering was, in what way does this psychological anxiety relate to the type of neoliberalism that Emily was talking about?

Then I came across an article by this political philosopher named Wendy Brown. She wrote this piece called "Neoliberalism and the End of Liberal Democracy." What she talked about is that one of the key components of neoliberalism is educative, in that it tries to produce people who think of themselves as risk-calculative subjects with preferences. In other words, neoliberalism structures our relationship with the economy in the following way: we are risk-averse, we want to reproduce our material privilege, and in order to do this we have to give administration of the economy over to the experts, who clearly know what is best for continued economic growth. So in other words, neoliberalism contains this component that makes us into passive subjects. Rather than being a part of the economy, rather than being subjects with ethical commitments, a propensity for struggle, antagonism, conflict, questioning, imagining, and desiring, we actually have an investment in our own passivity. Don't rock the boat, and things will go swimmingly, right? Even young people coming from really privileged families seem to have bought that idea. In spite of their relative privilege, they feel like they are not in a position to worry about anything other than themselves.

Challenging this idea, challenging people's own investment in their own passivity, calling on them to be a differently politicized subject in relation to the economy is a big challenge for me as an educator. It shows up in different forms for people who are more from my class background. There is a different set of anxieties, the thought "I've just got to worry about surviving" – that sort of mentality. It also shows up in me.

It's very difficult to be an academic proletarian, teaching four classes this fall and trying to retain my activist commitments. I need to continue to have an investment in this sort of work of exploring and fostering community based economies. The most effective way to do this is to engage in collective activist-academic research projects. This can take a variety of forms, including a two day road trip with colleagues to the USSF.

Germai Medhanie:
One challenge we have is how to obtain public space for our market project. We have to go about choosing which space is the best suited to bring more people and it has to be an affordable space. We have to deal with permits, with insurance, with public policy, as well as with politics. Sometimes it is difficult to know who owns the land, and then deal with a police and fire detail. To do all of these things costs money, and it is always the case that it is very challenging for small organizations to raise funds.

The other challenge we have is how to maintain the trust of some leftist progressive people in the movement. They may think that creating a market and promoting consumption is too capitalist and business-oriented. We need to assure them that this is also a transformative way to bring change, and we will build that trust through communicating with them by including them in the process.

Those are the kinds of challenges that we face. We are new, small organization, and we need to work within our limits as a small organization. We want to do a lot, but to a certain extent, we need to recognize our limits. It is a challenge to recognize these limits while we are working and holding on to the mission of the organization

First Round of Questions:

A discussion ensues about the structure of the corporation. Dan Swinney thinks that the distinction between high road and low road is more helpful, because, as he says, "there are non-corporate structures that can be corrupt. I've been accused of turning workers into capitalists because 'if you own a company, how can you help but be corrupt?' The most corrupting influence, I think, is a union office. So we have to build a movement that understands the limits and possibilities of these structures, and fights for the values and the systemic change we want within their context." He talks about how we have to be expansive in our language so that we can also be expansive about who we work with, because there is a lot of creative ferment going on in forming economic alternatives.

An audience member talks about his organizing with the *Northwest Bronx Community and Clergy Coalition* in the Northwest Bronx, and the trade-offs he has to make to ensure that there are true and attainable benefits to the community. They are contending to develop retail space, and get a community benefits agreement and a labor peace agreement. Although the stores that will be going in the development will still be traditional "big-box stores," this will give community members access to better jobs and lower-priced products. Hopefully, this organizing can be a springboard for more efforts to build an alternative local economy.

David Korten defines one of the main problems with corporate structure is that corporations are currently defined as people under the law, and therefore they are protected under the Bill of Rights in the same way a person would be. One audience member acknowledges that, "Yes, there are ways that we can move towards our vision of another world using existing legal structures, but I would love to see part of the solidarity economy focus on challenging this relatively new status of corporations. It must be challenged and revoked, so that corporations are no longer considered as "people" with rights," He wants to hear more about what kind of political movement might be able to mobilize against the current legal corporate structure.

Julie Matthaei first points out that our consumer decisions influence the economy. We can all influence the economy at the individual level by being involved in democratic workplaces, or by building citizenship to build a participatory democracy. Currently, most people are very passive in relation to the economy, and the profession of economics generally encourages this. Economists teach mainstream propaganda, that everything is fair, and that we should all leave the curves to the economists. We are taught to be more self-interested and more materialistic.

Bringing the point about democratizing the workplace and the economy to a more concrete level, Adam Trott tells a story about solidarity in his own worker cooperative, Collective Copies. Recently, Collective Copies started selling products from other cooperatives in order to promote and support them. This past year, they sold $20,000 in chocolate bars from Equal Exchange at a very small mark-up, and this set-up makes everyone happy: the worker-owners at Equal Exchange, the worker-owners at Collective Copies, and the customers. In regards to ownership, he says that, "I would just like to promote with all my heart local leadership and local ownership. But who owns these companies? I don't want just one owner, even if they work really hard, I want them all to be owners. Because if the local economy means that only not one person gets exploited, then I don't know if that's the type of economy that I want."

The discussion turns to the connection between political democracy and economic democracy. One audience member argues that we need to work for the former before we can ever hope to achieve the latter: "It's not 'we have to pass these laws, we have to change these corporations,' we actually have to build democracy from the grassroots. And it's only by people working on a day-to-day basis and deciding things democratically do they develop the skills that they can recognize and work on a political level democratically. We have been trying to focus on doing it the other way around."

Among the resources that were brought up in this discussion were: Open Capital www.opencapital.org, and Social Enterprise Coalition www.socialenterprise.org.uk,

Comment on the overall process of economic transformation in the U.S. and in the world, in terms of opportunities and challenges, including solidarity economy networking

Stephen Healy:
To speak from my own professional context, Julie Graham and Katherine Gibson, as geographers, have been talking about what we are calling here the soli-

darity economy for about ten years or more. Ten years ago, the spirit of the economics discipline, which is very Marxist in its orientation, was "that's crazy talk!" There was an enormous investment in taking on the huge behemoth capitalism, and it was a really masculine and macho thing to do, and here Julie and Katherine come along talking about gift economy, and volunteering, and cooperative businesses, and people dismissed it as small, interstitial, and ineffectual. But of course the thing they didn't think about was if a lot of small things are happening everywhere, like photosynthesis... then maybe it's not a small thing. Ten years later, who's laughing now? Me – I mean them. There was just this explosion of interest in this way of thinking about local development on different scales. It's just so inspiring for me, and I feel like I'm swimming in a sea of possibilities, and places to learn, and things to talk about, and people to talk with. It's just so much less lonely. That whole town v. gown, community group v. scholar thing, at least in our own region, is going away, partially out of necessity. As the issues of resource depletion and global climate change become self-evident realities to increasing numbers of people, my suspicion is that interest in developing locally based regionally linked systems of production, exchange and consumption will continue to expand. So I think things are changing pretty rapidly, and I am happy.

Dan Swinney:

I actually want to go back to the point about optimism. I'm scared to death. There's a crisis that's global, that's environmental, that's economic, and that is destabilizing our world. We are at a moment when we could either face decades of darkness that could see enormous destruction, or an opportunity for real fundamental change. While I'm heartened by what we're doing, I know that we're way behind the growing power of the Low Road, and we are losing at this point. We urgently need a program that speaks to how we would differently organize the economy in a comprehensive way from the micro to the macro level.

I think that the scale of the issues of the environment and poverty do not allow us comfort in being marginal. In this work we have to recognize there's a continuum from very little influence with small projects to very large-scale projects. Working with that continuum is the function of a social movement that really is committed to being a truly transformative movement rather than just a feeble light in a hostile dying world.

Finally, we need to be bold in creating alliances. In the work we're doing we find that the political coalition around that is remarkably large. I work as much with Republicans as I do with Democrats, Independents, and Greens. At this point, I think the ideas we're talking about can really be the catalyst for a movement that's broader than anything we've seen in the last 60-70 years.

Emily Kawano:

I completely echo the feeling that we are on the verge of a crisis. When I say that there are these huge cracks in neoliberalism, and that I believe that it's coming down, that doesn't mean that I'm unreservedly optimistic. I am hopeful, but also feel that it's a very dangerous time. Things could go just as easily in a very bad direction, a dark age of fascism, xenophobia, greater social fragmentation come to mind. That's why it's so important to build a base of actual practice and solidarity – to provide evidence that there are viable alternatives that exist all around us.

Just to step back a little bit - for those of you who might not be familiar with the term "solidarity economy," I'm sure you've picked up a sense of it, but it's not a term that's bandied about much in the U.S. So, to elaborate a bit: the solidarity economy is more of a framework than it is a model. It doesn't have a blueprint; it doesn't have rigid prescriptions. It's a framework built around principles of solidarity, cooperation, egalitarianism, sustainability, and democracy. Also, it is relatively new, and it's very much in the early stages of being defined. There's a lot of debate about the definition, the framework, and how it's going to grow. So don't worry if you've never heard the term before. It just doesn't have a lot of currency in the U.S., but that's something that we want change - to build awareness about the solidarity economy, to simulate debates and constructive dialogue.

The last thing that I want to say goes back to the values issue. We've been hashing this out all morning. Is the solidarity economy defined by good values: corporate social responsibility, socially responsible investment, ethical consumption and the like? I argue that values are important, but in order to enable those values, we need to think about structural, systemic change. Yes, there are capitalist corporations that behave responsibly – provide decent wages, benefits, working conditions, minimize pollution, and maybe even give workers some say in the running of the business. But the problem goes beyond good intentions to the dynamics that are driven by the system, the competition and the rules of the game.

At the heart of neoliberal cut-throat capitalism is a system that drives even well-intentioned capitalists to do bad things. For example, CEOs (corporate executive officers) are answerable to their stockholders, and if they don't produce a high enough rate of profit, then the value of their stock will go down and they become vulnerable to a hostile takeover. They don't want that want because they'll lose their job. So there's pressure to boost profits by cutting wages, benefits, outsourcing and so forth, particularly if the competition is doing so. Small retailers feel the pressure of competition from big box retailers like Wal-Mart. They may be committed to good practices and supporting the local economy, but are often driven out of business, forced to relocate, outsource, cut wages and so forth by the competitive game that companies like Wal-Mart play. Appealing to people's values, or moral suasion, is by itself, not sustainable given the way our economy is structured. It might work in the short term, but it won't work in the long term. In the long term, we need a systemic change along with a shift in the values underlying the whole system, not just the values of individual capitalists.

Germai Medhanie:
I am hopeful about what is going to happen. I don't think it is going to get much worse than it already is – the economy is in terrible shape, and the Bush administration is in denial. There are many people who are overwhelmed by debt; they are swamped, and they can't get out of it without making hard choices. The high stakes that are attached to these crises are forcing people to figure out new ways to tackle economic and environmental crises at all levels.

For example, one group that I belong to, the New Haven Bio-Regional Group, doesn't have many people of color – I'm probably the only one in the group. It's a serious problem in terms of lack of diversity. In order to help bring change, they are finding new ways to get to know their community. They created a project called "walkabouts." The group gets together once a month or every other week, and they find a neighborhood – it could be a Hispanic neighborhood or a Black neighborhood – and they walk through it and explore how the neighborhood is doing. They meet the community, and they introduce themselves, and they try to relate and see how similar and how different it is from their predominantly white neighborhoods. The idea is to create a sense of community, because New Haven belongs to everyone.

When they do the walkabouts, they also choose topics to talk about; I think it's really a new way of organizing – it is like field work, learning by being there. You see it, you feel it, and you smell it. You meet others, and build community.

I have had experience with walkabouts and talkabouts when I was back home in Asmara twenty-nine years ago. During the Eritrean revolution, we found out that it was dangerous to stay in one place and talk politics. If we did, the authorities assumed that we were talking politics, so a lot of our organizing was done by walking and talking. When we walked and talked, they thought that we are going home, but in fact, we had an agenda. We needed to use whenever method worked to organize, and to walk while talking was the best way to mobilize for social change. The Bio-Regional Group is also working on small local business development. They want to bring together small businesspeople together. It is often difficult for small, local businesses to survive in competition with large corporate competitors. This group is strategizing to pressure the city, state, and federal government for policies to support local businesses.

David Korten:
I think there is enormous potential in what you're doing in the solidarity economy network. We are each so involved in our own initiatives that we rarely take time to step back and look at the broader picture in the way we are here.
The combination of climate chaos, peak oil, and the collapsing U.S. dollar are going to dramatically shift the economic incentives from the global to the local. Those communities that are working to build local self-reliance in food and energy are going to have a huge advantage.

I was very taken by Dan's recent point that we should not confine ourselves to a particular part of the political spectrum. If you look at polling data you find a huge consensus on key values that transcends the normal division between conservatives and liberals. The bottom line is people want to see greater priority given to the needs of family, community, children, and the environment. And that's what we are talking about here, shifting from an economy that is focused on money and financial values to an economy that actually serves life – children, family, community, and nature. I think we have enormous potential to draw in people who otherwise would identify as conservative or even Republican. An important piece of this is the statistic that 72 percent of Americans believe that big companies have too much power over too many aspects of American life.[4]

I very much side with Emily's position that we need to deal with the structural issues around corporations, and particularly publicly traded corporations that institutionalize the most perverse form of absentee ownership and embrace short-term financial gain as their only value. As she notes, the argument that we can make the system accountable through our individual decisions as investors and consumers is specious. Pitting large unorganized groups of ordinary investors and consumers against highly organized global corporations is folly, especially in the situation of an unregulated market designed to benefit the irresponsible at the expense of the responsible. The incentives are backwards. We need to change the rules to favor doing the right thing.

I differ, however, with another part of Emily's argument – the argument that the problem rests exclusively with the system. In my book, *When Corporations Rule the World,* I self-consciously kept the focus on the system, rather than on personalities. More recently, thanks to George Bush, Ken Lay, and a host of other deeply flawed personalities, I have come to realize that we are also dealing with certifiable sociopaths who are psychologically incapable of making sound moral judgments. A recent article in *Fast Company*, called "Is Your Boss a Psychopath?" makes this point.[5] We need to keep in mind the fact that we are dealing with a combination of dysfunctional institutions and dysfunctional individuals. The most frightening piece is that dysfunctional personalities tend to be particu-

larly attracted to the power that high-level positions in government and corporations give them and these organizations are prone to elevate them to positions of
power because they embody the values of the predatory system. In this way the
institutions of the current global suicide economy actually suppress the development of a healthy moral consciousness and sensibility, and actively reward pa-
thology. It is a crime against humanity.

Second Round of Questions:

Questions are asked about the problems with the current linear growth model of
neoliberal economics. Emily Kawano talks about redefining growth in more social ways, with human indicators rather than financial indicators, and also about
distinguishing between the real need for growth in developing countries, and
over-consumption in developed countries. Essentially, they are on different parts
of the marginal utility curve. Julie Matthaei points out the connection between
our current monetary system and an insatiable need for growth: "The nature of
that system where there is not enough money in circulation for everyone to even
repay their debts plus interest, because there's not enough money in the economy, fundamentally creates a necessity for growth. We have to keep chopping
down rainforests, and have to keep mining and destroying the earth just to keep
the economic system from completely crashing."

Another audience member points out that developing countries are often harmed
by neoliberal growth, where wealth is distributed so unequally. She argues that,
"in developing countries, we don't need that type of growth either. For example,
in Venezuela, we have an economy that's been growing all the time because we
have oil, and in spite of that we had 80% of the population living in poverty for
many years. So the concept of growth has to be tossed out, along with demand
and supply curves." Instead she argues for more humanistic and spiritual measures of progress.

The conversation turns to socially responsible investment and shareholder activism, and questions are asked about how to find institutions where we can invest
our money responsibly. Yvon Poirier mentions the International Association of
Investors in the Social Economy (INAISE). David Korten cautions, however, by
saying that, "investing in the solidarity economy is better than investing in the
predatory economy, but it's not enough until we figure out how to make it work
in a framework of redistribution. A lot of it is moving beyond a society that is divided between what I call the "money people," who are the investors, and the
working people who live by their labor. This is where you get the worker-
ownership. We should all be doing some kind of productive work, and we all

ought to have some ownership stake in productive assets – that's when we begin to get a balanced community."

Questions are then asked about how we can move past the concept of economic scarcity. Stephen Healy provides an example where the laws of scarcity don't apply, and where the traditional economy is a supplement to the informal caring economy – elder care. He states that, "a quarter of the population in this country is involved in informal chronic elder care. That is about 25 million people, and, in terms of value, some researchers at Harvard estimate it $200 billion. This is almost twice the size of the nursing home care and visiting nurse care industry combined. In this case, the market economy is the supplement to the caring economy that really takes place in the households. So if we're going to have real health care reform in this society, for instance, we need to think about supporting the informal market. This would be a chance to exercise some solidarity…"

Stephen Healy continues by discussing how movements for economic alternatives can't wait for the perfect crisis; they need to start building the groundwork for their movements right now. The Argentinian Autonomista movement, for example, started during the boom years when public sector employees were being displaced. Radio programs, mutual credit systems, and other alternatives were already in place before Argentina's economy crashed in the early 1990s. He continues: "And this makes me think about the conditions in which we can build really impressive solidarity economies. Well, let's think about one. How about after a civil war, amongst an ethnicity that was being severely repressed by a nasty dictatorship, oh yeah, that's when the Mondragon cooperative got started, right? By the Basque people, under the nose of Franco, using the language of the nineteenth-century Catholic social doctrine. These initiatives really could start anywhere, or anytime."

Among the resources that were brought up in this discussion were: "Money as Debt" hosted on Google Video, and Post-Autistic Economics Network www.parecon.net/

Notes

[1] Matthaei, Julie and Barbara Brandt. (2007). "The Transformative Moment," in Richard Westra et al (Ed.). *Political Economy and Global Capitalism: The 21st Century, Present and Future*. London: Anthem Press. See also: Matthaei, Julie and Barbara Brandt, excerpted by Jenna Allard. (2007, June). "The Transformative Moment: An Introduction for Activists" *Transformation Central*.
http://www.transformationcentral.org/publications/tmforactivists.pdf
[2] Ernesto Laclau and Chantal Mouffe. (1985). *Hegemony and Socialist Strategy*. New York: Verso. was one of the first left/socialist books to legitimate "social movements" as radically transformative.
[3] "Capital Strategies" is the term that has come to describe labor's entry into issues and concerns historically reserved for the private sector in the traditional economic paradigm. These strategies are becoming more complex and effective as labor gains experience. Their use involves research, technical work, organizing, finance, politics, legal tactics, and pure power. They usually require finding individuals within the firm or industry who share our objectives–at least in part. They require a dramatic shift in the attitude of leaders who want to use them. Capital strategies acknowledge the strengths of the marketplace and require mastery of the skills necessary to use those strengths for labor's advantage. Taken from: Swinney, Dan. (1998) "Building the Bridge to the High Road". Center for Labor and Community Research.
http://www.clcr.org/publications/btb/index.html
[4] Aaron Bernstein, Micheal Arndt, Peter Coy, and Wendy Zellner. (2000, September 11). "Too Much Corporate Power?" *Business Week*. Issue 3698, 144-58.
[5] Alan Deutschman. (2005, July). "Is Your Boss a Psychopath?" *Fast Company*, Issue 96, 44-51.

8
Building Community Economies Any Time Any Place

Stephen Healy, Janelle Cornwall, Ted White, and Karen Werner
Community Economies Collective

Introduction and Summary
Stephen Healy

> *Stephen Healy is an assistant professor at Worcester State College in Massachusetts in the department of Physical and Earth Sciences. He is a long-time member of the Community Economies Collective. Much of his work has revolved around educating people about using the diverse economy framework to reimagine work life and health care. Working and learning together is what makes life enjoyable. Stephen is also an avid fan of film, cooking, and MMA.*

The Community Economies Collective (CEC) is composed of a network of activist- minded scholars and scholarly-minded community members whose goal is to think about a different and innovative approach to the issue of regional economic development, social and economic justice and sustainability. Ted White, Janelle Cornwell, Adam Trott, Karen Werner and I made the trip to the USSF by car over the course of a few days, wondering what sort of experience we were going to have at one of the largest gatherings of political progressives in the United States in recent years.

The session "Building Community Economies Any Time, Any Place" concerned itself first and foremost with the process of engendering a different set of desires and a sense of possibility in relation to economic space, however modest or tentative in nature. In our view, cultivating a different vision of the existing range of economic spaces of production, exchange and consumption expands our capacity to imagine what kind of economic justice we might desire by enlarging the tools at our disposal to produce it. Janelle Cornwell started us off with a brief pedagogical intervention that asked the members of the audience to think of market exchange, capitalist production and wage-based compensation as only the tip of an economic iceberg. Floating beneath the waters there might be other forms of economy, already practiced every day, just not bobbing above the waters in our conscious mind. The audience reacted with ready enthusiasm to this intervention, shouting out economic spaces and practices of various sorts that could not be seen as simply "part of capitalism." The vital production of goods and services in households and communities (from child rearing to eldercare) clearly take place outside of the "capitalist" economy because they do not involve wage work or production for markets. While people readily identified these non-capitalist spaces, others insisted that even within the space of wage work there is a production that goes on in "excess" of what is required (what we on other occasions have called "volunteering on the job"—something recognizable to many in progressive non-profits and the academy but also the building trades). Just as the space of production is readily differentiated other people pointed out that things are exchanged in a variety of ways—from the barter economy to Fair Trade. Recognizing what already is different allows us to imagine what might be economic development differently. What followed was a series of presentations on the elements of this diverse economy that, alone or in concert, might allow us to produce a society more in line with our values and desires.

Adam Trott's presentation consisted of a series of powerful reflections upon his role as a worker-owner in Collectives Copies, Amherst, Massachusetts. Adam emphasized that being a worker-owner both requires and produces a different relationship with the economy, as well as a different economic conception of self. The two great potentials of the cooperative, according to Adam, are collective self-determination in the workplace and engagement with the broader community. Collective Copies members all contribute to the governance of the firm. As well as being able to pay themselves well above industry average (in addition to patronage dividends), worker-ownership allows coop members to donate a portion of enterprise surplus to the local community. This practice started as a form of further payment for a community loan that had been given to the collective members during the coop's inception.[1]

Karen Werner's presentation again focuses on the role that activist scholars can play in fomenting connections amongst local communities and across generations through the use of a time bank. Karen began by treating us to a brief discussion of the four main aspects of money—who issues it, what are the bounds of circulation, how prices are determined, and whether or not there is interest—and went on to recount her efforts (along with her undergraduate students) to start a time bank-based currency in the North Quabbin region of Massachusetts.

Ted's meditative piece, in addition to containing images of farm stands throughout the Pioneer Valley, revolved around the ability of a marginal economic practice of exchange to produce a different sense of community. While many farm stands are little more than vegetables and a lock box, they provide us with a rare opportunity in U.S. society to trust one another and to feel the trust of others in us. Ted leaves us with the question of what would happen if this sense of trust were to become our general economic condition.

Janelle, Adam, Karen and Ted's talks all feature places and practices where it becomes possible to *see* and inhabit the economy in a new way. Worker cooperatives, local currency and local agriculture not only allow us to remake the economy, it both requires and allows us to remake ourselves. Production, transaction and consumption—rather than being spaces of domination, alienation and exploitation—become sites of possible connection, spaces of mutual aid and trust.

The Iceberg Exercise
Janelle Cornwell

> *Janelle Cornwell is PhD student of economic geography at the University of Massachusetts. She is a graduate of Prescott College (BA in environmental studies), the University of Denver (MA in international administration) and the Peace Corps (Guatemala). She resides in the Pioneer Valley of Western Massachusetts where, in the company of the Community Economies Collective, she studies non-capitalist community enterprises. She is especially interested in worker-owned collectives, local agriculture and the proliferation of joy—such as that found in salsa dancing, hiking, giggling children and the communion of 2 to 20,000 people who know another world is here. We ARE everywhere!*

In our workshop as the Community Economies Collective, we presented on several transformative, non-capitalist economic processes. In line with the diverse economies perspective of J.K. Gibson-Graham, our aim was to open a discursive space in which to present, discuss and imagine non-capitalist presents and futures. We felt, however, that to jump into our presentations without conceptual framing would have been like presenting a play in a theater without lights. We wanted the audience to participate in drawing the framework by locating themselves and their neighbors inside it: in the myriad of diverse economic processes that we practice in our communities and households every day. In this way, we hoped the texture of our presentations might be felt within the context of the rich noncapitalist world which can often be obscured by the thin but opaque curtain of capitalism or the "capitalocentric" imagination.

In order to break the ice (so to speak) and to "give the full diversity of economic relations and practices the space to exist in all their specificity and independence,"[2] we started with the "iceberg exercise" that J.K. Gibson-Graham have used in their action research. We drew a diagram of an iceberg, like Ken Byrne's in *A Post-Capitalist Politics* from which we borrowed the idea. The top, or *visible* part of the great iceberg, represented what is usually called "the economy," capitalist economic processes (waged labor and production in capitalist firms for a market). The bottom of the iceberg—the submerged or *invisible* portion—was, like a real iceberg, much greater in size than its frosty top. Citing Gibson-Graham's work, we noted that noncapitalist economic processes make up more than ½ of economic activity world-wide and asked the participants to help us "populate" the lower-half of the diagram with the kinds of activities that make up the other half of our economic lives. Participants shouted enthusiastically: "barter," "gift," "volunteer," "public services," "library," "baby-sitting," "alternative currencies," "churches," "schools," "community gardens," "cooperatives," "theft," "slave labor"... We were surprised and excited by the enthusiasm and ease with which non-capitalist processes poured out of participants' mouths and as they came from the audience we wrote them in the bottom of diagram.

Located in the *invisible* portion of our diagram, the household for example, is just one site of economic activity that informs a broader conception of society that cannot accurately be defined as solely capitalist. Despite the importance of production and distribution of goods and services in the household including the largely unpaid, non-capitalist labor of care, cleaning and meal production, this work remains invisible in economic terms until it is performed *outside* the house for a wage. These activities (and many more) rarely cross our minds as *economic* in part because of the stories we use to explain what *is* economic. The economic narratives that shape our daily perceptions tell us that the economy *is* a capitalist system.

Whether we know it as a force of liberation or destruction, the CAPITALIST ECONOMY has become the overarching story with which we explain "the economy" to ourselves. This colonization of our economic minds (and spaces) is what J.K. Gibson-Graham call the "capitalocentric" imagination. It limits what we are able to see as economic (and therefore "valuable" in terms of "well-being" or "worth"). Upon inspection however, as Gibson-Graham demonstrate, capitalism surfaces as just one among many economic forms.

In *The End of Capitalism (as we knew it)*, J.K. Gibson-Graham deflate the bloated imagery of capitalism, in order to shed light on the economic diversity that economist and popular dialogue so often miss.[3] They open the space in which we can think, talk about and imagine noncapitalist presents and futures. They suggest that,

> By marshaling the many ways that social wealth is produced, transacted and distributed *other* than those traditionally associated with capitalism, noncapitalism is rendered a positive multiplicity rather than an empty negativity and capitalism becomes just one particular set of economic relations situated in a vast sea of economic activity. [4]

By beginning our workshop with the iceberg, we hoped to dislodge a capitalo-centric grasp on the economic imaginary in our small room and enter into a discussion of what *else* the economy *is* and what it could be. Each presentation that followed represented our specialized interests, including economies of trust, worker-owned cooperatives, and alternative currencies and exchange networks and for at least two hours, the energy in the room suggested that indeed another world is not only possible but that other worlds are already here.

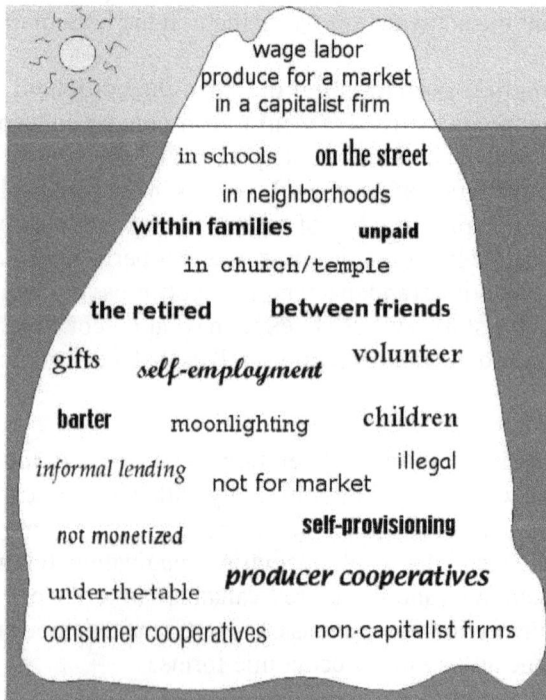

Diagram by Ken Byrne

Resources

You can find more about the *iceberg exercises* used in J.K. Gibson-Graham's research and about the economic imaginary of diverse economies in: J.K. Gibson-Graham's *A Post-Capitalist Politics*, and on the Internet links below:

http://www.communityeconomies.org
http://www.nd.edu/~econrep/essays/2002EconomicRepresentations.pdf
http://www.nd.edu/~econrep/papers/graham.html

Economies of Trust
Ted White

Farmstands: Economies of Trust
Photo: Ted White

Ted White is a geographer and documentary filmmaker who lives in Amherst, Massachusetts. He is a member of the Community Economies Collective (communityeconomies.org) and also part of an offspring group, Community Economies Research Group, which is associated with the University of Massachusetts Amherst. He and his fellow researcher pals investigate, participate in, and promote economies of trust, local/complementary currencies, diverse economies, and sustainable development.

One way that economies can transform us is when opportunities are created for producers and consumers to go beyond their usual roles.

The actual point of exchange can in some cases be the place where this transformation happens– where we can experience a new awareness and feel within ourselves a different economic identity start to emerge. With this idea of transformation, I have begun to investigate what I call Economies of Trust.

Much has been said and written of the culture of fear that has dominated American politics since 9/11. It's not just potential terrorists that we are to be wary of though–we're also encouraged to fear a host of others, from identity thieves to child-predators. In the commercial sector, the industries of mistrust (locks, alarms, paper shredders, surveillance cameras, etc.) are flourishing. Many people make their living by selling products or services that rely on widespread mistrust.

But despite what seems to be a growing culture of fear in the U.S., I've decided instead to explore a culture of trust and see if, in its own quiet way, it is also growing. My research focuses on a vibrant trust-based economy that exists where I live in the Pioneer Valley of Western Massachusetts: Farm Stands.

The tradition of farm stands enables farmers to sell their produce "direct"– at the same location as it was grown, with no middleman, thus making a higher profit. Since many of these farmers are either too busy to staff their farm stands or are away from the farm itself—working other more lucrative jobs—many farm stands must operate on an honor system. Therefore farm stands represent an economy which is based on trust.

In Western Massachusetts farm stands of varying sizes are both abundant and prolific. Why are they so popular? Why do people start farm stands? Mark Lattanzi, a staff member of the regional advocacy group Community Involved in Sustaining Agriculture (CISA), explains, "they have the legal permission to do so and they have the economic incentive to do so…and there's a growing culture and interest in buying produce directly from farmers." And CISA has itself played a big part in promoting this culture of buying local.

It is true that some farm stands are staffed (often by teens), but in pursuit of investigating more genuine economies of trust, the farm stands I've studied rely entirely on the honor system for transactions. This means no one is watching the stand. So in place of a cashier and a cash register, there might be an old tackle box, a jar, coffee can or bucket, and it's up to the customer to put in the correct amount.

The abundance of farm stands in Western Massachusetts form a type of community economy which has several noteworthy characteristics, which I will describe in detail. Most important perhaps is that this trust-based exchange system is fundamentally different from our usual methods of purchasing. The honor-system exchange provides both the producer and consumer a different way of experiencing and considering each other's character, each other's needs, each other's vulnerabilities.

In Massachusetts, state laws permit farmers to sell direct from land that is zoned agricultural—but many other folks also operate farm stands who don't have "ag-zoned" land. So farm stands represent informal temporary (seasonal) economic realms set up by individuals. Like tag sales or lemonade stands, farm stands are often so informal that they are largely unregulated.

Their physical infrastructure is informal too–a few planks are nailed together to form a table. Covering the table might be an old patio umbrella or other make-shift roof which shades the various vegetables, eggs, berries, goat cheese, maple syrup, flowers, holiday wreaths, etc. These are usually grown or produced on the premises, but sometimes are bought or traded locally (laws stipulate that the majority of items sold at a farm stand must have been produced on-site—this is to discourage farm stand operators from becoming simply retailers rather than producers). The following noteworthy characteristics attempt to describe and explain the ability of these farm stands to operate and usually thrive on trust.

Uninhabited

Many farm stands have an unusual quality of being uninhabited: no owners, no employees, no anyone. They are sites where goods are sold but where only the customer is present. "Sounds like a vending machine," one might think. But farm stands reflect specific farming cultural characteristics of the regions they are located in. Unlike a "Coke machine" which offers items marketed and sold in a globalized economy, farm stands are tied to geography, to seasons, to climate, and to cultural traditions (i.e. pumpkins for Halloween, etc.)

Conspicuous

Most farm stands are located on high-visibility arterial roads. Their presence encourages proliferation. If someone is running a farm stand down the road from you—why not you too? And for customers, the abundance of farm stands acts as a strong validation for this particular sector of the agricultural economy.

Personal/Educational

From the earliest stages of my research I discovered that in several cases farm stands have been set up by parents for their children to run or participate in. Parents want to provide their children with an income-generating opportunity based on producing goods rather than the more typical providing of services, like mowing lawns or babysitting. Parents who start farm stands for their kids also appear to value the educational experience of having their children grow and sell products within their own geographic or cultural communities. Participating in honor-system transactions introduces children to the concept that an economy could be based not on fear, growth and competition but on fairness, sufficiency and trust. Says one farm stand operator:

"I think it's a really important lesson for kids—a lesson that most kids in this country miss. My husband being from somewhere else and having immigrated—from a place where people are really poor—really feels its important that the kids know that nothing comes for free—and it's work. And I think that they have learned that." And in many cases the child might become a more visible contributor to his neighborhood. One teen I spoke with said he didn't realize that his farm stand "would get so famous."

Vulnerable

Farm stands are vulnerable. But as the pioneering urban theorist William H. Whyte observed, it is often this vulnerability and openness that breeds positive behavior. Whyte advocated that managers of public space should trust the public more readily and was famous for convincing managers of Bryant Park in New York City to put out moveable chairs, rather than bolt them down. Years later, it's still a successful approach. Whyte also noted that parks and playgrounds which are fenced and gated create a dynamic of suspicion amongst users. In stark contrast, farm stands present themselves as defenseless sites.

"Put money here," "Please pay for what you take"–these are the gentle reminders posted at farm stands that help the honor system to work. At one farm stand a metal sign hangs on a rusted wire and offers the following message: "Security – God on watch –all the time." Another farm stand operator I interviewed had actually set up a mock surveillance camera as an experiment to deter theft, but ironically continued to receive payments in an old coffee can. Though he was experimenting with fortifying his own security system, he also worried that this camera might be seen as an insult by the vast majority of his customers who were honest and loyal.

Most farm stand operators found that security was enhanced if the stand was located close to their house. Therefore if a roadside farm stand experienced too much theft, then a common response was for the farmer to move the stand closer to their residence. Most of us see the roadside as a public space or perhaps even some sort of "no-man's land." But we see the home as a private space. So, it is interesting to notice that with farm stands, the economy of trust is more successful in private space than in public space. The roadside after all is a place where we might be tempted to throw trash, but its unlikely that we'd throw trash on our neighbor's lawn. So even with farm stands, we see a bit of tragedy of the commons.

Defenseless sites in an overly defensive society
Photo:TW

Fortifying the physical vulnerability of farm stands is the awareness by many customers that hard physical work is synonymous with growing and harvesting food. This notion implores customers to honor the farmers effort with respect, conscientiousness—and fair payment. Said one farm stand operator: "I think people have in the back of their mind, that farming is kind of a long and hard road...and they're more than happy to put the money in."

Intimate

In addition to being vulnerable, farm stands often provide a glimpse of the farmers' personal space. Most farm stands are located on the premises of the farmers' own property: many are located on a front yard, and some are even located at the farmer's house—for example, on the front porch. So a visit to a farm stand can also be a fairly intimate look at someone else's living space, and this intimacy breeds trust.

Though farm stands are typically placed on private property, they are purposely very accessible. There is an interesting and transformative role reversal that takes place at farm stands where the customer must also become the clerk, cashier, and bagger. In some cases, the customer must even become the fieldworker too, since some farm stands offer "Pick-your-Own" fruits or vegetables. This role reversal can stimulate for the consumer a heightened class consciousness, and a chance to momentarily step into the shoes of the farm worker.

Many farm stands function like rural convenience stores where selections and transactions can be made quickly and quietly. Farm stands help save resources by selling at the site of production rather than transporting first to a wholesale distributor and then on to a retailer. Thus, the comparison of "food miles" between products at a farm stand and a typical convenience store demonstrate how vastly more sustainable farm stands are.

Photo: TW

Solitary Activity

Except for the occasional running into a fellow customer or perhaps the farmer himself, shopping at a farm stand is a solitary activity. Financial constraints, and in some cases personal preference, have driven farmers to value labor in the field (producing goods) more highly than labor spent sitting at the farm stand (service sector). This marks an historical shift in approaches to farm sales. In the past, farmers were not invisible and participated in more of a "meet and greet" form of exchange with their customers.

Small-Scale (Occasionally Miniscule)

Some farm stands operate on a scale so small they barely seem to qualify as a business at all. This might mean that the stand is offering only a tiny inventory of one product and nothing else– a few small flower bouquets, a couple dozen eggs, three baskets of blueberries for example. So in these cases the term "farmer" seems like quite an exaggeration; probably "gardener" would be more accurate.

These micro-scale farm stands beg the important question: why? If monetary gain is marginal, then what are some of the other motivations for farm stand operators? A need to contribute to their community, a reluctance to let surplus go to waste, a desire to "feel" like a farmer – these are some of the reasons I documented.

Farm stand income is often used for a specially designated purpose: i.e. kid's college fund, a trip to Australia, a nest-egg for future land purchase (for a couple who lives in a rented mobile home) – this all leads to a fragile situation where little bits of money are supporting big dreams. Perhaps money earned this way is infused with a greater sense of possibility?

Though minimal, signage is important to the success of most farm stands. Advertising is not absent from farm stands, but its rustic presentation pointedly rejects, whether intentionally or not, the legacy of corporate slickness. Instead it is done "in-house" and may only consist of a large hand-painted sign reading "Fresh Eggs" or felt-pen scrawled on a piece of cardboard stating "Sweet Corn, Our Favorite." The overt lack of advertising and of promotional pretense underscores the element of trust. Farm stands operate based on an unspoken notion which might be something like, "You know this is good fresh food, grown right here, at a very fair price" and indeed this appears to be all that customers need to know. Farm stands as an economic sector defy easy classification or comparison to other sectors because they are often un-regulated, idiosyncratic, non-growth oriented, non-networked, temporary (seasonal), and non-capitalist. In short, the farm stand economy doesn't seem to behave or aspire to behave like other market economies. And despite its radical informality as an economic sector, it does provide a significant means for production and consumption of agricultural products.

Promote Exchanges Based on Trust

It's interesting to note that when I interviewed various farm stand operators they generally referred to their stands as "self-service" rather than "honor system." None of those I interviewed outright rejected the term "honor system," but it is worth noting that the term "self-service" emphasizes a more neutral functionality. "Honor system," on the other hand, denotes a method of exchange that is clearly based on personal responsibility and ethics. There appeared at times a reluctance for farmers to discuss the uncomfortable issue of mistrust or exploitation (theft). Rather the most appealing topic for interviewees to discuss was what they grew and how much the customers appreciated their products
.
At various times during this research, I worried that my inquiries might make my subjects too self-conscious about trust. I felt that the notion of trust might be best left undisturbed and that calling attention to it might be like mentioning to a tightrope walker that there was no net below—perhaps a self-destructive fear would set in, and those using unlocked cash boxes would convert to heavy locked boxes, etc. Fortunately, by the conclusion of my first study I felt that I had provoked more thought about trust amongst my subjects but hadn't actually damaged the fragile foundation of trust itself. Ultimately, some interviewees admitted to being very trusting with their farm stands and with society in general, while others simply said that most customers paid their money and that was good enough for them.

Neuroeconomist Paul Zak, who studies trust in economics, has pointed out that exchanges based on trust are apparent (though not necessarily commonplace) even within the business dealings of huge corporations. However, the level of trust inherent in farm stand economy is fundamental, and explicit, and has a potential to strengthen a larger sense of trust within local communities. Perhaps it can even have a ripple effect into other communities.

My ongoing research on farm stands has broadened my awareness of the possibilities for proliferation, not just of farm stands, but of other trust-based economies. One interesting example is a café called Terra Bite which recently opened in Seattle, Washington. Like rural farm stands, this urban café also uses the honor system for transactions. The café features a food and drink menu, staff who take and prepare orders, and a place to eat. What they've chosen not to include is a price list. It is up to the customer to decide how much they want to pay—if at all. Terra Bite says patrons "are encouraged to pay what they would elsewhere;" however, they add, "We also cheerfully serve those who cannot pay, in a non-stigmatizing customer setting." Early reports suggest that consumers appreciate this transformation of roles and the ethical reciprocity of exchange it presents. The café is a place where they can trust and feel trusted. So far, the café's income seems to be comparable to traditional cafes where trust is not a featured item on the menu. The café has generated lots of fans who are deeply moved by the trust concept and many of them express interest in this as an inspiring business model which should be replicated.

One customer's comment listed on the café's website succinctly expressed the power of trust: "When I see good, I like to do good." Though Terra Bite has received a lot of visibility from the press, there are also other examples of honor-system restaurants in Berkeley, California; London, England; and Ahmedabad, India.The goals of justice, equality, solidarity and sustainability may seem lofty as cornerstones to our economy. But honor system-based exchanges provide us with a practice space for the act of trusting, and certainly trust is a prerequisite to realizing those goals.

Resources

Godbout, Jacques T. (1998). The World of the Gift. Montreal; Ithaca: McGill Queens Press.

White, Ted. (2007, Spring). "Building an Economy based on Trust." *Yes! Magazine*.

Whyte, William H. (1980). The Social Life of Small Urban Spaces. Washington, D.C: Conservation Foundation.

Zak, Paul J. (2003, April). "Trust." *The Capco Institute Journal of Financial Transformation*. 7, 13-21.

Zak, Paul J and Stephen Knack (2001, April). "Trust and Growth." The Economic Journal. 111, 295-321.

www.karmakitchen.org

www.terrabite.org

Understanding and Reclaiming Money Creation:

Our Experiences Creating the North Quabbin Timebank

Karen Werner

> *Karen Werner is a sociologist on the faculty of Goddard Col-*
> *lege in Plainfield, Vermont; a Visiting Lecturer in Social Wel-*
> *fare at Smith College and University of Massachusetts, Am-*
> *herst; and a member of the Community Economies Collective.*
> *Working with students from the University of Massachusetts,*
> *Amherst, Karen helped start a web-based currency called a*
> *time bank in the nearby towns of Orange and Athol in north*
> *central Massachusetts. The time bank is now run by a board of*
> *residents, non-profit representatives, and students and faculty*
> *from the university..*

Most of us think that money is a natural, obvious, and value-free system, just a piece of paper we use to record our exchanges. But monetary systems are not natural and value-free. The money we use affects our experiences of scarcity and abundance, our sense of place, and the values we place on the work of ourselves and others. As this paper shows, we have choices about how to construct our monetary systems. But first, it helps to have a basic understanding of what money is.

This paper is divided into three parts:

Part 1: Understanding Money and Envisioning Complementary Currencies
Part 2: Five Steps for Implementing a Complementary Currency
Part 3: The Value of Complementary Currencies in Theory and Practice

Part 1: Understanding Money and Envisioning Complementary Currencies

All currencies, including national currencies like the U.S. dollar, are infused with values and choices.

Any printed currency conveys some of its values right on its surface, in its illustrations and graphic design (e.g. in the case of the U.S. dollar, illustrating certain historical figures and buildings).

Going past this physical surface, we can identify four more values and choices regarding:

1. How the money comes into being
2. What its boundaries of use are
3. How price is determined, and
4. Whether one can earn interest.

Below I explain each of these four choices in more detail, explaining a range of ways that money can come into being, the variety of geographical boundaries possible within a currency system, and options in terms of price calculation and interest. These four choices reflect the values of the community that uses that currency. To visualize these options and underlying values and see how they can be combined to create a variety of currency systems, consider the children's toy Mr. Potato Head in which one constructs a potato head from various ears, eyes, nose, and mouth options. I find this visual tool helpful for clarifying the multiple choices we have when designing a currency. Monetary policy has erred for so long on the side of mystification that I hope you will indulge me in this effort to explain currency design as clearly as possible with visual aids.

The first choice, how money comes into being, can be represented by the <u>ears</u> of our potato head.

These ears mean that money is created by <u>fiat,</u> which means "let it be made" in Latin. Fiat money comes into being out of the power of the word; in the case of the U.S. it is the word of the Federal Reserve, an appointed group that decides whether more or less money should be circulating. Fiat systems require some scarcity so that the money keeps its value.[5]

These ears mean that money is a <u>backed currency</u> –a claim to a given quantity of a pre-determined commodity, which typically requires that a central bank have that commodity on hand to meet any such requests. When the U.S. dollar was "on the gold standard" it was an example of a backed currency.

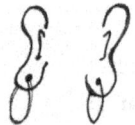

These ears mean that money emerges out of <u>mutual credit,</u> which means that the currency is created at the time of the transaction as a corresponding credit and debit for two parties, as in a barter exchange or in a Timebank, a currency discussed

below. No central bank is needed, but a system of keeping track of credit and debit is helpful.

The eyes represent a range of choices about geographical boundaries in the monetary system.

These eyes mean that the money has continental boundaries of use, such as all of Europe.

These eyes mean that the money has national boundaries of use, such as Canada.

These eyes mean that the money has local/ regional boundaries of use, such as Ithaca Hours used in Ithaca, New York, or Berkshares, used in Berkshire County, Massachusetts.

The nose represents choices about how price is determined within the monetary system.

This nose means that price is negotiable. Parties can decide the price of a person's skill or products. Some skills may be worth more or less than others –this is the "market," also known as supply and demand, a system of price and is the most common way that price is determined.

This nose means that price is non-negotiable. The price of everyone's skills and services is predetermined, as in the Timebank system, where everyone's hour of work is seen as equal in value. In Japan's *fureai kippu* program, the price is pre-determined, but different services are given different values.

The mouth represents whether or not interest is permitted within the currency. This mouth means that interest is permitted so that people with the currency can lend it out in exchange for a profit. A currency that allows interest enables people with currency wealth to accrue more –and such mass accruals have enabled big economic changes like the

Industrial Revolution, which needed a lot of capital investment.

This mouth means <u>interest is not permitted,</u> so people are not able to lend the currency out for profit. People have less of an incentive to save in a system without interest –thus keeping the currency actively circulating and helping people exchange services and goods.

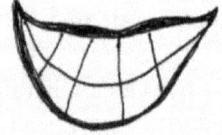

Consider the following two currency systems (one mainstream and one not) represented as potato heads, made up of combined ears, eyes, nose, and mouth choices. Each of the two currencies embodies values about scarcity and abundance, sense of place, how to measure contributions in the world, and how to distribute resources. After seeing these two examples, try crafting other potato head currencies out of the described ears, eyes, noses, and mouths described and identify the values they embody.

The U.S. Dollar potato head:

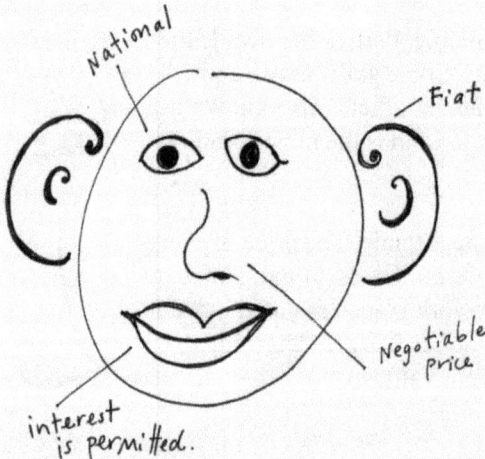

Each of these four choices has both complex implications. The U.S. dollar currency comes into being from fiat, and the Federal Reserve that oversees the money creation requires that the currency be somewhat scarce. There is never enough money for everything that needs to be done –this is a choice that is rarely examined, but has a big impact, particularly on cash-poor parts of the society. At the same time, fiat money creation is one way to manage an economy.

The dollar has national (and in some instances international) boundaries for use; such boundaries reinforce a sense of commonality and connection to a nation-state over, say, connection to a town or to the whole world. The nation-state sensibility prioritizes the well-being of the nation-state over these other boundaries – distinct local and broad global identities may both suffer as a result, with negative peace-keeping and environmental implications. At the same time, having a small, local geographical border within one's monetary system could lead to disconnection and lack of cooperation with other regions. It can become complicated to trade easily.

Price in the dollar monetary system is determined by supply and demand (the "market"). This system is criticized for valuing abstract concepts of supply and demand over people's actual needs. The market way of determining price is also embedded with sexist and racist values, demeaning the work that women and people of color do and according it lower prices. On the other hand, the market is defended as a self-regulating system, giving feedback to producers and workers in an economy about what work does or does not need to be done.

Finally, one can earn interest on money one has in the dollar system–as noted above, this prioritizes savings and consolidation of wealth (which can be used for capital investment and technological or scientific innovation) over the frequent use of money for exchanges.

Compare this to the Timebank potato head. A timebank is a currency run as a community-based website where people list all kinds of services they are willing to provide or need help with. People exchange these services without the use of cash. Every time someone does a service for someone in a timebank, they earn hours that they can then spend in the timebank. Everyone's hour of service is valued equally. A timebank can be illustrated as such:

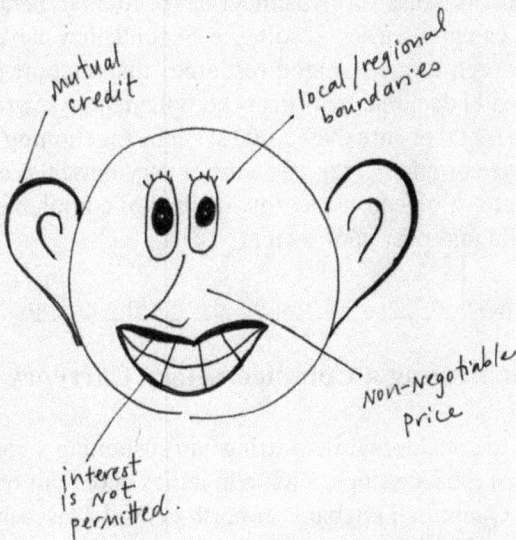

In contrast to the pervasive scarcity in the dollar system, the timebank's mutual credit means that as long as someone is willing to do the work and someone else is willing to go in debt, the work can get done. Scarcity is far less of an issue than it is in a fiat system. In terms of boundaries, the timebank encourages connection to locality, valuable for building community and trust with neighbors of all generations, something lacking in many communities in the U.S. Price in the timebank system is non-negotiable; specifically, everyone's hour is valued equally –this can be very empowering for people whose work, such as caregiving, is not highly valued in the market system. At the same time, if this were the exclusive monetary system, there might be less entrepreneurial incentive. Finally, interest is not allowed, putting all the energy of this currency into the exchange of services rather than into speculative activities, investments, or savings. This may be at the risk of having capital investment, which is helpful for many technological and scientific innovations.

While I am sympathetic to the values within the timebank currency system, I am not suggesting that timebanks are better than dollars or that they should replace national currency systems like the dollar. Rather, I agree with Bernard Lietaer, a former currency trader and one of the designers of the Euro, who argues compellingly in his book *The Future of Money* that we need multiple currencies. I endorse having a timebank and the U.S. dollar accepted in my own locality. As Lietaer argues, having multiple currencies can enable a society to balance competitive, consolidating, and hierarchical values embodied in currencies like the dollar with nurturing, equalizing, cooperative values embodied in currencies like the timebank. Invoking the yin/ yang balance, Lietaer argues that both competitive and cooperative energies have a social role.

Two additional reasons for having multiple currencies are, first, that if a national currency fails or leaves a country because of investment or speculative behaviors, complementary currencies can prevent social collapse. Second, they can enable a community to build the "commons," shared resources that support the common good, often democratically decided. How many complementary currencies are there? Lietaer estimates that there are over 5,000 systems functioning all over the world. I can think of nine complementary systems of varying scales and types in my state of Massachusetts. You can see a growing map of complementary currencies all over the world and post your own at:

http://www.complementarycurrency.org/ccDatabase/maps/worldmap.php

Part 2: Five Steps for Implementing a Complementary Currency

Below I describe five key steps to consider while starting and sustaining a complementary currency. For each of the five steps, I write in italics about our own process establishing the North Quabbin Timebank in north central Massachusetts, which we started in January 2007.

Step One: Getting Started

The first step in starting a complementary currency is to get the lay of the land: clarifying intentions, assessing resources, and doing research.

Intentions

What are you trying to achieve by introducing a complementary currency? Is your aim:

To encourage people to shop locally?
To build community?
To empower people who have been excluded by the national currency, helping them reframe themselves as economic contributors?
To help people meet practical needs and get supplies in a cash-poor region?
To have a safety net in place in case the national currency crashes?
To meet the needs of a particular demographic or social sector, say elders or education?
To provide a competitive edge for a business or sector (as in frequent flyer miles)?

Resources

Assess your people, national currency, and technological resources.
In terms of the people-power behind this currency effort, do you have a core group of people on board? Who are your allies?

In terms of using national currency as a resource for supporting the complementary currency development, is this effort something that can be incorporated into a paid job–for instance, work in a social service agency or university service learning program? Are there potential community funders? Are there schools nearby that could lend students (say, in exchange for giving them service-learning credit) or other resources like access to grants? Having a real commitment to compensate the coordinators of the currency is crucial for developing a long-term system. In terms of technology, consider whether potential users of the currency have Internet access and familiarity.

Research on currency systems

In light of your intentions and resources, choose a well-suited complementary currency system. Two good websites for researching the range of options are:

http://www.appropriate-economics.org/ and http://www.transaction.net/

You may be inspired to create your own hybrid system. Contact coordinators of existing systems with your questions about organizing and sustaining the various kinds of currency systems.

Our actual "Step One" experiences at the North Quabbin Timebank:

Our complementary currency started as an experiment in an undergraduate "Social Welfare" class that I taught at the University of Massachusetts, Amherst. The course explored a range of social welfare tools, including ones like community currencies that are still outside the mainstream social welfare discourse. Students in the course were able to experience a class-wide timebank for the semester, and then considered whether a complementary currency could be a useful intervention in a cash-poor region.

To my delight, at the end of the semester three students in the class proposed that we team up to do an independent study: starting a real timebank in a nearby low-income town, Orange, Massachusetts, where these three students grew up. One of the students had worked at a non-profit in Orange, Young Entrepreneurs Society (YES), that was very sympathetic to complementary currencies and was willing to sponsor a timebank, so we jumped at the opportunity. As a sociology instructor, I received some departmental funding and an outside service-learning grant to cover my involvement in the project (this was not an easy sell to the department) as well as a university arts grant to fund a short video about the project. The students each received credit for developing the timebank, which we named the North Quabbin Timebank. You can see the video we created at www.nqtimebank.org.

Since the students grew up in the region, they were able to tap community resources – extended family and friends, the high school where they graduated, relatives who ran the Rotary club, a sympathetic radio station, a grocery store and local business that made financial contributions. Their connection to YES has been invaluable. The director of YES is on our core organizing committee and connected us with key allies, including two town managers who are now members of the North Quabbin Timebank.

In terms of why we chose the timebank model rather than another complementary currency system, we went with what was familiar–the timebank worked well enough in our class. We knew the web system was very user-friendly. And, we liked the radical logic of timebanks (everyone's hour of service is valued equally) to balance the logic of the national currency, which values people at such different rates. We sensed that a timebank was simpler to organize than most printed currency systems, which require a larger scale to thrive. The director of YES had been one of the main organizers of a regional complementary currency that has since folded, so he was well-versed in currency-thinking and excited by the timebank model.

We also had a sense of the computer and Internet accessibility in the region –there is a free cyber café at YES in the center of Orange in addition to public libraries with computer access. We did not do a comprehensive search on other currency systems like LETS (Local Exchange Trading System), which may have had some insights for us along the way if we had chosen to include the exchange of goods in addition to services. We did contact several of the successful timebanks in our state and in other parts of the country , and have received very useful tips from them.

Step Two: Creating The Organizational Structure

As the instigators of a complementary currency, you'll need to think about how the system will be managed and organized. Even if you are anticipating minimal management, it is good to be clear about this. Issues of governance, funding, membership, liability, and orientation are important to think through as you get people involved and plan for the long term.

Governance Process

Who will make decisions about maintaining the system, and how will these people be selected? What will the expected terms of service be and how many people will govern? Will these people get compensated for their governing work? Will some decisions be made without collective input?

Try to anticipate the kinds of decisions that will need to be made. One kind of issue that gets raised is: What kinds of policies will there be regarding people who are in long-term, extensive debt in the system? Another question is: how will the system deal with state and federal taxes? (Timebank exchanges are legally tax-free, but most other complementary currency systems have tax implications.) Either the governing council or the starting organizers will also have to consider important issues of funding, membership, liability, and orientation, all described in more detail below.

Business Plan/ Funding

Business plans involve anticipated budgets and can also be opportunities to envision the growth of a project. An important issue to consider in developing a currency is what the expected annual costs will be and how you plan to raise needed funds. As mentioned in Step One, keep in mind the compensation of the currency coordinator(s), since coordinating can be a substantial amount of work.

Membership Rules

Some questions to consider:
Will this currency system be open to everyone, or only to those within a certain business sector, demographic, or geographic region?
Will members need to have references? A criminal record background check for certain kinds of services?
Will there be a cost to join? Will members be given a unit of the currency upon joining, to entice them to start using the currency?
What kind of communication will occur with currency users to clarify liability issues? What are the options for getting insurance coverage for your currency system?

Orientation Process

It is good to consider having a member orientation meeting or booklet. One advantage for orienting new members is that people will be clear about rules of conduct and liability issues related to engaging in the currency. And people may be more willing to join, knowing everyone has received the same training/orientation. Having a clear orientation to the currency may also prevent future confusion for users, keeping the system flowing smoothly. Orientation is also a chance to educate users about the social implications of the currency.

Our actual "Step Two" experiences at the North Quabbin Timebank:

We are getting to these issues nine months after starting our timebank. We wanted to get a core of people, many of whom we knew, signed up as timebank members before we invested time in governance and orientation details. With hindsight, some of us feel that that having a clear orientation system from the start would have been helpful–as it is, we will have over twenty members who have not been properly oriented. They were also admitted to the timebank without the references we are now asking from members.

In terms of governance, we took some advice early on from Timebanks USA (see their website http://www.timebanks.org) and gathered together a core organizing committee comprised of the three students from the University of Massachusetts, one of their parents who lived in town, myself, the director of YES, and two other community members who are leaders in the community. We meet every 5-6 weeks at YES for an hour and brainstorm how we can grow and what needs to be done. The members of this committee have connected us with funding opportunities and important venues for recruiting. We compensate each core organizing member with a timebank "hour" for each meeting they attend.

In terms of a business plan, we made one in our early days –a calendar grid listing outreach and publicity, fundraising, and membership goals and tasks. We barely looked at the plan thereafter, though arguably it was a good exercise for getting us to think through the tasks of our first six months of existence. Not everyone agrees with the step of mapping out a formal business plan. Paul Glover, who started the Ithaca Hours system in upstate New York said, "My business plan is to start and see what happens."

Six months after we started, we received a community foundation grant that will cover our costs for the next year of operation, but we need to start thinking long term: how will we ensure we can exist for the next ten years? This will involve an assessment of both cash and people power and realistic thinking about what we need to keep the currency going. We are also researching ways of tapping local college students who are given credit and, in the case of one forward-thinking community college, tuition in exchange for service learning.

We are just starting to work out more details about our membership rules. Our core organizing committee decided that anyone 16 years or older who resides or works in the nine towns that comprise the "North Quabbin" region can join. Membership is currently free. We have connected with several regional senior centers and groups who have been very interested but are concerned about safety. Will they be able to trust the people they contact for services in our timebank? We are researching how other timebanks manage this issue, and have been hesitant to ask for members' criminal background checks, but are considering asking for a reference. Timebanks USA suggests that members use common sense when connecting with someone for a service– making the same judgments as they would when doing an exchange with national currency.

We have decided to get liability insurance, since it is quite inexpensive, and since we are affiliated with a non-profit that we don't want to put in any legal danger.

We have just initiated a one-hour orientation, and we are now requiring this for all members. In hindsight, we should have required this for everyone who joined from the start, but we were so eager for members in our first few months that we made the process as easy as possible–just sign here. Now, we will have face-to-face contact with all members (which helps us make the timebank work best for them) and members will know that almost everyone has received a similar introductory training. We are publishing an orientation book, culled from the work of other timebanks. We will hold a group orientation periodically at YES and will also be available for one-on-one or small group orientations by appointment.

Step Three: Doing Outreach

Part of introducing a currency is getting people to believe in it and feel like it is worthwhile to be part of the system. Outreach is thus crucial for getting the word out and encouraging people to participate. Consider these opportunities for outreach:

Speaking about the currency at places like social clubs (in the US: Rotary, Lions, and Elks) as well as schools and senior centers and other community events;
Writing press releases and sending photos to local newspapers;
Creating your own website where you can post photos and sign-up information;
Being interviewed on community cable access television;
Contacting social service agencies –going to any community coalition meetings;
Contacting the chamber of commerce –ask them to mention the currency in their literature;
Organizing potlucks with potential members;
Contacting religious organizations –finding religious leaders in the community who can recruit their parishioners;
Talking to people one-on-one –this is a BIG one;
Inviting community leaders to governance meetings to get their outreach tips;
Riding around town on a bicycle, getting everyone you know to sign up;
Creating and placing brochures everywhere;
Harnessing the energy of anyone who expresses serious interest in the system – ask them to help recruit or invite them to join the organizing committee.

Our actual "Step Three" experiences at the North Quabbin Timebank:

We did a LOT of outreach in our first few months, and it paid off, to our delight. People in the region have heard about our timebank. We did our first presentation at a high school volunteer club, where some of our core organizers had close connections, and we recruited one member there. Then, we moved on to the Rotary Club and to a regional coalition of service agencies that meets monthly. We invited the town managers to an organizing meeting and they joined the timebank and invited us to be on a cable access television show. We invited the president of a senior citizens group to one of our meetings and she offered us recruiting ideas. We emailed a sympathetic journalist to do an article about us. We hosted a potluck and made many of our family and friends come –and we signed them up right there, after we ate and showed a video explaining timebanks. We spoke at a local "Public Conversations" dinner, did a press release, posted updates in a community coalition newsletter and created a website, www.nqtimebank.org, where we have now posted the short video we made about our timebank.

It was helpful that we had five people for this intense outreach phase; we were able to split up some of these tasks. We found that we became better at explaining our currency system with practice. People have been very supportive, which has been a pleasure and keeps us going.

Step Four: Doing Inreach

Inreach is just as important as outreach in making the currency a success. Having members is one thing, but do they actually *use* the currency system?

Make sure there is a system in place to count the number of exchanges done with the currency. Inreach can involve any kind of research, incentive, or technical refinement to encourage people to use the system. It can also connect with outreach when it involves recruiting members with particular skills that are requested within the currency. It is important to listen to members as well as those reluctant to join in order to strategize both inreach and outreach strategies.

Our actual "Step Four" experiences at the North Quabbin Timebank:

Since we were so focused on outreach, we were caught off-guard by the inreach needed to make our system thrive. We are finding that we still need to be in people's f aces to get them to use the system. We asked that core organizing members take leadership roles and promise to do one exchange per month, though all of us have been slack with this, still getting used to thinking of the timebank as a real resource we can use! Whenever we make a strong plea for our organizing members to use the timebank, we get a flurry of activity: people have exchanged babysitting, cooking, housecleaning, and assistance with a wedding. I am helping one organizing member apply to graduate school, and with my earned hour I am getting a haircut.

We are now embarking on an extensive inreach effort: one of our organizers will contact each member and ask him or her how to make the system best work for them. We will help members list more services that they need and want to offer; sometimes people need help thinking of service and requests. Another part of our inreach effort is making sure that all the services and requests listed are up to date.

Step Five: Documenting Your Experience

Documenting your efforts in organizing a currency system is important for a few reasons. First, documentation, whether on the web, on video, or in writing, can be a source of practical tips for others starting a currency system like yours. Second, documentation gives visibility to your particular currency project –a form of public relations and outreach. Third, documentation is an asset to the global complementary currency movement. As the World Social Forum movement attests, many people around the world are eager to learn about a range of ethical community development experiments. Complementary currencies are a vital part of these global conversations, and documentation helps make these efforts more concrete, tangible, and present for others. Finally, documentation about use and impact of the currency system (though it is always complicated to measure impact) can be useful for grant applications and other funding requests.

Our actual "Step Five" experiences at the North Quabbin Timebank:

We are documenting the creation of the North Quabbin Timebank in a few ways. First, we have video footage from our first six months of existence, and, as mentioned above, we used this to create a short promotional video which is posted on our website. From the start, I have been taking notes on the whole process and plan to write an academic article about creating a currency in the context of community economies, action research, and community-university partnerships.

The documentation of our currency project serves several audiences: residents of the North Quabbin who are curious and want to learn more before joining, people from other communities who want to consider their own currency systems, academics interested in rethinking what an economy is, and academics and activists looking for ways of collaborating and thinking about scholar-activism or community-university partnerships.

Part 3: The Value of Complementary Currencies in Theory and Practice

As mentioned at the start of this paper, the currencies we use affect us in relational and practical ways. They affect how we connect to place, how we relate to neighbors and feel about our own contributions, and how resources and services get distributed.

To be more specific, complementary currencies like timebanks affect us by valuing our contributions equally, prioritizing relationships and community-building over supply and demand. They can help construct a local economic identity, as is the case of the North Quabbin Timebank, and create a way for services to be exchanged and needs to be met, even when there is little national currency available in a region.

People are often supportive of complementary currencies, given these relational and practical advantages. But at our Atlanta U.S. Social Forum presentation on community economies, a few audience members posed questions about the political value of complementary currencies, arguing that timebanks and other seemingly small-scale community economy projects are tangential to the political project of fighting neoliberalism.

Along with others working from a community economies perspective, I see the political and strategic value of working on projects like a local timebank. Projects that may seem to be disparate and small-scale actually constitute an exciting global movement of social and economic innovations. Such efforts are documented in recent books,[6] and practitioners abound at the World Social Forum (embodying the spirit of "one no, many yeses.") Seeing the numbers of such disparate projects is staggering and inspiring, challenging assumptions that projects like a timebank are stand-alone and insignificant. In terms of currencies, for instance, consider the fact that there are over 600 complementary currencies in Japan alone, some government-sponsored, some grassroots-organized.[7] For more information about the prevalence of the global complementary currency movement, see the map referenced earlier:

http://www.complementarycurrency.org/ccDatabase/maps/worldmap.php
Documenting community economies projects is an important part of constituting and nourishing this movement of economic alternatives. This knowledge affects our sense of what is possible, in turn opening up the spectrum of activist projects we choose to pursue.

References

Cahn, Edgar. (2004). *No More Throw Away People: The Co-Production Imperative.* Washington D.C.: Essential Books

Gibson-Graham, J.K. (2006). *A Post-Capitalist Politics.* Minnesota: University of Minnesota Press.

Gibson-Graham, J.K. (2001). "Imagining and Enacting Non-Capitalist Futures" *Socialist Review,* Vol. 28, No. 3 + 4, 93-135.

Gibson-Graham, J.K. (1996). *The End of Capitalism (as we knew it).* Malden: Blackwell Publishers Ink.

Lietaer, Bernard. (2004). "Complementary currencies in Japan today: history, originality, and relevance." *International Journal for Community Currency Research* 8, 1- 27.

Lietaer, Bernard. (2001). *The Future of Money: Creating New Wealth, Work, and a Wiser World.* London: Random House Century Books.

Notes

[1] Editor's Note: Adam Trott's Presentation on Collective Copies can be found in Chapter 12: Transformative Businesses

[2] J.K. Gibson-Graham. (2006). *A Postcapitalist Politics.* Minneapolis: University of Minnesota Press, 59

[3] J.K. Gibson-Graham. (1996). *The End of Capitalism (as we knew it).* Malden: Blackwell Publishers Ink.

[4] J.K. Gibson-Graham. (2006). *A Postcapitalist Politics.* Minneapolis: University of Minnesota Press, 70.

[5] The members of central banks like the Federal Reserve are in a constant state of managing the economy. Their goal is to maximize employment while minimizing inflation, and so they make decisions that allow banks to lend more or less, depending on how they see the employment/ inflation balance.

[6] For instance, Paul Hawken. (2007). *Blessed Unrest: How the Largest Movement In the World Came Into Being and Why No One Saw it Coming.* New York: Viking Press.

[7] Bernard Lietaer. (2004). "Complementary currencies in Japan today: history, originality, and relevance." *International Journal for Community Currency Research* 8, 1-27.

SECTION III:

BUILDING THE SOLIDARITY ECONOMY THROUGH SOCIAL MOVEMENTS

9
Feminist Economic Transformation

Julie Matthaei and Barbara Brandt[1]

Barbara Brandt is a long-time social change activist. She was the founder and chair of the Boston Area Urban Solar Energy Association, and served on the Executive Committee of The Other Economic Summit (TOES). She was the National Staff-person for the Shorter Work-Time Group, founded the Sustainable Living Institute, and is on the Board of Directors of Take Back Your Time. She is the author of <u>Whole Life Economics</u> (1995), which predicted the emergence of the solidarity economy, and is an internationally recognized authority on "the new economics." With Julie Matthaei, she is co-authoring <u>The Transformative Moment</u>, a forthcoming book about the seven transformative processes.

Julie Matthaei has been active in anti-war, feminist, ecology, lesbian/gay, and anti-racist movement in the U.S. since she went to college at Stanford in 1969, and is a big fan of (and participant in) the Social Forum movement. She has been teaching economics – including Feminist Economics – at Wellesley College for 30 years, and is currently Co-Director of Guramylay: Growing the Green Economy. Julie has written two books on gender in U.S. economic history, <u>An Economic History of Women in America</u> (1982) and, with Teresa Amott, <u>Race, Gender and Work: A Multicultural Economic History of Women in the U.S.</u> (1996), and has been researching and writing about feminist economic transformation with Barbara Brandt for the past seven years. Julie was a member of the Working Group for the US Social Forum, which planned the caucuses and sessions which are documented in this book, and is currently a member of the U.S. Solidarity Economy Network Coordinating Committee. She lives with her husband Germai Medhanie, her *daughter Ella, and her three cats, at Cornerstone Cohousing in Cambridge, Massachusetts.*

Author's Note: This session was moderated by Nan Wiegersma, of the International Association for Feminist Economics (IAFFE). Along with two of her Wellesley College students – Alexis Frank and Hiywete Solomon –Julie presented on the topic of feminist transformation, and on the website she created with her Feminist Economics class on TransformationCentral.org. Avis Jones de Weaver spoke on the work of the Institute for Women's Policy Research (IWPR). The other two scheduled speakers, Kristin Sampson (Gender and Trade Network) and Kavita Ramdas (Global Fund for Women), were unable to attend. For the session report, Julie submitted this paper which she wrote on Feminist Economic Transformation with Barbara Brandt.

We are living in one of the most exciting times in history. It is a time of crisis and breakdown, and a time of potential transition to a new and more evolved economic and social stage. Diverse and vibrant movements for social transformation are springing up all around the world. The United States, while playing a reactionary role through its imperialist state policies and globalizing corporations, is also a locus of significant post-modern transformation. We call this time in the U.S. "the Transformative Moment," to emphasize its potential for paradigmatic and systematic economic and social change.

Feminism is playing a key role in this Transformative Moment. Far from being "dead," as many pundits have proclaimed, it is a vibrant and multifaceted movement. Here we will outline the various feminist transformative processes which are working to break down not just gender inequality and the devaluation of the feminine, but also to transform our economic and social institutions from the bottom up.

The Hierarchical Polarization Paradigm

To understand the present historical conjuncture in the United States, and the various forms of feminist movement now active, we have created the concept of the "Hierarchical Polarization Paradigm." The Hierarchical Polarization Paradigm preexisted capitalism, and was built into the U.S. capitalist economic system in the 18th and 19th centuries. It still undergirds U.S. economic and social values, practices, and institutions today, and is so deeply engrained in our ways of thinking, being, and acting that it is difficult for us to even see it. The Hierarchical Polarization Paradigm divides people and life itself into a number of distinct, purportedly independent, "hierarchical polarizations." Each hierarchical polarization is composed of two polarized, mutually exclusive, and unequal groups. Most of the hierarchical polarization create divisions among people: men vs. and over women, whites vs. and over Blacks, heterosexuals vs. and over homosexuals, U.S. citizens vs. and over foreigners, et cetera. Another set of hierarchical polarizations divide realms of life: man vs. and over nature, God vs. and over man, materialism vs. and over spirituality.

Because feminist movements have brought together women across race, class, gender, sexuality, and nationality divides in order to fight gender hierarchy and polarization, they have gradually incorporated and integrated anti-racist, anti-class, anti-homophobia, anti-nationalist and other anti-oppression politics into their values and platforms. It is thus extremely helpful, in analyzing feminism, to use this broader framework which encompasses the other hierarchical polarizations. In this piece, we will use the Hierarchical Polarization Paradigm framework to understand gender, the ways it intersects with other hierarchical polarizations, and the ways in which the feminist movement has evolved and connected with other issues and movements.

Hierarchical Polarization Processes and the Production and Reproduction of Gender

The Hierarchical Polarization Paradigm views men's domination and women's subordination – and the other hierarchical polarizations – as inevitable and God-given. However, as feminist and other social theorists have shown, gender and the other hierarchical polarizations are actually economic and social constructs. We call the social concepts, values, practices and institutions which produce and reproduce gender and other hierarchical polarization, "hierarchical polarization processes." We have identified eleven such processes, shown in Figure 1 (see next page), which are present in nearly all of the various hierarchical polarizations which have occurred in U.S. history. Here we will show how each helped construct gender polarization and hierarchy in its traditional, pre-feminist form. Note, however, that these processes also produce all of the other hierarchical polarizations, such as race, class, nationalism, etc.

Hierarchical Polarization Process #1. Categorization

The categorization process begins hierarchical polarization by creating pairs of mutually exclusive categories. These categories are used to classify all people in the U.S., and often the world, and to differentiate humans from other life forms. In the gender hierarchical polarization, the categories are man or woman; for race in the U.S., they are white or Black, white or Indian, white or colored, et cetera.

According to the Hierarchical Polarization Paradigm, the categories of man and woman, and of race, are determined by nature, not society. However, in fact, a significant share of humans – some experts estimate up to 1% of all people[2] – are born with genitalia (and chromosomes) that can not be characterized as either male or female.   And there is no shared biological basis for distinct racial categories.[3]

Figure 1. The Eleven Hierarchical Polarization Processes, as Applied to Gender

Categorization	People are separated into two groups: "men" (those with penises) and "women" (those with vaginas).
Ascription	At birth, people are assigned a gender identity based on their sexual organs, as per above; people who cannot be easily categorized in this way are assigned as their parents or medical authorities see fit.
Essentialism	All men (or women) are seen as having the same basic qualities, as defined by middle class white roles; thus poor whites and all people of color are seen as less manly or womanly because they can't live out the husband/breadwinner – wife/homemaker polarization.
Polarization of People, Traits, and Work	Men are the opposite of women, "opposite sex" ; men are masculine, women are feminine; sexual division of labor.
Hierarchization	Men are heads of their households; represent their households as citizens; women are seen as lesser social beings, and are denied political and economic rights
Domination/ Subordination	Men are given legal and economic power over women, in terms of citizenship, civil rights, and property rights, pay for work.
Violence	Wife beating, rape, murder, and threats of this violence.
Rationalization	Religions teach gender roles and men's dominance as head of family; science claims women lack brain capacity, are overly emotional.
Internalization	Parents, schools, and religious institutions teach children (and adults) that the above-defined gender roles are natural, inevitable, and good, making them an intrinsic part of a person's identity
Stigmatization	Parents, siblings, authority figures, and peers stigmatize and "make an example of" anyone who doesn't conform, that is, of anyone who deviates from their prescribed gender roles, as delineated above.
Institutionalization	Gendered categories and identities are built into the fabric of economic and social institutions.

Hierarchical Polarization Process #2. Ascription

Categories are applied to people – and people assigned to categories – through the ascription process.   Each person is assigned to one or the other category within each hierarchical polarization. This assignment, usually made at birth, is based on some aspect of a person's being that they cannot control. For gender, this aspect is one's biological sex; for others, disability, skin color, sexual orientation, or parents' group assignment/s (race, religion, nationality, aristocracy).

Once a person has been assigned a gender identity, his/her parents actively take on the work of establishing and reinforcing this gender identity. The child accepts his/her gender identity as established by his/her parents, and takes on the active "gender identity project" of being a man/masculine or a woman/feminine. This project is a continuous and active one throughout one's life.

One way in which feminist theorists have tried to draw attention to the process of ascription is to create different terms for biological sex and social sex or gender. People are born into a sex: male or female (or somewhere in between).   Males are ascribed to the gender identity of manhood, and to masculinity, while females are ascribed to the gender identity of womanhood, and to femininity.

The historical phenomenon of a "passing woman" is a good illustration of the processes of categorization and ascription. Historically, females have "passed as men," wearing men's clothes and acting masculine so as to gain entrance into men's higher paid jobs, go to war, or live openly with women partners.[4] At present, many transsexual or transgendered individuals find themselves in a similar position – living out the gender role of the "opposite sex," and pretending that their genitalia match their chosen gender role, or changing them so that this is the case.   The transgender movement has shown all of us how very oppressive gender categorization and ascription truly is. Indeed, some transgendered individuals simply refuse to take a fixed gender identity.[5]

Hierarchical Polarization Process #3. Essentialism

The first two hierarchical polarization processes create a series of binary oppositions and assign each person to one or the other pole of each opposition. Each of these group assignments is made integral to the social identity of the person: for example, a gay white disabled U.S. woman. As individuality and freedom emerged in the U.S. with the development of the market and of civil rights, these various identities severely limited and differentiated the types of agency that any individual could exercise.

However, the creation of identities under the Hierarchical Polarization Paradigm is contradictory. On the one hand, a person's gender identity – man or woman – is seen as a characteristic which is shared by all who have that identity. In other words, womanhood is understood to have the same meaning for all who are categorized as women. All men, in turn, are assumed to share something essential, as men. At the same time, women are differentiated by the other hierarchical polarizations: for example, white women are differentiated from Black women, and disabled white women from able-bodied white women. Economic class further differentiates each of these categories.

For this reason, the meaning of the category "woman" is not the same for all women. For example, in the nineteenth century, womanhood meant delicacy, asexuality, and a protected life for upper class white women, yet for enslaved Black women it meant hard physical work, vulnerability to legal rape by one's owner, forced separation from one's family, and violence. What it means to be a woman, then, varies, according to whether one is white or Black, aristocrat or commoner, heterosexual or lesbian, rich or poor.[6] Thus, womanhood has no consistent, shared meaning for all women, other than the actual fact of being in a subordinated position vis a vis the men of one's race/class group. Nevertheless, the category of "woman" remains, and has social significance.[7]

How does the Hierarchical Polarization Paradigm, with its impetus to create two homogeneous groups which are polarized from one another, deal with this differentiation of women? The nineteenth century cult of domesticity defined womanhood in a middle class, white, heterosexual fashion: full-time homemaker/mother, supported by a husband who earned a family wage. As a path-breaking collection on Black women's studies noted in its title, "All the Blacks are Men, All the Women are White, but Some of Us are Brave."[8] The universalization of the experience of one subgroup of women and men creates social pressures on those women who are not in the universalized subgroup. For example, working class or unemployed white men who were unable to support full-time homemakers were seen as unmanly. Similarly, because most Black men were excluded from family-wage jobs by racist labor market practices, they were seen as less manly than white men, justifying theories of Black inferiority. Similarly, Black women who worked in the fields as slaves, or who were unable to be full-time homemakers after abolition, were disapproved of by whites as unfeminine and uncivilized.

The truth is that, when there are multiple hierarchical polarizations among people, there cannot be a shared identity and experience for any category of people created by the Hierarchical Polarization Paradigm, even on the most abstract of levels. All women share the feminine gender identity, supposedly innate and essential, but are differentiated by their different racial, class, sexual preference, and national identities. This contradiction is at the root of a very creative and transformative feminist economic process, the combining process, which we describe below.

Hierarchical Polarization Process #4. Polarization

Once people are divided into mutually exclusive genders – men and women – each gender group is made different from "the opposite sex" by the polarization process.

One of the basic ways in which polarization of people into different and opposed genders is accomplished is through a sexual division of labor. Boys are trained for, and assigned as men to, "men's work," while girls are trained for and assigned to "women's work," and the two categories of work are mutually exclusive. The fact that males and females are trained for and employed at these different types of activities makes them into different, polarized "genders," masculine men and feminine women. In most known societies, there has been a sexual division of labor which assigns women predominantly to the intrafamilial work of homemaking and childrearing, and men to the interfamilial work of hunting, producing for the market, war, and politics.[9] This polarization underlies the heterosexual family in that it makes the genders need "the opposite sex" to live a full social life.

In the urban United States, since the mid-nineteenth century, the sexual division of labor assigned women to heterosexual marriage, child-rearing, and homemaking, and men to "bread-winning" in the capitalist market, as workers, entrepreneurs, and investors. If and when women entered the paid labor force, most often before marriage, they were segregated into lower-paid, lower-status women's jobs or a few, lower-paid women's professions (and women's jobs were, in turn, segregated by race and class). However, all women didn't do "women's work" of homemaking, in the sense of caring for families of their own. Upper and middle class women hired poorer women, often immigrants or women of color, to care for their children. These poor women, in turn, were unable to marry and have families of their own, or were forced to leave their children in the care of others while they cared for the children of wealthier, usually white, women. Sterilization policies aimed at women of color have further prohibited their performance of "women's work."[10]

While these differences show that the sexual division of labor does not assign a common work to all women (or men), it does not mean that all women (and men) do not experience gender polarization, or that sexual divisions of labor do not exist between women and men of the same race-class group. Work activities, both paid and unpaid, have consistently been race-class-gender typed, at least in a particular locality or firm – such as the white middle class women's job of secretary in the late nineteenth and early twentieth centuries. Further, differentiating oneself from the "opposite sex" through one's social and work activities is a key part of the gender identity project which both men and women engage in throughout their lives.

A related part of the gender polarization process is a division of personality traits between the genders, usually in ways that complement the sexual divisions of labor. Women are supposed to be feminine, which means caring, sensitive, emotional, dependent, and weak, while men are supposed to be masculine, which means assertive, tough, smart, independent, and strong. The definitions of gender-related traits often vary by race and class, but the gender differentiation of personality traits within each race-class group is a constant.

A key aspect of gender polarization is that it makes males and females into men and women who need one another to live full lives. For example, in order to be able to do their work of homemaking and mothering, middle class women in the nineteenth-century U.S. needed husbands who could be fathers for their children, protectors and bread-winners. Men, in turn, needed homemakers to bear and raise their children, and to care for their homes, or supervise this process.

Hierarchical Polarization Process #5. Hierarchization

A key aspect of gender hierarchical polarization – which distinguishes it from other, less noxious or even beneficial processes of differentiation and polarization – is the placement of men above women in the social hierarchy. In theory and ideology, every man is socially superior to every woman. In reality, the gender hierarchization process is more complicated, because there are many, cross-cutting hierarchical polarizations, and men and women belong to other superior and some inferior categories. However, being a woman, or a member of any "inferior" group, always decreases one's status in the social hierarchy.

Hierarchical Polarization Process #6. Domination/Subordination

The gender domination/subordination process gives men power over women. In some hierarchical polarizations, the domination/subordination process can be the result of self-conscious violent struggles of one group to subordinate another group, such as the U.S. government using its military to displace Native Americans from the land it wanted to settle with "whites." In contrast, while the man/woman hierarchical polarization involves domination/subordination, its roots seem to lie not in an historic defeat of women by men, but rather in cultural misinterpretation and exaggeration of the significance of biological sexual differences. Whatever its origins, once a hierarchical polarization has been self-consciously established and entrenched, the domination/subordination process becomes institutionalized in law and internalized in people's self-conceptions and social roles.

The gender domination/subordination process is exercised in all social realms: political, economic, familial, and cultural. Political domination/subordination has involved the exclusion of women from the right to own property, to vote, to speak in public, et cetera. Economic practices and institutions are a second key part of the gender domination/subordination process. In particular, the sexual division of labor in capitalism has assigned men to the highest paid jobs, and women to low-paid work or to unpaid work in their homes. Domination/ subordination in the family involves husbands commanding their wives (and wives obeying).

Hierarchical Polarization Process #7. Violence

Violence is an intrinsic part of the Hierarchical Polarization Paradigm, and of the gender relations it creates. There is an explicit or implicit understanding in this paradigm that it is acceptable for men to use physical force against, or even kill, women, especially if the latter refuse to accept their subordination. Common forms of male violence against women are incest, battering, and rape. Most urban women are afraid to walk alone on a deserted street at night without a male companion, for fear of being raped.

Hierarchical Polarization Process #8. Rationalization

Gender hierarchical polarization achieves stability through three seemingly nonviolent processes: rationalization, internalization, and stigmatization.

Rationalization is the use of "reason" to claim that gender hierarchical polarization is inevitable. The two main reasons given are religious dogma and "science." Most traditional religions, including Judaism, Christianity, and Islam, inscribe gender roles and men's domination over women. The rise of scientific investigation to increasing predominance from the 18th century onward introduced freedom of the mind, and the potentially democratizing principle that no claim was to be accepted simply on face value, or due to the fact that it had been uttered or written by an authority, religious or other. However, supposedly "objective" science has been used to justify hierarchical polarizations such as race, gender, and sexuality, as much as to overturn them. For example, nineteenth-century scientists claimed that those who were female and/or Black were intellectually inferior because they had smaller brains.

Hierarchical Polarization Processes #9 and #10:
Internalization and Stigmatization

Two important psycho-social processes that are key to the production and maintenance of hierarchical polarization are internalization and stigmatization.   In the internalization process, an individual takes the Hierarchical Polarization Paradigm and all its attendant hierarchical polarizations, into his or her psyche, accepting it as the way things are and should be. As feminists used to say in the early 1970s, "It's difficult to fight an enemy who has outposts in my brain." The prime locus of gender internalization is authoritarian parenting: parents, especially mothers, teach their children how to be and act, according to their dictated gender roles. Mothers reprimand any gender-deviation or homosocial/homosexual behavior, and teach their daughters that they must marry men, and serve their husbands.

This gender socialization is continued in schools, churches, and all other social institutions.[11] Since children usually internalize gender roles early in life, they then become active creators and defenders of their prescribed gender identities. Females take on the gender identity project of being women, and actively strive to be feminine and differentiate themselves from men; males do the opposite.

Social stigmatization of anyone who deviates from the prescribed gender roles cements people in their roles and identity projects. Anyone who dares to deviate from their assigned gender role is excluded from his/her peer group, teased, laughed at, and otherwise humiliated and ostracized. It is important to note that stigmatization applies forcefully to people on the dominator side of each polarization – e.g. men – as well as to those on the subordinated side – e.g. women – such as with the merciless taunting and beating of boys who are gentle and feminine, or gay. Further, as "out" gay people have learned, those who feel internally insecure about their own prescribed identities (i.e. closeted and self-hating gay-behaving people) are often the most ruthless stigmatizers.

A general outcome of the polarization and stigmatization processes is that difference becomes bad, even dangerous. Individuals are afraid to be different from their group's way of being; they try to conform or be like others of their group. They internalize the stigmatization that they see around them, berating themselves for being too ugly (a girl), or too emotional (a boy).

Hierarchical Polarization Process #11: Institutionalization

The final hierarchical polarization process is institutionalization: the building of the hierarchical polarization into social institutions. The institutionalization of gender goes beyond the dividing up of activities among men or women; the very ways in which social and economic categories are defined embody gender (and other) polarizations. For example, the elite jobs in the emergent capitalist economy were constructed for white masculine bread-winners, who were assumed to be supported by full-time homemakers, and when corporations developed, they embodied white masculine qualities of competition and narrow self-seeking in their core missions of profit-maximization and growth.

Transforming the Hierarchical Polarization Paradigm

Because gender and other hierarchical polarizations restrict freedom and cause deprivation and inequality, they have engendered resistance in many forms, e.g. labor unions and worker rights, civil rights and anti-racism, feminism, ecology, gay and lesbian liberation, et cetera. Each of these movements focuses on a particular hierarchical polarization – class, race, gender, man/nature, heterosexual/homosexual, et cetera – but, as we will see below, they all end up integrating struggles against other hierarchical polarizations into their movements, and coming together with the other movements in a "movement of movements."   It is important to keep in mind that feminist movement is a distinct but integral part of this larger transformative process. Along with anti-racist, ecological, antipoverty, and other transformative processes, these feminist transformative processes are creating the basis for an economy and society based on solidarity, cooperation, freedom, democracy, economic and social justice, diversity, and sustainability.

Just as the various hierarchical polarizations are produced and reproduced by the same eleven hierarchical polarization processes – so the movements to transform them share similar transformative processes. We have, in fact, identified seven distinct transformative processes at work in each social movement. Each transformative process attacks and transforms different aspects of the hierarchical polarization they are attacking. Figure 2 (next page) outlines the basic aspects of the seven transformative processes.

The remainder of this paper is devoted to exploring the different feminist transformative processes which are at work in the United States today, and their interactions with transformative processes in the other movements. The different feminist transformative processes have emerged more or less sequentially, each

Figure 2. The Seven Transformative Processes

Transformative Processes	Aspect of Hierarchical Polarization Paradigm Challenged	Basic Thrust of Transformative Process
Questioning/ Envisioning	View of social identities and relationships as natural or God-given, i.e. ascription (can also challenge Hierarchical Polarization Paradigm itself); belief that "there is no alternative"	Why are things this way? Isn't that particular social practice or institution unfair? Are people really naturally different as categorized? Are people inevitably unequal and violent? What better ways of being, and economic and social system, can we imagine?
Combining	Assumption that hierarchical-polarization-created groups are homogeneous, and disconnected from one another	Expansion of social movements beyond single-issue, identity-politics-based awareness and organizing; expansion of one's sense of solidarity in standing against the oppressions suffered by others
Equal Opportunity	View that certain people are naturally superior to others; resultant restriction of rights, privileges, and occupations of subordinated group	All are created equal; members of a devalued group should have the rights and privileges that the valued group has, including access to the higher-paid higher-status occupations
Valuing the Devalued	Devaluation of subordinated peoples, along with their traits and activities	The values, traits and works of the devalued group are important and valuable, and need to be recognized and revalued
Integrating	View that certain kinds of people, ways of being, values, character traits, and works cannot/ should not be combined; polarization/segregation of people, traits, and types of work	It is healthy and balanced to integrate social spaces and relationships; to combine the two poles of a hierarchical polarization in a person and in an activity; and to combine in one's life activities that previously were polarized, such as active parenting and paid work
Discernment	Negative aspects of ways of being, values, character traits, and work resulting from hierarchy and/or polarization	Critical reexamination of the basic building blocks of our social order – including masculinity, femininity, spirituality, materialism, whiteness, nature, success – so as to free them from their distortion by hierarchization and polarization
Diversifying/ Unifying/ Globalizing	Inevitability of polarization, domination, and violence; fragmentation of individuality and of social movements; the Hierarchical Polarization Paradigm itself	Unity amidst diversity; globalization from below; social forum movement, solidarity economy, socially responsible economic behavior, constructing a new paradigm

process building on the preceding ones. We will discuss each feminist process briefly here, putting more emphasis on the latter processes, which are more recent and less understood.[12] It is important to note that these feminist transformative processes are at work both in organized feminist movements, and in individuals' everyday, personal and work lives. Individual feminist transformation and organized feminist movements for social and institutional transformation coexist and complement one another, as expressed in the feminist saying, "the personal is political."

The Feminist Questioning/Envisioning Process

The feminist questioning/envisioning process challenges the rationalizations, and internalization of these rationalizations, that undergird gender, by asking questions about aspects of gender relations that have been taken for granted – and then envisions futures without this inequality and polarization. Questioning/envisioning processes are supported by self-conscious reflection, by true scientific investigation and education, and creative and visionary thinking.

Feminist questioning/envisioning was present in the so-called "first wave" of feminism, at the Seneca Falls Convention in 1848, when Elizabeth Cady Stanton and other participants declared, "We hold these truths to be self-evident: that all men and women are created equal," as well as in the famous "Ain't I A Woman?" speech of Sojourner Truth, a former slave'. This process was also embodied in second-wave feminist Betty Friedan's identification of the frustrations of white middle class housewives as "the problem which has no name," in her book, *The Feminine Mystique*.[13]

In the questioning/envisioning process, feminists question the biological and religious arguments that women are naturally intellectually and politically inferior to men, or only fit for child-rearing and homemaking. They ask whether the sexual division of labor, as expressed in the sex-typing of jobs, is really natural and efficient, and whether women's lower pay is fair. They protest against male domination in all of its forms, as in the Redstockings Manifesto of 1969:

> Women are an oppressed class. Our oppression is total, affecting every facet of our lives. We are exploited as sex objects, breeders, domestic servants, and cheap labor. We are considered inferior beings, whose only purpose is to enhance men's lives. Our humanity is denied. Our prescribed behavior is enforced by the threat of physical violence.... We call on all our sisters to unite with us in struggle. We call on all men to give up their

male privileges and support women's liberation in the interest
of our humanity and their own.[14]

The Berkeley-Oakland Women's Union Statement expresses the envisioning
part of this process in its opening sentence: "We come together to form a
women's union to develop a position of increasing strength and to transform our
society into one that will meet our needs and the needs of all people as full human beings."[15]

The Feminist Combining Process

In the combining process, feminist activists realize that their movements will be
strengthened, deepened, and made more transformative if they incorporate struggles against hierarchical polarizations other than gender. The feminist combining process is instigated by women who are multiply oppressed – that is, who are
also of color, working class, lesbian, and/or disabled – that is, by women whose
experience itself combines multiple oppressions.

Women of different classes, racial-ethnicities, and sexualities came together in
the grassroots "women's movements" that swept the U.S. in the mid-nineteenth
century, and again in the 1970s. However, when women came together to raise
their consciousnesses, fight sexism, and liberate *"women,"* privileged women
took the helm of the movement. Women who were working class, and/or of
color, and/or lesbians were marginalized, and their political issues were down-
played or ignored.

The first-wave feminist movement was characterized by overt racism and classism. While some feminists sought to combine the struggles for Blacks' and
women's rights, Elizabeth Cady Stanton, a key white suffrage leader, refused to
support Black suffrage unless women were guaranteed the vote first, and most
white suffrage groups excluded or marginalized Blacks.[16] Margaret Sanger, up-
held by feminists as the trail-blazer in the struggle for women's reproductive
rights, advocated birth control especially for poor white women and women of
color, as a eugenics measure.[17]

Race, class, and sexuality differences and inequality also surfaced early on in
second wave feminism. Educated white women tended to take control of feminist organizations because of their race and class privilege, and had difficulty
seeing the ways in which their behavior, and their definitions of women's issues,
oppressed and marginalized other women. These "other" women – especially
women of color, and lesbians – reacted with anger and disaffection. Many felt
the need to split off from the white-heterosexual-middle-class-dominated main-

stream feminist movement. They formed feminist groups of their own – especially lesbian feminist groups and Black/Third World women's groups – and created feminist theory and practice that spoke to their issues. *This Bridge Called My Back* expresses the sentiments of early second-wave feminists of color, many of them lesbians, as well as their insights into the intersection of race, class, gender, and sexuality.[18]

This polarization within the "women's movement" set the stage for the complicated, many-faceted combining process, which began to extend feminist movement beyond the compartmentalization of polarizations, issues, and identities created by the Hierarchical Polarization Paradigm. In order to convince women and women's groups which were working class, lesbian, and/or of color to join their movements, or work in coalition with them, white middle class heterosexual feminists had to examine their own internalized classism, homophobia, and racism – and state their commitment to transform these other forms of oppression. And they needed to realize that their views of any particular feminist issue were partial, tainted with the lens of their other privileges. Indeed, many white, heterosexual, and/or middle class feminists have learned to look to multiply-oppressed women – e.g. to women who are working class, disabled, lesbians, and/or of color – to find the most liberatory stance towards the issue they are theorizing about or working to transform.

As part of the combining process, many feminist groups have become multi-issue movements that aspire to truly address the issues of *all* women. Indeed, the National Organization of Women now lists on its platform of key issues "racism, lesbian rights, and economic justice."[19] Julie has participated in a similar combining process in the class-centered Union for Radical Political Economics. Groups which have expanded their focus as a result of the combining process also actively seek to organize in coalition with other groups working on issues which affect their constituency.

The Feminist Equal Opportunity Process

Equal opportunity processes are struggles by members of the subordinated groups, and their allies, to gain political and economic rights, social treatment, and economic opportunities equal to those of the dominating group. The United States itself was established as part of an equal opportunity process. With their famous, liberatory claim that "all (white) men are created equal," the Founding Fathers not only declared political independence from their British colonizers, but also formally overturned the aristocrat/commoner hierarchical polarization, and asserted equal opportunity for white men. The hierarchy among white men, instead of being based on ascription and aristocratic privilege, was replaced by a flexible, semi-meritocratic hierarchy.

The developing capitalist economy became a competition among white men to dominate or "better" each other in their struggle for wealth, a process called "bread-winning." A white man's wealth and ability to support a full-time home-maker, not his pedigree, became the measure of his worth or level of success. The true winner in this new system was seen to be the "self-made man": the man who, through his own effort, earnings, savings, and investments, worked his way up the economic hierarchy from entry-level worker to head of a large and power-ful firm.

The new flexibility in the economic hierarchy let loose a flurry of effort and in-vention which, coordinated by the market, fueled a new, dynamic economic sys-tem we call capitalism.   The competition of white men to dominate one another in the market was institutionalized in capitalist firms.   By the end of the nine-teenth century, this process had created a new, immortal individual – the corpo-ration – which abstractly embodied this competitive struggle for profits and growth, and in turn harnessed self-interested, competitive white men to its ser-vice, as managers and workers, in complex internal labor markets.[20]

Women's struggle against their exclusion from this declaration of equality, from the exercise of political rights, and from competition for the higher-paid, higher-status jobs is at the root of the feminist equal opportunity process.   The feminist equal opportunity movement is based in "identity politics" in the sense that it sees itself as a "women's movement," fighting to be equal to men.   Inspired by the abolition movement, women (with some male supporters) fought for and won women's suffrage and property rights in the nineteenth and early twentieth centu-ries.   And then, in the second half of the twentieth century, inspired by the Civil Rights movement, women (again, with some male allies) fought for and won the right to enter the higher-paid, higher-status white men's jobs.   What had been accepted as a natural, God-given sexual division of labor came to be viewed as discriminatory and unfair to women, something to be remediated through public policy.

The feminist equal opportunity process has made major strides in eliminating married women's restriction to unpaid work in the home, as well as the exclusion of women from higher-paid, higher-status "masculine" jobs.   The percentage of married women in the paid labor force has risen from 6% in 1900 to 61% in 2005.[21]   Women's share of traditionally male-dominated managerial and profes-sional jobs has increased dramatically.   Nevertheless, a "glass ceiling" still im-pedes women's advancement to the highest echelons of the economy, and statistical studies continue to find that women suffer from wage discrimination – that is, they are paid less than men with equal jobs and qualifications.[22] Thus, the feminist equal opportunity process continues today, because sex discrimination and gender segregation persist.

The Feminist Valuing-the-Devalued Process

The feminist valuing-the-devalued process reacts against and strives to transform a key part of gender hierarchical polarization which accompanies women's subordination by men – the devaluation both of women, and of the feminine traits and activities associated with them. This feminist process seeks recognition for the "invisible heart," the devalued and ignored feminine caring work which is crucial to economic and social life.[23]

The feminist valuing-the-devalued process both responds directly to the devaluation created by the Hierarchical Polarization Paradigm, and compensates for imbalances created by the feminist equal opportunity process. In the feminist equal opportunity process, women struggled for the same rights and opportunities as men. This meant that women's struggles tended to set their sights upon gaining what men (especially educated, white, heterosexual men) had. For this reason, feminist equal opportunity movement implicitly accepted and even reinforced the reigning social and economic *devaluation* of women and their traditional work. For example, when second-wave feminists fought for access to and success within high-status, male-dominated jobs, they implicitly or explicitly accepted and reinforced the reigning devaluation of the work of mothering and of full-time homemakers as "just housewives." At the same time, equal opportunity feminists were not fully aware of the personal and familial sacrifices which would be required of them and of the women who followed their lead, as they entered the competition for "top" jobs against men served by full-time homemakers. Many women postponed parenting until it was too late, or simply chose not to parent at all; other struggled miserably with "the double day."[24]

The valuing-the-devalued process redresses this problem both personally and politically. On the personal level, it responds to the unhappiness of women who regretted giving up mothering, or to the frustrations of women who suffered and sacrificed family time under the pressures of the double day.[25] The feminist valuing-the-devalued process validates women's choices to actively participate in homemaking and mothering, even the choice to "opt out" of high-paid jobs in order to do so.[26] On the political level, this process notes how crucial reproductive work is to our economy and society, demands its inclusion in output statistics, and advocates for public support of it through paid parental leaves, parental education, and other policy measures.

The Feminist Integrative Process

The feminist integrative process combines and builds on the feminist equal opportunity and valuing-the-devalued processes. If the former strives to give women access to the masculine sphere, and the latter asserts the importance of women's traditional feminine work, the feminist integrative process expresses and supports women's (and men's) desire to combine masculine and feminine work and ways of being, and advocates for the transformation necessary for this to happen. Since homemaking and bread-winning were constructed to be mutually exclusive and complementary – not combined – this desire to integrate these two spheres of life requires personal as well as social and institutional transformation. Participation in the equal opportunity process taught women the fallacy of believing that homemaking can be easily adjusted to meet the demands of one's job – through having few or no children, hiring others to care for them, and/or depriving oneself of sleep and balance. Learning from this, advocates of the feminist integrative process realize that work/family balance requires familial restructuring (particularly, men taking on traditionally feminine tasks), job restructuring (flexible and more reasonable work hours, flex-place, paid leaves), and social policies to support these (shorter work week policies, mandated paid parental leaves, parenting supports).[27]

Individuals and movements engaged in the feminist integrative process essentially reject the polarization of people into masculine or feminine beings, doing *either* men's or women's work, respectively. They view this polarization as restrictive, unbalanced, and unhealthy, and set out to combine things which were previously seen to be mutually exclusive. The work/family, work/life and parents' rights movements express this process.[28]

The Feminist Discernment Processes

Whereas the feminist integrative process combines masculine and feminine, the feminist discernment processes subjects masculinity and femininity, and the values, practices and institutions constructed around those gender polarizations, to serious critical evaluation. The polarization of people, works, and traits into mutually exclusive gender categories distorts and unbalances humanity. As feminist economist Julie Nelson has shown, the combination of previously polarized gendered traits allows more positive forms to emerge.[29] For example, when polarized between men and women, the basic human traits of directivity and receptivity degenerate into arrogance, insensitivity, and domination for men, and self-effacement, oversensitivity, and subservience for women. These distorted traits are then built into unbalanced and dysfunctional economic and social institutions. The integrative process, which we discussed above, combines poles and transcends polarization; the discernment process follows up as we redefine ourselves, our values, and our paid and unpaid work, freed from restrictive polarizations.

A key current area of the discernment process is occurring as a result of work/family integration. Women's equal opportunity struggles to compete in the masculine economy led to the emergence of a gender-neutral form of bread-winning, which we call "competitive careerism." At the same time, firms' efforts to increase their profits by boosting sales led to aggressive marketing and advertising campaigns which have institutionalized "competitive consumerism." The two "cc's" support one another – competitive careerism has the added carrot of increased consumption, and competitive consumerism's expansion of needs requires redoubled effort to stay afloat financially through competitive careerism. The addictions to money, stress, and disease which result from a life centered in these values is only heightened and exposed by feminist integrative efforts to combine paid work and family life. In particular, the exhaustion, imbalance, conflict, and squeezing of family time which results from trying to juggle competitive careerism with family life has led increasing numbers of women and men to "downshift." That is, it had led them to reject the prevailing competitive, money-centered, materialistic values which motivate their work lives, in favor of less demanding and/or more fulfilling but less paid work, along with a simpler pattern of consumption, and emphasis on quality of life, family, friends and community.[30]

The Feminist Diversifying/Unifying/Globalizing Process

The feminist diversifying/unifying/globalizing process has two aspects: the interconnection of feminist movements across the globe, or global feminism, and the interconnection of feminist movement with other social movements in a "movement of movements."

Global feminist organizing began almost as soon as the second wave of feminism emerged. The first world conference on women took place in 1975 in Mexico City, followed by conferences in Copenhagen (1980), Nairobi (1985), and Beijing (1995). Early conflicts between Northern/Western women's focus on equal rights and sexuality, and Southern women's focus on issues of economic survival, were mitigated by subsequent developments. Northern women began experiencing the economic dislocation resulting from globalization and offshoring, magnified by the decline in the welfare state – making them more concerned with economic issues. At the same time, the rise of fundamentalism led Southern women to be more concerned with women's rights. This confluence, along with the growth of Internet communication, facilitated the emergence of transnational feminist networks such as DAWN (Development Alternatives with Women for a

New Era) and WLUML (Women Living Under Muslim Laws) in the mid-1980s, and WEDO (Women's Environment and Development Organization) in the 1990s.[31]

At the same time, over the past fifty years, the feminist transformative processes have developed in the U.S. in parallel with anti-racist, ecological, and anti-class transformative processes. As a result of the combining process, which operates in all of these movements, U.S. feminism has become interlaced with anti-class, anti-racist, and other progressive principles – just as other U.S. social movements have begun to integrate women's and feminist issues into their goals and practice. The combining process has laid the groundwork for the transcendence of identity politics, and for the emergence of a new kind of consciousness which is opposed to *all* forms of hierarchical polarization – truly committed to liberty and justice for all. These two developments – the globalization of feminism, and the interconnection and coalescing of the various social movements – intensified at the turn of the millennium as a result of the rampant economic dislocation and environmental destruction brought about by corporate globalization, with its neo-liberal agenda of Free Trade and its new institution, the World Trade Organiza-tion (WTO). The famous Seattle anti-WTO protest of 1999 brought together for the first time organized labor and environmental groups, who had usually been in conflict, in what became a "blue-green coalition." This marked the coming of age of a vibrant anti-globalization movement which has united a broad range of groups around the world against corporate abuses, a process which has been called "globalization from below."[32]

The diversifying/unifying/globalizing process is leading people all over the world to reject the prevailing competitive, materialistic values and say no to business as usual in all that they do. As the Zapatistas say, "Un solo no, un mil-lion de si": a shared "no" to the global neoliberal capitalist economic system, and a million "yeses" to the multiplicity of different positive alternatives that people all over the world are constructing. What are the yeses? As the diversify-ing/unifying/globalizing process develops and extends across our country and the world, it is inventing new economic and social values, practices and institutions which can heal the individual and social wounds and imbalances created by the Hierarchical Polarization Paradigm. We'll discuss a few key examples here.

One example of the diversifying/unifying/globalizing process is a new form of political organizing for peace, justice, democracy, and sustainability, exemplified by the annual World Social Forum, and the hundreds of other similarly-organized forums that now take place yearly throughout the world. These fo-rums, with the motto "Another World is Possible," emerged as a way for the anti-globalization "movement of movements" to focus on building alternatives to neoliberal economic values, practices, and institutions. World Social Forums, and more regional and issue-focused forums such as the US Social Forum, bring together people of all ages, classes, genders, sexual preferences, race-ethnicities, and nations who are engaged in social and economic justice, environmental, peace, and democracy activism. The focus is on listening to one another, learning from one another, forming cross-country alliances, and creating and advocating new values, practices, and institutions which respect all of life.[33] A jointly written book, *Alternatives to Economic Globalization: A Better World is Possible*, has emerged from these meetings, and the groups which they have catalyzed. It lays out what is becoming a growing consensus around the necessary direction for economic transformation out of global capitalism into a post-Hierarchical-Polarization-Paradigm economy.[34]

A second example of the diversifying/unifying/globalizing process is the growing "solidarity economy" movement, which seeks to support, network and make visible the new economics which is emerging from the diversifying/unifying/globalizing process. Solidarity economy is a new conception of economic life which flows out of values of sharing, ecological sustainability, mutual support, and economic democracy.[35] Solidarity economy challenges managers and boards of directors to find win-win solutions that benefit all of their firm's *stakeholders* – all of those affected by its behavior – not just the stockholders, as traditional profit-motivated firms do.[36] Solidarity economy advocates *socially responsible* decision-making by consumers, workers, managers, entrepreneurs, and investors – that is, making decisions that are good both for the decision-maker AND for others and society at large.[37]

In these and similar ways, the diversifying/unifying/globalizing process holds out the promise of what Martin Luther King called "the beloved community." Beloved community is a "society in which every person [is] valued and where all conflicts [can] be reconciled in a spirit of goodwill and mutual benefit unified …where all of us can live together in a climate of understanding, cooperation and unity."[38]

*   *   *

The seven feminist transformative processes, developed and honed through over a century of struggles, provide us with the tools to truly liberate both women and men from the chains of gender polarization. Further, alongside and intertwined with the other social movements, feminists are in the process of dismantling the Hierarchical Polarization Paradigm, building more egalitarian, peaceful, loving, free, and democratic economic and social values, practices and institutions for everyone. We are blessed to have been born into such an historic, transformative moment, and it is up to each of us to do what we can to help guide our world to this possible future.

References

Amott, Teresa and Julie Matthaei. (1996). *Race, Gender, and Work: A Multicultural Economic History of Women in the United States*. Boston: South End.

Berkeley-Oakland Women's Union Statement. (1979). In Zillah Eisenstein (Ed.). *Capitalist Patriarchy and the Case for Socialist Feminism*. (pp. 355-361).New York: Monthly Review Press

Brecher, J., Costello T., and Smith, B. (2000). *Globalization from Below: The Power of Solidarity*. Cambridge: South End Press.

Blair, M. and L. Stout. (1999). "A Team Production Theory of Corporate Law," *Virginia Law Review*, 85, 2.

Blau, Francine, Marianne Ferber, and Ann Winkler. (2006). *The Economics of Women, Men and Work* , 5th ed. Upper Saddle River: Pearson Prentice Hall.

Brien, Kevin M. (2006). *Marx, Reason, and the Art of Freedom* , 2nd edition. New York: Prometheus Books.

Cavanagh, J. and J. Mander (Ed.). (2004). *Alternatives to Globalization: A Better World is Possible*. San Francisco: Berrett-Koehler.

Denny, Dallas. (2006) "Transgender Communities of the United States in the Late Twentieth Century." In Currah, Paisley et al. (Ed.). *Transgender Rights*. Minneapolis: University of Minnesota Press.

Fausto-Sterling, Anne. (2000). *Sexing the Body: Gender Politics and the Construction of Sexuality*. New York: Basic Books.

Fisher, W.F. and T. Ponniah (Eds.). (2004). *Another World is Possible: Popular Alternatives to Globalization at the World Social Forum*. London: Zed Books.

Folbre, N. (2001). *The Invisible Heart: Economics and Family Values*. New York: The New Press.

Friedan, Betty. (1963). *The Feminine Mystique*. New York: W.W. Norton.

Goodman, Alan, Deborah Heath, and M. Susan Lindee, (Eds.). (2003). *Genetic Nature/Culture: Anthropology and Science beyond the Two-Culture Divide*. Berkeley: University of California Press.

Gordon, Linda. (1976). *Woman's Body, Woman's Right: A Social History of Birth Control in America*. New York: Grossman Publishers.

Hewlett, Sylvia and Cornell West (1998). *The War Against Parents*. Boston: Houghton Mifflin Co.

hooks, bell. (1984). *Feminist Theory: From Margin to Center*. Boston: South End Press.

Hull, G. T., P.B. Scott, and B. Smith (Eds.). (1982). *All the women are White, all the Blacks are Men, but Some of us are Brave : Black women's studies*. Old Westbury: Feminist Press.

Joseph, G. and J. Lewis. (1981). *Common Differences : Conflicts in Black and White Feminist Perspectives*. New York : Anchor Press/Doubleday.

Kelly, Marjorie. (2001). *The Divine Right of Capital: Dethroning the Corporate Aristocracy*. San Francisco: Berrett-Koehler.

Levi-Strauss, Claude. (1971). "The Family." In Arlene Skolnick and Jerome Skolnick. (Ed.). *The Family in Transition*. Boston: Little Brown.

Matthaei, Julie. (1982). *An Economic History of Women in America: Women's Work, the Sexual Division of Labor, and the Development of Capitalistm*. New York: Schocken Books.

Matthaei, Julie. (1996). "Why Marxist, Feminist, and Anti-Racist Economists Should be Marxist-Feminist-Anti-Racist Economists." *Feminist Economics* 2, 1.

Matthaei, Julie, and Brandt, Barbara. (2001). "Healing Ourselves, Healing Our Economy: Paid Work, Unpaid Work, and the Next Stage of Feminist Economic Transformation," *Review of Radical Political Economics,* 33.

Moghadam, Valentine. (2005). *Globalizing Women: Transnational Feminist Networks*. Baltimore: Johns Hopkins University Press.

Mohanty, Chandra. (2003). *Feminism Without Borders: Decolonizing Theory, Practicing Solidarity*. Durham: Duke University Press.

Moraga, Cherie, and Gloria Anzaldua (Eds.). (1981). *This Bridge Called my Back : Writings by Radical Women of Color*. Watertown.: Persephone Press, c1981

Nelson, Julie. (1996). *Feminism, Objectivity and Economics*. London: Routledge, 1996.

Redstockings (Bitch) Manifesto. (1969). Accessed Feb. 17,2008. http://www.hippy.com/article-310.html

Juliet Schor. (1998). *The Overspent American: Upscaling, Downshifting, and the New Consumer*. New York: Basic Books.

Scott King, C. (2004. January 22). "Building the Beloved Community." http://www.hum.wa.gov/Diversity/coretta%20scott%20king.html

Spelman, Elizabeth. (1988). *Inessential Woman: Problems of Exclusion in Feminist Thought*. Boston: Beacon Press.

Stanton, Elizabeth C., Susan B. Anthony, and M.J. Cage (Ed.). (1969). *The History of Woman Suffrage, Vol 1*. New York: Arno Press

Terborg-Penn, Rosalyn. (1998). *African American Women in the Struggle for the Vote, 1850-1920.* Bloomington: Indiana University Press.

The Combahee River Collective. (1979) "A Black Feminist Statement." In Zillah Eisenstein (Ed.). *Capitalist Patriarchy and the Case for Socialist Feminism.* (pp. 363-372).New York: Monthly Review Press

Waring, Marilyn. (1988). *If Women Counted: A New Feminist Economics*. New York: Harper & Row.

Notes

[1] A shorter version of this article was presented at the Rethinking Marxism conference in Amherst, October 2006, and it has been published in a different version as: Julie Matthaei and Barbara Brandt (2007) "The Transformative Moment," in Richard Westra et al. (Ed.). *Political Economy and Global Capitalism: The 21st Century, Present and Future.* London: Anthem Press. Heartfelt thanks to Donna Bivens, Janice Goldman, and Germai Medhanie for their help with previous drafts, and to the students of Econ 343, Feminist Economics, at Wellesley College, over the years, and especially the Spring 2007 class, for their questions, insights, and website contributions.
[2] Anne Fausto-Sterling. (2000). *Sexing the Body: Gender Politics and the Construction of Sexuality.* New York: Basic Books.
[3] Alan Goodman, Deborah Heath, and M. Susan Lindee, (Eds.). (2003). *Genetic Nature/Culture: Anthropology and Science beyond the Two-Culture Divide.* Berkeley: University of California Press.
[4] Julie Matthaei (1982). *An Economic History of Women in America.* New York: Schocken Books, 192-3.
[5] See Dallas Denny. (2006). "Transgender Communities of the United States in the Late Twentieth Century." In Paisley Currah et al. (Ed.). *Transgender Rights.* Minneapolis: University of Minnesota Press.
[6] Elizabeth Spelman. (1988). *Inessential Woman: Problems of Exclusion in Feminist Thought.* Boston: Beacon Press; Chandra Mohanty. (2003). *Feminism Without Borders: Decolonizing Theory, Practicing Solidarity.* Durham: Duke University Press.
[7] Kevin M. Brien. (2006). *Marx, Reason, and the Art of Freedom* , 2nd edition. New York: Prometheus Books, p. 272, employs the notion of a "concrete universal" to understand the existence of socially meaningful categories that do not, however, describe a shared experience.
[8] G. T. Hull, P.B. Scott, and B. Smith (Eds.). (1982). *All the women are White, all the Blacks are Men, but Some of us are Brave : Black women's studies.* Old Westbury: Feminist Press.
[9] Claude Levi-Strauss. (1971). "The Family." In Arlene Skolnick and Jerome Skolnick. (Ed.). *The Family in Transition.* Boston: Little Brown.
[10] Teresa Amott and Julie Matthaei (1996). *Race, Gender, and Work: A Multicultural Economic History of Women in the United States.* Boston: South End, Chapter 2.
[11] We are not saying here that all socialization and internalization are oppressive, only that the internalization of these polarized and hierarchical structures do.
[12] Because of space limitations, we discuss them only briefly here – for more, see the "Feminist Transformation" pages of www.TransformationCentral.org.

[13] Elizabeth C. Stanton, Susan B. Anthony, and M.J. Cage (Ed.). (1969). *The History of WomanSuffrage*, Vol 1. New York: Arno Press; Betty Friedan. (1963). The Feminine Mystique. New York: W.W. Norton.
[14] Redstockings (Bitch) Manifesto. (1969). Accessed Feb. 17,2008.
http://www.hippy.com/article-310.html

[15] In Zillah Eisenstein (Ed.). (1979). *Capitalist Patriarchy and the Case for Socialist Feminism*. New York: Monthly Review Press, p. 355-361.

[16] Rosalyn Terborg-Penn. (1998). *African American Women in the Struggle for the Vote, 1850-1920*. Bloomington: Indiana University Press.

[17] Linda Gordon. (1976). Woman's Body, Woman's Right: A Social History of Birth Control in America. New York: Grossman Publishers.

[18] Cherie Moraga and Gloria Anzaldua (Eds.). (1981). *This Bridge Called my Back : Writings by Radical Women of Color*. Watertown.: Persephone Press, c1981; see also G. Joseph and J. Lewis. (1981). *Common Differences : Conflicts in Black and White Feminist Perspectives*. New York : Anchor Press/Doubleday; G. T. Hull, P.B. Scott, and B. Smith (Eds.). (1982). *All the women are White, all the Blacks are Men, but Some of us are Brave : Black women's studies*. Old Westbury: Feminist Press; bell hooks. (1984). *Feminist Theory: From Margin to Center*. Boston: South End Press; and The Combahee River Collective, "A Black Feminist Statement," in Eisenstein, 363-372.

[19] http://www.now.org/history/history.html

[20] Matthaei 1982, Ch. 5.

[21] U.S. Census Bureau. (2008, January). "The 2008 Statistical Abstract", pp. 132-3, www.census.gov/compendia/statab/index.html

[22] Francine Blau, Marianne Ferber, and Ann Winkler. (2006). *The Economics of Women,Men and Work* , 5th ed. Upper Saddle River: Pearson Prentice Hall.

[23] This expression was coined in: Nancy Folbre (2001). *The Invisible Heart*. New York: The New Press; an early example: Marilyn Waring. (1988). If Women Counted. New York: Harper & Row.

[24] Julie Matthaei and Barbara Brandt. (2001). "Healing Ourselves, Healing Our Economy," *Review of Radical Political Economics* 33.

[25] Ibid. I often find that my students who had overworked, unavailable double-day mothers learned from their experience the problems with the equal opportunity feminist model.

[26] Lisa Belkin's controversial article, "The Opt-Out Revolution." (2003, October, 26). *New York Times Magazine*, highlights the valuing-the-devalued process.

[27] Matthaei and Brandt (2001); see also Joan Williams. (2000). *Unbending Gender: Why Family and Work Conflict and What to do About it*. New York: Oxford University Press; and Mona Harrington. (1994). *Care and equality: inventing a new family politics*. New York: Alfred A. Knopf. See the Integrative pages on Transformation-Central.org for links to resources on this issue.

[28] Sylvia Hewlett and Cornell West (1998). *The War Against Parents*. Boston: Houghton Mifflin Co.

[29] Julie Nelson. (1996). *Feminism, Objectivity and Economics*. London: Routledge, 1996, Chapter 2.

[30] Matthaei and Brandt (2001); Juliet Schor. (1998). *The Overspent American: Upscaling, Downshifting, and the New Consumer*. New York: Basic Books.

[31] Valentine Moghadam. (2005). *Globalizing Women: Transnational Feminist Networks*. Baltimore: Johns Hopkins University Press.

[32] J. Brecher, T. Costello, and B. Smith. (2000). *Globalization from Below: The Power of Solidarity*. Cambridge: South End Press.

[33] www.forumsocialmundial.org.br; Fisher, W.F. and T. Ponniah (Eds.). (2004). *Another World is Possible: Popular Alternatives to Globalization at the World Social Forum*. London: Zed Books.

[34] J. Cavanagh, and J. Mander (Ed.). (2004). *Alternatives to Globalization: A Better World is Possible*. San Francisco: Berrett-Koehler.

[35] Editors' Note: See Chapter 2: Social and Solidarity Economy: Transformative Concepts for Unprecedented Times?, in this collection.

[36] Kelly, Marjorie. (2001). *The Divine Right of Capital: Dethroning the Corporate Aristocracy*. San Francisco: Berrett-Koehler; , Blair, M. and L. Stout. (1999). "A Team Production Theory of Corporate Law," *Virginia Law Review*, 85, 2.

[37] Editors' Note: See Chapter 19: Live Your Power, in this collection, for a detailed discussion of these movements.

[38] Scott King, C. (2004. January 22). "Building the Beloved Community." http://www.hum.wa.gov/Diversity/coretta%20scott%20king.html

10
Immigrants, Globalization, and Organizing for Rights, Solidarity, and Economic Justice

Germai Medhanie

> *Germai Medhanie is a long-time economic activist. He is co-founder of Guramylay: Growing the Green Economy (a project of EDINA, the Ecological Democracy Institute of North America), and he is an editor of TransformationCentral.org. Germai served as the Executive Director of The Union for Radical Political Economics (URPE) from 1995 – 2006, and on the editorial collective of Grassroots Economic Organizing (GEO) from 1992 to 1996. He has taught at the School of Human Services of Springfield College in Springfield, MA and at the Common Ground High School in New Haven, CT. An immigrant from Eritrea, Northeast Africa, Germai has a B.S. in Accounting and Economics, and an M.S. in Community Economic Development.*

My name is Germai Medhanie. I work for Guramylay: Growing the Green Economy, and for TransformationCentral.org. One of our focuses is promoting green businesses and green solidarity values. We are interested in how people are running these kinds of businesses so that we can spread the word and inform others. That is the main focus of our organization, but we also have an interest in immigration.

This panel will focus on immigrants, globalization, and organizing for rights, solidarity, and economic justice. I will discuss my experience as an Eritrean immigrant, including the global conditions causing Eritrea immigration to the U.S., and the depoliticization of many first-generation Eritrean and Ethiopian immigrants. I also want to discuss the use of recent African immigrants as token Blacks in the labor market, and the need for African immigrants to build solidarity with African Americans and other people of color. In addition, as an immigrant, I would like to explore what this country stands for, and what kind of opportunities it offers. Finally, I would like to invite members of the audience to share your experiences as immigrants, and the lessons you have learned about immigrant organizing.

Current Immigrant Organizing in New Haven

First, I would like to report on my colleague, John Lugo, who was supposed to be speaking here with me here today. He is from Columbia, and he is in New Haven right now because there is a crisis there for immigrant people. New Haven was one of the first cities to give a city identification card to all residents, including all immigrants. Anybody can apply for a resident card, whether they have a Social Security number or not. The plan is supported by the mayor and also the Chief of Police, because in this way, all residents of New Haven will be able to apply for services and conduct business. The card issued by the city should allow immigrants to open a bank account, but not all banks are currently accepting this card as a valid form of identification. At the same time that the city was planning to do this, federal immigration officers conducted raids and imprisoned several undocumented immigrants, because many people from outside of New Haven had been complaining about undocumented immigrants. John Lugo is very active with this issue, and he decided that this fight was more urgent than coming here to speak. Today, he is in Hartford trying to free those who are still in prison, and to get more citizens talking about the issue.

New Haven is a very important city for immigrants. There are many big schools located there, like Yale University, Southern Connecticut University, New Haven University, and Gateway Community College. Immigrants come to New Haven to work, but have the possibility of studying as well. The immigrant movement in the city was not visible until 2006, when it joined forces with the May Day Celebration Committee. For 20 years, this Committee has organized a yearly multicultural festival that honors and celebrates labor history and labor, peace, social service and social justice groups. Two years ago, these two movements formed a coalition to celebrate May Day and to address immigrant issues, and they have drawn thousands of people to the festivals since that time. In many places, these kind of alliances are not being formed, and immigrants still feel very isolated from other communities, but in New Haven this coalition is bringing new hope and the realization that we are all immigrants.

My Immigration from Eritrea

I emigrated from Eritrea in 1979. At that time, I felt isolated, and I had limited connections to people in the Eritrean/Ethiopian community, or to people that were working and going to school like me. We all had part-time jobs, and we were working mainly on one street, Chapel Street, and its surrounds, because there were many restaurants in the area, and we did not have cars to explore other job opportunities.

I came to the United States, like many immigrants, because had to: I did not have a choice. In 1962, Eritrea was annexed as a province of Ethiopia. Six years later, the Eritrean revolution began, with a goal of independence from Ethiopia. This revolution was ignored, in particular by the United States, until Ethiopia formed a socialist government in 1975. In a student revolution, the Ethiopian people had overthrown Haile Selassie, who had been in power for the previous forty years, and the military wing of the revolution set up a new government in Ethiopia, the Derg. The military was able to take power because they were the only organized group, and they had the resources. The students were organized, but they did not have a practical vision of how to take power; they never anticipated that the fall of the Haile Selassie regime would happen so quickly. So here, as in other situations, when a movement for change does not have a practical vision for taking power, another group, who might not share their ideals, can come in to fill the vacuum – in this case, the military.

When Haile Selassie was still in power, the Eritrean revolution was marginalized by Western countries, the United States in particular, because Haile Selassie had a good relationship with the U.S. government. When the Derg came to power, however, the U.S. started to sympathize with and support the Eritrean revolution, in order to destabilize the socialist government in Ethiopia. At the same time, the Soviet Union and the socialist bloc was supporting the Ethiopian socialist government. In a sense, Eritreans won their independence, not because the West recognized their suffering or their cause, but because we were pawns in a strategic battle in the Cold War. For the Eritrean people, it was clear that they were fighting for their country, but for the leadership, it was a game; they knew the real relationship between the revolution and the U.S. government. The leaders of the revolutionary movement used patriotism and nationalistic rhetoric to emotionally charge up the masses, while concealing their true intentions and connections with the U.S.

By then, many Eritreans who were active in the independence movement began to get discouraged. It was hard to stay in Eritrea once they realized what was happening to the country. There was a shortage of jobs and of food. Restrictions on movement, including a 6 pm curfew (before sunset!) and a lack of electricity at night made the people feel like prisoners. So people were starting to leave Eritrea. At that time, the only viable option for emigration was Khartoum, Sudan – and that was where I went first, with many of my brothers. Immigrants, especially refugees, go to whichever country opens its doors to them at the time – it is unpredictable and outside of their control. The flow of immigration is directly connected to the policies of the countries they go to.

When I came here, the U.S. was not accepting many Eritrean refugees, but they were open to Ethiopians fleeing the socialist government. I came as a student and I had family connections here. Once I came as a student, my request for political asylum was rejected, and I was not entitled to pay in-state fees for my tuition. So I had to get a job to pay for school in order to stay in the U.S. under a student visa. Yet, with a student visa it was difficult to find a well-paying job, because I did not have a green card or resident status.

Encountering the African American Experience in the U.S.

By now, I felt like an immigrant, trying to make a new life in the U.S. I was new to the culture and even to the immigrant mindset. I did not know anything about African American culture and history. Sometimes whites and Hispanics treated me as African American, and sometimes I would be treated as a different kind of Black, because I was an immigrant. Once I became established here, I began to be active in progressive economic groups, and generally was accepted by the whites in these groups perhaps because of my education or my politics. I also have found out that many white working class people here are humanist; race is not an issue for them. I met many African Americans when I was working for the Housing Authority of New Haven, CT, and when I was working in the restaurant business. They had respect for me but the relationships were more work-related.

For our own sake, we, as Black immigrants, need to develop a relationship with the African American community. We need to learn about the African American experience, and about their struggle against racism in this country, in order to appreciate and value it, because we, the new Blacks, are often the beneficiaries of their struggle.

One of the things that I see happening within my own community of first-generation immigrants is that they came here and got jobs as token Blacks. They do not question what the companies that employ them do, or what the government does, as long as they benefit. We African immigrants count as African Americans in affirmative action statistics, but we do not represent the true African American experience. In a sense, we are being used to achieve racial diversity, but because we want to succeed in this society, we are timid about questioning it. But there is a cost to this timidity. I may not feel that I am an African American, but my children will feel that they are African Americans, and will be treated as such. I still reflect my country of origin, Eritrea – I am first-generation, and still my culture is in me – but my children, my grandchildren, born here, they will be truly African American. If we do not tell them about the true experience of African Americans – how they were treated unequally, and how they fought in order to create new a social structure – and if we do not participate in anti-racist, immigrant rights, and other economic justice struggles, we will not be able to be good role models for our children, showing them how to bring justice and equality to the United States.

Just as it is my responsibility to educate my children about how, as Blacks, we came to be free and enjoy the freedom in this country, it is also equally important for me to reflect on the country I left, Eritrea. Being educated here and staying here, I feel I left a vacuum back home. At a minimum, I need expose the injustice there, and its toll on the Eritrean people. In Eritrea, which is now "free," the leaders of the revolution did not bring democracy; they did not bring anything to the country, except for misery. The leaders of the Eritrean government drove out the intellectuals, because they understood the danger of intellectual freedom that allows students to organize and radicalize. They brought in teachers from other countries, such as India; teachers who do not participate in national politics. These foreign teachers cannot serve as a model for their students, because they do not share the same national, political, and economic interests. After disempowering the students by not allowing them to get teaching jobs, the government took a step further and even closed the university. They have kept the whole country in the dark. In contrast, in Ethiopia, many Ethiopians teach at the university, and the students and teachers always talk politics and are constantly opposing the government. This is one of the differences between the Eritrean and the Ethiopian governments.

Both the Ethiopian and Eritrean governments are open to neoliberal capitalism. They receive funds from the World Bank. They adopt policies that the United States supports. They want to bring multinational corporations into the country, rather than foster a national economy. Right now, we are witnessing that Ethiopian troops are fighting in Somalia in order to protect U.S. interests. The Ethiopian leaders are serving the interests of the U.S., rather than those of the Ethiopian people. It is very sad scenario.

Opening up the Discussion: Immigrants and Globalization

I really want immigrants to understand the bigger picture of how globalization is impacting our lives. I do not think anybody would want to move from their homeland and come to a strange country. Like many immigrants, this kind of life was forced on me. The forces of globalization were working on me personally, but I did not understand it at the time. When I came to the Eritrean community in Washington, D.C., I saw that they were trying to recreate their own culture in that place. Yet this culture is very removed from Ethiopia or Eritrea. Whatever they do, it cannot be the same as "back home." In order to understand where you are, you need to understand both where you came from, and the culture you came to. That means, we need to know about African American culture and their experience – our experience is akin to theirs – and eventually, we are them.

Enough about me, I am going to stop there. But I would like to hear about everyone, and about what brought you to this workshop, or to this country. If you are not here as a first-generation immigrant, what brought your parents or your grandparents here? I think if we share insights from our own migration experiences, it would help us to understand the sources of discrimination against us, as immigrants. Everyone came here for a different reason, and I would like to know what that is, and that is why I have shared mine. Let's go around the room and tell us your experience or your families' experiences as they arrived to the United States.

A second question I would like you to address is whether you and your families, as immigrants, have faced the same sort of problems as many people of color are facing here. How would you compare their experiences here with the experiences of people of color in the U.S.?

Discussion: Voices of a New Immigrant Generation

On Reasons for Attending the Session

Audience Member 1:
I personally, through my work in higher education, interact with a lot of African students and teachers, and I think that sometimes we don't understand, as African Americans, how they've migrated, and their experiences. There's a lot of ignorance, a lot of stereotypical ideas about who they are and what they represent, and this session provides a different perspective of the "new" immigrant.

About the issue of illegal immigration, I think, like anything, you need regulation. I don't really want to get into my feelings too much, but I do believe that regulation is the key, and informing people as to what's going on, what are the issues that we're really dealing with, what is the effect on Americans, and what is the effect on me personally.

Audience Member 2:
I came here mainly to learn about the connection between immigration, globalization, and organizing for the rights of people – solidarity and economic justice – because I think people come here because they leave poverty or injustice, and I

think there is a real connection between immigration and these issues. We are all in this together, and it is a question how we resolve these issues. It makes me very happy to see other people who are dedicated in a very real way to trying to work it out and to listen.

Audience Member 3:
I am here because immigrants are what built this country up. Ever since 1795, the Naturalization Act, there have been so many reforms and acts against immigrants and refugees, and this hostility does not make any sense.

On the Connections Between Immigration and Globalization

Audience Member 4:
I did some legal observing with a group that organizes day laborers, and the people that I met, doing that, were from all over the place. It made rhetoric around immigration seem really stupid and shallow. Obviously globalization is deeply tied to immigration, and I think there is a real discussion to be had about these issues in the U.S., but we're so far away from having it in this country. It is really disappointing.

Audience Member 5:
Where I live, in Iowa, I'm part of an Immigration Coalition. Of course, the issue in our part of the country is more with Mexican immigrants, but immigration is a global issue, and many nations where the economies are going relatively well are experiencing it. Europe is experiencing it. Australia is experiencing it. This is a global phenomenon.

As it relates to the United States, one of the reasons why immigration is such a controversial issue is because of race. There are many European or white Americans who still see this country as a white homeland. When they see immigrants who are darker, they see them as a threat. The notion of being overrun is very strong in this country. This is what I believe is stimulating anti-immigration fervor in this country. We are a nation of immigrants, yet a lot of it depends on the skin color of the immigrant. Those who are opposed to the anti-immigration movement have got to talk about race and stop beating around the bush. We are dealing with people who are racist, and they are trying to use non-racist language, because overtly racist language is no longer seen as politically acceptable. So they are using everything but the racial pejoratives to rile up the "white masses" against what they see as an "invasion."

Julie Matthaei:
Your point about race is really important. Americans have to wise up, understand the big picture, and not allow ourselves to be divided and manipulated by racist ideology. The race card has been played every time there is a recession, every time there is unemployment. The powers that be use the media to blame immigrants and people of color; they play the race card and say, "The reason why low wages and poverty exists, the reason why there is unemployment, is because of these immigrants." In the 1930s, Mexican citizens who had grown up in this country were deported and their land was taken. In earlier times, it was the Chinese. So we really have to get smart, and come together with people all around the world to work towards a better economy. This is what is entailed in global citizenship.

If firms can take their capital anywhere in the world, and move to the cheapest place—somewhere with no environmental or labor regulations—then we ought to be able to move around too. We need to support the rights of working people around the world, and try to move, gradually, towards increasing the standard of living and rights of everybody. We have to globalize our movement. That is what is so good about the Forum movement – it's a global movement. Our welfare state, our social safety net, has been destroyed in this country – destroyed for everybody. It is not just the immigrants who use the safety net, it is white people, it is middle class people. Most of us are one job away from being poor, and firms have now less and less loyalty to their workers. But we are getting smart. We are realizing that, in order to wrest power back from the corporate elite, we have got to unite. And to be able to unite, we have got to fight our racism and nationalism and ethnocentrism and religious bigotry. One key way to do this is to learn about each other, learn one another's stories, as we are doing here today.

Emily:
The story of Eritrea—of dictators and coups and U.S. intervention—is also the story of Latin America, and so many other countries around the world. My mother is a Guatemalan immigrant. She came here in 1979, and gradually all of her family has come here too. Some of them are illegal, some are legal, but basically they are like every other immigrant to this country. I think it is foolish to say that illegal immigrants are criminals because they fled from U.S. intervention in their own country. They came here because of bad government and poverty.

I have cousins that came to the U.S. when they were really young, but they are not considered citizens, and they can not work normal jobs because they do not have documentation. They will never attain citizenship, but their children are citizens. They are in this limbo of never really being able to fully provide for their family, and they can not maximize their potential.

On Immigrants as "Other"

Fred Matthaei:
My grandfather came her from Germany back in the 1880s as a kid, and worked his way up – he had to work in a grocery store, drove wagons, became a butcher, and started a small store. So I am third generation, but I am an immigrant. During the First World War, the German community in Detroit was ostracized, just like the Eritrean community in New Haven. They were set on, they were put aside, because the United States was fighting Germany. They were citizens at that time, but they were German. Then when I was in high school, during the Second World War, it was the Japanese and the Asians. I witnessed how the Asians were ostracized, or kept different, or treated as immigrants.

So now we have got people coming in from different countries and the newest people on board are the ones everybody is afraid of. On the other hand, I think there's growing resistance to that attitude; you know, we are all here together, we have so many opportunities here. If we get together, and talk to other communities, we can make it work.

John:
I am from the Boston May Day Coalition and the Industrial Workers of the World, and we came down from Boston to participate the immigrant rights talks and workshops here at the US Social Forum. Perhaps rather than calling the U.S. the land of immigrants, you should call us the land of refugees. My family was from Scotland, and was kicked off their land and sent here in the late 1700s. The Irish were chased out after the Civil War they had with England. The words "immigrant" and "refugee" were created to make distinctions between groups; again, that is another clever tactic. But there is a long history of documented and undocumented people organizing together to fight back, so that is the one thing that we can draw on, moving forward into the future, that can make real change in society. Let's go back to the 1900s, incredible struggles in Lawrence, Massachusetts, for instance, or in McKees Rocks, Pennsylvania, or in California with migrant farm workers, where people from fifteen or twenty backgrounds came together and tried to make the world a better place. That is the positive thing that we can see in this land of refugees here.

Kristin:
Hi, I am Kristin. I am from Chicago, and I work for a national organization called Interfaith Worker Justice (www.iwj.org). We do a lot of organizing in

faith communities, particularly around work justice issues, and obviously right now the immigrant worker issue is huge. What is intriguing to me, and what is concerning to me, is that I can not tell you how many people in "Middle America" think that the word "immigrant" is synonymous with "terrorist," with "the other." There is a reason why we have been unable to get any sort of good immigration reform on the table, despite the fact that all the statistics, all the polls, say that the majority of the people in this country want some sort of immigration reform. I think it is so tragic, because I continue to have conversations with "nice religious folk" who are fine on a whole bunch of justice issues until they get to immigration.

I think part of that is a racial issue; I think part of it is that people are really unable to connect with what they see as "the other." Despite the fact that we are a country of immigrants, except for the native American folk who I guess are long, long-term immigrants, we can not get beyond our primary values of wanting security.

When I spoke at the National Convention of Unitarian Universalists last week, I was shocked because a number of folks came up to me to talk about overpopulation and all sorts of incredibly ridiculous things concerning immigration. I thought, "Oh my God, this is one of the more progressive faith denominations out there, and they are still really grappling with how to understand that we are all connected, and that there is space for all of us at the table. What are we going to do about the rest of the folks, the rest of 'Middle America'?" I feel like we are really good at talking to each other in this room, because we all agree that we are all connected and that we need to fight for justice for all immigrants, and yet, how do we get this message to the broader population?

Recently, Interfaith Worker Justice came out with a booklet called *"For you were once a Stranger: Immigration in the U.S. through the Lens of Faith."* It is a hundred page booklet; about half of it is immigrant stories, statistics, and resources that people can use, and the other half is stories about what different organizations are doing around the country, and scriptural references from all the different faith denominations and texts.

Jesse:
My name is Jesse, and I am a student from South Carolina. Unfortunately, many people there are, like you were saying, nice religious conservative white folk, and a lot of my family members are even that way. My grandmother just recently told me that she asked her yard worker if he had a green card. So I want to learn as much as I can, because I know I am from a place, and I am connected to a place, that has a lot of racism, and many of awful things going on, and a lot of

ignorance. I want to be able to combat that in some way. I want to help, because I am really afraid for all of these people, and I want to do something to help them, because you see it over and over again throughout history, people being oppressed, and I do not want it to happen again.

Tim:
My name is Tim from Tulsa, Oklahoma. All of this is very new to me. I was in a bubble, and the bubble recently burst. I have dedicated my own resources to building a media company, with the hopes of bringing this center-stage. That's why we are here videoing the session. We feel like this is our role and responsibility in these endeavors.

We have actually created a media-screening environment on the Internet called www.culturalcreatives.tv. So we will pop up most anywhere, gathering information, documenting things, and making them available to raise consciousness. I see the solution as being primarily of a spiritual nature: we have to evolve past this notion of separatism, because we are all one whether we realize it or not. So I think that there needs to be some effort to raise the consciousness of people, particularly of Americans. By that, I mean actually exposing and really looking at our value system, because all of our decisions and notions and beliefs grow out of that.

On their Personal Stories of Organizing from Immigrants' Rights

Abdulla:
My name is Abdulla, and one way to get the message out for the immigrant community is to get progressive media involved. It is really unfortunate to see how progressive media has failed many immigrant communities and also progressive-minded people. I work with a group in New York; we go to organizations such as the ones represented in this room, and teach them how to do media. We teach them because the mainstream media is not coming to them, which obviously no one should expect. We teach them so that they can report on what is going on in other communities. For instance in New York, we are doing some work with groups of street vendors. They are mainly people from the West Indies and Africa and Asia, but also people from here in the U.S. We also work with groups of cab drivers, with domestic workers, and with construction workers. We train them to do media, and some activists have even been able to file stories at a local radio station.

Audience Member 7:
I am an immigrant; I am from New York; and I am a youth producer from the Global Action Project (www.global-action.org). African Americans say "these

immigrants have just come here, and they are so different from us." But we have so much in common. African Americans who were brought here as slaves in chains, and the chains that these new immigrants have, they are not obvious, but they are there. Immigrants to the U.S. do not leave home because they want to leave—they are attached to their land and country, just like Americans are.

High-school students from New York come to the Global Action Project, and make videos about these sorts of issues. In one video, they went out on the street and interviewed people in New York. They talked about HR-4037, which was a law that would allow the authorities to deport immigrants after just going up to them in the street and asking for their ID. We asked people in the street, "What rights do you think that undocumented people should have?" We interviewed one lady, and she said, "Well, should they have any?" These people think that immigration does not affect them, but it affects you! It is something real that is happening in your backyard.

This video also talks about the IMF and the World Bank, and how it is all connected to immigration. These institutions always say they are there "to help the poor countries," but in reality they are mainly constructed to make those poor countries even poorer. In my country, Guinea, the land is so rich, they have diamonds, they have gold, and they just found oil there, but the people are so poor, and there is so much corruption. Guineans went to D.C. and they protested, but nobody saw it on the news. The mass media does not show all that they are supposed to show.

Americans think that immigration does not affect them. It does affect you. People who are in this country want to study, and want to go to college and do other things, but if they do not get these opportunities, they end up on the streets. That's why it makes me sick...

Juana:
My name is Juana, and I am part of two groups, POWER, which means People Organizing to Win Employment Rights, and also the Brown Berets from Watsonville, California. I am here to talk about specifically the raids happening in California and all over the U.S. Moving to the U.S. is basically an act of survival for immigrants. People here have called them refugees, but in my group, we call them economic refugees. There are also political and religious reasons for immigration, but basically, it is usually a matter of economic survival.

I do not have a specific answer for how immigrants affect your family and your children, because that is very situational. However, I can say how the third-world countries which are sending immigrants to the U.S. impact Americans:

Americans profit off their cheap labor. We like to go to Wal-Mart and buy these really cheap articles, but if you think about how your actions affect people in third-world countries, that is why these people are basically getting paid nothing; that is why these people are losing their jobs in their home countries; that is why these people are coming here.

NAFTA in 1994 opened up the borders for money and investment to flow freely without tariffs, basically setting up factory sweatshops with cheap labor. At the same time in 1994, Operation Gatekeeper in San Diego put up this big border, making people who want to cross the border go around through the desert. We allow a flow of money, but not flow of labor, not the flow of the actual human bodies that produce this labor. We like to get these cheap things but we do not like to see the people doing the labor.

Legislation like HR-4037 criminalizes immigrants for the act of survival, and the people that help them. How does that make sense? School officials, teachers, and priests would not be able to help anymore. Global citizenship, I think it is a great idea, but I think that until we can reach that point, until it becomes an agreement that is set in stone, we really need to address the issues that are impacting our communities, such as the raids.

In Watsonville, California and all over the country, immigrant people are experiencing raids at their workplaces, outside of churches, and in local markets. People are scared to go out. People are afraid to live their lives, to go to work, because they might be taken away and separated from their families.

I came here to share my experience in organizing in California, with the Watsonville Brown Berets and in the Californian network that we have, called MigraWatch (www.migrawatch.org). We have established a network with a hotline number that is posted all over the community. You can call that number, and tell the person who is in charge of that phone, "We heard that immigration raids are happening here, can you go check if that's true?" MigraWatch checks to make sure it is not just someone spreading rumors, so that immigrants are not scared to go into that area. If they find that people there are doing raids, MigraWatch sends people with video cameras there to observe, even though they can not really intervene legally, because a lot of people are experiencing physical abuse at the hands of the authorities. They are getting pinned to the ground; they are being handcuffed; they are being hit; a lot of women are being molested.

Having people observing prevents many of these things from happening. MigraWatch is very local now, but we are trying to spread it out all over California to see how that works. We have started posting our logo up in a lot of businesses.

People in our community know that if they are ever in need, if they see ICE (U.S. Immigration and Customs Enforcement) and they want someone to help them, they can go to this business that has the logo, and they will call somebody. People will network, and call each other to say, "Stay in your houses, don't open the door, you are legally able to stay in your house and you don't have to open the door, unless ICE wants specifically someone in your house." MigraWatch is providing a support system for these people who are very scared.

The most recent thing is that we did is that we made our city a sanctuary city, so that our police and law enforcement will not cooperate with ICE. We also have been trying to get notification laws. People have told us that local law enforcement knows almost a week before any ICE raids because they get notified, but they are not giving this information to people. They know that ICE is going to come, and the damage that that does. So we are trying to get a notification clause through the city council, to get it passed, so that they tell people at least a day in advance, so that people know, to prevent these things from happening.

Rosa:
My name is Rosa, and I am a second-generation immigrant. My parents came from El Salvador during the U.S.-backed civil war. My experience is very frustrating, because even though I am a U.S. citizen, and my parents are now either U.S. citizens or permanent residents, we have a lot of family and friends that are currently undocumented. I would like to stress that I personally appreciate when people say "undocumented immigrant," because "illegal" has this connotation that a human being has the possibility of being illegal, and that is just impossible.

I am from Colombia Heights, which is in Washington, D.C., and we are a very heavily Salvadoran and Mexican populated area. I am here as a representative of the FMLN D.C. Chapter, which is a leftist political party in El Salvador, and as a member of the D.C. Committee for Immigrant Rights. Right now, we are trying as a committee to have D.C. declared a sanctuary city. Currently we have weekly vigils at a well-known community park every Friday. We encourage families from the community to come out if they have received deportation notices, or if they have had some sort of confrontation with police, or with ICE – to come talk to us, so that we can connect them with the different resources in our community.

It is frustrating how incredibly easy it is for people in this country to forget their history, and how things just keep repeating. We are all immigrants. This is something so important, and I don't understand how people miss sight of it. I also do not understand the huge lack of accountability, not just by this government, but by its citizens, because they do not know what their government is doing in their name. It is infuriating how the topic of immigration is talked about in

Congress like it is a domestic issue, like it is a separate issue not connected to anything else. This creates this illusion that this is a simple issue. But that is not the case; immigration is connected to many issues.

When people ask me, "Why do these people come here?" or, "Why do they deserve rights that we are working towards with our tax dollars?" first I say that human beings are human beings and human rights are human rights. Everyone deserves them. It does not matter if you have a piece of paper or not. Secondly I say, there is no real domestic solution to the immigration problem, because as long as the U.S. keeps its foreign policy as it is now, people are going to flee their countries. There is this lack of understanding of the fact that people do not want to leave their homes, that people do not want to leave their families to come to a place that they know nothing about – or if they do know about it, they know horrible things about it – they know that it is actually accountable for the reasons why they are coming here. They do it, they sacrifice for their families. I know that personally, each person has to have sacrificed something for their family or for their friends, so I do not understand this inability to connect on a human level. It boggles my mind.

Then we are being even more confused by the different proposals about "comprehensive" immigration reform. People who do not really know, but so very much want to help, are very easily misguided. I say, listen, if you are being proposed something, being told about a "comprehensive" immigration reform, pay attention to who is presenting it, because a proposal from a labor union is going to be completely different from a proposal from an immigrant rights organization, because there are vested interests that you do not know about.

All of these issues are embedded in the immigration reform discussions, and I guess my question would be, "What's the next step?" On a grassroots level, we are doing what we can; in each community, they're doing what they can. What's the next step? How do we connect all these communities? How do we make a bigger stronger movement towards justice for these communities?

Viviana:
My name is Viviana, and I work with an organization in California called TIGRA (the Transnational Institute for Grassroots Research and Action, www.transnationalaction.org). We are an immigrant rights organization. It was interesting coming to this workshop because of the economic justice focus that you gave to the conversation. That is very much what we focus on at TIGRA, because we believe that economic justice is the next frontier in immigrant rights work.

Rosa, thank you so much for posing the question: what it is that we do next? What is it that we can do because we are doing everything can we can do at the grassroots level? That is very much what TIGRA has set out to do. When we started the organization, we thought for a long time about what is going on right now in the world with globalization. Everything has been taken over by corporations, and corporations are able to set the agenda for how governments interact with each other.

Now we see more and more mass migration all over the world. I believe that over the last year, something like 300 million people around the world were migrants, and that is not even counting internal refugees – meaning people being displaced inside their own countries from the countryside to the towns, etc. This number is projected to grow. We need to start looking at migration from a global perspective. We have a constituency that is global, and that feels and sees itself as global. I actually grew up in Argentina myself; we came to the United States as political refugees a long time ago already, in the late 1970s. I have always said that I have a foot in another country. My family is there, and all my interests and my passions.

Migrants all over the world are expressing their love for their communities in the same way, because they keep sending money home to their families. It is that money that people are sending home which is one point of unity for all migrant communities – be they Latino, or African, or Asian. It is one thing that unites us all, and one issue that we can all work on together. It is that money which is being sent home that has become an alternative economy that is global. That is one thing that migrant communities have not realized yet: that we have a lot of economic power.

Migration is expected to grow more and more, at something like 30% per year. Even as we focus within the United States on keeping people from coming in, countries from all over the world are coming to the UN and to the WTO, and saying that their economic strategy for the next ten years is to grow their emigration, so that more people will send money home. They want to use that money for infrastructure development, for building roads, building schools, fixing up churches. So that is the strategy of these countries: to grow migration while here we are trying to keep them out.

TIGRA is focusing our attention on remittances. We are building "million-dollar clubs" all over the United States. We are working in about ten cities right now, and we are having people fill out a survey in order to gain consciousness of how much money they are sending home, because sending money home to your family is a very individual act, but it signifies the love and commitment that you have to your family. Even as little as 400 people, when you add up how much money they are all sending home, it adds up to a million dollars. That is why we're forming million-dollar clubs, so people can feel like they are millionaires.

The numbers are staggering for remittances. Last year alone, $260 billion was sent around the world. For some countries, like El Salvador, the amount of remittances for last year alone surpasses the amount of foreign aid that the country received in the last ten years. This is money that is being sent from people only earning $5 an hour, or even less sometimes, working sometimes with no rights. What we have also seen is that the fees that people pay to the companies to send their money home are incredibly high. Western Union, which is the biggest remittance company, made $400 billion. They charge $15 to $25, sometimes even more, while it costs them $2.50 to send that transfer. They are making incredible amounts of money, and they have absolutely no regulation. In the United States, there is a law called the Community Reinvestment Act that was passed by communities coming together and saying, no, banks can not just make profits, they have to invest in the communities that they have businesses in. That is why you are able to get a loan to buy a car or to buy a house—you used to not be able to do that from a bank. All of that is through this law that is in place, but these money transfer companies are not regulated by the same law. Yet they are located in the poorest neighborhoods, where there are no banks, so they are the banking industry of our immigrant community.

The focus of TIGRA is to make these money transfer companies accountable to our communities. We are not saying that people should not to use the companies. They have to use them, especially the biggest ones like Western Union, because Western Union is like Coca-Cola: it is everywhere. You see them in the smallest most remote towns. They are providing an important service, but what we are saying is that they need to be accountable.

Discussion Summary and Conclusion

As I hear the people from all walks of life speak in this workshop, they quest for fair immigration reform. White, immigrant, or Black, they recognize the correlation between the U.S foreign policy and immigration issues. Until the U.S. plays the role of an honest broker all over the world, promoting democracy and economic justice instead of grooming dictators, we will see a continuous flow of immigrants coming into the United States. The U.S. needs to stand for justice and peace around the world – that would be the first step to take in resolving immigration issues, rather than building walls and prisons.

11

Just Between Us: Women in Struggle in Africa and the African Diaspora

Rose M. Brewer

Rose M. Brewer defines herself as a scholar-activist. She has been a Professor of African American & African Studies at the University of Minnesota-Twin Cities for over fifteen years. She has been a member of the board of Project South: Institute for the Elimination of Poverty and Genocide, a past board member of member of United for a Fair Economy, and a founding member and current member of the National Council of the Black Radical Congress. Her involvement in the U.S. Social Forum was fueled by a long-term commitment to fundamental social transformation in this country and globally. It represents another phase of her involvement in the Black Freedom Struggle, continuing a legacy of study and struggle. As a university professor and activist, Rose's commitment to social change is a matter of radical vision and action. It is a matter of legacy, and an imperative. At core for her is acting in concert with women of Africa and the African diaspora to transform our lives, creating a new order. This commitment is forged by her history and her present. She must do this work because her life depends upon it.

There was clearly a moment when lifting up the visibility of the women of Africa and the African diaspora seemed self-evident for some of the member organizations of Grassroots Global Justice; when we were preparing to go to Nairobi, Kenya for the 7th World Social Forum in January 2007. If earlier forums in Brazil, India and Venezuela gave little attention to race and gender - Black women's struggles - surely Nairobi would be a space where the women of Africa and the African diaspora could come together and be featured front and center. It turned out not to be that easy. Even on the African continent, the idea that Black women must be connected transnationally and engaged in struggle across borders was poorly understood. Our workshop in Kenya was given a bad time; it was scheduled against the Women's Court! We ended up with only a handful of attendees.

It was clear to us that we must try again at the U.S. Social Forum in Atlanta, Georgia, slated for late June 2007. Our workshop was accepted for the USSF, and this time our efforts were met with a substantially more positive response: nearly 50 were in attendance (mainly women). Not all the attendees were of African descent but the great majority were, and many were involved in struggles for social change. Activists came from across the United States, the Caribbean and Africa. Nearly all were involved in Black and nonblack women's struggles around economic justice, sexual violence, AIDS and women, education and schooling, working closely with women on the ground. It was very gratifying to have quite young women in the room, between the ages of 15 and 18, who were active in AIDS work in the AIDS Housing Network in New York.

We shared those struggles and fight-back efforts in the workshop by listening and being in dialogue with one another. The workshop itself was collaboration among Grassroots Global Justice, The AIDS Housing Network, Southern Anti-racism Network and a Kenyan organization, Akili Dada. The women representing these organizations facilitated and centered the workshop on three key questions: When did you first become involved in the struggle for African and African diasporic women's struggles (or struggle for women's rights and justice generally)? What are some of the key issues confronting women of Africa and the African diaspora today? And, how must the struggle continue? Because it was clear to us that identifying and locating Black women structurally in this era of corporate globalization and neoliberalism was critical, we dialogued about the current political moment and locating Black women within it. Thus the remainder of this essay will focus heavily on the structural context of African and African diasporic women's lives in this political moment, and conclude with some reflections from the workshop on the question of resistance and how resistance is/must occur among women of Africa and the African diaspora. All of us agreed that women of Africa and the African diaspora are profoundly impacted by the social and political forces of race, class, gender, imperialism, and neoliberal state polices, corporate globalization, and repression today. It was also a source of frustration for us that Black women are often missing from political conceptualizations and left analyses analysis (except as asides). This needs to change. Black women globally need to be centered in our analyses of the current political moment. Thus some time was spent identifying and locating Black women structurally in this period of neoliberalism and transnational capital.

The Current Political Moment: Women of Africa and the African Diaspora in Struggle

African and African diasporic women must be understood in complex ways and within a historical and comparative framework. Moreover, this means that women of African descent can be studied from a shared cultural, political, economic, and social framework in the midst of tremendous national diversity. Africans have long moved from the continent to other parts of the globe since ancient times but, the last 500 years have been rooted in enslavement, colonialism and imperialism that has crafted what we think of today as the African diaspora. These violent disruptions and destruction of African peoples were always met with intense resistance. The self-determining move of articulating and rendering visible the interconnection of global African peoples is, indeed, a resistive move. Thus, the dispersal as well as linkages and interconnections are the core ideas that should be drawn upon in utilizing an African diaspora framework. But the framework must be given political potency through a movement-building lens. Just to assert an African diaspora is not enough. The struggle for Black women's lives must be built intentionally, strategically and transnationally.

Clearly the policies of the IMF, World Bank and international trade polices in the global South have hit African diaspora women and those on the African continent hard. Within the global North, and the U.S. in particular, dismantling the social welfare state, the criminalization of Black women's lives and the assault on Black women's bodies are core realities. Wealth is highly concentrated globally, on the Continent, and in the diaspora, and Black women are some of the poorest people on the face of the earth.

The expropriation of human and material resources continues pretty much unabated in this new era of "Empire." Wars and conflict in countries such as Somalia, and political corruption across the African Continent have also generated human suffering and chaos. These realities are certainly precipitated and shaped by the new imperialism of the U.S. Countries on the Continent have been hard hit by debt, privatization, and the neoliberal and structural adjustment policies put into place by the IMF, World Bank, and the International Monetary fund.

These are the institutions organized by global capital. In this context the economic and political plight of African and African diasporic women remains harsh. Economic exclusion continues. Health, HIV-AIDS, land, girls' education, women's rights, sexual and child labor, control of water and resources, among other things, are some of the burning issues confronting Black women. Indeed, these issues were front and center in the discussions at the workshop.

The legacy of colonialism continues on the Continent. The persistence of racism and white supremacy in the context of patriarchy and sexism are the global systems that mark women of Africa and the African diaspora. The face of imperialism is still raced but many of the elite beneficiaries are indigenous to the cultures. This sector represents a class integrated into the logic of transnational capital for the benefit of the capital and their own wealth accumulation. The South African post-apartheid neoliberal agenda is a case in point.[1]

The consequence of this "new world order" is that the "200 richest people in the world have wealth of over $1 trillion. This is greater than the combined income of 41% of the world's people This also means that 1.3 billion people live on less than $1 a day."[2] These practices, operating in conjunction with neoliberalism and privatization, are at the crux of the current political dynamic.

The global South is pressed into policies which destroy the social wage and structure nations to operate in the interest of maximizing transnational profits. Structural adjustment has been the key tool of the International Monetary Fund to accomplish this agenda. It is only recently acknowledged widely that these policies haven't worked (as though they were ever meant to work).[3]

Nonetheless, capital is organized. The transnationals are supranational entities with their own laws often transcending those of any particular nation state. Imperial globalization may not be new, but the degree of transnational integration is a shift. Thus transnational trade agreements such as AGORA (African Growth and Opportunity Act), NAFTA (North American Free Trade Agreement) and The General Agreement on Tariffs and Trade (GATT) are the tools for the integration into the global system of national economies.

Given this 21st-century reality, it is fact that many sectors of the Black women in the United States, the Caribbean, Europe, Africa, and the diaspora in general are in social, economic, and political crises. In advanced Western capitalist societies such as the U.S., the dismantling of the social wage–destruction of social welfare state supports which reach the poorest women and children, a disproportionate percentage of whom are Black–is part and parcel of global restructuring and privatization.[4]

These processes in the economically dominant North are mirror-imaged in the South through the policies of the International Monetary Fund (IMF) and World Bank. Accordingly, race and class are deeply enmeshed in gender, sexuality and nation, simultaneously shaping and being constructed by political economy and ideology.[5] This means that the current situation for African women and women of the African diaspora reflects the 21st-century realities of corporate globalization and neoliberalism. The impact of these policies for Black women throughout the diaspora is the shared fate of poverty, racism, oppression and exploitation. Five hundred years of the economic underdevelopment of African women by enslavement, colonialism, imperialism, and capitalism is expressed today in the new imperialism of transnationalism and articulated ideologically in the cultural commoditization of Blackness–stereotyped and vilified in the new international division of labor.

Given this, we must be very clear that the problems of women of African descent have never been simply the expression of class exploitation, but are deeply conditioned by racial practices and gender ideologies. The systems of race/class/gender history are deeply interconnected and relational-they are profoundly shaped by one another. This means that racism is redefined in the context of the changed political economy of advanced capitalism. Advanced capitalism continues to be shaped by racism where the poorest people on the face of the earth are Black, young, female children. This social reality is expressed as a set of complex social relations involving multiple sites of oppressions.[6]

It is within this conceptual frame of multiplicity of oppression that the continuation of Black women's exclusion, economic exploitation, and violation must be understood in the current period. At the center of the global economy are women whose labor is used to enrich small economic elites, but who also do the socially reproductive work of the world –cleaning, cooking, caring—the unpaid labor and super-exploitation that goes unnamed and unrecognized. This socially necessary work is central to the labor exploitation of the international division of labor. It is a sexual division of labor.[7] In its public and cultural expression, the African woman's incorporation into the logic of transnational capital too often means the disruption of the traditional female informal economic sectors.

In Senegal, for example, the women's market has been heavily destabilized by structural adjustment demands of the IMF. As these women's economic networks are destroyed so are the foundations of communal life–communities with some degree of economic and cultural autonomy. So, too, often destroyed is the spiritual and social glue of life, of possibility for whole communities of African descent peoples. Networks of Black women have been central to this community construction. Significantly under conditions of transnational patriarchy, women are expected to perform unpaid labor in the home and be intensely exploited in the labor force.

Economy and state in the global South and North are reflected today in the integration of conservative and liberal state practices–neoliberal state practices in the U.S. This signals a move to the right strikingly expressed in the "dismantling of welfare as we know it" – as stated by Bill Clinton – when he signed welfare reform into law in 1996. These welfare-to-work policies, predicated on the heavy vilification of African American women, forces work under the onerous conditions of low pay and persistent poverty – even as women work fulltime.

Thus, the neoliberalism of the global order is reflected in microcosm within U.S. state decision-making and the locating of African American women and men within the political economy as expendable labor.[8] It also means that tens of millions American children, women and men have no health insurance in this country. For women being forced to work, it means, in most states, no Medicaid, no housing subsidies and no child care. These women have been made to work for their poverty.[9] The destruction of the public sector and social wage have placed a large number of Black women at the center of wage exploitation in the interest of private capital.

Nonetheless, the class structure of the Black population in the U.S. is complicated. The middle classes have grown in the post Civil Rights era, but appear quite vulnerable given the shrinkage of the public sector. Even still, notable is the growth of a Black managerial-professional class which appears to be much less race identified, much less centered in ethnic alliances and who are located in the conservative political, economical and academic circles of this country. As political power brokers they go against the will and energies of a good many African-American people. Condoleezza Rice and Clarence Thomas come to mind.

Having said that, we also know that these structural realities have hit young Blacks in the U.S. very hard. This generation of 16-to-24 year old young women has been born under the rules of capitalism, and a reconstituted racism which is coded "colorblind." So the struggle for work and meaning is on for these young women. They enter a formal economy of mainly low-paid service work or no work. This lack of formal work has contributed to their growing participation in the informal sexual services economy, an economy inhabited by female, male, straight, gay, lesbian and bisexual youth. This trafficking in sex is, of course, global in the diaspora. Nonetheless, it is young women who are heavily exploited, even enslaved into sex slavery. The social, health and economic realities that these women face is most powerfully seen in the AIDS epidemic affecting Black life in the U.S., the Caribbean and on the Continent.

Women across the diaspora are used as exceedingly low paid labor in the context of incarceration and the growth of the prison industrial complex. In the U.S., for example, the privatization of prisons and use of prison labor means that African American women are increasingly caught in its snare. Their numbers are increasing more quickly than the Black male population. In fact, crime is down overall but sentencing and drug policies that target nonviolent crimes have fueled the bulk of the growth in mass incarceration matched by the growth in the private prison and the development of prisons for profit.[10] So whether in Africa, the Caribbean or the U.S., violence, coercion, incarceration and the police state are used to manage these inequalities. This is the political moment and framework embraced by the workshop attendees.

Women of Africa and the African Diaspora in Struggle: The Fight Back

A central piece of the fight back is organizing and educating, and our workshop highlighted the work of Akili Dada, an organization providing scholarships to poor girls for secondary education. Akili Dada intentionally targets girls who are most likely to lack access to secondary education. Its founder, Wanjiru Kamau, facilitated this discussion. The important work of Akili Dada in advancing educational opportunities for poor Kenyan girls was lifted up as a concrete example of how African women are resisting the forces of exclusion and inequality. Rural girls often end their education at eight or nine years of age. Wanjiru emphasized that literacy is absolutely a key piece to the tools that need to be in place to build consciousness for political struggle. This is imperative on the Continent where too few African girls get access to education beyond the first few grades.

Other women spoke of a broad range of fight-back efforts: labor organizing, protests, rebellion, and cultural resistance in music, art, dress, stance and attitude. These are also sites of class, race, and gender and sexuality struggles, but also, resistance to state impositions, male domination and heterosexual privilege. In turn, these fights have the potential to reshape state/economy/cultural practices. Indeed, Black women's struggles and resistance must be considered an essential element in the transformational possibilities of the current period. We need to organize ourselves by building networks and in so doing, create a force which speaks more powerfully to the international community than we can as individuals. We must organize beyond our local communities and transnationally across Africa and the African diaspora. This sentiment was expressed loudly and clearly by the participants in the workshop.

Why Now? This call to organizing reflects the crisis of the current moment. The social forum movement globally and in the U.S., in particular, expresses several new and old moves:

1. It concretely articulates an anti-sexist, anti-racist, anti-imperialist, anti-capitalist and anti-homophobic politics.

2. It is yet to be but must be centrally concerned with a radical political economic critique of transnational capitalism, white supremacy and patriarchy and its impact on African peoples, the women of Africa and the African diaspora– those most excluded.

3. The movement connects scholar activists with movement activists and activists- scholars, but not easily.

Nonetheless, it was clear to us that as a space for Black women's struggles, the social forum movement faces the same challenges from within and without as other oppositional efforts historically and many of the dilemmas of left movements in the U.S.:

a. How does such a radical collective cohere?
b. What is our ongoing connection to on the ground struggles?
c. What is the vision of social transformation?

Indeed, these are chilling times for the peoples of Africa and the African diaspora. In the U.S. case, there is a concentrated attack on affirmative action, escalating violence against people of color and anti-Black racism expressed in the Jena Six and the racist symbol of the noose. Indeed this Jena Six story makes visible how quickly Black youth can be can be snared into an aggressive prison-industrial complex which has locked away over one million Black people in a prison population of 2.2 million. Thus the challenge for those of us who believe in freedom is not to embrace but to reconnect to a radical Pan Africanist perspective that understands a complicated global economy, racism and sexism and our deep connection to the multiple struggles of the world's peoples. Past Pan African efforts which go hark back to the movement's turn of the century inception under the leadership of Dr. W.E. B. Dubois offers lessons. Certainly any new movement must center gender. It must articulate a complex diaspora framework of race, class and gender intersectionality.[11] The idea of rebuilding a movement in this country and globally is an imperative. It is work that must be done. On that, we all agreed.

References

Brewer, Rose M. (2004). "A Critical Sociology of African Americans, the U.S. Welfare State, and Neoliberalism in the Era of Corporate Globalization," in Race and Ethnicity-Across Time, Space and Discipline, Rodney Coates (ed.), New York: Brill Publishers, pp.117-131.

Chang, Ha-Joon. (2003, January). "Kicking Away the Ladder: Neoliberals Rewrite History." Monthly Review: 10-15.

Dahms, Harry F. (2000). Transformations of Capitalism: Economy, Society, and the State in Modern Times. New York: New York University Press.

Davis, Angela. (2005). Abolition Democracy: Beyond Empire, Prisons, and Torture. New York: Seven Stories Press.

Desai, Ashwin. (2002). *We Are the Poors: Community Struggles in Post-Apartheid South Africa* New York: Monthly Review Press.

Fusfeld, Daniel R and Timothy Bates. (1984). *The Political Economy of the Urban Ghetto*. Carbondale: Southern Illinois University Press.

Human Rights Watch (1999).World Report. http://www.hrw.org/worldreport99

Kuumba, M. Bahati. (2001). Gender and Social Movments (Gender Lens). Lanham: AltaMira Press

Law, Sylvia A. (1983). "Women, Work, Welfare, and the Preservation of Patriarchy." University of Pennsylvania Law Review.   131:1249-1339. McClintock, Anne. 1995. Imperial Leather. New York: Routledge.

McClintock, Anne. (1995). *Imperial Leather: Race, Gender and Seuality in the Colonial Contest*. New York: Routledge.

Mies, Maria. (1986). *Patriarchy and Accumulation on a World Scale*. London: Zed.

Moody, Kim. (1997). Workers in a Lean World: Unions in the International Economy. London: Verso.

Squires, Gregory. (1994). Capital and Communities in Black and White. Albany: State University of New York Press.

Notes

[1] Ashwin Desai. (2002). *We Are the Poors: Community Struggles in Post-Apatheid South Africa* New York: Monthly Review Press.

[2] Human Rights Watch (1999).World Report. http://www.hrw.org/worldreport99

[3] Ha-Joon Chang. (2003, January). "Kicking Away the Ladder: Neoliberals Rewrite History." Monthly Review: 10-15.

[4] Harry F. Dahms. (2000). Transformations of Capitalism: Economy, Society, and the State in Modern Times. New York: New York University Press.

[5] Anne McClintock. (1995). *Imperial Leather: Race, Gender and Seuality in the Colonial Contest*. New York: Routledge.

[6] Rose M. Brewer. (2004). "A Critical Sociology of African Americans, the U.S. Welfare State, and Neoliberalism in the Era of Corporate Globalization," in *Race and Ethnicity-Across Time, Space and Discipline*, Rodney Coates (ed.), New York: Brill Publishers.

[7] Maria Mies. (1986). *Patriarchy and Accumulation on a World Scale*. London: Zed.

[8] Daniel R. Fusfeld, and Timothy Bates. (1984). *The Political Economy of the Urban Ghetto*. Carbondale: Southern Illinois University Press.

[9] Sylvia A. Law. (1983). "Women, Work, Welfare, and the Preservation of Patriarchy." University of Pennsylvania Law Review. 131:1249-1339.

[10] Angela Davis. (2005). *Abolition Democracy: Beyond Empire, Prisons, and Torture*. New York: Seven Stories Press.

[11] Kuumba, M. Bahati. (2001). Gender and Social Movments (Gender Lens). Lanham: AltaMira Press.

SECTION IV:

BUILDING THE SOLIDARITY ECONOMY THROUGH COOPERATIVES AND SOCIALLY RESPONSIBLE BUSINESS

12
Growing Transformative Businesses

Germai Medhanie, Jessica Gordon Nembhard, Ann Bartz, and Adam Trott

Moderator's Introduction
Germai Medhanie

My name is Germai Medhanie from Guramylay: Growing the Green Economy and TransformationCentral.org. This session focuses on the truth that businesses do not have to be narrowly self-interested and bottom-line-oriented to succeed in our economy. Indeed, green, socially-responsible, community-rooted transformative businesses must play a key role in the building of the solidarity economy. We have invited Jessica Gordon Nembhard, an expert in community-based business development; Ann Bartz, staff person for the Business Alliance for Local Living Economies; and Adam Trott, a worker-owner in the successful worker cooperative, Collective Copies, to speak to you today about their experiences growing transformative businesses.

Community-Based Economic Development
Jessica Gordon Nembhard

Jessica Gordon Nembhard is a political economist and assistant professor in African American Studies at the University of Maryland, College Park. She specializes in the emerging field of democratic community economics, which includes cooperative economic development and community-based asset building, and has published several articles on those subjects. She is completing a book on the history of African American cooperatives, and is co-editor of the book Wealth Accumulation and Communities of Color in the U.S: Current Issues (2006). As a scholar activist Gordon Nembhard is a member of the editorial board of Grassroots Economic Organizing Newsletter; and is a founding member of the U.S. Federation of Worker Cooperatives, The Eastern Conference for Workplace Democracy, and the U.S. Solidarity Economy Network. She is also a board member of The Association of Cooperative Educators, Organizing Neighborhood Equity in DC (ONE DC) community development corporation, and CEJJES Institute.

Overview: Models of Community-Based Economic Development

Community-based businesses are local enterprises that are owned, run, managed, and/or shared by members of the same community – either a geographic community (locational affiliation), or a community of interest (based on cultural, ethnic or economic affiliation). They are elements of the solidarity economy because they exemplify local control, democratic participation, and economic organizing at the grassroots.

Here I will provide some nuts and bolts of community-based business development, focusing on three or four strategies for developing worker-owned and community-owned businesses.

An Example of a Community-Owned Business: Big Wash, a Community-Owned Laundromat.

The founders and shareholders of Big Wash in Washington, D.C. were members of a church choir in the neighborhood. There was no Laundromat close enough, and they needed one on their block. The group pulled together, studied other Laundromat businesses and machinery, and worked with a non-profit to do a feasibility study. They then went door-to-door in their neighborhood, and sold 30 shares of stock for about $100 each. They were able to secure loans for the rest of the enterprise. They opened their own Laundromat in a strip mall in their neighborhood that was owned by a community development corporation (CDC).

CDCs are community-based non-profit organizations that organize to promote the physical and social improvement of low income neighborhoods, particularly the infrastructure, often by owning and developing property. Unfortunately Big Wash had some problems with the CDC. They signed a lease with them, but the CDC followed a commercial development mode, and cared more about their profit margin than about supporting community-owned businesses. As property values increased in the neighborhood through processes of gentrification, the CDC raised the rent. Big Wash sued them once to keep the rent agreed upon in the lease and won. But once their lease expired they could not afford to sign a new lease at the new higher rent, and so had to sell the business to a traditional owner.

When I interviewed one of the founders and owners of Big Wash two years into the enterprise, they had already been written about in the *Washington Post* newspaper. Five points stood out to me from their history and from the interview:

1) Community of interest and need – there was a need for the service, and it was not simply the profit motive that got them going. They wanted to jointly own and share the risk and profits of a business that was needed in their community.

2) Neighborhood based – they saw themselves as a very neighborhood-specific business, and they did not want to franchise, or open another Laundromat. The woman I interviewed asked me, "Why would I do that? If they want one they should open their own!" They did, however, consider writing a manual to help other community groups start their own Laundromat.

3) Business success - Although the original shares were sold for $100, one member sold a share after three years for $600. Other members were able to use their equity to leverage other assets.

4) Spill-over effects – they worked on developing and supporting small connected enterprises: they encouraged someone to sell small boxes of detergent, and bleach, and they allowed some women to run a folding business at the Laundromat. One member even trained himself to repair the washing machines and dryers; he gained a skill and additional employment, and the business saved money.

5) Community ownership and safety – because the community owned the business and residents knew this, they were never broken into. Their storefront had a picture window, for example, without gates or grates over it; and, unlike many other storefront windows in the community, it was never broken. The Laundromat also became a community center of sorts. It had chairs on the side where people could come and meet, and the neighborhood felt welcome and connected to the enterprise.

Models for Cooperative Business Development

There are a variety of start-up models for cooperative businesses. Cooperatives are enterprises owned by the people who use their services, those who formed the company for a particular purpose and are the members of the enterprise, i.e. member-owners. Cooperatives are created to satisfy a need - to provide a quality good or service at an affordable price (that the market is not adequately providing). They are also formed to create an economic structure to engage in needed production or facilitate more equal distribution to compensate for market failure. The International Cooperative Alliance, a nongovernmental association founded in 1895 that represents and serves cooperatives worldwide, defines a cooperative as "an autonomous association of persons united voluntarily to meet their common economic, social, and cultural needs and aspirations through a jointly-owned and democratically-controlled enterprise." Cooperative businesses range in size from small-scale to multi-million dollar companies. Cooperatives are usually classified as consumer-owned, producer-owned, and worker-owned. I focus on worker cooperatives.

Workers form cooperatives to jointly own and manage a business themselves, to save a company that is being sold off, abandoned, or closed down, or to start a company that exemplifies workplace democracy and collective management. Worker-owned businesses offer economic security, income and wealth generation, and democratic economic participation to employees, as well as provide meaningful and decent jobs and environmental sustainability to communities. Here I will discuss three main models for worker-owned cooperative development: the agency-initiated model, the succession/conversion model, and the community of interest initiative model.

1. Agency-Initiated Model

In this model an outside agency or organization starts the cooperative, finds capital, provides training, and then afterwards turns it over to worker-control.

a) A nonprofit or other organization raises money, puts together a feasibility plan, and recruits people to start the business. For instance, I am on the board of a temporary employment services co-op, Enterprising Staffing Solutions in Washington, DC. It was started by a local CDC and a worker ownership technical assistance company; they hired a manager, and used foundation grant money as start-up capital. The co-op's purpose is to create employment continuity for unemployed people who cycle in and out of temporary jobs, that is, to guarantee workers full-time employment in temporary work, or to secure temporary-to-permanent placements for them. The idea is that even if the work is temporary, if a worker continues to work with the company, they will always have a job even if it is not the same one. Ultimately, the mission is to make this employment agency profitable, and then turn it over to the workers. The workers in the agency would be able to buy shares and sit on the board or elect board members. Presently, as the company is developing, it is the community members who sit on the board and work with the manager to run the company. The co-op's other mission is to make temporary service more permanent by actually looking for replacements for the temporary jobs, or by piecing together some temporary jobs that would then make a permanent job with our agency. Again, our mission is to hire and give new employment opportunities to people in a local neighborhood of Washington DC, which has high unemployment levels of Black youth. In this business model, a local community development corporation comes together to raise money to start a new cooperative business. The CDC runs the business until it is more on its feet and then "sells" it to the workers and trains them to run it.

b) An existing co-op or local business creates a development arm and helps initiate new cooperatives. A prime example of this is Arizmendi Bakeries, a for-profit cooperative development cooperative that is partnered with a successful worker-owned bakery, Cheeseboard, to reproduce their model. Again, the original bakery was not interested in the traditional path of franchising a successful business. They were happy with where they were and what they were doing, but they realized that they had a very *innovative* model that was working. The original company, Cheeseboard, is located in the San Francisco Bay Area. Recently, they were named one of the 10 best pizza places in the country by *US News*. Instead of franchising their model in order to expand, however, they instead put 25% of their annual profit into this co-op development initiative, called the Association of Arizmendi Cooperatives. There are three co-op developers who work to reproduce the model of the original bakery. They find a location for the store, recruit employees, and train them. The employees train once a week at the Cheeseboard store, and learn how to make pizza and bread from the original bakers. The development cooperative works with them for a year or two on how to establish their own business, provide training and orientation, as well as manage it. Gradually they turn these new businesses over to the workers. This is a kind of agency-based model, but not exactly the same as the nonprofit model. This is more internal, within the co-op community. Other worker cooperatives that also support replication are Cooperative Home Care Associates in the South Bronx, and ChildSpace in Philadelphia.

c) A franchise or branch store/office creates a new branch. In this case the cooperative actually does create an affiliated second or branch store which uses its name (or derivative), shares resources, and is owned by the first cooperative. Collective Copies in Amherst, MA, with its branch store in Florence, MA, is one example. Many cooperative grocery stores have used this strategy to better serve their members as well as to grow and expand.

As opposed to the replication model (b) above, the branch model does not start a new business entity but expands an existing business to a second or third location, increasing members but maintaining the original ownership. The replication development model uses the first company as the model but a new company is created with new member-owners and a separate charter. In the replication model the development team is usually not even direct members of the original cooperative, though some may once have been members. Rather the team consists of developers who have studied the model, have some autonomous relationship with the original cooperative, and work with members from the original cooperative to recreate the cooperative by creating a new and different business based on the model of the former co-op.

2. Succession, Conversion Model

In successions or conversions, the workers in traditionally-owned businesses show interest in buying and maintaining the company, raising equity either from outside or among themselves. They figure out how they can run it themselves or get themselves trained, sometimes by the original owner. They buy the company from the initial owner and set it up as a cooperative or worker-owned company. There are a variety of different scenarios that can give rise to such a process, some are ESOPs (Employee Stock Ownership Plans) which provide stock ownership for employees and some measure of employee input, depending on the extent of employee ownership; and I focus on worker cooperatives which provide full employee ownership and governance. Worker cooperatives and ESOP are similar but operate under different tax and association laws (I describe a few more of the differences below).

a) The original owner retires or shares ownership. The owner either wants to retire, or is tired of running the business, and so he or she sells the business to the workers, and helps them to be able to buy and run the business. In some succession models, the owner actually stays with the company, provides employees with a financing plan, and works with the employees as one of the worker owners to keep the company going, as at the Little Grill restaurant in Harrisonburg, VA. In most of the conversion models, however, the owner just sells out and moves on, and the workers take over. For example, in the case of Good Vibrations in the Bay Area, a sex toy mail-order company, the original owner got tired of being an owner, and decided to sell her company to the employees, and they started a co-op. For many years it was a very successful worker cooperative. The workers had worked with the former owner to run the company and learn the business, and converted the ownership to a cooperative. These employees actually recently sold out, and all of them made great profits on their shares, and then all moved to lateral positions in other types of businesses.

b) The original owner abandons the business. In the case where the owner(s) actually wants to move the company to another country or to another location – that is to close the current business, and to take the assets and equipment or to sell them off - there is sometimes a chance for the workers to buy the business. The workers join together to petition to buy the company. The conservative version is an Employee Stock Ownership Plan (ESOP) where workers buy stock sometimes as full owners but often only as partial owners and with only minimal representation on the board of directors. Many steel mill conversions have happened this way. ESOPs have increased dramatically over the past 30 years, but the majority of them are not run democratically and employees only own some percentage of the stock, usually not all; and have no real control over the company (the board of directors or management policy).

The more democratic strategy is to buy the company as a worker-owned cooperative or worker-owned democratic corporation with employees owning 100% of the stock, controlling the board of directors, and self-managing or engaging in management-labor teams. This model requires workers to find funding, or finance the buyout through the original owner(s). They may also need technical training about business operations from an outside source. Employees also often need government support to stop the owner from taking all the assets overseas or dismantling the physical capital/inventory before leaving or selling. The worker cooperative version of this model has become known from the publicity about the efforts of Argentinean workers to take over abandoned factories and start worker cooperatives. There are examples here in the U.S. such as Once Again Nut Butter in Nunda, NY. Sometimes the workers cannot buy the existing business but together start a new company doing the same business, such as with the Workers' Owned Sewing Company, Inc., in Windsor, NC, started by some of the workers of Bertie Industries, and a sympathetic farmer, after Bertie shut down in 1979.

c) Worker-ownership is precipitated by a drive for unionization. I call it the union model, although no one else goes by this term. This model is built out of labor activism. It is one of the ways that connects worker co-ops with labor unions. In the 1930s and 40s some progressive labor unions actually started consumer and worker cooperatives. That hasn't happened as much recently, but this model keeps unions and worker-owned businesses in close collaboration. This type of succession or conversion model is illustrated by the histories of Collective Copies in Amherst, MA, or Lusty Ladies in San Francisco. The first step is when the employees decide that they need a union to help them gain rights and better working conditions. They usually do a huge drive; it is usually a long struggle – it can be a one or two-year long process - for better working conditions and unionization. Once the workers actually win the bid for a union and vote to be a union shop, the owners close the company down and attempt to move away because they do not want to operate with unionized workers. In the Collective Copies example, the workers then figured out they could run it themselves. They went through training, capitalization, and self-management. They also engaged the local community by keeping them informed, involving them in the struggle, and using community support both in the struggle for unionization and later as a stable clientele for their copy and printing business. In the Lusty Ladies example, they won the union, but the owners wanted to shut the operation down after that.

The women sex workers joined with the janitors and bought the business to run as a worker cooperative.

3. Community of Interest initiatives

In this model the cooperative actually begins with a group of people who want to work together similar to the Big Wash company. This would be a community of people who want to have meaningful work, who want to work together and who want to start a business. And usually what that means is that they start out with some kind of a study group or an organization model, then talk through what their own talents are, what the needs of their communities are, and come out with a plan of action of what to do to start a business. There are many examples of this. Immigrant women, for example, who figure out that they can cook and cater, clean houses, or sew for a living. They follow a similar pattern of education and training, conducting a feasibility study and writing a business plan, raising money, etc. They then start a small co-op if all goes well. Sometimes they use a non-profit sponsor or developer to help them or to support them.

One example of a community of interest initiative is Equal Exchange in West Bridgewater, MA. They came together with a community of interest in the sphere of fair trade in coffee. They decided that to do fair trade in coffee would require that they cooperate with non-exploitive coffee growers, preferably cooperatives, internationally; and that their own company should be a worker- owned non-exploitive community business. They chose their business model based on the *nature of the business*, because fair trade is a solidarity economy concept. Equal Exchange is now one of the largest worker cooperatives in the U.S. and one of the fastest growing cooperatives, adding tea, chocolate and nuts to their products, and increasing the number of worker owners each year. They are self-managing, run the company by committee and have developed an extensive orientation process for new members. They also educate their consumers on their packaging and through their website.

There are other models of cooperative development for worker- as well as consumer- and producer-owned cooperatives; however these are the major models that tend to be used today particularly for low-income communities. There are many similarities among all the models. In particular, all the models operate with a mission to produce a thriving business as well as a "good" company that does not exploit workers, consumers, or the environment; that provides living wages and benefits to workers; that provides excellent service and produces quality products; that is a learning organization; and that is a good neighbor and a stable community partner committed to remaining in a community. In addition to wanting to familiarize people committed to building a solidarity economy with the variety of ways to develop a cooperatively-owned business, one of the objectives of delineating the major cooperative development models is also to point out that there are many ways to accomplish or create transformative businesses. There are almost as many strategies as there are democratic businesses, and new models are created constantly around the world, particularly at the grassroots. Most important is to understand the principles of economic solidarity and that there are a variety of ways to achieve it.

Resources

Websites:
The US Federation of Worker Cooperatives website, www.usworker.coop, has information about how to start a co-op, as do International Cooperative Alliance www.ica.coop , and National Cooperative Business Association www.ncba.coop, and National Cooperative Bank www.ncb.coop. The ICA Group is a technical assistance provider and its website gives examples of both ESOP conversions and worker cooperatives they have helped; www.ica-group.org. A site that has articles about some of these examples is GEO Newsletter website www.geo.coop.

Articles:
The Democracy Collaborative at the University of Maryland. (2005). *Building Wealth: The New Asset-Based Approach to Solving Social and Economic Problems*. Washington, DC: The Aspen Institute.

Fairbairn, Brett, June Bold, Murray Fulton, Lou Hammond Ketilson, Daniel Ish. (1991, revised 1995). *Cooperatives & Community Development: Economics in Social Perspective*. Saskatoon, Saskatchewan: University of Saskatchewan Center for the Study of Cooperatives.

Feldman, Jonathan Michael, and Jessica Gordon Nembhard. (2002). *From Community Economic Development and Ethnic Entrepreneurship to Economic Democracy: The Cooperative Alternative*. Umea, Sweden: Partnership for Multiethnic Inclusion.

Gordon Nembhard, Jessica. (2007). "Cooperatives." *International Encyclopedia of the Social Sciences* 2nd Edition. Editor in Chief: William A. Darity. Farmington Hills: Macmillan Reference USA (Thomson Gale), pp. 123-127.

Gordon Nembhard, Jessica. (2006, Summer). "Principles and Strategies for Reconstruction: Models of African American Community-Based Cooperative Economic Development." *Harvard Journal of African American Public Policy* Vol. 12, 39-55.

Kaswan, Jaques. (1999, September-October). "Cooperatives as a Socioeconomic Alternative to the Mainstream: Are We Ready?" *Grassroots Economic Organizing Newsletter* Issue 38, 2-3, 12.

Kreuberm Sherman. (2003, Fall). "Sectoral Strategies in CED: Critical Factors in the Success of CHCA and Childspace." *Making Waves* 14:3, 4-10. (http://www.cedworks.com/files/pdf/free/MW140304.pdf)

Labelle, Luc. (2000/2001, 2 Winter) "Development of Cooperatives and Employee Ownership, Quebec Style." *Owners at Work* XII, 14-17.

Logue, John, and Jacquelyn Yates. (2005). *Productivity in Cooperatives & Worker-Owned Enterprises: Ownership and participation make a difference!.* Geneva, Switzerland: International Labour Office.

Mathews, Race. (1999) *Jobs of Our Own: Building a Stakeholder Society, Alternatives to the Market and the State.* Sidney, Australia: Pluto Press.

McCulloch, Heather and Lisa Robinson. (2001). *Sharing the Wealth: Resident Ownership Mechanisms.* Oakland: PolicyLink.

Megson, Jim, and Janet VanLiere. (2001, Spring). "The Role of Worker Cooperatives in Urban Economic Development." *Journal of Cooperative Development* 2: 4: 2 and 18.

Shipp, Sigmund C. (2000, March). "Worker-Owned Firms in Inner-City Neighborhoods: An Empirical Study." *Review of International Cooperation* 92-93:4/99-1/00: 42-46.

Videos:

Headlamp Productions. (2004). "Made in the USA: American Worker Cooperatives" [motion picture]. Center for Cooperatives, University of California, Davis.

Smith, Margot and Bob Purdy (Producer/Director). (1999). "Democracy in the Workplace: Three Worker-Owned Businesses in Action." [motion picture]. Berkeley, CA: Off Center Video.

The Business Alliance for Local Living Economies
Ann Bartz

> *Ann Bartz, network development manager for the Business Alliance for Local Living Economies (BALLE), has a degree in English from the University of California, Berkeley. In her working life, she has sold books, tended grapes, elected a senator, helped develop the California solar industry, edited an academic journal of economics and several award-winning national magazines, recruited small manufacturers for a climate protection program, and helped launch the Ella Baker Center's Green for All program. She holds a certificate in permaculture design; for more than twenty years she has taught strategies for leadership development and eliminating racism. She has written on the environment, economics, health, and social change for Not Man Apart, Mother Earth News, Health, YES! and In Business, the San Francisco Chronicle, and the Millennium Whole Earth Catalog.*

The Business Alliance for Local Living Economies (www.livingeconomies.org) has worked since 2001 to build networks of locally-owned independent businesses in communities around the US and Canada. These businesses collaborate to green and strengthen their local economies.

Some of the businesses we work with see themselves as transformative and others probably do not. Jessica Nembhard's list of qualities of transformative businesses is certainly ideal. We organize all sorts of businesses, transformative and otherwise, to work together for economic transformation.

So far, BALLE has organized business networks in about fifty-two communities around the United States and Canada. The businesses involved are in many different sectors of the local economy, including sustainable agriculture, renewable energy, green building, downtown retail, community capital, zero-waste manufacturing, and independent media.

Many of these businesses see themselves as transformative in that they are organizing to help each other move toward more sustainable or "green" business practices and a more sustainable local economy. Others have joined a network as part of a Local First consumer education campaign to keep their business financially viable, or because they were already a member of, say, a chamber of commerce that joined our organization. Then we help them look at the local economy in their region - whether it is an urban neighborhood or a rural small town, a big city or an entire state - and learn from other communities in our organization how to build a strong local food system, for instance, or a stronger retail environment for independent businesses. We also help them figure out economic and materials linkages between companies in the various sectors we work with. We have worked with local government and business leaders to help them do green economic development as well.

We worked with a rural county south of San Francisco, where our headquarters is, that was facing a lot of pressure to develop productive farmland into a bedroom community for Silicon Valley. The local integrated waste management board, tasked with giving loans to businesses that use recycled feedstocks (recycled materials as inputs for new products), had been unable to find any such companies in the county to loan money to. They found out about BALLE and called us. We got community economic stakeholders - farmers and ranchers and local small business people - to the table to discuss what sorts of businesses they really wanted in their area that would enhance the economy and environment there, and to discover business opportunities that would leverage regional assets and existing businesses.

They came up with the idea of a local food and wine emporium that would showcase the products of the county. They found out that a local cedar shake company was producing enough waste that they could think about bringing a biomass facility there – which would qualify them for a loan from the integrated waste management board. They found out that a local grass-fed beef operation was spending a lot of money, time, and energy to ship cattle to the other end of the state for slaughtering. So a local slaughterhouse emerged as a business opportunity. A dog biscuit company using the entrails of the slaughtered beef has relocated near the ranch. Some of the new businesses have started up, and BALLE is trying to replicate this model in other communities.

Many people working in the local economies movement are interested in community-based financial systems. Our annual conference this past year hosted a daylong seminar on local currencies organized by Current Innovations, based in Santa Rosa, California (local currencies encourage people to employ local labor and materials). BALLE also works with community banks and credit unions as a way of keeping money local - if you bank in a locally-owned institution rather than a larger banking conglomerate, it is one more way of keeping money circulating through the local economy rather than shipping it off to corporate headquarters somewhere else. Patronizing locally-owned retail stores has the same community benefit. Another financial strategy for growing the local economy is the loyalty card. One BALLE network, the Santa Fe Alliance, has created one for independent businesses that collects money for local nonprofits and also increases consumers' awareness of and loyalty to locally-owned businesses. This is a plastic card usable only at local independent businesses in Santa Fe. You can get more information at www.locals-care.org.

Transformative businesses in themselves can build a local economy just by virtue of their being locally-owned, which keeps money circulating in the community by employing local workers and buying from local vendors. But businesses can exponentially increase their economic effectiveness and well-being by working with other locally-owned independent businesses to market themselves to the public, strengthen local supply chains, explore methods of collaboration such as group purchasing, and learn together how to implement best practices in green economic development and business problem-solving – all the things that a BALLE network does.

The Story of Collective Copies
Adam Trott

> *Adam Trott is in his third year as a worker/owner of Collective*
> *Copies in Massachusetts . Along with the Cooperative Capital*
> *Fund, Adam sits on the board of the Eastern Conference for Work-*
> *place Democracy. He cherishes his participation in the Valley Alli-*
> *ance of Worker Cooperatives, and in the Community Economies*
> *Research Group, as well as the four years he spent at the Fourth*
> *Street Food Co-op in Manhattan , with two years on their Finance*
> *Committee. Adam graduated from the University of Massachusetts,*
> *Amherst with a BA in Theater and a BA in Social Thought and Po-*
> *litical Economy.*

My name is Adam Trott, and I work at Collective Copies, a twenty-five-year-old print shop in Massachusetts. Collective Copies was formed in 1982 when workers at Gnommon Copy, a Boston area copy chain, went on strike to form a union. After months of striking, Gnommon closed its doors. The workers and their union, the United Electrical Workers, turned their efforts to forming a worker collective and with money given in advance for copies by community members, doors opened in 1983.

I would like to address three things. 1) What a worker cooperative is and why it is distinct from other types of cooperatives, 2) how Collective Copies as an example of worker cooperatives is a transformative business for workers, and 3) how Collective Copies, again as an example, is transformative for communities and regional social movements.

Part I: What is a worker cooperative, and why is it distinct from other types of co-ops?

One of the beautiful things about working in a cooperative is that it means different things to different people. Among the 300 or so worker cooperatives in the United States,[1] worker cooperators experience many unique benefits: the dynamics and challenges of a cooperative business, shared control over conditions and compensation, ability to gain expertise in new areas, application of ideology or politics, or just a feeling of sharing the experience of work. I feel there are two things that make all these things possible in worker cooperatives and worker collectives (worker collectives are one form of worker cooperatives, typically smaller in size – less than twenty people – and decisions made by consensus). First is one member, one vote, and this is true for each of the approximately 4,000 worker-owners in the U.S. In worker cooperatives, only workers are members, and all own an equal share. This ensures that those who are affected by decisions of the organization or business are the only ones who make them. One share per worker maintains a sense of equality and protects against some workers having less investment than others. Furthermore Collective Copies, as well as most collectives, operates on consensus, where everyone has to agree or abstain from the decision in order for it to pass. The second principle is that workers decide where the surplus goes, that is, what's left over, or what in a capitalist firm is called profit. It is in the control of the surplus where we are offered the chance to apply our beliefs in the process of what we do.

So what makes worker cooperatives unique from other types of cooperatives - consumer, producer, and purchasing? It is important and useful to cooperate around renting or owning a home, as in housing co-ops. Purchasing co-ops benefits members through lower cost items, like in a buying club or business association. Just as important is to cooperate around what food we buy, where members in food co-ops have a real say. But what about the product or service itself? Worker cooperatives are unique and exciting in that they do not focus on where we spend our money, but rather on how we earn our money. Worker co-ops operate on multiple bottom lines – environmental impact, workers' rights and compensation, anti-sexist and anti-racist movements, etc – prices are decided by workers earning that living in tune with their beliefs and not owners maximizing a profit. At Collective Copies we interact on a community basis and cultivate local relationships to create a business to meet our community's needs. Workers' controlling the surplus of a business makes a difference in these powerful parts of a business. At Collective Copies we use our surplus to offer workers a great benefits package: medical, dental benefits, Simple IRA retirement contribution, vacation, sick days, and holidays. For our work we use nearly exclusively recycled paper, and we use 100% post-consumer recycled paper for our self-serve machines used by the public. We also donate 10% of our surplus to local organizations. I feel that our structure has as much to do with these aspects of our business as we do. In the cooperative our beliefs and the mission of the business support each other.

Part II: Collective Copies as an example of a transformative business

Work is consuming, and it takes up a large part of our lives. The day-to-day life of work and the influences it has on our lives make up a big part of our outlook and our contribution to society. In speaking with another worker-cooperator, I was asked how can we have a democratic society when most people work outside of a democratic process. Worker co-ops may be alone in succeeding to transform workers into worker-owners who have a real say and true benefit in their daily working lives. This transformation is very powerful with tangible results. Using recycled paper, compensating workers with medical benefits, having paid time off – all costly choices that we feel are the right things to do. A little research (using the National Resources Defense Council's facts) into our use of recycled paper tells us that in a year we save over 300 trees, 70,000 gallons of water, 40,000 kilowatts of electricity and 600 pounds of air pollution.

A less tangible transformation, and perhaps my favorite to try to unravel, is how people in a cooperative grow and challenge themselves. The difficulties and demands of running a business give plenty of opportunity to challenge yourself as a worker-owner: marketing, retirement plans, customer service, accounting, etc.; sometimes the list is overwhelming. As we're learning together, I see we're trying different parts of ourselves out, sometimes taking certain parts of ourselves seriously for the first time. Many people characterize consensus as arduous or too difficult and slow, and this is true at times. I insist, however, it is worth it all for that powerful and motivating moment of having 13 people behind a decision. Learning about our business and how I can benefit it has been a wonderful road towards learning about myself. I see it as one of the best opportunities I have during my day to try to push myself, and in this practice, with the support of my co-workers, I have become my better and truer self. It is more than the work my co-workers and I perform. It is ourselves that are changing and improving, being pushed as we are supported. I cherish this process of finding myself as much as my work being the subject of transformation as I work cooperatively.

Part III: How Collective Copies, again just as an example, is transformative for communities and regional social movements.

I see Collective Copies and worker cooperatives in general as transformative agents in two major ways. The first way is through our donation programs. Collective Copies is one of many worker cooperatives whose donation method is based off of the Mondragon Cooperative Corporation, though many cooperatives choose their own donation processes. We give away 10% of our gross profits each year to community organizations from animal shelters and health clinics to the Valley Alliance of Worker Cooperatives and Save the Redwoods. We also make donations monthly, usually for organizations trying to make their printing budget or to improve on their printing choices. Secondly, I find many of my co-workers and friends within the worker cooperative movement are very active. Whether it is the democratic atmosphere carrying over, or the flexibility of our schedules, many of us volunteer our time in organizations fighting for social or economic change in our neighborhoods. In working at Collective Copies I have the time and energy for the meetings, conference calls and work for the projects that I care about.

Conclusion

It strikes me that for how well worker cooperatives work for so many of those involved that there aren't more of them. At Collective Copies we spend more money on paper, more money on workers, use what is considered a slow, difficult decision-making process with no accounting or business degrees awarded to any of us, and we are succeeding. So far Collective Copies has not had a money-losing year, no lay-offs, better pay and benefits for workers than industry average, and steady growth resulting in a $1.5 million year in 2007. I wonder if a little copy shop, by introducing equal, fair and transparent practices in their business makes such a difference, what else we can do? What about our schooling or public transport? What about agriculture? Or restaurants, for that matter? If this is what can happen with thirteen people in one shop, what would happen if, instead of the 4,000 worker-owners in the U.S., there were 4 or 5 million? Worker cooperation is in a growing fresh new wave of organizing, and is a prime model for transforming their members and their communities. The economic equality that worker cooperatives strive for is a constant, vibrant catalyst for equality among sexes, nations, and races, through a drive towards democracy, first in our workplaces, and then in our communities and societies.

Notes

[1] Facts concerning the worker cooperative movement, as well as lots of other great information, came from the United States Federation of Worker Cooperatives-www.usworker.coop.

13

Competing by Cooperating in Italy: The Cooperative District of Imola

Matt Hancock

Matt Hancock is assistant director of the Center for Labor and Community Research. Before CLCR, Matt worked as a Researcher at the Institute for Labor, in Bologna, Italy. Matt has a Masters in Cooperative Economics from the University of Bologna where he studied under Professor Stefano Zamagni. Between 2003 and 2005, Matt studied the cooperative movement of Emilia-Romagna, with a particular focus on the cooperative district of Imola.

Introduction: The Cooperative Movement of Imola, A Community Economic Asset

The District of Imola is located in the province of Bologna, Italy, and is made up of the capital city, Imola, and the surrounding towns of Castel San Pietro Terme, Dozza, Medicina, Castel Guelfo, Mordano, Casalfiumanese, Borgo Tossignano, Fontanelice e Castel del Rio.

Imola is the largest city of the district—population-wise—with 64,348 residents, as of the 2000 census. The total district has a population of 119,417,[1] about the same population as Stamford, Connecticut in the United States, in an area almost 200 square kilometers larger than Chicago.

Imola is home to one of the world's most robust, dynamic and deeply-rooted cooperative movements. Today, there are 132 cooperatives, active in all sectors of the economy. Each year the movement has added at least one start-up to the family of firms. Between 2005 and 2006, four new co-ops were born. Rarely does a co-op fail. One out of two residents is a member of a co-op and 17% of the area's workforce (9,204 people) is directly employed by a cooperative.[2] And when subsidiary firms—businesses owned by the co-ops but not themselves co-ops—are considered, jobs created by the cooperative movement increases to more than 13,487.[3]

Fundamentally, the cooperative movement is an engine for wealth and employment creation for the local community - a community asset. As we will see later, the business and market strategies pursued by the cooperatives are guided by the deeply-held notion that the cooperative is a community resource. The extent to which the co-op is able to compete in the market (increasingly an international market) and be profitable determines the level of benefit that flows to the local community.

The combined annual revenues of the cooperatives of Imola in 2006 were €2.4 billion. The combined net worth of the co-ops was €1.4 billion. Fixed employment between 2005 and 2006 increased 2.76%. Since 2002, the cooperatives have increased fixed employment between 2% and 7% each year. In what may seem like a paradox to some readers—particularly American readers accustomed to declining employment in manufacturing—Imola's economy and employment are driven by a robust, sophisticated and globally competitive manufacturing sector.

The main engines for this kind of growth and wealth creation are the district's fourteen worker-owned manufacturing cooperatives, the most important of which are: 3elle, Cefla, Cooperativa, Ceramica d'Imola and SACMI. Together, these four co-ops produce 47% of total fixed employment in the cooperative movement, 47% of annual revenues and 71% of the total net worth of all the cooperatives combined.

Economic and Social Impact on the Local Community

In the absence of a significant, positive economic impact on the local community there would be little reason to study the cooperative district of Imola, aside from an academic interest in cooperatives per se. What is interesting about Imola is the convergence of one of the highest concentrations of cooperative firms in the world and extremely positive economic and social outcomes: a globally competitive economy that drives wealth and employment creation for the benefit of the local community. This convergence is by no means casual.

According to the latest available census figures, unemployment in Imola is 3.1%, compared to a national average of 9%. Disposable annual income per family in Imola (income after *all taxes* are paid) is €45,538—nearly €6,000 a year more than the national average for Italy. Per capita disposable income in Imola is €18,324, €3,288 higher than the national average. Residents of Imola also consume more than a typical Italian: €16,199 compared to €12,955 a year respectively.

To put these numbers in perspective, the *pre-tax,* median household income in the United States is currently $48,451.[4] At today's exchange rate, that means that a typical household in Imola enjoys annual disposable income of $66,604, $18,000 *higher* than the median, pre-tax household income in the United States. While by no means scientific, this "back of the envelope" calculation should leave no doubt as to the high standard of living enjoyed by residents of Imola.

As I mentioned, the high concentration of cooperatives and positive economic and social outcomes in Imola is not a casual convergence. In fact, these positive results are driven primarily by the cooperative movement. 17% of Imola's workforce is directly employed by the cooperatives—even more when private subsidiaries owned by the cooperatives are taken into account. The cooperatives are also significantly larger than the average firm in Imola—in some cases by a factor of almost 200. Not only do Imola's cooperatives employ a sizeable percentage of the local workforce, in a highly fragmented business environment they represent the highest *concentration* of employment in the private sector of the local economy.[5]

Imola is located in Emilia-Romagna, a region studied by scholars throughout the world for its globally competitive manufacturing economy, networks of small, locally-owned firms and cooperatives, low unemployment and high standard of living. Given this, it's interesting to note that Imola has outperformed the larger provincial and regional economy by some measures. For example, between 1991 and 1996, industrial value added in Imola grew at a 3% annual rate, compared to just 1.6% in the province of Bologna and 2.5% in the Emilia-Romagna region. Looking at growth in value added in manufacturing, a subset of industry, the numbers are even higher: 4.6% in Imola compared to 3.1% in the region and 1.7% in Bologna. More than half of Imola's industrial output is produced by cooperatives.[6]

In terms of employment, again, it's manufacturing that leads. Between 1991 and 1996, employment in industry in the province of Bologna *dropped* by 8 percentage points. In Imola, employment in industry held steady (increasing by .1%), driven by a 2.7% *increase* in employment in manufacturing, particularly in ceramics and automatic machines, sectors dominated by cooperatives like *Ceramica di Imola, SACMI* and *CEFLA.*[7] Strong performance in manufacturing also resulted in collateral benefits, with corresponding increases in employment in sectors that provide services to manufacturing.[8]

In 2006, Imola's co-ops produced total revenues of €2.4 billion, and net profits of €91.5 million. But looking beyond profit, to value added, gives us a better idea of just how much new wealth the cooperative movement produces for the community.

Value-added is a measure of total wealth created by a business in the production or distribution of a good or service and is calculated by subtracting from revenues the cost of purchased goods and services. What's left over is what the company itself has produced. This new wealth is where wages and profits come from.

In 2006, Legacoop Imola surveyed a representative sample of 40 cooperatives. These cooperatives produced €389 million of value added, or new wealth—one fifth of their total revenues. Out of this total, €259 million, or 67% of wealth produced, went to labor in the form of wages, 12% to amortization of capital, 12%, or €45 million, to net profits and Legacoop's cooperative development fund, and 9%, or €35 million, to the state in the form of taxes.[9]

The cooperatives also distribute wealth and drive job creation in the local community through purchases of goods and services. Each euro spent locally by a cooperative creates more jobs in other businesses in the local economy. In 2006, out of total purchases of €1.3 billion, the cooperatives spent €270 million—over 20% of the total—in Imola. By purchasing locally, the cooperatives maximize their positive multiplier effect on the local economy.

Finally, the cooperative movement has impacted Imola positively by allowing the local community to effectively face the challenges of globalization—challenges that so many communities have been struggling with. Imola's manufacturing base is export-driven, and it has been the cooperatives—which have positioned themselves as global market leaders in a diverse range of sectors—that have allowed Imola to project itself globally, while maximizing benefits locally.

Imola's leading industrial firm—SACMI—produces 85% of its revenues through exports, for example.[10] And 30% of the entire cooperative movement's revenues are generated by sales outside of Italy.

By seeking positions of leadership in manufacturing in the global economy—and not retreating from competition—the cooperatives have been able to continue to drive wealth and employment creation locally. By aggressively competing to be the best globally, the cooperatives of Imola have contributed significantly to the creation of a vital local economy and to maintaining the high standard of living and low unemployment enjoyed by residents, even in the face of new and intense competition from developing countries.

The Imola Model

It should be mentioned that Imola is not a lone cooperative district in a sea of private enterprise. Emilia-Romagna, a region of about 4 million, is home to over 4,000 cooperatives and Italy boasts one of the highest concentrations of cooperatives per capita in the world. While cooperatives have flourished in Italy and elsewhere in the world, Imola is truly unique. Imola's cooperative movement has demonstrated an ability to combine outstanding economic performance over time, integration into the global economy, and competitiveness with a commitment to democracy in the workplace, community development, and solidarity within and across generations. Imola's experience is perhaps matched only by the Mondragon Cooperative Corporation in Spain.

Intergenerational Solidarity

The analysis of the Imola model has to start from the unique view that Imola's cooperators have of their cooperatives. Today's cooperative leaders see the cooperatives as a community economic asset. Current members are simply beneficiaries of wealth created through the sacrifice, investment and careful management of their forebears. As such, members have the very serious responsibility of protecting that wealth and expanding it for future generations, just as the cooperators before the current generation did.

3elle, a worker-owned cooperative started in 1908, is today among the top three producers of wooden door and window frames in Italy.[11] Founded by 15 carpenters, technicians, teachers and others, 3elle's first headquarters was the covered portico of the church of San Domenico (this fact, and the political orientation of the founders, earned them the nickname "the Red monks").[12] Today, 3elle has revenues of €62.28 million,[13] exports 10% of its production[14] and employs 301 people. When I spoke with Giuliano Dall'Osso, the president of 3elle's board of directors and a worker-member, I asked him if he saw the cooperative as a part of the labor movement. He reflected a moment, and answered that he saw the cooperative as a part of the "patrimony of the local community... wealth for the territory, something for my children... wealth for future generations."[15] This sentiment was expressed by all of the cooperative leaders I interviewed.

Dall'Osso's words capture what I would consider to be *the* core value of Imola's cooperators today. It is this particular notion of the cooperative, an asset for future generations and part of the local community's patrimony, that drives much of the behavior of the cooperatives, both in regards to how they compete in the marketplace, and how internal democracy manifests itself.

The most significant manifestation of this notion of wealth creation for future generations is the cumulative retained earnings, or "indivisible reserves," of Imola's cooperatives. The notion of indivisible reserves was codified into law with the 1947 Basevi legislation. In brief, the law required that all co-operatives establish indivisible reserves: earnings that the co-op will retain and account for on the balance sheet separately from shareholders' equity. At no point during the life of the co-op can members receive any portion of these reserves as dividends or in any other form; they can not be "divided." Further, the law required that, in the event the co-op ceases to operate, the indivisible reserves be "devolved" in their entirety and utilized in the "public interest."[16]

In 1977, to further encourage co-ops to self-finance, the Italian parliament modified the cooperative legislation to exempt from corporate income tax any earnings retained by the co-op, as long as they were placed into the indivisible reserves. Under the 1977 legislation, at the end of a co-op's fiscal year the co-op had the option of retaining up to 100% of earnings, tax-free, as long as those earnings were placed in separate, indivisible reserves. Today, Italian law requires that, in the event a co-op is liquidated or privatized, all remaining indivisible reserves be devolved to one of the national cooperative development funds, managed by the national cooperative business association of which the co-op is a member.

This law has had a powerful, dual effect on co-ops in Italy: on the one hand, by exempting indivisible reserves from corporate income tax, cooperators have a material incentive to focus on long-term growth of the co-op through self-financing; on the other hand, they have a disincentive to speculate on a healthy co-op by cashing out through privatization. If a cooperative were to be sold, almost its entire net worth, minus the member dues plus interest, would go to the cooperative movement.

As Giuliano Poletti, former president of the Cooperative League of Imola and current president of the Cooperative League of Italy, put it: "members give up individual profit to invest profits into the indivisible reserves (which the members give up forever) that are then used to reinforce and develop the firm."[17] In Imola, each year, members voluntarily give up a majority of the profits they produce, in favor of the long-term health of their co-op. In 2006, for example, the cooperatives invested 69% of total profits into the indivisible reserves. This massive reinvestment of profits provides the co-ops with the financial resources needed to compete effectively in the marketplace. But fundamentally, the indivisible reserves represent a form of inter-generational solidarity, guaranteeing current and future members stable employment and high wages as well as insuring that the local community will continue to benefit from the current and future wealth created by the co-ops.[18] Thanks to the sacrifice of past members, Imola's cooperatives today have total reserves (roughly equivalent to net worth) of over €1.4 billion.

For Imola, the cooperative legislation doesn't drive investments into indivisible reserves; it is merely the legal codification of this form of "external" mutual aid long practiced by the cooperatives here. In 1904, for example, in the absence of legislation requiring them to do so, the founding members of the Cooperative Bank of Imola chose to reinvest 90% of that year's profits back into the bank. The founding members of the bank also voluntarily decided to require that a part of the bank's reserves, should the bank close, be used in some way to benefit the collective interest.[19]

These are choices that are both entrepreneurial (long-term growth of the business) and social (wealth should be set aside for the benefit of the larger community, not just the individual members).

Market Competition and Social Values

The business strategies pursued by Imola's industrial cooperatives are the result of the tension between social values and what it takes to remain competitive in the global marketplace. The result has been bold, and sometimes controversial, business strategies. I would argue that these strategies are consistent with, and even promote, the social values at the core of the cooperative movement: local development, dignified work opportunity and employment stability and intergenerational solidarity.

All of the industrial cooperatives have sought and achieved market leadership nationally, and in many cases globally, by focusing on producing the highest quality products in diverse sectors from machine tools, to ceramics, to packaging lines, to carpentry. To do this, Imola's cooperatives have made significant investments in new technology, R&D, and process and product innovation.

Growth has been driven almost entirely by exports. All of the industrial cooperatives have pursued a strategy of internationalization—not delocalization[20]—to a greater or lesser extent. Some have focused on simply increasing sales abroad of products produced locally. Other cooperatives have pursued an aggressive strategy of internationalization through acquisition of private companies and setting up sales and service offices, as well as production plants, throughout the world, including developing countries from China to Brazil. SACMI has by far been the most aggressive in this regard, with 80 subsidiaries in 24 countries. Over 80% of SACMI Imola's sales are exported.[21]

In many ways, Imola's cooperatives flip the common perception of globalization on its head: instead of going abroad to take advantage of cheap labor, opening up production plants in other parts of the world has allowed Imola's firms to increase their percentage of market share by increasing their ability to be close to their global markets. This strategy has allowed the co-ops not only to increase sales and market share, but employment in Imola as well.

While aspects of production are sometimes decentralized to the subsidiaries, the "brains" remain with the cooperative. Research, technological innovation, strategic, high value-added production or high knowledge-content production is kept inside the cooperative, or as close as possible to the cooperative. Overall, as certain aspects of production have been decentralized, total employment in the cooperative has increased through a corresponding *increase* in design, marketing, finance and research done *inside* the cooperative. In 1989, for example, SACMI created – at the main plant and headquarters in Imola – a Center for Research and Development which carries out R&D for the entire group. The Center includes chemistry and physics labs, a "technological" lab for packaging, and experimental areas for prototype testing. In addition to the production of packaging machinery, SACMI has been testing new, high-tech olfactory systems that will allow a company that packages perishable goods to detect possible problems before an entire order is packaged.

As many of the managers and cooperators I have met with have stressed, any firms that are acquired and operated by the cooperatives through their holding companies are "instrumental" to the mission of the cooperative and serve to reinforce the competitive position of the co-op. The networks of subsidiaries owned by the cooperatives allow them to continue to grow productive capacity and create new jobs at home, while frequently creating new jobs in other parts of the world, contributing to increasing productive capacity elsewhere, and introducing new technology into developing economies. The industrial cooperatives, with SACMI in the lead, have successfully integrated themselves with the global economy in ways that are consistent with their values, and that increase employment and productive capacity at home, while safeguarding and increasing that patrimony that has accumulated over the last century, and that will continue to benefit future generations.

Conclusion

Most communities aren't really in control of their own futures. Even in modern democracies like the United States, most communities—though they may vote for their elected officials in government—do not have control over the major economic decisions that determine their standard of living and livelihoods. As a result, communities, more often than not, suffer the consequences of the economic decisions made by others.

Imola is an example of a community that, through cooperative ownership of economic assets, *is* in control. At several critical historical junctures over the past 150 years, Imola's cooperative movement has proven to be an indispensable community asset. It was largely through the cooperative movement that landless peasants and small farmers were able to secure for themselves a fair return for their labor and a decent standard of living. The early experiments with credit unions contributed to the development of small industry in Imola.

It was the cooperative movement that literally rebuilt Imola following the devastation of the Second World War, helped abolish sharecropping and developed a modern industrial economy. And it is the cooperative movement, particularly in the manufacturing sector, that has projected Imola onto a global scale and maintained a high standard of living and low unemployment, even in the fact of intense competition from low-wage countries. While we see the impoverishment of many communities that were once wealthy as a result of the recent wave of economic globalization, Imola shows how a local community can become a positive factor in helping firms more effectively compete in the global market.

I would argue that we are currently in one of the most complex and potentially dangerous historical periods yet. On the one hand the globalization of the economy has created many new opportunities; on the other hand, the emergence of transnational, hyper-mobile capital (no longer linked to a particular community or nation-state) and the dominance of low road, speculative business practices represent new and serious threats.

In the face of such dramatic, historical changes, labor, community movement and even states have been unequipped and ill-prepared to manage this period. The traditional instruments of the strike, the protest and state intervention—all instruments that tend to keep people away from the process of wealth creation— have proven ineffective as the suffering of communities has only increased. This is why Imola's experience is more important today than ever.

While the damage to many communities has already been done by low road globalization, Imola offers an important example of how we can begin to rebuild our communities (just as they did after the Second World War) around an economic and social model capable of competing in the global market through a focus on people, mutual aid and a profound sense of solidarity, especially toward future generations.

References

Benati, Benito (1998, October 2). "Sacmi: Partecipazione Sociale e Successo Imprenditoriale," *L'Impresa al Plurale*, n. 2, 265-282.

Bilancio Esercizio. (2004). 3Elle.

Bilancio Sociale. (2003). SACMI.

Billi, Paolo. (2005). SACMI, Company Profile.

Casadio, Quinto. (2002). Legacoop Imola, Vent'anni di vita che hanno radici lontane, Imola.

CEFLA. (2005). Company Profile, Annual Report.

Fornasari, Massimo & Vera Zamagni. (1997). Il Movimento Cooperativo in Italia, Florence.

Galassi, Nazario. (1986). La Cooperazione Imolese dalle Origini ai Nostri Giorni (1859- 1967), Imola.

Imola Insieme. (2005). Annuario 2005 della Cooperazione Imolese, Confcooperative & Legacoop di Imola.

Imola Insieme. (2007). Annuario della Cooperazione Imolese, Confcooperative & Legacoop di Imola.

Relazioni e Bilancio. (2004, December 31). Cooperativa Ceramica d'Imola.

Poletti, Giuliano, (2005, September). Editorial, "Il Sole 24 Ore."

Pfeffer, Jeffrey. (1995). "Producing Sustainable Competitive Advantage Through the Effective Management of People." Academy of Management Executive, Vol 9: 1.

Pontiggia, Andrea. (2001). Le Cooperative Industriali del Comprensorio di Imola e Faenza, Assetto Istituzionale e Modelli Organizzativi, Ravenna, ITACAlibri.

SACMI, Company Profile. (2006).

Stefanelli, Renzo. (1975). L'Autogestione in Italia, Bari: De Donato.

V Rapporto Sociale della Cooperazioen aderente a Legacoop Imola (2007). Imola.

Zamagni, Vera and Massimo Fornasari, (1997). Il Movimento Cooperativo in Italia, Un Profilo Storico-economico (1854-1992), Firenze.

Notes

[1] 2000 census data, accessed online: http://www.regione.emilia-romagna.it/statistica/pop_prov/

[2] 2000 Census, accessed online: http://www.regione.emilia-romagna.it/statistica/pop_prov/lavoro_ottobre.htm

[3] Legacoop in numeri, Bilanci consolidati, http://www.imola.legacoop.it/web/index.php?option=com_content&task=view&id=51&Itemid=65

[4] US Census, http://www.census.gov/prod/2007pubs/acs-08.pdf

[5] As in the Emilia-Romagna region, most businesses in Imola can be classified as small and micro, with an average firm size of just 7.7 employees. By contrast, the largest co-op headquarted in Imola, *Ceramica di Imola,* employs 1,435, not counting employment in subsidiary firms.

[6] Zamagni, 176.

[7] Analisi e studi, 24.

[8] Analisi e studi, 8.

[9] Legacoop Imola, V Rapporto Sociale della Cooperazione Aderente a Legacoop Imola, 16.

[10] SACMI Annual Report 2006, 12.

[11] Personal interview.

[12] Personal interview.

[13] http://www.3elle.it/3elle_cifre.htm

[14] Personal interview.

[15] Personal interview.

[16] Basevi Law of 1947, http://www.movimentocooperativo.it/index.php?id=330

[17] Poletti, Giuliano, Editorial, "Il Sole 24 Ore," 3 September 2005.

[18] Imola Insieme, 2007, p. 8.

[19] Galassi, 139.

[20] By "delocalization" I mean shifting productive capacity from one area to another, rather than adding to overall productive capacity. When people generally think of globalization, they think of delocalization. "Offshoring" is the more commonly used term in the US.

[21] Sacmi, Annual Report 2006, 8.

14

Another Workplace is Possible: Co-ops and Workplace Democracy

Melissa Hoover

Melissa Hoover has worked in cooperatives and collectives almost all her working life. Currently the Executive Director of the US Federation of Worker Cooperatives, she is also a member of the Arizmendi Development and Support Cooperative in the Bay Area, and does consulting in financial literacy and financial management for worker cooperatives and small businesses. She has presented at local, regional and national worker co-op conferences, at the Center for Popular Economic summer institute, and at the US Social Forum. Her co-op movement work is informed by the belief that economic literacy for all workers is not only possible, it is essential for strong co-ops, and especially critical to building an economic alternative to capitalism. She is a passionate believer in the possibilities of real democracy and would like to convene an 8-hour consensus meeting to discuss this premise.

Introduction

This is not a theoretical workshop, but a practical one. I'm not an economist, not a researcher; I am not an expert on worker co-ops. I do have years of experience working in, thinking about, and supporting the growth of worker co-ops. That said, I hope I can address in some small way the "How do we get there?" question by looking at a real-life alternative with radical roots and potential that's actually working. In this talk I will:

- Explain a little about worker cooperatives, define some terms and give a basic explanation of the form.
    - o   Explore some elements of worker ownership.
    - o   Explore some elements of democratic worker control.
- Give an overview of the worker co-op movement in recent history and right now.

- o Talk about some of the strengths and possibilities of worker ownership: why it's the most exciting thing happening right now.
- o Point out some tensions in the worker cooperative structure.
- o Look at some hopeful new directions in the movement and give some real-life examples of worker cooperatives doing movement-building work.

Background

What is a worker cooperative?
A worker co-op is a business or social enterprise that is owned and controlled by the people who work in it. There are a lot of other names floating around out there: democratic workplace, collective, worker-owned business, etc. At the most basic level, worker cooperatives boil down to two things: the workers own it, and the workers control it. We'll get to what this can mean in a minute, but for now let's get an overview of worker co-ops in this country.

We estimate that there are about 300-400 worker cooperatives in the US, employing more than 3000 workers. This is only a rough estimate because there's not much hard data on worker cooperatives right now. They are concentrated in a few areas: the West Coast, particularly the Bay Area, the upper Midwest – Minnesota and Wisconsin – and Massachusetts and Vermont on the East Coast. Worker cooperatives exist in all sectors of the economy and lots of different industries, though we see concentrations in things like grocery, cafes, and recently in health care. We've also started to see growing interest in worker co-ops from around the country and from several different quarters, particularly from nonprofits doing economic justice work who are interested in developing co-ops.

The common image of a worker co-op is small, probably countercultural, maybe societal dropouts, maybe middle class white people. Certainly hippies. We all know co-ops are for hippies, right? Well, this image is outdated. Worker co-ops have changed and grown tremendously over the past 20 years, from a countercultural cottage industry to a more mainstream mode of community economic development in the US. Today worker co-ops run the gamut from small collectives to several hundred person jobs, from service industry to manufacturing, from semi-skilled work to highly skilled trades, from businesses to social enterprises that exist to provide a community benefit.

We also estimate that up to half of the worker co-ops that exist today were founded in the past twenty years. The 1990s saw a real explosion of growth and, more important, of organizing among worker co-ops. This was a specific kind of growth, an intentional growth. To back up a little, in the 20th century there were a couple of big co-op growth spurts, one in the 1930s and one in the 1970s. The co-ops that survived from the 1970s into the 1990s were a significant catalyst for the growth that took place in the 90s. Many of them were thriving; they had demonstrated that the model was viable and they were committed to helping grow it, through replication, spinoff, and technical assistance. These older 1970s co-ops provided resources, inspiration and in many cases directed capital to help those new co-ops get started in the 1990s. So there's this older generation saying, "Look at this crazy idea from the 1970s – we've found a way to make it actually work," and a younger generation looking for creative economic alternatives to an increasingly corporate world. And throughout, there have been cooperative development and support organizations like the ICA Group in Massachusetts, which has been helping create and support worker-owned businesses for thirty years.

There are several examples of this "seeding" approach. The Cheese Board bakery in Berkeley (founded 1971) provided some money, expertise and their recipes to a group of people who wanted to create co-op bakeries based on the Mondragon model in Spain. That was ten years ago, and now there are three new Arizmendi bakeries and a growing association of all those bakeries and the Cheese Board, called the Arizmendi Association, after the priest, Father Arizmendiarrieta, who founded the Mondragon cooperative system. Another example is when the designers from Inkworks Press (founded 1974), also in Berkeley, wanted to spin off and create their own co-op, Inkworks supported them by helping financially, sharing their customer list and creating a working relationship with the new design shop. The design spinoff, called Design Action, is in turn helping other political design shops in the area research and learn about converting to worker-ownership. Cooperative Home Care Associates in the Bronx, the biggest worker co-op in the country with nearly 1000 workers, has provided consultation and technical assistance in replicating their model to other home care co-ops in Wisconsin and Philadelphia. CHCA and its sister organization, Paraprofessional Healthcare Institute, have been a major catalyst for the growth of democratic home health care jobs in the last decade. And North Country Cooperative Grocery in Minneapolis created the Northcountry Cooperative Development Fund to make sure that co-ops could get access to money just like regular businesses. These are just a few examples of worker co-ops consciously sustaining and growing a movement.

Back to the 1990s: there was also a new sort of radical politics developing in the 1990s, the anti-corporate movement, and the movement against globalized capitalism. Many of the people who got involved in worker co-ops and co-op development in the 1990s were people who were consciously trying to build a movement to support alternatives. They approached co-ops that way, less the sort of utopian approach that many of the co-ops may have started with in the 1970s (and many of those didn't last or evolved beyond utopian tendencies) and more with an eye toward building something bigger.

In the mid-1990s we started to see local and regional co-op groups start to form – the Network of Bay Area Worker Cooperatives (NoBAWC) and the Western Worker Co-op Conference on the West Coast, and the Worker Owned and Run Cooperative Network (WORC'N) in Boston, who got together to create social bonds and share ideas and skills. Those groups focused on sharing skills and strengthening our workplaces, but they also started to think about federating to get bigger things done. In the late 1990s and early 2000s, the Eastern Conference for Workplace Democracy and Federation of Workplace Democracies in Minnesota formed. And in 2004, out of all those regional groups there was a national conference and from that emerged the national Federation.

It's also worth mentioning, with credit to the amazing group Incite! Women of Color Beyond Violence, that there has been a growing consciousness among people, and young people especially, about the limits of nonprofits to effect social change, what Incite! dubbed the "nonprofit industrial complex." They coined this phrase at a conference in 2004, and recently published a book on the same topic, *The Revolution Will Not Be Funded.*   Many co-op developers today are looking at co-ops as a strategy for economic justice, as a way to build assets in poor communities, and as an income strategy for people who have few options – basically as a way to create jobs that does a lot more than just create jobs, as it has the potential to create skills, investment and community benefit.

There have also been some significant and inspiring international movements that bear mentioning. The Canadian worker cooperative movement is amazingly well-developed and funded, and the Quebec co-ops in particular have an impressive degree of self-sufficiency. Mondragon in Spain is of course a long-standing inspiration and model for co-ops around the world.[1]

But more recently, there's been growth in the Emilia Romagna region of Italy, which has an entire worker co-op economy; in the reclaimed factories movement in Argentina, where workers took over their factories after the economy collapsed in 2001; and the government-sponsored co-op growth in Venezuela under the Chavez regime.

This locates our current growth in the US as part of an international movement that exists alongside and in some cases in direct opposition to the growth of global corporate capitalist models.

Nuts and Bolts

So that's where we sit, but what *is* a worker cooperative, exactly? The first thing to know is that there is no standard incorporation form for worker cooperatives – and in many cases there's no form at all, so we're talking about a variety of structures and arrangements. We'll start with the general umbrella term Democratic Workplaces. This is a workplace where decisions are made democratically, where workers practice democratic self-management. There are a variety of democratic management and decision-making structures, and a variety of corporate structures. Pretty much any workplace can structure itself as a democratic workplace if it wants to: (privately held) corporations, partnerships, Limited Liability Corporations (LLCs), even nonprofits, though they have to work a little harder because there is some hierarchy built into their structure. The key to being a democratic workplace is that the people affected by decisions are the ones making the decisions. This can mean anything from direct democracy to representative democracy to everything in between.

This workshop will focus on one example of a democratic workplace – worker cooperatives, but will touch on the variety of forms and structures that exist.

What is a co-op?

A co-op is a particular kind of democratic workplace with two components:
　　　　1. Workers own it
　　　　2. Workers control it

For practical purposes, the U.S. Federation of Worker Cooperatives calls any enterprise that is worker-owned and worker-controlled a worker cooperative. In reality, 'cooperative' is specific legal designation – it's an incorporation form – and it's not uniform from state to state. In fact in many states a business can't even incorporate as a cooperative, so we use a functional definition – one that's aligned with international practices and principles – rather than a legal one. There are seven principles of cooperatives, and CICOPA, the international worker cooperative body of the International Cooperative Alliance, also has a statement of principles called the 'Oslo Declaration' that we use to judge whether an enterprise is a worker cooperative. [2]

Democratic ownership: 'we own it!'

Ownership is pretty straightforward in the legal cooperative form – it is written into the legal structure of the business. The member-owners of the cooperatives are the workers. For every other incorporation form, owners figure out how to structure democratic ownership within existing laws (which of course are not written to facilitate this). Here are two basic elements of ownership with just a few possibilities for each:

1. Buy-in
   o   Standard worker ownership: Each worker contributes some amount of money to the equity in the business. This is an investment in the business, and represents their ownership. In businesses not incorporated as cooperatives the ownership structures vary by incorporation form.
   o   Community ownership/trust: Some democratic workplaces don't have ownership, or treat the concept of ownership as a community holding. Community groups, social enterprises, and businesses that conceive of themselves as a public resource set up a trust to hold the assets of their business, or incorporate as a nonprofit corporation (this is not the same as a 501c3, what we usually think of as a non-profit) whose assets are not owned by individuals but belong to the community.
   o   Outside investors or hybrid ownership: Some worker cooperatives are actually hybrids, with both the workers and the community holding ownership shares in the business.

2. Profit-sharing
   o   Patronage : In a conventional business, the surplus that the business generates at the end of the year is called profit. In a cooperative, it is called 'surplus.' The distribution of the surplus to the members is called 'patronage.' Understanding these terms helps you understand some fundamental differences between co-ops and traditional businesses: surplus is simply the extra cash generated by the business after expenses are taken care of. Whereas profit is the goal for conventional businesses, member benefit is the goal for co-ops. The term 'patronage' comes from consumer co-ops where the members were patrons of the buying co-op and if there was a surplus at the end of the year it was re-distributed to the members based on their investment. There's a similar idea at work in worker co-ops: if you have surplus left, it is re-distributed to the members, because it's theirs as a return on their investment.

o   Profit-sharing: Democratic workplaces not incorporated as cooperatives can still share profits among workers; they just don't get some of the same tax advantages as cooperatives.

The ownership question is pretty straightforward. What's trickier and more individualized, and what people always want to know about, is self-management. So let's explore that.

Democratic self-management: (how) does that work?

Democratic self-management is often the hardest thing for people to wrap their minds around. Does it work? How does it work? True, it is often the most difficult, unique, and time-consuming part of setting up, converting, or improving a worker co-op, and it's also what makes the form so powerful, flexible and inspiring. How often can you say you have been in a room full of people who have all made themselves heard, understand each other's position, and agree on a course of action? That's a strong thing. And getting there is a strong process. There's an old SDS saying that 'freedom is an endless meeting,' which of course sounds horrific, but viewed through a different lens can be interpreted as the notion that being free and working together is an ongoing and constant negotiation and communication.

There are as many ways to do self-management, or democratic governance, or worker-control, or whatever you may have heard it called, as there are people and ideas in the world. The key element is: the workers choose the structure, control it, and are accountable to it. There are examples on all scales; one method is going to work for a small collective and a different one works for a large multi-site workplace. There's no question that most jobs require some kind of management. Notice I didn't say manage*er,* I said manage*ment,* the function of managing. You can think of management as a job role. It can be a role that rotates among different workers. Or elements of management can be part of each worker's role. Or if a management job role is filled by one person, you can think of management being that worker's job just like doing tech support or selling vegetables is another person's job. Of course management job roles carry some different privileges and responsibilities but once you begin to think of management as a job role, you can take apart the power that many people think is automatic in a management role, and hold managers accountable the same way you hold other job roles accountable. Rather than getting too specific, I'll focus on two important elements of worker self-management:

1. Accountability.

Mutual accountability is the key to democratic management. Usually we think of accountability going one way, from worker to boss. How often have you felt that you could hold your boss accountable for anything?

You can't because they can fire you! When you build in mutual accountability, that power structure is immediately disabled. For smaller co-ops, this might mean face-to-face evaluations. For larger co-ops, it could mean a board of directors composed of workers, to whom people in management roles are accountable. Or smaller departments might be accountable to the general membership meeting. However they work, structures of accountability are crucial to effective self-management. (Examples of Management Accountability Structures are illustrated in Figures 1-3).

Some Possibilities for Management Accountability Structures:
No management job roles (collective form)
Management elected by the workers
Management appointed/part of job role
Certain job roles take part in a management group
Steering group performs some management functions
Committees for different management functions (i.e. finance, personnel)
Managers for Operations (day to day), but Governance (big picture) by members
Board of Directors
Autonomous departments with/without management

2. Decision-making.
A process for making decisions – or more commonly, several processes for making several different kinds of decisions – is the other element of self-management to consider. In a hierarchical model, decisions flow one direction, with less and less autonomy the further downhill you get. In a democratic model, it's important to consider both management and accountability in creating decision-making structures. What decisions does the whole group need to have a voice in (hiring/firing, compensation, major purchases)? What decisions can be delegated (what kind of paper to buy)? How will those decisions be made? Consensus? Majority vote? Required voting? Optional? How will the group hold decision-makers accountable and give them support? There are models for all these options, as we'll see in a minute. First some basics:

Some Possibilities for Decision-making Processes:
Consensus
Modified consensus

Majority   vote
Consensus for small group decisions, vote for large-group decisions
Consensus for some types of decisions, vote for other types
Elected   representatives

It is important to note that in both accountability and decision-making, the most effective structures are usually a combination of several of the above-listed options, and some that are created to fit a situation. Effective democratic management is generally not a question of 'either/or,' but rather of 'both/and,' and the combination depends on the people and the nature of business. There are several functional, inspiring models, but no single boilerplate, one-size-fits-all solution, because each workplace is different and must create the management structures that make sense for it.

Accountability and Decision-Making: Some Democratic Management Models

Figure 1. Conventional Management Model

CONVENTIONAL MODEL

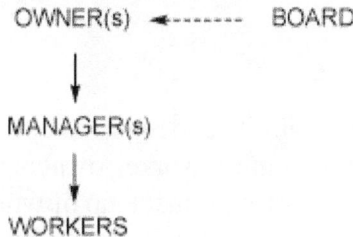

OWNER(s) ◄------- BOARD

↓

MANAGER(s)

↓

WORKERS

Decision-making responsibility and requirements for accountability flow in one direction only, from owner to manager down to workers.

Figure 2. Worker Self-Management Model, Flat

FLAT DEMOCRATIC MODEL

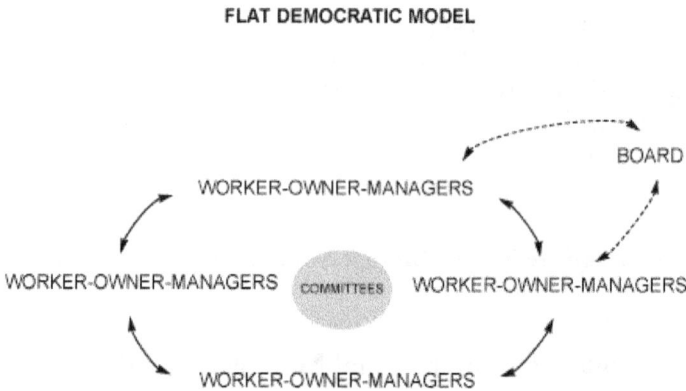

Decision-making responsibility and requirements for accountability flow in all directions among member worker-owners who are also their own managers. There may be a Board made up of worker-owners that shares some decision-making responsibility and is accountable to all other workers. Committees may make certain types of decisions and are accountable to all workers. Many smaller workplaces use this model; some larger workplaces use this model for departments which compose the general membership (workforce).

Figure 3. Worker Self-Management Model
with Management Job Roles

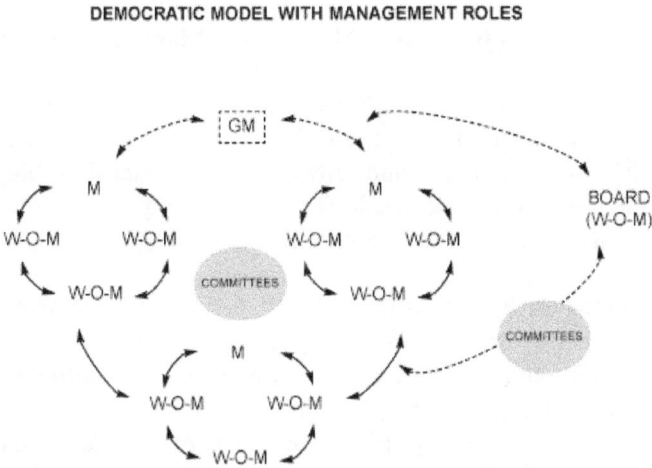

DEMOCRATIC MODEL WITH MANAGEMENT ROLES

Decision-making responsibility and requirements for accountability flow in all directions among member worker-owners, including those with management job roles. There may be management roles in each department and/or a general manager. Note that worker-owner managers are accountable to other worker-owners. As in Figure 2, some decision-making responsibility may be shared by a Board of worker-owners that is accountable to all workers, and by committees that make certain types of decisions.

Activity

In order to get participants acquainted with the hands-on process of creating cooperative structures, they were split into a group for a participatory exercise. You are starting a housecleaning business. You have several interested people who are experience house cleaners. You want it to be democratically owned and governed. Divide into groups to answer these questions:

Who will make the following decisions? How will they make them?
-   Policies
-   Operations (how to do the work)
-   Big picture and long-term planning
-   Hiring and firing, personnel

-   Financial
-   Office duties

Reconvene and share different groups' approaches.

Some Practical Things to Keep in Mind When Starting a Cooperative

One of the first things you'll need to ask yourself as you move forward in planning and before you commit to anything: Is the worker cooperative a good form for you? What are the benefits and drawbacks? Consider how the particulars work with the group of people you have, the industry you're working in, your geographic location, and a host of other factors.

The next thing to bear in mind is that you will be running the business you will be working for. This means you will be engaged in a competitive market, making financial decisions, and assuming a lot of responsibility. It's like owning your home rather than renting it: if the plumbing breaks, you have to fix it. Are you ready for that? Are you ready to think about money more than you might want to? Are you ready to think ethically and in a principled way about money? And if you are not talking about a business, but a social enterprise, how will you support it financially? Either way, you'll have to know your numbers and be ready to understand the financial world in which you are operating.

Just as important, you are talking about running a business or an enterprise democratically. This is no small feat. You will need to commit to an ongoing process of training. You will also need to commit to a thoughtful setup of structures, an honest assessment of the people involved, and a deep, abiding flexibility and patience. Democracy comes naturally to us in some ways, but we're also working against a lifetime of having very little training in real democracy; that is, listening, compromising, and thinking in terms of the common good. The more time you take to set things up thoughtfully and anticipate problems, the better chance you have of not being frustrated or caught by surprise.

Cooperation is everywhere – you already know how to do it, now you need to formalize that knowledge into structures. At the same time, it's not easy because we spend our whole lives enmeshed in hierarchy with very little formal training in democracy. Be aware of this. Research how it's been done in the past. Other people's mistakes are your best teachers.

You need a good group of people, a vision and clear mission, a commitment to structure, a commitment to democracy, and last but not least, some money. There's money out there for startups and conversions. (See resources section following.) There's also technical assistance out there – cooperative developers, conventional business and nonprofit groups, and most important, other co-ops. Other co-ops will help you, and this is the best help you can get. Seek it out! Use it! You'll have to lasso everything that looks good and piece it all together, but there is help out there.

Resources

All the network-building and resource-building of the last ten years has started to pay off. If you want to start a co-op, convert your business, or improve and strengthen your co-op, there are people and materials to help you. There is a worker co-op conference every year now, national conferences every other year and regional conferences on the East and West coast in the other years. Many cities and states have worker co-op groups: the Bay Area, Portland, Minneapolis, Boston, Western Massachusetts, and soon Madison, Wisconsin.

If you are lucky enough to live in an area with a concentration of co-ops, find out if there's an organized group that meets, and go to one of their meetings. If there are several worker co-ops but no group, how about organizing one yourself? Many of the local worker co-op networks started with social events or basic skill-sharing. If you do not live or work in an area with many worker co-ops, you could make it a point to attend one of the annual worker co-op conferences held in different parts of the country each year. These conferences are an institution for worker co-op people; they're where we gather to share skills, meet each other, generate ideas, and build our movement. You can find out about worker cooperative events across the country at the US Federation website, www.usworker.coop. Another good place to start is in the resource list that follows this chapter.

As for materials, how-tos, training curricula, that sort of thing, an excellent new handbook has just been published by the Northcountry Cooperative Development Fund called the Worker Co-op Toolbox: available online at: http://www.ncdf.org/documents/worker_coop_toolbox.pdf

There are books and other handbooks available on our website: www.usworker.coop

But really, your best resource is other worker cooperatives. They've done the work to develop good systems; they can tell you from experience what works and what doesn't. They are on the whole incredibly generous with their time and documents. With that in mind, the US Federation has gathered these working and model documents into a Worker Co-op Document Library that's available online.

We are also starting to put together a technical assistance network of experienced worker co-opers and professionals that support worker co-ops, like attorneys and accountants. Our dream is that when someone calls with questions and a plan for starting a co-op, we can send a little team of experienced worker co-op members to consult and give assistance. That's still far down the line as a formal program, but it's already happening informally, especially in areas where the worker co-op economy is strong, like the Bay Area.

Why Worker Cooperatives Matter

The strength (and some would argue the weakness) of worker cooperatives is that they are deeply practical. For many people, they are also political, part of a larger movement for economic democracy, political democracy, labor rights, sustainability, and social justice. While individual worker cooperatives may (and do!) disagree on this point, from my perspective, worker ownership is structurally anti-capitalist, or at the very least a rejection of a core tenet of capitalism, that is, the commodification and exploitation of labor (workers) by capital (owners). Worker co-ops still use capital and function in the market system – we all do, it's inescapable unless we want to barricade ourselves in the hills (we tried that, it didn't work) – but they are now an alternative to capitalism, and it's my hope that at some point they will constitute a real challenge to it.

First and foremost, the worker co-op is a living, vibrant, inspiring alternative. We all know capitalism doesn't work, but there is a dearth of workable economic alternatives. This is the value of the co-op - it's something you can say yes to, something that demonstrates that we can meet our human needs in another, less destructive and inequitable, way. And let's not forget that our jobs are where most of us spend the majority of our time. If we can make money in a non-oppressive, non-exploitative way, then we have achieved some measure of justice and sustainability in the very act of working.

In addition, worker cooperatives provide training in democracy . They foster the skills and engagement we need to build successful movements. Most of us have few chances and virtually no training in democratic decision-making, in regarding one another with respect as equals, or in exercising our own power. If we are to create successful movements for social change, we must have this training and these examples in place *before* capitalism self-cannibalizes and collapses, so that we are strong and prepared to build a new economy. Even before such a collapse, worker cooperatives are well-suited to the instability in our current economy. They can fill the widening gaps that capitalism creates, provide basic services, and meet basic needs.

Because co-ops are rooted in their communities, they tend to have more sustainable practices, civic connections, and investment in doing right by the community. Worker cooperatives were among the first "green" businesses, long before green was a trendy marketing term, because they actually cared about the safety and health of their workers and community (which were often one and the same).

Lastly, co-ops provide jobs that are stable and offer the asset of ownership to their workers. In this way, co-ops can build assets in communities that traditionally haven't had assets or access to it. This ownership of capital empowers workers and can alleviate pervasive economic inequities like the racial wealth gap.

Challenges and Strategy

Worker co-ops are growing, interest in them is growing, and federating institutions are growing. I would hesitate to call it a movement, but maybe it's a mini-movement. There are still some challenges. Workplace democracy efforts in the U.S. so far have been small-scale. Can they work in bigger industries and on larger scales? How will we deal with growth? How can established co-ops pass on their resources and knowledge to the new generation of democratic workplaces started by people of color, immigrants, and people organizing traditionally low-wage jobs? What happens when we compete head-on with capitalist enterprises in the marketplace? Can democratically-managed co-ops be strong, flexible and savvy enough to fight corporate hierarchies that are single-mindedly focused on profit? Are our principles strong enough to keep us rooted in justice?

I would argue that these tensions are one of the most vibrant things about the worker cooperative movement, because they are an indication of real people struggling with real issues, from a principled perspective. Worker co-ops are engaged in the world as it stands, and attempting to work within the system and structures we have right now. But the worker co-op movement is going to have to face some hard questions with principled intention. Sometimes we like to think of ourselves (and other people like to think of us) as a shining example, but the challenge is to remain a shining example while broadening scope, forging alliances, growing, and diversifying. We are charged with both growing our movement and collaborating with other movements. We may fear that we cannot do this without corrupting our ideals, or getting consumed or destroyed by globalized free-market capitalism. But we have to try. What's the alternative?

Notes

[1] The Mondragon Cooperative Corporation in the Basque region of Spain, founded in the 1950s and now the largest cooperative in the world with over 150 subsidiary companies. For more on Mondragon, there is a book: Morrison, Roy. (1991). *We Build the Road as We Travel: Mondragon, A Cooperative Social System.* Philadelphia: New Society Publishers.

[2] This can be found online at:
http://usworker.coop/public/documents/Oslo_Declaration.pdf

SECTION V:

BUILDING THE SOLIDARITY ECONOMY THROUGH NETWORKING AND COMMUNITY ORGANIZING

15
The Solidarity Economy as a Strategy for Changing the Economy

Ethel Cote, Nancy Neamtan, and Nedda Angulo Villareal

Editors' Introduction: Activists and academics in the U.S. have much to learn from the practices of other countries, many of whom have long histories of social/solidarity economy organizing. In this exciting session, Ethel Cote and Nancy Neamtam of Canada, and Nedda Angulo Villareal of Peru, shared lessons from their experiences in this area.

The Canadian Community Economic Development Network: Focusing on a Marginalized Community in Ontario through the Building of a Solidarity Economy Movement
Ethel Cote

> *Éthel Côté has been involved in the economic, social, cooperative and cultural fields for 30 years. She holds a certificate in Agricultural Leadership and a Masters Degree in Community Economic Development, and teaches Community Economic Development at Boreal College and Concordia University. She took part in several fact-finding missions in Europe and Latin America to investigate the cooperative movements, the mobilization and socio-economic consensus-building processes, and the impact of globalization on the socio-economic development of rural communities in these countries. Through Uniterra, she participated in skill-strengthening missions in Mali, Niger and Senegal for the social and solidarity economy networks of these countries. She was also part of the organizing committee for the 3rd World Conference on Globalization and Solidarity held in Dakar in 2005, and is the Canadian representative on the Board of the International Network for Promotion of Social Solidarity Economy (RIPESS). Since the year 2000, she has mentored hundreds of communities and promoters of social*

enterprises, and during the last three years, she has been actively involved with the Center for Community Enterprise, training the trainers in social enterprise development. She has been involved with the Canadian Community Economic Development Network (CCEDNET) for several years and sits on both the National Policy Council and the International Committee. She currently chairs the Ontario Solidarity Economy Network. She is also the CEO of L'Art du développement, a small business involved in Social Enterprise, CED & co-op development.

Definition of CED Community Economic Development

Action by people locally to create economic opportunities and enhance the social and environmental conditions of their communities, particularly with those most marginalized, on a sustainable and inclusive basis.

I will take a few minutes to present the Canadian Community Economic Development network (CCEDNET) and also one of its newest members, a very young provincial network: *Economie solidaire de l'Ontario* (ESO). For the last seven years, I have been a volunteer on the Board of CCEDNET and this year, I have taken on the duties of Co-Chair of the Policy Council. I am also a Community Economic Development (CED) practitioner, so on a daily basis, I provide technical assistance to support local development strategies, co-op development, social enterprise development, leadership and governance training, strategic planning, etc. As a Francophone who lives outside of Quebec, I am very actively involved with a minority community which has been marginalized in many ways.

Today, I will talk about the Canadian network and also about a new and emerging network inspired by *Le Chantier de l'Économie Sociale* in Québec. These networks are part of a vibrant solidarity economy movement being built in different regions of Canada, as well as on the national scene. We use strategic planning to mobilize and to develop the national movement. In Ontario, mobilization for the ESO has been mainly organic until now, but the steps we took in the last five years are quite impressive, and we have learned by listening to others and by sharing our experience.

The Canadian Community Economic Development Network

Let's begin with the Canadian Community Economic Development Network. CCEDNET is a national, nonprofit association of community organizations working to enhance social and economic conditions of communities based everywhere in Canada. CCEDNET has 650 members, and that represents between 4,000 and 5,000 network organizations throughout the country. In that membership base, there are community-based organizations, aboriginal organizations, youth groups, women's groups, co-operative organizations in all sectors, immigrant associations creating their own social enterprises as well as urban and rural initiatives. CCEDNET also mobilizes actors from the public and private sectors, universities, social enterprises and financial institutions. Before I continue, I will invite my colleague Mike Lewis, one of CCEDNET's founders, to share information about the history and the progress of this movement.

Mike Lewis on the origins of CCEDNET

Some of the inspiration from our early work came from the United States. In 1981, when I was in northern Alberta, I came across the newsletter of the *National Economic Development Law Center* in Berkley. They work with legal service corporations across the United States. They were talking about a bunch of pieces that I was beginning to become aware of, and I started working with the *National Economic Development Law Center* on projects.

Through my work with them, I became aware of the 25-year anniversary conference on the War on Poverty that was held by the Center in Chicago in 1988. I thought that this was a good opportunity to convene some Canadians in Chicago and show what we were doing in Canada in the area of community economic development. Twenty-five Canadians went to Chicago, and met in our own parallel sessions.

CED: a multi-faceted approach, conceived and directed locally, for revitalizing and renewing community economies by managing and strengthening community resources for community benefit.

CED: an alternative to conventional approaches to economic development, founded on the belief that problems facing communities – unemployment, poverty, job loss, environmental degradation and loss of community control – can best be addressed by community-led, grass roots, holistic approach.

Many of the initial relationships and discussions that emerged out of this meeting were the seeds for a ten-year organizing process of trying to bring people together across the country, creating the basis for the formation of the Canadian CED Network. Nancy Neamtan, in her previous incarnation, was managing a community development organization in the poorest neighborhoods of Montreal - an area that is now really managing growth rather than dealing with depletion and disinvestment. That was going on in Quebec, while other CED organizations were emerging in different parts of Canada, partly inspired by what had happened in the United States. So we worked to put together a research project to explain the innovations which were occurring in the urban context. We wrote a couple of books on this topic, and out of that process, began to think about how we could organize the CED movement, how we could bring people together. We began to think about the practices of the work we had been doing, and began to try to learn from them. Out of that process, we were able to weave things together and form the Canadian CED Network, which was finally incorporated in 1999.

Social Economy

Community nonprofit organizations and co-operatives are the engines of the social economy, creating economic and social outcomes for their communities.

We refer to these organizations and the strategies they use in much of English Canada as "Community Economic Development," by which we mean integrated approaches to creating social and economic opportunities through local action by people to reduce disadvantage and generate greater self sufficiency.

Building a Social Economy

Building assets and enterprises collectively owned by communities to generate both social and economic benefits
♦ Social Assets (housing, child care, cultural facilities)
♦ Social and community enterprises including co-operatives
♦ Equity and debt capital for community investment

Ethel Cote on CCEDNET today

So CCEDNET is a **member-led, democratically governed network that:**
- Supports practitioner development and peer learning amongst community-based organizations.
- Advocates policy to all levels of government and key sectors to strengthen support to citizen-led efforts to reverse social and economic disadvantage.

- Promotes community economic development and the social economy as an alternative model: citizen-led; community-based; integrating social, economic, cultural and environmental objectives.

CCEDNET is a very active network that is implementing various initiatives. However, I think that at the same time, the network is at a crossroads in its development. Being a member-led organization means that members have always given direction as to the organization. They do this through broad consultations during CCEDNET's national conference and through committees and board discussions from which a strong strategic plan is established, one that was just recently updated. In the last two years, CCEDNET has faced financial issues for which social and financial solutions have been identified. Very interesting projects were developed, and CCEDNET turned to the government to fund them. Some funding was confirmed and now the network has a lot of work to deliver. More than ever, CCEDNET needs to continue to implement projects that are important for its members, but at the same time, I think that, more than ever, it necessary to explore ways to be financially independent and thus not become an organization that is driven by projects and funders. CCEDNET needs to continue to be driven by its mission, its core business, and I am convinced that we will get there.

One of CCEDNET's key initiatives is the research and development component. CCEDNET is Co-chair of the National Social Economy Research Hub and many of its members are involved in Regional Research Centers which received five year Social Sciences and Humanities Research Council funding. There is one hub in Quebec, two in Ontario and a few more throughout Canada. Through this research, CCEDNET is working actively on:

- CED & Social Economy Mapping (Solidarity Economy Mapping)
- Immigrant-led CED
- CED and Social Inclusion
- Place-based Poverty Reduction
- And CED Funding Models: solidarity finance

In regards to Social Inclusion and Poverty Reduction, CCEDNET truly thinks that crime prevention and the involvement of offenders in activities that build social responsibility should be a major focus for CED organizations in many communities. CCEDNET believes there are major opportunities to use the social economy as a means to reduce crime and enhance public safety. Another example is child care offered by non-profit and co-operative groups which are being developed alongside other assets and opportunities for families such as skills and training, self-employment, English or French as a second language, culture, recreation, and self-help programs. These models of providing child care as part of a continuum of supports and opportunities for families have great potential for scaling up. Immigrant and refugee settlement and economic integration through the development of co-operative and social enterprises is a focus for an increasing number of immigrant serving and ethno-cultural groups. CCEDNET currently has a pilot project that is testing new approaches to using co-operatives and community economic development by immigrants to enhance their economic self-sufficiency. The network's objective is to see public policies and programs become more informed about CED as a component of immigrant integration and settlement in Canada.

In Quebec, they have ten years of experience in documenting their story and it is very impressive to observe the movement-building, the mapping, the various stakeholders involved in the field, and the results.

In regards to Solidarity Funding, CCEDNET was involved in a roundtable on community investment and thus had an opportunity to learn about and share different and sustainable funding mechanisms and models.

As Co-Chair of CCEDNET's Policy Council, I can confirm that the network is actively involved in policy-building. A very active Policy Council is in place that is working on a National CED Policy Framework, Funding, and Labor Market Development. In some parts of Canada, provincial governments and municipalities are looking at ways that they could efficiently support CED. In Nunavut, they have elaborated a CED policy, and in Manitoba there is a lot of support. In Ontario, there is momentum now, after ten years of very conservative governments. We have a great opportunity with the current government to move things forward and involve them at different levels, such as policy, and funding incentives.

CCEDNET's Learning Activities

Where action learning activities are concerned, a National Conference is organized every year. The 2007 conference was held in Newfoundland, and the 2008 national conference will be in the middle of Canada in Saskatchewan. Those events provide good networking opportunities for members and partners, learning experiences through workshops, and also a democratic experience by participating in the Annual General Meeting of the Network. Regional peer learning events are also organized because the proximity and the similarities provide a whole different and efficient dimension for sharing, learning and regional networking. We need to regroup more closely with organizations that share the same reality. So in Alberta, British Columbia, and Ontario, groups are establishing Regional platforms, sometimes as a chapter of CCEDNET, or as in Alberta, as an independently incorporated co-op. We mobilize nationally to be a strong national voice, but we also support regional mobilization.

CCEDNET also has a partnership with *le Chantier de l'Économie Sociale*: the two groups operate under a memorandum of understanding to engage the strengths of both networks, mainly around policy-building at the national level. Learning, strategic thinking and sharing are very important between networks of networks.

Regarding Social Enterprises, two national conferences have already been organized, bringing practitioners, funders, partners and technical assistance providers together to support social enterprise development, as well as many other key players involved in the field. CCEDNET sees this interest growing and will facilitate a roundtable to maintain the relationship between the key players and to continue to support the movement that is building, or in other words, "connect the dots." Good debates on themes such as: "Should we all be involved under the same umbrella organization or network, or should we build various sector networks have been initiated?" Practitioners, partners and funders will continue to have those debates and I truly hope we will find the best strategy to continue to grow as a movement representing Solidarity Economy in Canada.

Over the last few years, at the national meetings, the room was filled with a majority of gray-haired people and not that many young people. However, we all know that there are a lot of young people involved in social, economic, and green initiatives, but they were not actively involved in the CED movement. Some young people who were involved in co-ops came a few years ago to the National Conference and decided to do something to mobilize and to get a voice. CCEDNET agreed to support the young people through the creation of an Emerging Leaders Committee. During the last year, this committee was made permanent, thus confirming a seat for their Chair on CCEDNET's Board of Directors. So far, having the opportunity for them to meet has given CCEDNET the opportunity to see who really needs to be engaged with, and hopefully to bring this new blood to network. So CCEDNET has organized four different initiatives:　⇒　The Emerging Leaders initiative with 50 young activists across Canada, because in order to know and acknowledge youth's experience, it is necessary to identify what's out there.

⇒　Profiles of youth engagement in CED were documented and posted on the website.

⇒　The CreateAction Program funded 60 paid interns who were involved in CED all over Canada over a three-year period.

⇒　And finally, with both intern and volunteer youth supervised by the youth committee, a National Report on the Effectiveness of Youth Inclusion was produced.

All of this research is very recent, thus representing the reality of our movement today.

CCEDNET's Policy Framework

To create its Policy Framework, CCEDNET mobilized with other national networks to strategize. The group agrees that the most advantageous model would be an integrated community-led model that builds and mobilizes community and individual assets to:

- Strengthen social capital
- Strengthen human capital
- Strengthen financial capital

For years, all of those networks were working side by side to negotiate a Social Economy Initiative with the federal government that would have provided the community $132 million. Some funds were also included for research and patient capital – loans that are paid back slowly at lower interest rates. The only province that managed to negotiate the transfer of some of these funds was Québec, and those funds were invested in a major trust fund.

Unfortunately, because of a change in federal government, most of the Social Economy Initiative was cancelled. However, after an initial period of shock and incredulity, the networks have decided to go ahead and pursue their strategy of working together in Ontario and elsewhere in order to establish a Community Trust Fund involving the provincial government as well as the private and social sectors.

I have been involved in CCEDNET in different capacities from the beginning, and I can confirm that the need for connecting with each other, and for connecting the dots between the stories and practices, not only in one province, but throughout Canada. This was a need long before CCEDNET was created, and it is only now that we are slowly but surely succeeding.

The Solidarity Economy in Ontario

The Francophone community has a history that is similar to what Nancy Neamtam has shared with us, so I won't go over that again. However, I would like to remark that there are 7 million Francophones in Canada: there are 6 million in

Quebec, and thus 1 million outside of Quebec. In Ontario, we are 550,000, and we think that in fact we would be more numerous if we were to include the immigrants from French-speaking nations. For example, if an immigrant enters their first language as Swahili in the census, the census will automatically count this person as having English as their first official language. All the immigrants from French-speaking African countries are thus probably being counted as having English as their first official language.

The reality is that living in French in Ontario is a real fight every day for services, education, etc. You breathe and fight every day. 10 years ago we fought to have our own school system, and 15 years ago to have our first community college put into place. The community continually needs to fight to be recognized, to have all the services that are provided elsewhere in Canada. We are a pacifist people, we like to work with all the key stakeholders, but when due processes do not work, the community has learned that it is necessary to engage in a power struggle. The Francophone community has thus sued the government more than once in order to defend or obtain our rights, and we have won every time. In the field of CED, the Ontario Francophone community is the only community in Canada who is bringing the government to court. We do this not only to have our rights recognized and thus have access to CED and Social Economy funding, but also in the hope that this process will force the government to officially recognize CED and the Social Economy and thus open doors to all other government departments for additional funding in the field of CED for both Francophone and Anglophone communities. We are fighting for ourselves, but hope that it opens doors for other communities.

So, inspired by CCEDNET, by the *Chantier de l'Économie Sociale*, and by RIPESS (The Intercontinental Network for the Promotion of the Social Solidarity Economy), a group of practitioners created an Ontario network in 2004: Économie solidaire de l'Ontario (ÉSO) which is a member of CCEDNET. We have been strategic, we have learned from our experience, and we have tried to bring all the key organizations involved in CED and the Social Economy to the table. Because we are a small community, we always relate to the private businesses in our community and the educational system because we know that we are stronger if we are connected together.

Économie Solidaire de l'Ontario is still a young network, but it has succeeded in sharing a lot of knowledge, and it has created a website. Not having the capacity to physically gather people from all over Ontario, we find that technology is a good way to connect. In collaboration with partners, two tele-learning sessions have been organized and both were successes. We decided to share information because we know that that is a good way to connect with each other. A newsletter named "Vision DEC" was created where key organizations and initiatives are highlighted. The 21st edition has now been published. 300 organizations were on the mailing list after two years and now there are over 1,000. Practitioners, researchers, organizations, and members of the non-profit sector from different components of the community receive the newsletters. Politicians have requested the newsletter and many Francophone media have asked for it in order to be able to promote this kind of development. A partnership with the Francophone municipalities has been concluded and ÉSO is helping them to organize their next Provincial Congress under the theme of Solidarity and Community Economic Development. We need to tell the world what is going on in our own part of the world and in Canada.

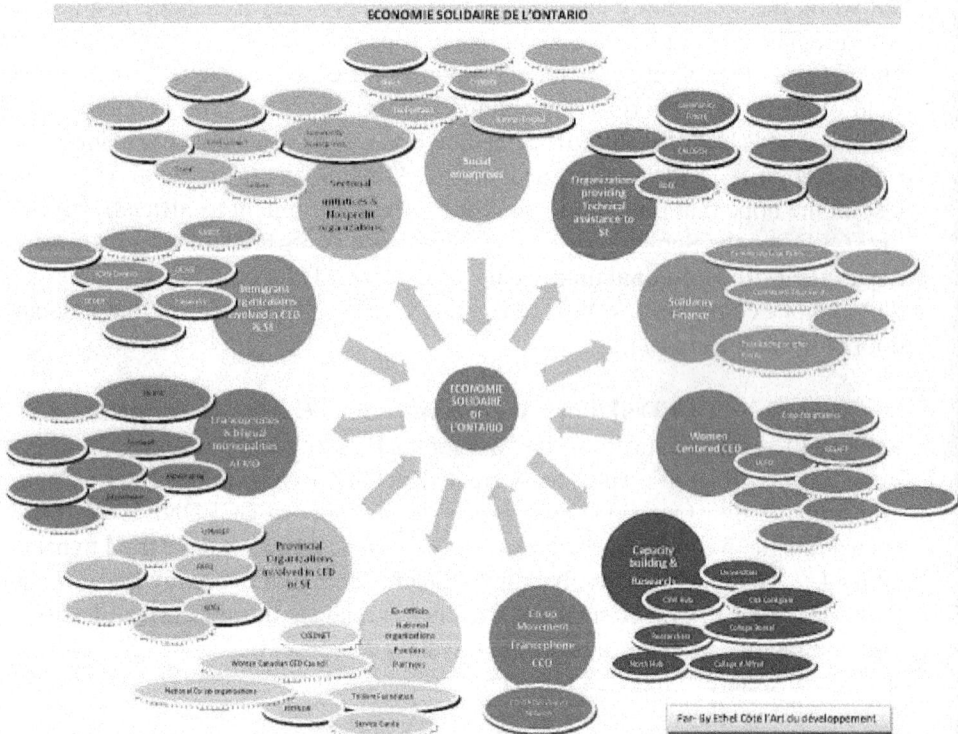

Five years ago, the solidarity economy map included co-ops and the non-profit sector. Today, our organic mapping shows all of these different elements.

Économie solidaire's website, www.economiesolidaire.ca (only in French), has much useful information and includes the 21 editions of our newsletter.

We knew that we did not have the capacity to put forward major initiatives like building a major trust fund alone, so we joined in a strategic alliance with Anglophone and First Nation groups in Ontario. A consortium has been created and there is an emerging CED Network in Ontario that is growing and that is also connected to CCEDNET.

During the last month and a half, a group has been working on what many were trying to do at the federal level for a year – to put together and find funding for a social economy initiative. We have met with five or six ministers and a few key bureaucrats, and have received a warm welcome for our trust fund concept. A critical element for us is to anchor this trust fund through the credit union movement, because, unlike the Quebec movement, we do not have the experience necessary to create an independent structure to manage this funding mechanism. We have momentum and doors are beginning to open to the idea of investing in this kind of work right now. We are documenting our experience and our practice to show how we can mobilize and manage our development as a community and link very strategically with all the components of the solidarity economy.

To sum up, we are hoping to establish a community trust fund very soon in Ontario to maintain the pace of the Ontario and Canadian movements, to continue building with municipalities, and continue to support them in the organization of a provincial and efficient Congress that will be involved more actively in CED and the Solidarity Economy.

The number of social and solidarity economy activities being implemented at all levels in Canada is increasing. As our movement grows and develops, we are resolving issues which we encounter along the way, and planning for the present and the future. We need to maintain the networking and continue to grow as a movement, and the key to this is to learn from each other, to share practices and lessons learned from different kinds of strategies to make things happen, and also to learn from the experiences of Quebec, Canada, USA, Europe, Africa, Latin America, and others. I think that, with our strength to fight and energy to mobilize, we will succeed together.

Chantier de l'Économie Sociale: Building the Solidarity Economy in Quebec

Nancy Neamtan

Nancy Neamtan is President and Executive Director of the Chantier de l'Économie Sociale, a non-profit organization administered by 28 representatives of various networks of social enterprises (cooperatives and non-profits), local development organisations and social movements. Since 1999 Ms. Neamtan has been Co-Director of ARUC-ÉS (Community University Research Alliance on the Social Economy). She was the founder and President of the Board of Directors of RISQ (Réseau d'investissement social du Québec), a $10 million investment fund dedicated to the non-profit and cooperative sector between from 1997 to 2006. Since November 2006, she has been President of the Fiducie du le Chantier de l'Économie Sociale, a new $53 million investment fund for collective enterprise. Ms. Neamtan is actively involved in civil society organisations in Quebec. She was named by the Quebec government to represent the community sector at the Commission des partenaires du marché de travail (Labour Force Partnership Commission). She is a board member of CECI, an NGO involved in international cooperation and of CIRIEC Canada.

My name is Nancy Neamtan and I work with an organization called the *Chantier de l'Économie Sociale*. The name of our organization is hard to translate because it has a double meaning in French. The word "chantier" refers to a working group but it also is the word for construction site. Despite the fact that our organization has existed for over ten years, we have kept this term because the image of the construction site is a good image for what we are trying to do: build a more democratic and equitable economy.

The Context of Building the Solidarity Economy in Quebec

Before I start talking about the solidarity economy experience in Quebec, it is important to understand the context. Quebec is a French-speaking nation within Canada. Its population is around 7.5 million, and as a small French-speaking society within North America, it has historically had to struggle to survive as a nation. This has created a context for social dialogue and cohesion that have been favorable conditions for the development of the Social/Solidarity Economy movement. Another element of context that has favorably influenced the development of the solidarity economy is the history of economic development in

Quebec. Until 1960 the Quebec economy was controlled totally by outside inter-ests: American, British, or English-Canadian fortunes. There was no French-Canadian bourgeoisie; there was in fact no modern state, and the clergy had a major influence in Quebec society, including in political and economic spheres. In the sixties, what we call the "Quiet Revolution" took place. The Quiet Revo-lution began through the electoral process, with the election in 1960 of a new government whose slogan was 'Maitre chez nous' (masters in our own house) and whose program was the building of a modern welfare state. In a very short period of time, Quebec went from being a very Catholic society to a very secular society. The welfare state was built in the 1960s. At the same time there was a very strong process of unionization that has sustained itself up until today. At the moment, the labor movement in Quebec represents over 40% of the labor force. This is a very important part of the context for the development of the so-cial/solidarity economy.

Over the past decades, our welfare state has "adapted" to globalization, but, de-spite this, there is still a certain culture, a certain reality of government interven-tion, not only in the area of social development, but also within the economy. It is important to understand that one of the first roles that was played by the Que-bec government in the 1960s during the "Quiet Revolution" was to create eco-nomic institutions that allowed the development of a Francophone bourgeoisie. This is important because this context has been very favorable for the develop-ment of government support for the solidarity economy. Of course, I do not want to minimize the great work that has been done by people in communities across Quebec, but it is important to appreciate its context.

Beginning with a Happy Ending:
The Summit on the Social and Solidarity Economy

I am now going to move on to tell the story of *le Chantier*. I thought I would start with a happy ending, which is not really an ending but at least the end of a really nice chapter. It is about a summit that was held in November 2007 in Quebec, called The Summit on the Social and Solidarity Economy. It brought together 700 people, and since it was not a conference but a summit, people who attended were delegates for their networks or organizations. They represented a wide range of networks of cooperative and nonprofit solidarity/social economy enter-prises, economic development organizations in local communities, networks for the different regions of Quebec, social movements, the union movement, the en-vironmental movement, the women's movement, and the community movement. We also had international visitors from twenty-three countries.

The Summit was organized to celebrate the tenth year of the beginning of an organized social/solidarity economy movement in Quebec. A declaration was adopted at the end of the Summit. The first paragraph of the declaration explains the context well:

> On the occasion of the Social and Solidarity Economy Summit, we actors of the social economy from the community, cooperative and mutual benefit movement and associations, cultural, environmental and social movements, unions, international corporations and local and regional development organizations, affirm with pride and determination our commitment to build a Social/ Solidarity Economy locally, regionally, nationally and internationally. For decades now across Quebec and even abroad, we have been constructing a social and economic project rooted in the notion that there should be no losers. It is a project based on the values of social justice, fairness, solidarity and democracy. Today we are very proud of the results and achievements of social economy actors and partners. Our continued efforts, especially during the past decade, have enabled us to create new instruments and reinforce existing ones. It has facilitated the emergence of new sectors and strengthened others. Our efforts have also contributed to this important creation of thousand of jobs and the improvement or formation of new spaces of social inclusion, mobilization and governance. And in doing so, they have enhanced citizen participation, and also enabled women to play a leading role in this values-added economy. (When we refer to values-added, we mean values like solidarity, democracy, equity etc.)[1]

The Summit on the Social and Solidarity Economy was a turning point for us. It was a manifestation that today, in Quebec, one of the strongest social movements is the movement for a social/solidarity economy. This movement has been built up over the years and, very importantly, from the bottom up: from local practices, from debates within social movements, and particularly from within the community and union movements. This movement has been based on the premise that, if we say that we want to transform the world and we want to transform our society, then we cannot just protest and ask the government to do things differently. We cannot just protest against the way neoliberal economics are destroying our planet, our social fabric. We have to start building alternatives; otherwise we are not credible; we are not responding to community needs. So this whole issue of taking economic development head-on, without losing our value system, has been the driving force for the creation of this movement. The initial debate took place within the labor movement in the 1980s in Quebec. The labor movement made a conscious choice of saying, "Our job is not just to negotiate collective agreements; our job is also to become actors in creating economic opportunities, and creating jobs, and becoming a major force in the development of our communities and our regions." The two major labor unions now control and manage labor pension funds, or solidarity funds, that are investing in economic activity across Quebec. Since the 1980s, community organizations and social movements have also become involved in community economic development in responding to the needs of rural and urban communities. There has been a learning process about what economics is, how economic development takes place, and how it could be done differently. There has been a process of re-appropriation, the taking back of certain economic concepts that, in the current ideological context, have been "privatized" by neoliberal ideology. This learning and demystification process has been an important part of building this movement.

History of the Movement in Quebec

In 1996, an important event took place in Quebec which created a context for the coming together of the social/solidarity economy movement. The event is a good illustration of this fairly unique Quebec political culture of working together among the business sector, unions, community organizations and government. *The Quebec Summit on the Economy and Employment* was convened by the Quebec government in 1996 in the context of a 12% unemployment rate and huge pressure to reduce government deficit. In fact, the Quebec government was being pushed by Standard and Poor's in New York to eliminate the deficit by cutting back government spending, to avoid seeing its credit rating decline. In this context of cutbacks and high unemployment, the Quebec government convened representatives from all spheres of socio-economic activities.

The Premier confronted the business sector, saying, "Government doesn't create jobs, you do. So why don't you present strategies and projects to create employment and the government will support and accompany you?" The social movements that were invited to the Summit, including the women's movement that had just organized a major women's march against poverty and violence against women, and other social movements, asked themselves what they could do. Because of the context, we were able to come together around a new concept, the social economy, a term that was very new for us in Quebec. The social economy term, widely used in Europe to refer to cooperatives, associations and mutuals, had been taken up in Quebec following the 1995 Women's March against poverty. The women's movement had demanded public investment in social infrastructure and in the social economy, referring specifically to the numerous women's and community organizations that exist across Quebec. Within the context of the summit, a working group on the social economy was created, providing an opportunity for us to use this new vocabulary to express both the realities of the cooperative and non-profit sector, and its aspirations.

Through this common vocabulary we were able to pull together and put forward a wide range of ideas, projects, sectoral strategies, and activities we could develop, and identify the kind of tools we needed to be able to develop them. We also understood (and this was our first recommendation in the plan we presented at *the Summit on the Economy and Employment*) the need to gain recognition of the importance of the collective sector – what we call the social economy – within the Quebec economy. In fact, the major battle that we have waged over the past ten years, and have not totally but almost won, is that if you want to understand and support economic development in Quebec, it is essential to recognize the plurality of our economy. It is essential to recognize that there is a public economy and a private economy, but there is also a collective economy based on cooperative and nonprofit organizations, based on collective control of economic tools that have social or environmental missions, where people have primacy over capital, and where there is democratic control.

This social economy has always been a part of the socioeconomic infrastructure of Quebec. Our premise, which we presented at the Summit and continue to defend today, is that the social economy has tremendous potential for development if we provide the appropriate development tools, if we recognize its existence and its specificities, and (as we have often said though we are far from having won this) if we give it a level-playing field with the private sector. In other words, we demand the same kind of support for our collective enterprises as the government has given to the private for-profit sector. The 1996 Summit was the birthplace of this coalition in favor of the social economy, of this coming together within an organization that I have had the privilege to head up since its foundation.

A Network of Networks: the Chantier de l'Économie Sociale

The Chantier de l'Économie Sociale is today a network of networks. It has a Board of Directors made up of 32 people representing a wide range of networks. One segment of our Board is made up of representatives of networks of cooperative and nonprofit enterprises organized by sectors, such as co-op housing, worker coops, nonprofit recycling businesses, parent-controlled non-profit day care, and non-profit manufacturing businesses whose mission is to create employment for the handicapped – all kinds of networks of social/solidarity economy enterprises. Another segment of our Board is made up of representatives of networks of community economic development organizations working on revitalizing local communities, both in rural and urban areas. These organizations work with different strategies and tools but have as their mission, or at least part of their mission, the development of collective or social economy enterprises. Another segment of our Board is made up of regional networks, because the social economy movement is now organized on a regional basis in every region in Quebec. A very key and strategic component of our Board's membership are representatives of social movements: the two major union movements have been part of the *Chantier's* Board since the beginning, as have been the environmental movement, the women's movement, the community movement, and so on. The reason we have included social movements in our membership is to never forget that, if our goal is to develop more and more collective enterprises, and more and more tools to support a democratic form of economic development, the fundamental goal is to contribute to a process of social transformation. Therefore we have integrated social movements into the very structures of what we do, in order to assure that we don't fall into the historical trap of just being concerned with our enterprises and not with what is going on in the rest of the world - the trap of forgetting how all this fits into a broader vision of social and economic justice in the world. That, in brief, is the structure of our organization.

What has the *Chantier* allowed us to do since we came together as a network of networks? The first major accomplishment is the building of a structured movement. This is very important to understand. For in fact, much of what is called the social economy in Quebec today existed before 1996; we didn't create it. But it had no common identity. It was identified primarily on a sectoral basis, as part of community media, or as parent controlled non-profit day care or co-op housing. We had no common vocabulary; we didn't have a way to come together and understand to what extent we were an essential part of the Quebec economy. We already had sufficient evidence that the social economy worked. We had expertise within our own networks. There was a lot we could do but we didn't have the political clout to get the support and recognition we needed. By coming together under a common banner and vocabulary, we were able to create a political force. So the first major accomplishment has been the creation of a movement made up of organizations and people who see themselves as part of this Social/Solidarity Economy.

The second major accomplishment is to have been able to give ourselves common tools. For example, one of the things we realized was that, in order for our enterprises to develop, we needed access to capital. There is no enterprise that can develop without access to capital. But the first obstacle to accessing capital was the fact that the available capital was oriented toward investment in enterprises whose first priority was to maximize financial return on investment. This obviously is not our goal with a social/solidarity economy. Our goals are to maximize social or environmental return on investment, and to assure positive impact on people and communities. The second obstacle was the fact that investors, and particularly venture capitalists, are only willing to invest if the money allows them control over the enterprise. By definition, outside control is impossible in the social economy; both nonprofits and cooperatives are based on worker control, community control or membership control, so we couldn't give traditional investors any form of control in return for financial investment. Another obstacle was the perception that a social economy enterprise, because of its social mission, is doomed to failure. Therefore investors considered the risk so high that they either refused to invest or demanded very high interest rates to compensate potential losses, or loan guarantees that communities and organizations were not able to offer. So, in order to support the development of collective enterprises, we started to create our own investment tools.

Solidarity Economy Investment: The Chantier de l'Économie Sociale Trust

In 1997 we were able to create our first $10 million investment fund that was exclusively for solidarity economy enterprises (non-profits and cooperatives). Over the years we have been able to prove that investing in collective enterprise is a good investment. We have been able to get other investors interested, and generate modest investment funds for collective enterprises across Quebec.

Based on this success, ten years later, in 2007, we were able to create a new fund, *The Chantier de l'Économie Sociale Trust*, which is a $54 million investment fund of what we call 'patient capital'. This trust is based a partnership with the Labor Movement (the two major labor pension funds, the Quebec Solidarity Fund and Fondaction) and with the provincial and federal governments. It allows us to invest real equity, and support a stronger development of our enterprises. This new fund has allowed us to scale up a lot of our work and allow our social entrepreneurs to be much more ambitious because of this new access to patient capital.

Another example of the kind of tools we have created is in the field of labor force development and vocational training. We have a sectoral council (*Comité sectoriel en économie sociale et action communautaire*) that works exclusively on issues related to labor force development and training in the social/solidarity economy. It has allowed us to analyze all the different skills and professions within the social and solidarity economy and to create training tools adapted to our realities and needs. It has even allowed us to identify new professions. For example, in the numerous nonprofit recycling businesses that were created by the environmental movement, we now have a new apprenticeship program that trains workers whose job is to sort used clothing and other recyclable objects, to realize the value of each textile or matter, and to work with all the material and make sure nothing is wasted. This skill has now been recognized as a profession, as we recognize plumbers, nurses' aides, or carpenters. This is an example of what we have been able to do by coming together under the banner of the social economy.

Another example is the research alliance that has developed over the past seven years. The Community-University Research Alliance on the Social Economy has become a vast network of researchers and practitioners in universities and regions across Quebec, whose mission is to develop new and useful knowledge for practitioners on the social economy and to support knowledge transfer and training with the expressed goal of improving practice. The partnership involves working together to define the subjects of research, to supervise the processes and to assure the dissemination of results.

No doubt the most important accomplishment that this vast coalition has allowed us to achieve is the negotiation of public policies to support the development of different sectors of the social/solidarity economy. We are far from a level playing field with the private for-profit sector but we certainly have made important gains.

Remaining Challenges

There is no question that many challenges remain. I don't want to create the illusion that we have taken over the Quebec economy and that it is now a Solidarity Economy. As we continue to develop, the private sector has begun to push back. Initially, they were not concerned about us; we were under the radar screen, and intervening in economic sectors or regions that were not financially profitable enough for private sector investment. Some even supported us, and allowed us to pick up the pieces they didn't want to deal with. But over time, we have become ambitious. We are taking on sectors where the private sector is present, and it doesn't appreciate us trying to move into these more lucrative markets. I see this as one of our major challenges: increasing our capacity to play an even more important role in the Quebec economy. When we do take on these new challenges, we have to get them right. In the current context there is no room for failure in the social/solidarity economy.

I want to end by mentioning two fundamental challenges for us at the *Chantier*. Firstly, in the current ideological context, there is the need to assure that the development of the social/solidarity economy is an integral part of a process of social transformation. For example, from an environmental perspective, we must make sure that we are integrating environmental concerns into the very way we are creating, producing, and doing business. The second fundamental challenge, and one of the reasons why we are here, is to make sure that when we build the social/solidarity economy, we are not trying to create some little utopia up in Quebec, but that we are part of an international movement for a Solidarity Economy. This is not only a desire; it is the only way to go. We will never be able to build a more democratic and equitable economy in isolation, on our own. Fundamentally, our economy is now global, and working together across borders is essential.

Resources
www.economiesocialequebec.ca
www.socialeconomyhub.ca
www.chantier.qc.ca
www.aruc-es.uqam.ca

Building the Solidarity Economy in Peru
Nedda Angulo

Nedda Angulo is a sociologist with a Masters in Social Management. She is Vice President of the Solidarity Economy Network Group of Peru (GRESP), and Latin American representative on the board of the Intercontinental Network of Promotion of Social Solidarity Economy (RIPESS). Nedda works as a consultant for NGOs and for entities of the Peruvian State. Her email address is: neddangulo@yahoo.com

To introduce the process of construction of the Solidarity Economy in Peru, I would like to start with a few characteristics of the Peruvian context. Peru is a country with a population of 28 million people. According to official statistics, 54 % of the people are poor and 24 % are extremely poor. We are talking about a country where the majority of the population is indigenous or racially mixed.

Even today, there are still a lot of ancestral practices. The majority of the population of the rural areas is organized in rural communities, modern forms of the "Ayllus" of the Inca epoch, social organizations that link the families who live in a territory to decide on common good. These rural peasant communities are spread throughout my country. Oftentimes they form collectives to manage the land. Other ancestral practices are the "Minka," a collective work group that does free work for the community or for the government, in public service and construction. Another ancestral practice is the "Ayni," a reciprocal exchange of work between families of the community. If I need to cultivate my land, I will work together with you and your family. We will all cultivate the land together; if I need to build my house, I would do it the same way. With the process of migration from rural to urban areas, this way of living has expanded even into urban areas. These are some of our first expressions of Solidarity Economy in Perú.

In 1968, the military government introduced new forms of social management in my country: cooperatives, agricultural societies, and industrial communities. Very few of these survive, because they did not have the technology to sustain the means of production, much less to finance the maintenance of these units of production, many of which have actually been privatized.

At the end of the 1970s, an economic crisis began in my country, which still continues, and there was a deindustrialization of what had been built during the sixties. Then a new expression of the Solidarity Economy began, connected to the survival of the family. Families came together around the issues of food and health, which before could be covered at a family level, and started community kitchens and self-managed healthcare services. They formed community kitchens to purchase, prepare, and serve food, in order to reduce the costs of meals, and so to increase food security. These cost reductions were made possible due to the application of economies of scale in the purchase of food and materials, the collection of subsidies in food or in money on behalf of the State, and operation according to a logic of subsistence, oriented exclusively to cover costs. In the community kitchen, work is performed in shifts, usually weekly, that are covered by worker "associates," whose numbers vary according to the size of the organization and the quantity of rations to prepare. The associates receive, as their daily salary, from three to four free meals. Another positive consequence is that women get some time for themselves, and have better control of the nutrition of their families. The community kitchen movement started in December, 1979 in Lima, and has spread to most of my country. A national organization of women was started, and it has registered 10,000 community kitchens. They all have the characteristics that I have described: women leave the domestic sphere to join the community environment, and they start a dialogue with the state about creating a community kitchen. They receive official recognition and regular funding. They are a subsidiary of the state, but the major work is done by the women of the community which is being served.

There are other experiences which are similar. There is a classic municipal milk program, which came about during the leftist government of Lima. In 1983 this program was present only in Lima, and then started a mobilization throughout my country; by 1984, the program had been institutionalized in all city governments. The "Committees of the Glass of Milk" are groups of mothers organized in a pyramidal structure for the execution of municipal programs of the same name. Each district has a local committee, which articulates and represents the committees constituted in the settlements of the district, which in turn articulate and represent to the grassroots committees formed at the level of four contiguous blocks within the settlements. The local committee participates in the Committee of Administration of the Program of the Glass of Milk: first, by putting out to bid the food to acquire, and then collecting these rations and delivering them to the grassroots committees, which take charge of the respective preparation and distribution to the beneficiaries.

So that the importance of these experiences is understood I need to mention one more characteristic of Peru: we have never had a public sector that pursues the public welfare. Political scientists call the practice of our state "patrimonialista;" this means that public goods are controlled by the politicians for their own benefit, as if they were private goods. Things are decided upon not as if those were public goods which belong to the people, and when the peoples' rights to these goods are recognized, they are seen as "concessions" rather than rights.

That is why these solidarity economy experiences are also building civic actions and rights in my country. From the community kitchen and Glass of Milk organizations have come other expressions, such as the expansion of health care, and the fight against domestic violence. Together, these initiatives are working to bring welfare services to the people, and they are partially subsidized by the government.

I also want to talk about some of the cooperatives that survive, connected primarily to agricultural production. By confederating, they have achieved a better position in the market, and increased their exports; many of them are connected to fair trade. I am going to mention particularly two national organizations that are members of the board that guides the Solidarity Economy network which I am in: the National Council of Coffee in Peru, a group of 35,000 coffee producers; and the Central Artisan Organization in Peru, with 1,600 artisans. Each of these groups is diversifying their activities and creating their own financial entities, including their own exporting companies. They provide us with examples of sustainable development for my country. Because we believe that the wealth generated by these economic expressions is really what is sustaining our economy, in 1994 we started a process of linking all these groups, in order to develop a project of mutual support, and to engage the state in encouraging the Solidarity Economy. That is the origin of the Solidarity Economy Network Group of Peru (GRESP), the organization which I represent here as its Vice President.

Up to this point, our Solidarity Economy Network has achieved   official recognition of the community kitchens and government support for these programs, and the approval of a law for artisan programs to encourage the growth of this sector, including some tax cuts. We are currently working on a number of other political initiatives on behalf of the agents of the solidarity economy in Peru, which we will plan to take up with the State.

In conclusion, the Solidarity Economy in Peru is a strategy that combines initiatives based on the individual or collective property of the means of production which facilitate   access to welfare services and to the labor market, and which are fighting for the recognition of economic human rights and for the construction of the democracy in my country.

Notes

[1] Social and Solidarity Economy Summit (2006, November 17). 2006 Declaration. Montreal.
www.chantier.qc.ca/uploads/documents/pages_descriptor/affichedeclaration_ang_8fev07.pdf:

16

High Road Community Development, Public Schools and the Solidarity Economy

Dan Swinney

Dan Swinney is the executive director and founder of the Center for Labor and Community Research (CLCR) and has 35 years of community and labor organizing as well as community-development experience. After graduating with a B.A. in history from the University of Wisconsin, Madison, Dan worked for 13 years as a machinist in the Chicago area. He organized Steelworker Local 8787 at G+W Taylor Forge in Cicero, Illinois, and served as Vice President. He is a Board member of the Leadership Greater Chicago Fellows Association. He has written articles appearing in Economic Development America, Social Policy, Business Ethics, New Labor Forum, Working USA, the South Africa Labour Bulletin, Yes! and other publications. He is part of the coordinating committee for the U.S. Solidarity Economy Network (U.S. SEN).

Introduction to the Panel

Most attendees of the U.S. Social Forum share the conviction that the current climate in the US is ripe for the advancement of an alternative vision of social and economic change. That vision must be based on a development policy that can compete at a very large scale and win very broad support among leaders in politics, in the market, and in civil society. In this panel, several speakers discussed their experiences and challenges organizing for this alternative vision. They included Erica Swinney, an organizer for GreenAction for Health and Environmental Justice in San Francisco; Nedda Angulo, a leader in the solidarity economy movement in Peru and on the Board of Directors of the Intercontinental Network for the Promotion of the Solidarity Economy (RIPESS); and myself, Dan Swinney, the executive director of the Center of Labor and Community Research (CLCR), as well as the Chicago Manufacturing Renaissance Council (CMRC). In this article, I will discussion the beginning of an exciting new project that I am involved in, Austin Polytechnical Academy, and its connection to the solidarity economy and high road development in Chicago.

Introduction to the Discussion

I'll start with my background. I'm a veteran of the 1960s, beginning here in Atlanta in 1965 as a volunteer for the Student Non-violent Organizing Committee, then a militant and multi-racial civil rights group of young people. My first organizing experience ever was in SNCC's efforts to promote school desegregation in rural and suburban communities in Dekalb County, GA. I next became active in the student antiwar movement, and then explored a potential career in the labor movement.

I spent 13 years as a machinist, and was the organizer and leader of a Steelworkers local in Chicago. When my company closed in 1983, I founded and now direct the Center for Labor and Community Research (www.clcr.org)—a 25 year old consulting and research not-for-profit in Chicago. CLCR is now focused on developing and advancing through theory and practice a comprehensive alternative to development that is economically, socially, and environmentally sustainable and restorative.

The Importance of Mondragon

I now want to jump across the Atlantic to Mondragon, Spain, to bring forward a seminal inspiration for our work and today's topic. This is a network of cooperative businesses—the Mondragon Cooperative Corporation (MCC), based in the Basque region of Spain, and focused, over 40 years, in creating manufacturing and other worker-owned firms. I'll provide a brief description and then return to its strategic significance later.

MCC was initiated by a visionary priest and opponent of the Franco regime—Father Jose Marie Arizmendi in the 1940s. He first created a polytecnical school that trained youth in technical skills and to assume leadership in the economy and society—providing them with the education necessary for production as well as the values essential to linking business with the broader concerns and interests of the community. This was in 1943.

In the mid-1950s, Arizmendi and five of his students took over a manufacturing company and organized it on a cooperative basis–one worker, one vote–with a pay ratio of 1 to 3 – the highest paid not making more than three times the lowest paid. This success of this first company led to more ventures. Today there are 85 companies comprised of 130,000 workers world-wide.   This network of companies is the cutting edge of Spanish industrial economy—and the hub of a network of housing, retail, financial, social and educational cooperatives. In a down-to-earth way, Mondragon serves as a model for global local development consistent with vision of the solidarity economy.

Chicago and the 'Low Road-High Road' Divide

Putting forward MCC as a starting point, I want to jump back to Chicago. This major urban center experienced dramatic destruction of its local communities in the 1970s through the 1990s due to de-industrialization. During those years, Chicago lost 4,000 out of 7,000 factory jobs and lost 200,000 manufacturing jobs paying, on average, $50,000 to $60,000 a year hour with benefits. Naturally, the number of families in poverty grew notably.

CLCR documented that this was not inevitable due to market, globalization, or new technology. We are certain that 80% of these losses could have been prevented. Many larger companies closed because of "low road" business strategies that could have been successfully challenged by alternative business plan reflecting "high road" values. For those not familiar with these terms, the "low road" is where business emphasizes short-term profitability and competes with third world labor markets by lowering wages, gutting benefits, breaking unions and ignoring environmental concerns. The "high road" is where business emphasizes long-term sustainability by increasing skills and compensation, worker participation, and environmental safety.

Many small companies closed simply because of an aging white owner with no successor. These companies could have become successful ventures for employee owners or Black and Hispanic entrepreneurs.

A failing education system also contributed to the decline of local companies. Those that remain competitive in the global market require employees with a quality education and high skill to compete in high value-added markets. I'll return to this point shortly.

The structural crisis caused by deindustrialization is also an opportunity for the solidarity economy. This reality—common in every city, large and small—created enormous openings for a competitive, practical model based on sustainable and restorative development. It requires that we:

- Advance a program for intervention to retain larger companies. Here we must protect jobs for workers, as well as retaining managers and creating new owners;

- Address the problem of succession in small companies. Many of these are quite profitable, but will fold unless we help the new owners find the leverage to pay full value for the company and maintain its market share;

- Address failure of education in public system. At present, many high road companies look abroad for skilled labor, since local schools have lacked the vision or plan for upgrading their vocational education to current standards and awakening the critical thought their students will need to thrive in the modern world.

This combination of issues created the opportunity to compete in the mainstream for objectives and resources that will build the capacity of communities to retake and develop the assets of their own communities, guided by the values of the solidarity economy.

The Critical Role of Education

In 2001, CLCR in partnership with the Chicago Federation of Labor completed a study (*Creating a Manufacturing Career Path System in Cook County*) that documented the failure of education to meet the needs of locally owned companies at their expense as well as the communities that depend on them for income and stability. The study attracted support of local manufacturers and the major manufacturing trade association—the Illinois Manufacturers' Association—a reality that gave us considerable influence with mainstream labor, governmental, and educational institutions.

This was one key factor in forming the Chicago Manufacturing Renaissance Council (CMRC) in 2005. CMRC represents the top business, labor, governmental, community, and educational leadership of the city. It has the objective of Chicago becoming the global leader in high value-added manufacturing—a development vision that should be embraced by most if not all countries. This is an approach to development that can profoundly link the public and private sectors.

A key priority of the CMRC is a comprehensive focus on education: public schools, community colleges, and not-for-profit training providers. Austin Polytechnical Academy, a new public high school in a low-income neighborhood and a project of the CMRC, represents our most interesting and potentially powerful tool to rebuild a community movement. All involved have agreed, to one degree or another, that part of APA's objective is creating a leadership pool of the next generation that is technically, socially, and politically competent to take control and develop the assets of their community in successful competition with traditional leaders in the market economy. APA represents a reform agenda for both schools and community development that is hard to beat politically. It is also a school that will be replicated in other communities—we already anticipate five other schools in other Chicago communities.

Austin Polytech: An Overview

APA is located in Austin, a West Side Chicago African-American community that has high rates of poverty, failing schools, and a deep level of cynicism about its future. Austin Polytech just started this year with a freshman class of 145 students. We are a small school by design, sharing a building and facilities with at least one other small school. By 2011, we will have 550 students. About 54% of the student body are female, and 15% have some form of learning or other disability.

With innovative methods and hard work, we are promoting career paths for these young people in high skilled production, management, and ownership of manufacturing companies. We have 26 companies on board serving as Austin Polytech Partners that will be providing internships, summer jobs, and intensive exposure to manufacturing.

The students who graduate will be college-ready, have industry credentials, and have work experience. They can go on to higher education, directly into skilled jobs, or both. The desire and capacity for life-long learning is built into the program, and the school is explicitly dedicated to the high road development of the community. Austin Polytech will create a leadership pool of the next generation that is technically, socially, and politically competent to take control and develop the assets of their community in successful competition with traditional leaders in the market economy with the objectives and values of the solidarity economy.

Critical Assumptions

Like Mondragon, we need to focus on advanced manufacturing. In the broader cooperative movement, this is not always easy or taken for granted. It is this sector of the economy that can provide the highest quality jobs; that can stimulate broader economic and social growth in the community; and that is where key decisions that have impact on the environment, and on the general development of society are made.

Modern manufacturing is the necessary foundation for an economy that can overcome or end poverty. It can be the anchor of a regional or national complex economy that can then support other services, a retail market, and the development of scientific knowledge. In the context of the local community, Austin Polytech is an explicit first step to creating an alternative to those who promote de-industrialization, gentrification, and low-end retail jobs such as Wal-Mart as a development strategy. Also like Mondragon the school can begin to create an opportunity for local control and participatory economic democracy.

In light of current realities of global competition, the high road qualities shared by schools and factories – participation, critical thinking, a democratic culture – provides a competitive advantage for forward-looking businesses and other agencies committed to change. If a school is organized on a participative or democratic basis, it can help transform the culture of a community at all levels.

Conclusion

The decline of manufacturing or the general economic decline of our communities is not inevitable. We need not surrender to it; indeed, it creates a huge opportunity for the movement for a solidarity economy if we are willing to:

- Go to scale and really compete for the control and management of the major institutions in our society;

- See the market as a terrain for struggle where we can prevail; and

- Build alliances with the section of the business community.

The last of these three points—alliances with a sector of business—often raises some controversy in the left and progressives movements. But the fact remains that some businesses, particularly high road productive capital, are an important ally we can't do without, and shouldn't want to do without. Austin Polytech is a case in point. While all progressives would affirm the need for school reform in the inner city, and the need to prepare its youth for a high-skilled, high-paying future, such a structural reform requires the participation of a sector of business. In fact, many of them are clamoring for just these changes. High road business often supports our tactical objectives because of a convergence of self interest. Some also share our strategic objectives opposing the low roaders, and bring essential opportunities, support, skills, and resources to our projects.

We must recognize that the corporate community is not a monolith, and that generalized 'anti-corporate' strategies don't help much, and often hold us back. There's a definite low road sector of capital—a portion of the 13,000 publicly traded companies that are larger and can typically roam the world to solve their production problems—at the expense of local communities. But there are 8 million privately held, usually locally owned companies that represent a large section of the business community that can and will be won to our side, even if only for a period, in the process of moving towards a solidarity economy.

But in order to succeed, we must end the simplistic anti-corporate rhetoric and programs of our movement. I feel that this is the most destructive intellectual construct in our movement at this time. The rhetoric is a symbol of a middle class movement of the radical intelligentsia that has the luxury of standing on the side of fundamental change rather than applying its organizational and intellectual skills in bringing about fundamental change.

SECTION VI:

BUILDING THE SOLIDARITY ECONOMY THROUGH PUBLIC POLICY

17
Participatory Budgeting: from Porto Alegre, Brazil to the U.S.

Michael Menser and Juscha Robinson

Michael Menser is Assistant Professor of Philosophy at Brooklyn College (BC) and is on the executive boards of the Environmental Studies Program at BC and the Center for the Study of Place, Culture, and Politics at the City University of New York Graduate School .Among his most recent publications are "Disarticulate the State! Maximizing Democracy in 'New' Autonomous Movements in the Americas" (in <u>Altered States</u>, forthcoming, Routledge 2008) and "Transnational Participatory Democracy in Action: the Case of La Via Campesina." (<u>Journal of Social Philosophy</u> 2008). He is a member of the Northeast Region Coordinating Committee of the US Social Forum and the U.S. Solidarity Economy Network Coordinating Committee. Mike participated in the fifth WSF and many local SFs in the U.S., but his first introduction to activism occurred in the 1990s as a member of an adjunct organizing project at CUNY and with Reclaim the Streets/NYC.

Juscha Robinson is a Local Democracy fellow for Liberty Tree Foundation for the Democratic Revolution, a nationwide non-profit that assists communities and organizations working for democratic change in their schools, local governments and institutions, elections, and so on. Robinson was a co-organizer of the participatory budgeting sessions organized at the U.S. Social Forum, in June 2007 in Atlanta, Georgia, and continues to help administrate the PB network that formed out of those sessions.

Throughout the U.S. left, but in particular among those groups participating at the first U.S. Social Forum and the global justice movement more generally, "participatory democracy" is a phrase one encounters in all kinds of different movements and organizations, from anti-war meetings and environmental justice organizations, to direct action affinity groups, to community-sponsored agriculture outfits, international solidarity organizations and prison abolitionists. It is certainly a central feature of the solidarity economy. In this essay, we will talk a little about what "participatory democracy"[1] (PD) has come to mean for such movements, but for the most part our remarks will focus on a particular mode of PD called "participatory budgeting," an innovation made famous in Brazil but recently spread across the globe to more than 1,000 cities.[2] The last section of the essay takes stock of conversations at and after the U.S. Social Forum, where a national participatory budgeting initiative was launched, and offers a few humble observations and suggestions about concrete plans of action for those interested is democratizing that most fundamental of all governmental functions: the budget.

Participatory democracy is that view of politics which calls for the creation and proliferation of practices and institutions that enable individuals and groups to better determine the conditions in which they act and relate to others. The term gained currency in 1962 after Students for a Democratic Society (SDS) issued their groundbreaking Port Huron statement, which, among other things, laid out a conception of democracy that called for citizens to seize their collective political fates by reclaiming the public sphere as self-determining agents, rather than lining up to listen to those campaigning to take the reins of the military-industrial corporate state. SDS's view was largely influenced by eminent social critic C. Wright Mills, but another key (now forgotten) figure was Arnold Kaufman, a professor at the University of Michigan, who first coined the phrase in an essay called "Participatory Democracy and Human Nature" (Miller 160).[3] It was one of Kaufman's students, Tom Hayden, who actually drafted the Port Huron Statement. For SDS and contemporary proponents of participatory democracy , *any* sphere of human activity could and should be made more "participatory;" not just the formally political (e.g. legislatures, courts, bureaucratic departments), but the social and economic realms as well (families, neighborhoods, communities, schools, associations, firms). This unbounding of democratic desire is evident in the vast range of institutions in which PD has taken root: from food cooperatives and collective households, to free schools and neighborhood associations.[4]

Although participatory democracy seems to share many of the values of mainstream liberal/Enlightenment tradition (freedom, equality, solidarity, democracy), *actual* liberal democratic states often impede or even actively undermine PD efforts. In recent years this has been especially evident in the growth of a bureaucratized (if private) "expert class" which considers the "average citizen" too stupid to make important policy decisions, much less understand the complexities of contemporary life because of its immense scale and technological sophistication.[5] Additional threats to PD are well-known: the dominance of big money

donors and corporate media in elections and the failure of campaign finance reform to adequately address either problem.

This inability (or unwillingness?) of the state to foster more democratic and
popular participation (all we get are scripted "town hall" meetings!) raises the
more difficult question as to the nature of the state and its role in building a more
progressive political future. Perhaps states are *essentially* anti-democratic, as an-
archists and (many) indigenous peoples believe. The argument here is that because the state claims a monopoly on both law-making and the deployment of
coercive force (i.e. only the state can pass laws and *legitimately* use violence), it
is at its core all about the wielding of incredible power by an elite against the
populace at large (also known as the "citizenry," but more accurately labeled the
"subjects" of the state). We must remember, after all, that the United States was
founded as a democratic republic, and republics are founded on the notion that
those who rule and those who are ruled belong to two different spheres, and that
the function of the police is to preserve the barrier between the two. In a republic,
a representative stands in for the citizens, rather than allowing the citizens to participate and govern themselves (letting those who are affected decide). At their
best, such republics may satisfy the *interests* of certain groups (usually elites),
and when crises or unrest threaten, "new deals" are sometimes struck (e.g. the
welfare state, and the Civil Rights Act of 1964[6]). For the most part, however,
when the state benefits (represents or "stands in for") some group, it sticks it to
somebody else (minorities, slaves, women, the colonies, or indigenous people).

Others argue that this need not be the case. Rather, it is neoliberalism or capitalism that renders states so violently inegalitarian. With the right political party, or
possibly with widespread social upheaval, they believe that states can be made
truly democratic. This is the view of socialism and liberalism, both of which are
driven by a view that the state is the best way to create a just political community, even if they differ drastically about methods, the extent of change (revolu-
tions v. elections), and who should lead it (vanguard party v. persons whose last
names are Clinton).

In the last two decades or so, whatever one's view, it seems clear that even liberal democratic states have become less and less democratic both in terms of
their political processes, and the results of these political processes. More and
more people have fewer opportunities to participate, and inequalities of all sorts
have intensified. Yet, even though cynicism and apathy are conspicuous features
of our socio-political landscape, over the same time frame there have been more
and more efforts to make various institutions more participatory. As one might
suppose (going back to SDS), the most robust examples of PD have occurred
outside of the state in civil society (for example, community gardens, Food not

Bombs, and indymedia outlets). If one expands the scope of inquiry and lets it drift a bit to the south, however, one of the best known PD experiments *in the world* has shown that it is possible to democratize that most central of all governmental functions: the budget.

Participatory Budgeting: Brazil and Beyond

Almost two decades ago the city of Porto Alegre, Brazil, developed what has come to be regarded as the definitive case of a participatory budgeting process. Despite the cultural and political particularities of its emergence there, PB has spread beyond Latin America to the Caribbean, Europe, Asia, and Africa, and has been used in over a thousand cities to democratize municipal, county, state, school, housing, and organization budgets. Although none have taken root in the U.S., there are projects active in several cities, including Lawrence, Massachusetts and New York City. In this section we shall give some more details on the PB process of Porto Alegre, and examine its manifold political and economic implications, especially since PB is not just about "participation" but also wealth redistribution, inequality reduction, capacity development, and the "right to the city." In the last section, we shall consider the possibilities of PB in the U.S., especially in light of the conversations that happened at the U.S. Social Forum last summer in Atlanta, Georgia.

Participatory budgeting consists of a process of democratic deliberation and decision-making in which ordinary city residents decide how to allocate part of a public budget through a series of local assemblies and meetings. It is characterized by several basic features: community members determine spending priorities and elect budget delegates to represent their neighborhoods, budget delegates transform community priorities into concrete project proposals, public employees facilitate and provide technical assistance, community members vote on which projects to fund, and a public authority implements the projects. Various studies have suggested that participatory budgeting can lead to more equitable public spending, higher quality of life, increased satisfaction of basic needs, greater government transparency and accountability, increased levels of public participation (especially by marginalized residents), and democratic and citizenship learning.[7] Most of the well known examples of participatory budgeting were the results of city administrations that turned over decisions about municipal budgets, such as its overall priorities and choice of new investments, to citizen assemblies. Other examples involve school budgets, housing project budgets, and the budgets of cooperatives and non-profit organizations.[8]

PB was first developed in the late 1980s when Brazil was undergoing the transition from dictatorship to democracy and there was serious public doubt about the legitimacy of the new government.[9] At this time, although Porto Alegre was the capital of the wealthiest state of Brazil (Rio Grande do Sul), one third of its citizens lived in shantytowns or slums, and the city as a whole faced a budget shortfall so severe, it was unclear how to best spend the funds available.[10]

In 1988, a new mayor was elected, Olivio Dutra of the *Partido dos Trabalhadores* (PT), the Workers' Party. The PT had played a key role in the opposition to the dictatorship, and was eager to implement its own brand of socialism. But Dutra and his vice mayor were also cautious; they had received only 30% of the total vote. Many within its ranks questioned more traditional socialist solutions to the present political and economic crises, such as creating mechanisms for the state management of various economic sectors. Brazil's recent authoritarian past seemed to call for an opening up rather than a new left authoritarianism, and this government needs to reach out to the broader public for the visions and coalition-building necessary for any chance at success. A decision was made, despite dissension within the party, to forgo an attempt to implement state socialism. Instead, a program was launched to invite participation. This participation was not just solicited from factory workers, but also from the "popular classes," including women's groups and civil society organizations, which built upon the PT's desire to break from more traditional workerist party models that privileged factory (usually male) labor as *the* subject for revolutionary change, and create a post-authoritarian democratic politics. After consultation with these various constituencies, the mayor issued a decree establishing the Participatory Budget. Note that no law was ever passed.[11]

The key features of PB in Porto Alegre are as follows: The process begins with neighborhood assemblies in each of the city's 16 regions, and, since 1994, in non-territorial thematic assemblies (e.g. environment, transportation). In these regional meetings (akin to municipal districts in the U.S.), any city resident may participate; some are attended by more than a thousand participants. The purpose of these meetings is to enable residents to voice their concerns with the municipal government and to express and deliberate over the most pressing needs. The discussion then shifts to a *ranking* of the top three needs.[12] Once the priorities are decided, delegates are elected to represent the region at the city-wide level in the city-wide "PB council" (Conselho do Orcamento Participativo or COP). At this assembly, delegates from across the city meet to decide what needs are most pressing *and* which region most lacks the services in question. After all the delegates' reports about their respective regions' needs are heard, the PB council deliberates to determine a ranking of priorities for the entire city.[13] During this stage of the process, delegates take trips to the sites deemed most in need and technical experts are made available to the COP by the mayor's office to make sure funding requests for specific projects are feasible. After completion of PB budget for the year, it is integrated into the mayor's budget proposal and submitted to the legislature. At the beginning of the following fiscal year a review of the past year is taken up and sometimes various procedures or criteria are altered to increase fairness or efficiency.[14] Because of its popular legitimacy, the PB section of the budget has never been modified by the legislature.

After some initial difficulties, the PB has routinely satisfied its primary goals: to deliver basic services to those most in need, to foster participation by a range of citizens, especially those most in need of city services, and to enable the delegates and residents to modify the norms and mechanisms of the PB process and COP. With regard to services delivered, the results have been tremendous, especially with respect to access to running water and sewage lines, housing assistance, and the creation of schools.[15] In terms of popular participation, the numbers of those joining the neighborhood meetings have increased as the process has matured over almost 20 years, although there has been unevenness in terms of participation by class and geography. In order to make sure that the PB did not reinforce hierarchies already present in society, the city responded to poorer and less educated residents' demands for the provision of technical education and training in public speaking for participants (especially delegates). The purpose of these programs for participant capacity development was to make sure that class power did not translate into deliberative power in the assemblies. As such, Porto Alegre's PB does not just *permit* participation by wide segments of the population, it *empowers* them to participate.[16]

At its inception, PB was responsible for only 2% of the total budget; the municipal legislature handled the rest. In this early phase, the process prioritized those most underserved and since the completion of its first year, basic services to the poorest and most marginalized have dramatically improved. This, in turn, justified the expansion of PB's portion of the overall municipal budget to 20%. Now PB handles social services, local school policy, and human rights enforcement as well as the budget of education, culture, health, and sports[17]. In general, PB has made great gains from the standpoints of quality and quantity of participation.

In addition, PB contains a mechanism for the evaluation of its process and enables the participants and delegates to make changes based upon these evaluations independent of the city officials and bureaucracy. Although the latter can give input, the delegates have the power to decide and implement. Significant changes have occurred over the evolution of PB with regard to the number of delegates and their length of term, the point system in which needs and regions are prioritized, and the range of issues considered. This is crucial because it shows that PB is not just a means by which the state, on its own terms, invites participation (to quell dissent or further its own legitimation), but that those operating outside the formal state set the terms under which they deliberate and the goals of the deliberative process[18].

Not surprisingly, much (but not all) of the interest in PB in the U.S. is coming not from elected officials or political parties, but rather from a range of advocacy groups and community organizations. These groups and organizations are building upon earlier local traditions in participatory governance (for example, the New England town hall meeting model,) or are forging new alliances with one another as part of the global Social Forum process. This process also began in Porto Alegre in 2001, and arrived in the U.S. in 2007.

Participatory Budgeting at the U.S. Social Forum 2007

Interest in Participatory Budgeting has been growing here in the United States, as communities and organizations face budget shortfalls and wake up to the fact that the politicians they elect are not spending tax dollars according to community priorities. The U.S. Social Forum in Atlanta in June was an ideal place to educate about PB, identify people in organizations and community groups across the country interested in working on PB, and discuss what is needed to support the work of those groups. Among the 900 workshops and sessions over the course of the week, two focused exclusively on PB.

The first session, "Participatory Budgeting: Community Control over Public Money" took place in the early afternoon, during the same time slot as 200 other workshops. Despite this competition, the session drew over 70 people. The participants started with a round of introductions, and got the sense of the incredibly wide variety of experience with PB in the room, ranging from former residents of Porto Alegre, Brazil, to those who had heard of PB, to people who had just read the session description and been intrigued by the idea of community control over resources.

The session started with a half-hour panel, aimed at presenting basic information on PB and highlighting some examples. Mike Menser, a City University of New York (CUNY) professor, PB organizer, and one of the authors, presented the history of PB and its nuts and bolts. Maureen Turnbull, recently finished with graduate work about PB in Brazil, talked about the experience and empowerment of women through the PB process. Jennifer Flynn, director of the NYC AIDS Housing Network, talked about how her organization interacts with the city around budget issues and attempts to integrate aspects of PB. Karen Dolan, from the Institute for Policy Studies' Cities for Progress Network, spoke about how this network coordinates with elected officials to pass progressive local legislation. Joe Moore, a city council member from Chicago, Illinois, and member of Cities for Progress, talked about his impressions of PB from his perspective as an elected official, and offered some tips on practicalities and obstacles that would have to be overcome in order to implement PB.

The conversation then opened up to the larger group, and what followed was a lively discussion following several threads. Several people expressed enthusiasm for PB in concept, but also doubt that such a system could ever work in the U.S., primarily because of low and unrepresentative public participation. Participants stressed that people need to see results from a PB system in order to continue participation (and to build participation). The group discussed the needs and methods for keeping participation and outreach diverse. Flynn warned that PB could potentially discriminate against small and vulnerable groups of people (e.g. AIDS survivors), unless inclusive measures were taken. This prompted discussion about what, if anything, is fundamentally different between Brazil and the U.S., what cultural differences might have to be taken into account, and how elements of PB might have to be adjusted to be more effective in the U.S.

The group also discussed how PB might look in the U.S. Although PB has usually been limited to capital rather than operating budgets, participants discussed other areas that might be fertile for experimentation. The session wrapped up with talk about how most PB programs depend on elected officials voluntarily giving up some budgetary power, and strategies for convincing officials to do so. A speaker concluded that PB in Brazil did not succeed overnight, and that no one model will work for every community.

The next day was the second session, "Participatory Budgeting: Making It Work in the U.S." Menser, Flynn, Dolan and Moore gave short presentations, and the group (around 50 participants) quickly got into a detailed discussion of how to move PB in the U.S. forward.[19] The first part of the discussion focused on organizing strategies and how an individual or organization would actually get PB started. The group concurred that in order for a PB project to succeed, just like any organizing, the group of initial organizers has to include the wider community stakeholders and those whose buy-in will eventually be needed. Organizers need to do their homework and figure out how and where PB would best fit into the budgetary process and address community needs. One person suggested that putting together a local social forum would be an excellent place to begin such a community discussion. There was general debate about whether PB would most likely be successful starting with a smaller or medium scale project. The group did agree, however, that as part of any PB project, public civic education about the budgetary process, interaction with government, and basic organizing is essential. There was also agreement that public participation must go beyond attendance at hearings; it must be much deeper and more authentically participatory, including participation in the actual decision making, enactment, execution and organizing.

The group moved on to discuss what infrastructure they would need to do PB organizing. They came up with the idea of a national network assisted by national organizations, providing administrative support, public relations help (for example, coordination of op-eds), education of elected officials about PB, spreading success stories, and providing information and education to organizers about PB. At the conclusion, participants reminded the group that while PB is the project, the discussion is ultimately about using PB as a vehicle for building community power and deepening democratic participation. The implications of this are manifold. Firstly, PB cannot solve all of our problems (racism, sexism, environmental degradation, war, etc.), but it can develop individual and group capabilities that can be used in areas other than the PB. Secondly, efforts to initiate participatory budgeting processes must be linked to broader social justice movements to ensure inclusiveness and a radical political pluralism at the beginning of the process. Such pluralism and inclusiveness would prevent PB processes from being perceived to be a pet project of a few knowledgeable persons who are really controlling its development. It would also make those involved feel that they are not spectators passively watching the action, but agents who will directly contribute to the outcome of the project. The inclusion of multiple diversities at the beginning (not only racial and ethnic, but cultural and ideological) not only increases fairness and equality (hallmarks of PB!), but also taps a greater range of knowledge and experiences than a program dominated by one tradition or ideology.

What Next? A National PB Network

Citizen participation in budget making is not a new idea. In North America, and especially in New England, citizens in small towns have decided on budget spending through over 300 years of town meetings[20]. Since the 1960s, many cities, large and small, have involved residents in budgeting through community boards and councils. In several cases, such as Dayton, Ohio and Portland, Oregon, these boards have developed into enduring institutional venues for dialogue and community input.[21] Increasingly, municipal governments are organizing open public consultations, in which individual citizens and organizations can express their views on budget spending. In some cities, such as Burlington [Vermont] and Seattle, small citizen boards are empowered to allocate community grants, through participatory grant-making schemes[22].

Lerner and Baoicchi, along with the authors of this essay, are developing a national PB network, building upon these many examples of PB that already exist in the United States, and also on the work that was done at the USSF. The network aims to promote and support participatory budgeting in U.S. local governments, agencies, and organizations. Drawing upon Lerner and Baiocchi's analysis, one might say that there are four possible scenarios for the emergence of new PB practices in the U.S. The first scenario is local precedent: there is some existing PD initiative (Dayton) or history of popular democracy (New England) which supplies a least a partial basis for the justification of PB. In other words PB is doable because some PD program is already in effect, or there is a local or regional history of it occurring. The second scenario is economic crisis, which is how PB came to be in Porto Alegre. Combined with a lack of faith in the state's ability to solve the problem, economic crises sometimes enable previously inactive or unaligned groups to form coalitions for basic survival purposes. Lerner and Baiocchi note the recent emergence of a robust PD project in Lawrence, Massachusetts. Called Lawrence Community Works, it works for sustainable economic and physical revitalization of the community. Another example is when the Toronto's Community Housing corporation (TCHC), the second largest public housing authority in North America, faced drastic budget cuts in 2000. A PB process was launched both because tenants wanted more decision-making power, and because the housing administration did not want to make tough choices, deferring instead to the newly emerging PB.

With this last example one cannot help but think of Katrina and the recent decision by the New Orleans city council to permit the demolition of 4,500 public housing units. There were many groups from the Gulf Coast at the USSF, including a few individuals who attended both PB sessions. Their presence and their questions reminded us of the urgency of this sometimes abstract phrase "participatory democracy." From homelessness to gentrification, and now, to the subprime crisis, the housing question is one that begs for a new conversation, and the political parties are not permitting it. With the emergence of the "right to the city" coalition last year and the formation of several other alliances at the USSF, forwarding PB proposals and connecting them to existing solidarity economy projects is not only a possible next step, but a necessary one.

The trick, of course, is to create a political space where a mix of groups and individuals can come together in a way that is open and empowering but focused. Here, the Social Forum process which helped to launch the PD national initiative can be put to use at the local level. A great way of checking out the possibilities of launching a PB project is to have a Social Forum first and make PB a central piece (maybe part of a plenary). This helps to create the space for a wider sense of ownership of the PB project, since most people are totally unaware of its present or past. Another strategy is to focus on bringing in organizations that have earned the respect of their communities combined with those that have knowledge of the intricacies of municipal government and law. Alternatively, if those seem too daunting or ill-suited to one's local situation, then why not take the path of the Ridgeview elementary school in Vancouver, Canada and let the kids try it! In this case, PB was launched with seventh-graders. After assessing the needs of their school with the help of teachers and administrators, the students voted to set up a school store to help them raise additional funds so as to take on an array of projects, including "cooking classes, a small indoor climbing wall, a water fountain, new sports equipment, and a school pet that students would take care of."[23] It is with this wonderful mix of basic needs and ludic playfulness that we conclude, so that all of you may contemplate the possibilities of participatory democracy in the places where you live and love, fight and dream.

References

Baiocchi, Gianpaolo. (2003). "Participation, Activism, and Politics: the Porto Alegre Experiment," in Archon Fung and Eric Olin Wright (Ed.). *Deepening Democracy: Institutional Innovations in Empowered Participatory Governance*. (Real Utopias Project). New York: Verso Books.

Berry, J, Portney, K and Thomsen, K. (1993). *The Rebirth of Urban Democracy*. Washington: The Brookings Institution.

Bryan, F. (2004). *Real Democracy: The New England Town Meeting and How It Works*. Chicago: University of Chicago Press.

Chavez, Daniel. (2004). *Polis and Demos: the Left in Municipal Governance in Montevideo and Porto Alegre*. Maastricht, Netherlands: Shaker Publishing.

Cunningham, Frank. (2002). Theories of Democracy: a Critical Introduction. London: Routledge.

Lerner, J. and Baiocchi, G. (forthcoming) "Could Participatory Budgeting Work in the United States?, *The Good Society*.

Menser, Michael. (2005). The Global Social Forum Movement, Porto Alegre's "Participatory Budget, and the Maximization of Democracy," in *Situations: a Journal of the Radical Imagination*, Vol. 1: 1, 87-108.

Menser, Michael. (2008). "Transnational Democracy in Action: the Case of Via Campesina." *Journal of Social Philosophy*.

Pateman, Carole. (1970). *Participation and Democratic Theory*. Cambridge: Cambridge University Press.

Santos, Boaventura de Sousa. (2005). "Participatory Budgeting in Porto Alegre: Toward a Redistributive Democracy," in Boaventura de Sousa Santos (Ed.). *Democratizing Democracy: Beyond the Liberal Democratic Canon*. New York: Verso.

Simonsen, W. and Robbins, M. (2000). *Citizen Participation in Resource Allocation.* Boulder: Westview.

Notes

[1] For the purposes of this essay we shall use the term "participatory democracy"
rather than "direct democracy" because the first category is broader; thus, DD is a
kind of PD, but there are others. It is worth noting that some believe PD is too close
to the liberal democratic state and that direct democracy (also called self-governance,
self-determination, or autogestion) is the real future of democracy. While we are
sympathetic to this view, we do not share it. For more on this issue see Menser, "Disarticulate the State (forthcoming, Routledge 2008).
[2] According to PB researcher Josh Lerner, the most robust example of PB is no longer
Porto Alegre, but Seville, Spain. Other cities that are undertaking PB projects include
dozens in the Dominican Republic, Bobigny, France, the London Burrow of Harrow,
Puntagorda, Canary Islands, and Guelph, Canada. PB has also occurred within different municipal departments such as in public housing in Toronto and in schools in
Brazil. A lengthy if incomplete list is found at www.participatorybudgeting.org
[3] We note the origin of the term not to proclaim Kaufman (or SDS, for that matter) to
be the sole originator of participatory democracy – PD has been practiced in many
different cultural contexts for millennia, but to note the intersection of theoretical innovations alongside emerging social movements and the productive interplay between
the two. This cross-fertilization between the theoretical and the action-oriented is
again at play in the current moment in what often gets called the global justice
movement. See D.L. Sheth's "The Reinvention of Participatory Democracy".
[4] Cunningham, Frank. (2002). Theories of Democracy: a Critical Introduction. London: Routledge, 127.
[5] Of course, this same elitist argument could be made against the leadership of the
current administration but we'll pass on that contradiction for the moment. What is
worth emphasizing, however, is that the existence and spread of PD and participatory
budgeting in particular demonstrates the falsity of the all too familiar argument that
"average citizens" are unable to make good decisions; (more below.)
[6] A wonderful instance of this understanding was in full display in January of 2008
when Hillary Clinton stated that "Dr. King's dream began to be realized when President Lyndon Johnson passed the Civil Rights Act of 1964, when he was able to get
through Congress something that President Kennedy was hopeful to do, [that] the
president before [him] had not even tried," she said. "It took a president to get it
done." Former community organizer and current presidential candidate Barack
Obama took offense, as did many others, and the two have agreed to drop the issue.
[7] Baiocchi, Gianpaolo. (2003). "Participation, Activism, and Politics: the Porto Alegre
Experiment," in Archon Fung and Eric Olin Wright (Ed.). *Deepening Democracy: Institutional Innovations in Empowered Participatory Governance.* (Real Utopias Project). New York: Verso Books.

[8] Again see www.participatorybudgeting.org for this information and many resources and documents on PB across the world. One can also join the US and international PB list serves there.

[9] This paragraph and the next are largely taken from Menser (2008).

[10] Chavez, Daniel. (2004). *Polis and Demos: the Left in Municipal Governance in Montevideo and Porto Alegre.* Maastricht, Netherlands: Shaker Publishing.

[11] Ibid.

[12] Shortly after the onset of the PB process, street paving, sewage infrastructure, and housing were frequently deemed to be the most pressing needs for many of the regions (Santos, Boaventura de Sousa. (2005). "Participatory Budgeting in Porto Alegre: Toward a Redistributive Democracy," in Boaventura de Sousa Santos (Ed.). *Democratizing Democracy: Beyond the Liberal Democratic Canon.* New York: Verso.)

[13] From its inception, PB was not merely designed to increase participation, but to deliver benefits to those who had been underserved by the municipality. While this framework has generally been adhered to over its existence, it has evolved in myriad ways. See Santos 2005.

[14] Santos (2005).

[15] Baiocchi (2003); Santos (2005).

[16] See Menser (2005).

[17] Baiocchi (2003).

[18] Santos (2005).

[19] Organizers of the sessions were Josh Lerner (Planners Network; http://www.plannersnetwork.org), Mike Menser (CUNY), Karen Dolan (Cities for Progress; http://www.citiesforprogress.org) and Juscha Robinson (Liberty Tree Foundation for the Democratic Revolution; http://www.libertytreefdr.org).

[20] Bryan, F. (2004). *Real Democracy: The New England Town Meeting and How It Works.* Chicago: University of Chicago Press.

[21] Berry, J, Portney, K and Thomsen, K. (1993). *The Rebirth of Urban Democracy.* Washington: The Brookings Institution; Simonsen, W. and Robbins, M. (2000). *Citizen Participation in Resource Allocation.* Boulder, CO: Westview.

[22] Lerner, J. and Baiocchi, G. (forthcoming) "Could Participatory Budgeting Work in the United States?, *"The Good Society".*

[23] Ibid.

18
The Sky as a Common Resource

Matthew Riddle

Matthew Riddle is a staff economist with the Center for Popular Economics, and a PhD Candidate in Economics at the University of Massachusetts, Amherst. His research has focused on the economics of resource depletion and climate change, with an emphasis on the distributional consequences of climate change policies.

Climate change has emerged recently as one of the key challenges facing humankind. The consequences of climate change are difficult to anticipate with much precision, but they could be enormous. Shifting weather patterns will likely lead to serious droughts in some areas, greater frequency of extreme weather events, and widespread extinction of species caused by changing habitats. Tropical diseases could become more common and could shift their ranges. Warming oceans and melting polar caps are likely to cause coastal flooding, kill coral reefs, and weaken the gulf-stream. Melting mountain glaciers will alter the flow of glacially fed rivers, disrupting water supplies in some of the most populous regions of the world (IPCC 2007).

The effects will be greatest in poor countries that are vulnerable to coastal flooding and changing weather patterns. Low income communities within each country will also be the most vulnerable because of their lack of mobility and their inability to pay for products that could help insulate them from the effects of coastal flooding, droughts and changes in the patterns of disease. At the release of the latest Intergovernmental Panel on Climate Change summary report on the impacts of climate change, IPCC Chairman Rajendra Pachauri told journalists that, "It is the poorest of the poor in the world, and this includes poor people even in prosperous societies, who are going to be the worst hit"[1].

On the other hand, it is rich countries and people who are most responsible for the damages. Developed countries, with 19% of the world's population, currently produce 58% of the world's carbon dioxide emissions (see Figure 1). Developed North America – consisting of the US and Canada – is the worst culprit, producing 26% of CO_2 emissions with only 5% of the world's population.

Within the US, the richest 10% of the population is responsible for over eight times more CO_2 emissions than the poorest 10% (see Figure 2).

Figure 1
World Population by Region, 2001   **Carbon Dioxide Emissions by Region**

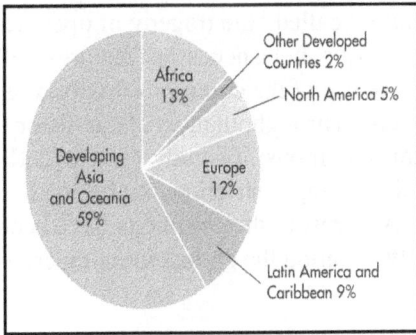

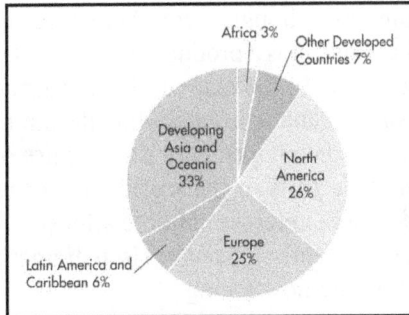

Source: Goodwin et al. (2005)

Figure 2
Contributions to carbon emissions by different expenditure brackets

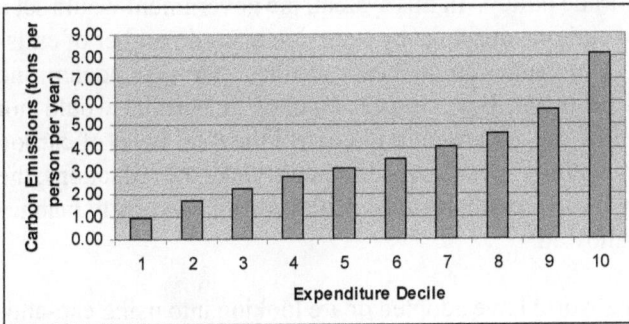

Source: Boyce and Riddle (2007)

The Need for Regulation

There is no single solution to this challenge. People all around the world must engage in activities that contribute to a shift away from fossil fuel consumption, through the development of alternative sources of energy, technologies that use energy more efficiently, and lifestyle changes that help to conserve energy. Much of this is already happening; committed individuals, businesses, cooperatives, non-profits and governments are finding innovative ways of helping to reduce greenhouse gas emissions.

But while these local initiatives are crucial to a successful strategy to reduce emission, it is also important to have national and international policies that create the right incentives so that people who are working to reduce their contribution to global warming are rewarded. The sky is an example of what economists refer to as common property, or as a commons. If society allows open access to the use of a commons, with no restrictions, there is a tendency for it to be over-exploited, because users do not take into consideration the negative effects that their use has on others. This situation is often described as "the tragedy of the commons," though it could be more accurately called "the tragedy of open access," since it is a product of inadequate regulation, not a necessary feature of all commons. In the case of global warming, the use of the commons involves releasing greenhouse gasses into the atmosphere. Throughout most of our history, there has been open access to the use of this commons; it is only very recently that some parts of the world have begun discussing restrictions on how much CO_2 can be released into the atmosphere. As a result, the commons have been overused; emissions have risen dramatically, creating the global warming crisis that we are now facing.

Cap-and-Trade Approaches

One approach to regulating greenhouse gas emissions that is frequently discussed is the idea of a cap-and-trade policy. In this system, the government would set a cap on the total level of carbon emissions by releasing a fixed number of emission permits each year. Companies could then trade these permits to determine where the cuts would be made, but the total number of permits would not change. This would allow the government to control the total level of carbon emissions in the country without specifying who should make the reductions; the flexibility should allow those reductions to be achieved in a less costly manner than if no trading was allowed.

Governments around the world have adopted or are looking into using cap-and-trade policies to fight global warming. The most extensive policy in place so far is in the European Union, which has adopted a program to limit carbon emissions by producers of electricity and other heavy industrial users of fossil fuels. In the US, several proposals for a similar national cap-and-trade program have been introduced in congress, and all the major Democratic candidates for president, as well as some Republicans, have their own cap-and-trade proposal. In addition, several states have already agreed to implement statewide cap-and-trade programs that would cover CO_2 emissions from electricity generation.

There are many different variations of the cap-and-trade idea. While all of them have the potential to reduce emissions, their effect on the people in the country could be very different. Any cap-and-trade program would raise the price of fossil fuels, which could hurt consumers financially. Since low income households on average spend a greater portion of their income on fossil fuels, the effect on these households would be particularly difficult to manage. Without any compensation for consumers, they could face an unfair and unnecessary burden.

Early cap-and-trade proposals were based on a free allocation of emissions permits to historic polluters – a system known as grandfathered permits. The cap-and-trade program that was implemented in Europe in 2005 was a good example of this type of system. In its first stage, at least 95% of the permits were distributed for free each year to the companies being regulated – the very companies that had been most responsible for emissions in the past. Yet, even though the permits were given out for free, the price of electricity and other products went up along with the price of permits. This allowed companies to reap significant windfall profits. One study in Great Britain showed that over a billion dollars of windfall profits were collected in Britain alone[2]. In other words, the net result of this policy was a billion dollar transfer of money from consumers to polluting companies.

This approach has been criticized on many fronts, with groups ranging from environmental groups to mainstream economists voicing their opposition. The alternative to grandfathered permits would be a system where the permits are auctioned to producers, instead of being given away for free. This eliminates the windfall profits for producers, and allows the government to collect this money instead. Consumers are still hit by higher prices, but if the government revenue from selling the permits is used appropriately, it can help to offset the negative impact on consumers.

Cap-and-Dividend Approaches

One option, proposed by Peter Barnes (2001), would auction the permits and use the revenues to distribute dividends to all households on an equal per capita basis. This proposal has been referred to by several names, including Sky Trust and Earth Atmospheric Trust, but the name currently being used by its proponents is Cap-and-Dividend. Barnes sees his proposal as a way of asserting the principle that the sky is a common resource that should be owned equally by all people. Any system of emission permits can be seen as a reorganization of the rights to the earth's capacity to absorb emissions. A system of grandfathered permits would be a huge giveaway of these rights to historic emitters. The principle of equal ownership of the commons requires that the permits, or the revenue from selling the permits, would be distributed equally to everyone.

This proposal has several attractive features. It helps to reduce emissions in all sectors of the economy by creating a significant financial incentive for households and businesses to reduce carbon emissions in any way possible. It allows the government to choose the emissions target for whole country, while allowing markets to determine the cheapest way of reaching this target. Just as importantly, this proposal satisfies some basic principles of fairness: people who are responsible for more than their share of the US's emissions have to pay more money through higher prices than they receive in dividends from permit sales, whereas people who use less than their share of emissions actually come out ahead financially. Because poor households are generally the least responsible for emissions, the net effect of a cap-and-dividend policy is a redistribution of income from richer households to poorer households. In the scenario shown in Figure 3, with a permit price of $200 per ton of carbon, the average household in the poorest 20% of the population could see a net rise in its income of 14.8%, instead of the 6.2% loss it would face if the permits were given away for free to polluters.

Figure 3

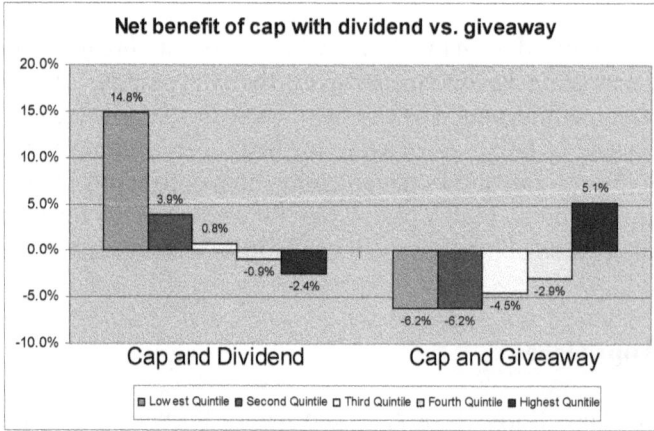

Net benefit of cap with dividend vs. giveaway

Source: Boyce and Riddle (2007). Based on a permit price of $200 per ton C.

Because of its attractiveness from both an environmental and social justice perspective, a cap-and-dividend system could be an important feature of a new, progressive economic system. Several features of the proposal have become more accepted in recent policy debates, suggesting that it could also be politically feasible. Environmental and consumer advocacy groups have played a key role in bringing about a shift in public views in favor of auctioning permits, and away from grandfathered permits. Massachusetts Climate Action Network led a coalition of environmental groups that pushed for 100% auctioning under the northeast's Regional Greenhouse Gas Initiative, and was able to persuade several states, including Massachusetts and New York, to commit to 100% auctioning. European countries have also faced pressure from groups such as CAN-Europe and Friends of the Earth Europe to auction more permits, and the pressure has paid off: the European Commission announced in January that it will propose 100% auctioning in the third phase of the agreement. In the US, The Federation of State Public Interest Research Groups (USPIRG) released a report in September 2007 calling for 100% auctioning that was endorsed by 43 prominent advocacy groups, including the Sierra Club, Oxfam, Greenpeace, and MoveOn.org. Since then, the momentum for 100% auctioning at the national level in the US has been increasing; presidential candidate Barack Obama has even included 100% auctioning as a key feature of his energy proposal.

There is less of a consensus as to what should be done with the revenues from the auction. This is a crucial question, as the value of the revenues could soon be in the range of $130 billion to $370 billion per year[3]. Barnes' cap-and-dividend proposal is not the only use of this revenue that progressively minded groups could support; there is a case for using some of the money for purposes other than paying dividends to consumers, such as investment in energy efficiency and renewable energy, or transitional assistance for affected workers. However, by establishing the principle that the revenues should be returned evenly to consumers, the cap-and-dividend proposal provides some insurance that the money won't be diverted to the wrong places – a very real possibility, as evidenced by current proposals, many of which include giveaways to fossil fuel companies.[4] It also helps to ensure that most poor and middle income households won't be hurt financially, which could be crucially important in gaining political support for the policy. Finally, it establishes the principle of equal ownership of common resources - a principle that can be applied to other aspects of the economy beyond climate change policy[6]. If environmental and social justice groups could come together behind this idea, it could be a unique opportunity to move toward a world with both a cleaner environment and less inequality.

References:

Barnes, Peter. (2001). *Who Owns the Sky? Our Common Assets and the Future of Capitalism.* Washington, D.C.: Island Press.

Barnes, Peter. (2006). *Capitalism 3.0: A Guide to Reclaiming the Commons.* San Francisco: Berrett Koehler Publishers, Inc.

Boyce and Riddle. (2007). "Cap and Dividend: How to Curb Global Warming while Protecting the Incomes of American Families," Political Economy Research Institute Working Paper # 150. Available at http://www.peri.umass.edu/fileadmin/pdf/working_papers/working_pape rs_101-150/WP150.pdf.

Carbon Dioxide Information Analysis Center (CDIAC) at Oak Ridge National Laboratory, "Trends: A Compendium of Data on Global Change." Available at http://cdiac.ornl.gov/trends/emis/em_cont.htm.

Environment News Service. (2007, April 6). "UN Climate Change Impact Report: Poor Will Suffer Most." Available at http://www.ens-newswire.com/ens/apr2007/2007-04-06-01.asp.

Friends of the Earth. (2007). "Windfalls in the Lieberman-Warner Global Warming Bill: Quantifying the Fossil Fuel Industry Giveaways." Available at http://foe.org/globalwarming/Coal%20Rush.pdf.

Goodwin, N., Nelson, J., Ackerman, F., & Weiskopf, T. (2005). *Microeconomics in Context*. Houghton Mifflin Co.

Intergovernmental Panel on Climate Change. (2007). "Fourth Assessment Report: Climate Change 2007." Available at http://www.ipcc.ch/.

IPA Energy Consulting (2005) "Implications of the EU Emissions Trading Scheme for the UK Power Generation Sector." Available at http://www.massclimateaction.org/RGGI/BritishEmissionsTradingIPA1105.pdf.

Paltsev, Sergey *et al.* (2007, April). "Assessment of U.S. Cap-and-Trade Proposals," Cambridge, MA: Massachusetts Institute of Technology Joint Program on the Science and Policy of Global Change, Report No. 146. Available at http://web.mit.edu/globalchange/www/MITJPSPGC_Rpt146.pdf.

Roberts, Brian. (2007, October 10). "Green Badge of Courage," *Guardian.* Available at http://commentisfree.guardian.co.uk/david_roberts/2007/10/obama_energy_plan.html.

Notes

[1] Environment News Service. (2007, April 6). "UN Climate Change Impact Report: Poor Will Suffer Most." Available at
http://www.ensnewswire.com/ens/apr2007/2007-04-06-01.asp.
[2] IPA Energy Consulting. (2005). "Implications of the EU Emissions Trading Scheme for the UK Power Generation Sector." Available at
http://www.massclimateaction.org/RGGI/BritishEmissionsTradingIPA1105.pdf.
[3] Paltsev, Sergey *et al.* (2007, April). "Assessment of U.S. Cap-and-Trade Proposals," Cambridge, MA: Massachusetts Institute of Technology Joint Program on the Science and Policy of Global Change, Report No. 146. Available at
http://web.mit.edu/globalchange/www/MITJPSPGC_Rpt146.pdf.
[4] Friends of the Earth (2007) "Windfalls in the Lieberman-Warner Global Warming Bill: Quantifying the Fossil Fuel Industry Giveaways." Available at
http://foe.org/globalwarming/Coal%20Rush.pdf; Roberts, Brian (2007, October 10),

"Green Badge of Courage," *Guardian.* Available at
http://commentisfree.guardian.co.uk/david_roberts/2007/10/obama_energy_plan.html
[5] Roberts, Brian (2007), "Green Badge of Courage," *Guardian.* Available at
http://commentisfree.guardian.co.uk/david_roberts/2007/10/obama_energy_plan.html
[6] Barnes, Peter (2006) *Capitalism 3.0: A Guide to Reclaiming the Commons.* San
Francisco: Berrett Koehler Publishers, Inc.

19

U.S. Economic Inequality and What We Can Do About It

Thomas Masterson and Suresh Naidu

Thomas Masterson is a Research Scholar at the Levy Economics Institute of Bard College, working on the Distribution of Income and Wealth and LIMEW projects. He received his Ph.D. in Economics from the University of Massachusetts, Amherst. He is a long-time staff economist with the Center for Popular Economics, teaching workshops on the U.S. Economy, environmental economics and the Living Wage.

Suresh Naidu is a graduate student in economics at UC Berkeley. Prior to attending Berkeley, he received an M.A. from the University of Massachusetts, Amherst. He is a long-time CPE member, teaching workshops on political economy and international economics.

U.S. economic inequality is a hot topic these days. This is due in no small part to what has been happening to it recently. Despite a period of economic growth in the 1990s longer than any previously recorded, most people in the US today are not much better off economically than they were in 1980. Most often economic inequality is talked about in income terms, while wealth inequality, though widely recognized to be larger, is discussed less. However, the economic status of households depends not just on their income or alternately on their wealth, but on income, wealth and a variety of other factors as well. When we look at a broader measure of economic wellbeing, a fuller picture emerges, and one that is different from the picture we get when only looking at income. The Levy Institute Measure of Economic Wellbeing (LIMEW) is an attempt to produce such a broader measure, and we will be describing it and some of the results we get in the next section. Getting a better handle on the nature of economic inequality can also lead to better policy for addressing it, such as the Basic Income Grant (BIG) that we'll be discussing after we talk about the LIMEW. More effectively addressing economic inequality, by tackling it at its roots as the BIG does, can free up people's time and energy for organizing themselves to make the Solidarity Economy work for them.

Measuring Inequality: the Levy Measure of Economic Wellbeing

The usual measure of economic inequality (calculated by the US Census bureau, for example) is money income (MI). It includes all receipts of cash by a household. This is a good start, but it has several deficiencies. First of all, it doesn't include the value of non-cash benefits associated with employment (such as employers' contribution to health insurance) or non-cash transfers from the government (such as Medicare). In addition, it does not deduct the taxes paid by households. The Census Bureau has developed a measure that addresses these deficiencies, which they call extended income (EI). However, there are still large gaps in this measure. Missing from the measure are the value of public consumption, that part of government spending on things like education and roads that benefits households directly, and the value of household production. Also, EI includes the *income from wealth*, which is not an adequate measure of the impact of a given *amount of wealth* on household economic wellbeing.

The Levy Institute Measure of Economic Wellbeing (LIMEW) addresses all of these deficiencies. It goes beyond EI, by including the value of public consumption and household production, as well as incorporating the amount of wealth a household owns rather than the income from wealth at a given time. The latter is not as straightforward as the former: what we do is to assume that the household spends its wealth down to zero over the expected lifetime of the household head and replace wealth income with the value of this annuity in the present. The LIMEW is thus a much better measure of household economic wellbeing. And the difference in the measure shows up very starkly when we look at what happened to household economic wellbeing over the 1990s.

Between 1989 and 2001, the median household (not the average, but the household with 50% above and 50% below them) MI went from $41,310 to $42,198 (adjusted for inflation), an increase of a little over 2% (See Figure 1, below).[1] Things look a little better for EI: increasing 6% from $40,742 to $43,199. But the LIMEW increased from $63,590 in 1989 to $72,014 in 2001, a jump of over 13%! A big part of this jump is the change in the median household's hours of paid work over the decade, going from 2,080 to 2,340. So, an additional six and a half weeks of paid work per year per household yielded a whopping additional $888 per year in MI, which is most directly affected by hours worked. Not exactly a great trade-off for most households.

In order to break down the changes by the components of LIMEW, we have to use averages. In 1989 the average household LIMEW was $80,080 while EI was $47,579, while by 2001 the average LIMEW had risen to $93,595 and the aver-

Figure 1: US Economic Wellbeing, 1989 & 2001

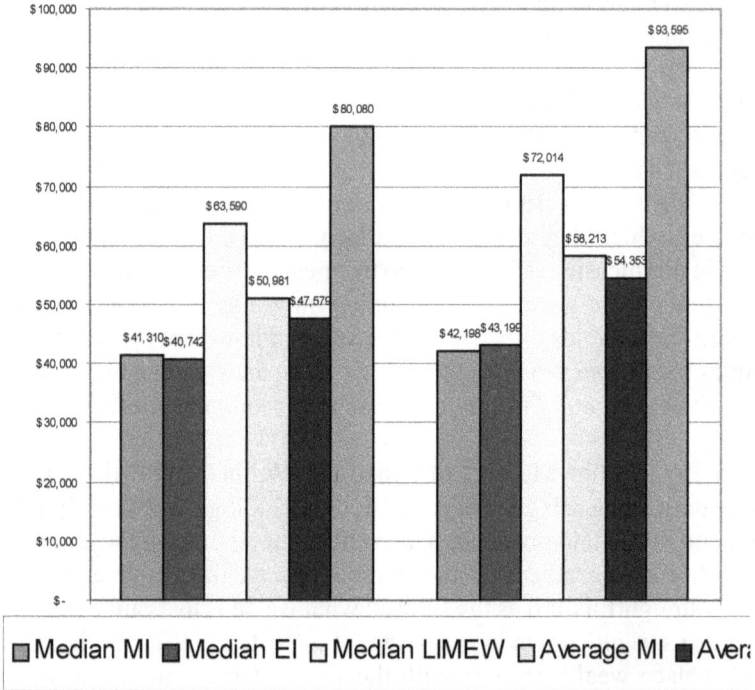

□ Median MI ■ Median EI □ Median LIMEW □ Average MI ■ Avera

age EI to $54,353. In percentage terms the average LIMEW grew by 17% while EI grew by 14%. The reasons for the difference are the change in the average amount of wealth compared to the income from wealth: the wealth component of the LIMEW grew by 21%, while the wealth component of EI shrank by 1%. Also, because EI does not include public consumption, the net government transfers in EI (which is negative) decreased by 21%, while that part of the LIMEW (which is positive) decreased by 15%. In addition, household production increased by 12%.

So, how do these measures compare in terms of inequality? Economists use something called the 'gini coefficient' to measure inequality. The closer to zero the gini coefficient is, the more equally economic wellbeing is divided up among households, while the closer to one it is, the more unequal the situation is. In terms of overall inequality, all three measures increased in inequality over the 1990s. However, the LIMEW has the smallest increase, from 0.39 to 0.41, while EI went from 0.37 to 0.41 and MI went from 0.42 to 0.46. These differences are not that great, but when we look at inequality in terms of demographic groups, the differences in the measures become much clearer. The elderly are frequently seen as being much more economically disadvantaged than the rest of the population. Certainly in terms of income excluding government transfers this is indisputable. However, what is infrequently talked about is wealth in terms of age. The elderly are much wealthier than the rest of the population. And in terms of net government expenditures the elderly are much better off than non-elders. In fact, in 2001, the average elderly household's LIMEW was 9% higher than the non-elder household average. For the median households, this was reversed, with the median elder household's LIMEW just 85% of the median non-elder household's.

Redressing Inequality: The Basic Income Grant

So the LIMEW shows that there is still a lot of inequality even when you adjust for government transfers. Surely we can design better government policy to redress inequality? Currently, the system of redistribution we have is a complex swamp of conditional transfers and tax breaks, all basically designed to make sure none of the "undeserving" have access to public cash. For example, food stamps are a program that exists to make sure that poor people can only purchase food with government largess. Earned-Income Tax Credits are designed to make

Figure 2: US Economic Inequality, 1989 & 2001

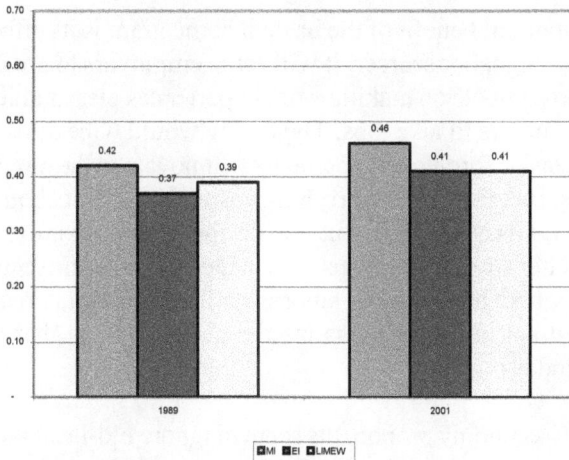

sure the poor work in order to qualify for a tax break. Social Security is a population that has both very wealthy people (as we've seen above) and very poor people in it. Can we radically simplify the government's transfer programs, reduce inequality, build a political bloc for other progressive policies, and promote alternative economic institutions? Maybe we can, with unconditional basic income grants.

A proposal that has been floated by progressives for some time is the idea of the unconditional basic income grant. The basic idea: ditch welfare as we know it, and write every adult a flat check funded out of a progressive tax system. If people want to work and earn more, that's fine; we don't want to punish work, but instead make it more fulfilling by removing desperation from the labor market. Obviously, this program would tax the rich and transfer to the poor, just like any good egalitarian economic strategy would, and thus reduce inequality. But in making the transfers universal, we might be able to generate not just a kinder capitalism, but also a space for building alternative economic institutions and longer-term political power.

A first benefit of the BIG is reducing the bureaucratic infrastructure we maintain to police the poor by "means-testing." A noxious dimension of our welfare system is not just that it is skimpy; it also keeps poor people jumping through a ridiculous number of hoops: appointments and regulations. Outside of the implicit moralizing and indignities that lie behind proving that you're a member of the deserving poor, this morass of red tape has economic consequences. It becomes a part-time job just to make sure the welfare checks keep coming, which is hardly the best use of an unemployed person's time.

An equally important benefit of the basic income grant is its effects on the labor market. By making labor scarcer, it will force employers to not only pay higher wages, but also compete on making work experiences pleasurable and empowering to induce workers to take jobs. The policy would wipe out a whole range of low-paid, trite tasks, forcing entrepreneurs to innovate in the direction of improving job quality. Imagine firms worrying constantly not just about how to build a better product for its consumers, but also putting resources into figuring out how to develop a better work experience for its employees. Some sectors, such as law and software, where high-quality labor is really important, already do this. The basic income grant might universalize the perks and pay that only the highly educated get today.

Some solidarity economy proponents seem to ignore old-fashioned economic redistribution programs. But in reality, an important feature of government redistribution could be that they complement building alternative economic institutions. Instead of letting the market run amok and relying on the government to fix the resulting inequality, we can design government programs that help foster and maintain a different, less market-based vision of the economy. So, let's consider what implications an unconditional basic income grant would have for the solidarity economy.

Firstly, the safety cushion that the basic income would provide could increase the amount of experimentation with alternative economic institutions, such as those promoted under the solidarity economy banner. People could not only spend more time with their kids and families, they could also spend more time volunteering for community day-care, experimenting with starting a small business or a cooperative.

Basic income grant proponents have perhaps understated the potential growth impacts of the entrepreneurial talents unleashed by the BIG. Freed from the day-to-day paycheck hustle, people might finally be able to realize the business ideas and innovations that have been shackled to the need to meet subsistence. This may be enough to offset the higher taxes and more expensive labor costs that the basic income grants entail.

Secondly, by making labor scarcer, the BIG gives cooperatives a competitive edge. If in fact worker-participation and democracy is more desirable than workplace hierarchy, then anything that makes labor scarcer will improve the business prospects of cooperatives, as they presumably have an easier time recruiting labor than a run-of-the-mill job. If it doesn't, then at least we'll have some more insight into the (complex) reasons why worker democracy is not more common in market societies.

Thirdly, and perhaps most importantly, the basic income grant is, like other universalistic redistributive policies, a device for building political power for the left. One of the things often neglected by promoters of the solidarity economy is the need not only for just economic institutions, but also the political support and mobilization necessary to preserve those economic institutions. We would like constituencies that are willing to fight to build and maintain progressive institutions and programs; designing institutions that build and maintain those constituencies is part of what will make those institutions persist.

When one considers two rashes of redistribution in the history of the U.S., the New Deal and the War on Poverty, it is easy to think of why the first substantially outlived the second. Witness the difficulty the Bush administration had in privatizing social security. Given that such a large fraction of Americans received it, it was really hard to mobilize people against it. There was a lot of "don't touch my check!" emotion flying around, even from moderately well-off people. Contrast this to Clintonian welfare reform, which passed easily, because it was possible to demonize the takers of AFDC (Aid to Families with Dependent

Children) as "those poor people" and withdraw their benefits. The recipients of AFDC were a narrow segment with low political power: taking away their pittances was political cake.

Given the realities of politics, in is important for progressives to worry about policies not only in terms of their outcomes for people, but also their effects on political support for those policies. By demanding programs, such as Basic Income Grants, that have a wide class of beneficiaries, and does not discriminate among them, we create a pro-redistribution political bloc, one that it will take the right substantial time to overcome. The virtue of this political power is obvious: it means that the left can implement more of the pro-poor, pro-solidarity institutions it favors, by bundling them with programs (such as the BIG or social security) that have wide appeal.

Economic inequality in the US has been increasing in the last couple of decades. There are a variety of ways to deal with this issue, some better than others (for example, the line of thinking that says that "inequality is a natural result of different choices that people make in their lives, so the best thing to do is nothing" is unsatisfactory). Obviously, we are on the side of doing something. The Basic Income Grant is a simple idea that would be relatively easy to implement and that would make a big difference for those at the bottom of the economic scale. While it is not a cure-all, the BIG lowers inequality, is politically self-sustaining and gives people more room with which they can innovate and experiment with alternative, solidarity economy institutions.

Resources
- Levy Economics Institute of Bard College. http://www.levy.org.
- The US Basic Income Guarantee Network. http://www.usbig.net.

References
Wolff, Edward N., Zacharias, Ajit, and Caner, Asena. (2004). "Levy Institute Measure of Economic Well-Being: United States, 1989, 1995, 2000, and 2001." Annandale-on-Hudson, NY: Levy Economics Institute of Bard College.
Redesigning Distribution. Basic Income and Stakeholder Grants as Cornerstones for an. Egalitarian Capitalism, edited by Erik Olin Wright., Verso, 2006

Notes

[1] All numbers regarding LIMEW, Money Income and Extended Income from Wolff, Zacharias and Caner, "Levy Institute Measure of Economic Well-Being: United States, 1989, 1995, 2000, and 2001," May 2004.

20
You Are What You Eat

Helen Scharber and Heather Schoonover

> *Helen Scharber has been a member of CPE and an Economics
> graduate student at the University of Massachusetts since 2005.
> Helen's interest in the food system stems from her background
> in Environmental Politics and was heightened after reading
> The Omnivore's Dilemma by Michael Pollan.*

> *Heather Schoonover has been a policy analyst at The Institute
> for Agriculture and Trade Policy (IATP) since 2001. Heather's
> current research focuses on linkages between U.S. farm policy
> and public health, specifically the role farm policy plays in in-
> fluencing the food environment and how such policy might be
> better directed to support healthier, more localized food systems
> that benefit public health, independent family farmers, rural
> communities and the environment alike.*

Introductions

We started by introducing the organizations hosting the session: the Center for
Popular Economics (CPE) and the Institute for Agriculture and Trade Policy
(IATP). CPE is a collective of political economists based in Amherst, Massachusetts, that teaches economic literacy to activists. IATP is based in Minneapolis, Minnesota, and promotes resilient family farms, rural communities and eco-
systems around the world through research and education, science and technology, and advocacy. All the workshop participants then introduced themselves to
the group and explained, briefly, why they came to the session.

After the large group introductions, participants broke into groups of four or five
to discuss their personal experiences with the food system in the U.S. We pro-
vided some questions to guide their short discussions:
- How much do you know about where your food comes from?
- Can you buy what you want? If not, why not?
- What factors influence what foods you buy?
- How much do you think about food?
- Are you actively working on food-related issues?

During a short debriefing, we learned that while lots of people in the room were actively working on food-related issues, many agreed that it is difficult to learn about where, exactly, our food comes from, and it is also difficult to buy fresh, local, and organic food.

Not-So-Fun Facts about the U.S. Food and Farm system

Each participant was given a fact about the food and farm system to read aloud, and it was wonderful to hear many different voices from the group. Here is a sampling of some of the not-so-fun facts that were shared:
- A typical vegetable in the U.S. travels 1,500 miles between the farm and the dinner table.
- One in four rural U.S. counties lost population between 1990 and 2000.
- 35 million Americans—12% of the U.S. population—are food insecure.
- Two-thirds of American adults are overweight; one-third are considered obese.
- Approximately 9 million children over the age of six are considered obese.
- Between 1985 and 2000, the real cost of fresh fruits and vegetables in the U.S. rose nearly 40%. The real cost of soda pop, sweets, and fats and oils, on the other hand, went down.
- In many places, particularly in low-income neighborhoods, it is easier to find a fast food restaurant or a convenience store than a grocery store.
- On average, only 19¢ of each dollar spent on food in the U.S. goes to the farm sector. The other 81% goes toward packaging, processing, transportation, advertising, etc.
- 70% of antibiotics in the U.S. are used for accelerating animal growth and compensating for overcrowded and unsanitary conditions in factory farms—8 times the amount given to humans to treat disease.
- There are more than 450 varieties of soda pop on the market. The average American consumes over 50 gallons of soft drinks a year.

After everyone read a fact, we discussed some common threads running through all the facts. We concluded that overall the U.S. food system appears to be good for some large agribusiness corporations but generally negative for family farmers, the environment, public health, and inner-city residents.

Mapping the U.S. Food System

In the next exercise, a large "map" was posted on the wall, which had a horizontal line running through the middle and four main parts of the food system marked: production, processing, distribution and consumption. Participants were given sticky notes and, after breaking up into groups, were invited to write down "players" in the food system, which could include anyone or anything involved in the system. Some players included:

- Small and large farmers/livestock producers/fishers from both the U.S. and other countries
- Agribusiness firms (ConAgra, Monsanto, etc.)
- Big food processing companies (Coke, General Mills, Nabisco)
- Grocery stores (mom and pop, Wal-Mart, etc.)
- Restaurants
- Policy-makers (USDA, trade negotiators, lobbyists).
- People who eat food (rich, poor, city, rural, etc.)

After each group had written down four or five food system "players," they were invited to post the sticky notes on the map where they fit best – near production, processing, distribution or consumption. If they thought their player was a "winner" in the food system, they put the note near the top of the map, while food system "losers" were placed near the bottom. Sometimes the right map location for a player wasn't clear—consumers both benefit and lose from cheap food, for example—but it was clear that big, multinational corporations seemed to be winning at the expense of everyone else.

Farm Policy 101

Heather provided a five-minute introduction to U.S. farm policy and Elizabeth Pixley-Fink, her co-presenter and an intern at IATP, provided an introduction to international trade policy, which helped to explain how government policy has helped create the food system we currently have. In the mid-20th century, U.S. farm policy focused on production management, aimed at keeping commodity prices stable by managing supply. Measures such as grain reserves and acreage set-asides helped ensure that commodity prices would not plummet if the country's ever-increasing production capacity surpassed demand for its products. Conversely, grain could be released back onto the market if supplies dwindled and prices go too high.

Throughout the second half of the twentieth century, however, the agribusiness sector chipped away at these policies. This sector had a vested interest in keeping commodity prices low and unstable and therefore preferred chronic overproduction and oversupply of commodities to any sort of supply management. Beginning in the 1970s, supply management programs began to be phased out and farm policy shifted toward encouraging overproduction—which drove down prices—and then compensating for the resulting low prices with subsidies.

This approach to farm policy continues today: rather than managing production and stabilizing prices, farm policy allows prices to fall—often below the cost of production—and then provides subsidy payments to farmers to make up the difference between price and production costs and enabling this system to persist.

Overproduction and low prices lead to many of the characteristics of our current food system. For example, low commodity prices represent a substantial indirect subsidy to industrial animal factories, enabling them to buy feed at prices below the cost of production and giving them a decided advantage over diversified livestock producers who raise their animals on pasture or grow their own feed. Low commodity prices also drive food industry investment into finding as many uses for these cheap raw inputs as possible, contributing to the prevalence of unhealthy products such as high-fructose corn syrup and partially hydrogenated vegetable oils. We also export commodities below the cost of production, which undermines other countries' food and farm systems.

Food System Values

After the policy lesson, Elizabeth and Heather posted two large sheets of paper on the wall and invited participants to identify 1) the values that drive the current food system and 2) the values that they thought *should* drive our food system. Many values were suggested. Some of the current values identified were efficiency, profits, convenience, and low price. Values that participants wanted to see represented to a greater degree included justice, health, environmental friendliness, accessibility, democracy, and vibrant rural economies.

Leading by Example

The last half hour of the workshop was set aside to allow participants to discuss what aspects of our ideal food system already exist and what people are already doing to create a better food system. Many inspirational examples were given, and in many cases, participants were actively involved in making food production and distribution more in line with the values identified earlier. Some of the initiatives and movements mentioned included
- Food movements and labeling programs, including local, organic, and fair trade
- Programs creating a more direct link between farmers and consumers, including those that bring fresh food to schools, nursing homes, and hospitals
- Introducing youth to food production through school gardening
- Greater community involvement in food production, especially in poor areas, through community gardening and farming

-   Marketing arrangements that shrink the distance between producer and con-
    sumer, including farmers markets, co-ops, and community-supported agrul-
    ture (CSAs)
-   Policy work at local through international levels to reform the food system,
    including local ordinances, Farm Bill provisions, and trade agreements

Summing Up

The *You are what you eat* workshop had three main goals. We wanted to
provide:
1. Greater awareness of how the U.S. food system works (and doesn't
    work)
2. Inspirational examples of how people are making changes at different
    levels
3. A forum for networking among people interested in food activism

We learned in the early part of the workshop that powerful corporations and poor
policies have built a food system that is good for corporate profits but bad for
just about everything else, including human health, farmer livelihoods, poor people, and the environment. While discussion of how the current food system operates can be both overwhelming and discouraging, we devoted a good deal of
time to discussing alternative types of food production, distribution and consumption. Efficiency, convenience and profits may be the values and motives
that drive the food system today, but they need not drive it tomorrow. Participants in the workshop gave personal examples to show how health, accessibility,
and justice can drive good food production and distribution. Another food world
is possible, and we can all help to make it happen.

Resources

Institute for Agriculture and Trade Policy's Agriculture Observatory.
http://www.agobservatory.org/index.cfm

"Farm Bill 101." Food and Water Watch.
http://www.foodandwaterwatch.org/food/us-farmbill/farm-bill-faq

FoodRoutes. http://www.foodroutes.org/
Community Food Security Coalition. http://foodsecurity.org/

SECTION VII:

BUILDING THE SOLIDARITY ECONOMY THROUGH DAILY PRACTICE

21

Live Your Power: Socially Responsible Consumption, Work and Investment

Julie Matthaei

Julie Matthaei teaches economics students at Wellesley College how to "live your power." She was born in 1951 in a white, upper class suburb of Detroit. When she arrived at Stanford University as a first-year student in 1969, she immediately became involved in the vibrant campus movements: the anti-Vietnam war movement; the planning of the first earth day (where students went door to door asking people to recycle); and the early feminist movement. Julie became a hippy, joined a vegetarian Gandhian anti-war commune, Columbae, and was arrested for nonviolent civil disobedience, while blocking a draft board. The spring of her sophomore year, she dropped out of school, and traveled the country on a "Free School Bus" to spread the counterculture and its radical politics. Thirty five years later she has been gratified to discover – in this session – a new generation of youth who are taking hippy patched blue-jeans and simple living to a whole other level!

Author's note: I organized this workshop, and invited Dennis Brutus (Graduation Pledge and TIAA-CREF Campaign), Victoria Cepidia-Mojaro (United Students Against Sweatshops), Trish Tchume (Idealist.org), and Denise Hamler (Co-op America) to attend; all confirmed except Denise. However, in the end, all of the scheduled speakers were unable to come to the session. So instead, I presented a brief introduction to the topic, which I summarize here. Then I opened the workshop up to discussion among the 80 or so participants. What I learned when the discussion started, which was true about all of the sessions I participated in at the US Social Forum, was that most of the participants were extremely knowledgeable and sophisticated. The session became a sharing of information on ways to transform one's everyday economic life, especially in community. I took notes and Jenna videoed the workshop and transcribed much of it, so I am able to share here a good deal of the insights shared by the participants.

Live Your Power Presentation

The movement we have been waiting for is finally coming to fruition – both as a movement of movements, epitomized by the Social Forum movement of which this first US Social Forum is a part – and as a new kind of consciousness, expressed in a plethora of new, solidarity-based ways of participating in our economic lives. Here we will focus on the latter. Economic individuality is being transformed from narrowly self-interested, materialistic, and competitive economic behavior to a new, post-materialist, socially responsible economic personhood – and this new type of personhood is beginning to transform economic values, practices and institutions, creating the basis for the emergence of the solidarity economy.[1] In 2000, Paul Ray and Sherry Anderson estimated that 50 million Americans belonged to this new category of persons, whom they identify as "cultural creatives."[2] This new type of economic personhood is much less competitive and much more communitarian than the old "economic man." The growth of community economy institutions is thus a key part of the economic transformation we are in the midst of.

This session is entitled "Live Your Power" because we have the power to transform our economy through our everyday economic actions, as consumers, savers/investors, workers, and citizens. We have been taught to leave our ethics at the door when we enter into the economy, to be materialistic and narrowly self-interested in our economic choices – and to let the "invisible hand of the market" take care of the rest. Mainstream economists tell us that doing so will create a free, efficient and just economy. By now, we all know that this is a suicidal strategy – we are confronted by global warming, growing inequality and unrest, and deep alienation from ourselves, one another, and nature. The way out of this morass, we are finding, is to inject our ethical or spiritual values into our everyday economic lives. We need to take and live our power in our economic lives, making them reflect OUR values, not those of the rich few, or of advertisers. The more we realize that we can do something to make a positive difference in the world, the more our alienation and apathy dissolves, and our compassionate caring emerges.[3] More and more people are beginning to "do the right thing," not out of guilt, but out of enlightened self-interest.[4]

Here we will look at some of the multitude of ways that people are finding to transform our economy through their everyday economic actions. We have so much to learn from one another, as we together, in all our creativity and diversity, create a solidarity economy—economic values, practices, and institutions based on cooperation, sharing, democracy, diversity, and sustainability.

Socially Responsible Consumption

Consumption is a key area in which people are "living their power" and transforming our economy. Socially responsible consumption is growing by leaps and bounds. Studies show that a majority of Americans want to consume in socially responsible ways. For example, in one survey, 65% of Americans said it was "extremely" or "very" important to buy products and services from those who have similar values and principles, and 76 percent said that a company's treatment of its employees plays a big role in their purchasing decisions.[5] Three of every four American consumers said they would avoid shopping at a retailer that they knew sold garments made in sweatshops, and 86% of Americans said that they would be willing to pay nearly 5% more for their clothes if this would ensure decent working conditions for those who produced them.[6] And a study reviewed by Public Agenda found that 70% of all consumers had purchased a product or brand because it was better for the environment.[7]

This new socially responsible or ethical consumption both punishes firms that are not ethical, and supports the development of firms that are. The burgeoning Fair Trade movement is a result of this new type of consumerism. It links ethical consumers to wholesalers, retailers, and producers who are committed to providing fair wages and good employment opportunities to economically disadvantaged artisans and farmers worldwide. Information is key to ethical consuming, and the fair trade movement also educates consumers about the importance of purchasing fairly traded products which support living wages and safe and healthy conditions for workers in the developing world.[8]

On 200 high school and college campuses, this movement has taken the form of "Students Against Sweatshops" (www.usasnet.org), who refuse to purchase products, especially clothing, made through the superexploitation of workers. The students have thus achieved leverage over suppliers.

Another excellent resource for socially responsible consumers is Co-op America – now their "Green Pages" are on-line, listing 2,500 ethical "business associates." Their website, www.coopamerica.org, provides a wealth of information about socially responsible consumption, and those on their e-mail list receive informative updates about products and actions.

Another aspect of socially responsible consumption is consuming less, treading lightly on the planet. The movie "Affluenza" and the associated website, www.pbs.org/tcts/affluenza, call Americans' dysfunctional pattern of overconsumption, overwork, debt, and stress "affluenza," and prescribe the solution of cutting down on one's consumption, and hence need for income. *Your Money or Your Life*, by Joe Dominguez and Vicki Robin, makes the same point, which is taught in seminars across the country.[9] The Simple Living Network (www.SimpleLiving.net) and the Center for a New American Dream (www.newdream.org) also support this type of downshifting.

Socially Responsible Work and Social Entrepreneurship

Socially responsible work is on the rise – that is, the desire to have a job which makes a positive contribution to people and the planet. Four-fifths of Americans say it's "extremely" or "very" important to work for those who have similar values and principles.[10] In her book, Making a Living While Making A Difference, Melissa Everett points out that, for a growing number of people, the desire to do work that serves society does not come from a sense of guilt or self-sacrifice.

Instead, it is rooted in a well-developed social self, a self which realizes that it is part of a larger process, and wants to "reintegrate individual vocational satisfaction with an ethic of spiritual development and service." Such people want to "connect [their] personal working lives with the work that needs to be done to restore communities and the planet."

Such sentiments fuel the Graduation Pledge movement, comprised of student groups at over 100 colleges and universities. College seniors encourage their fellow graduating seniors to sign cards which say, ""I pledge to explore and take into account the social and environmental consequences of any job I consider and will try to improve these aspects of any organizations for which I work." (www.GraduationPledge.org) This movement has a website with listings of not-for-profit and socially responsible jobs, as does www.idealist.org.

One strategy for finding socially responsible work is to create your own. Everett notes that self-employment is a key way to create such work for oneself.[11] Others such as Judy Wicks, the successful founder of The White Dog Café in Philadelphia advocates for the creation of "beautiful businesses" – locally-rooted businesses which serve a triple bottom line, people, profit, and planet.[12] Wicks helped found the Business Alliance for Local Living Economies (BALLE) which networks small, local entrepreneurs, with a focus on green technology and community development.[13]

Another slightly different expression of this desire to do socially responsible work is "social entrepreneurship:" people starting nongovernmental organizations (NGO's) or socially responsible businesses with the main goal of serving others and saving the planet.   Aware of the urgent need for change, frustrated with the failure of government to act appropriately, and better able to communicate with others and coordinate efforts thanks to the Internet, social entrepreneurs are innovating, "creating new models to create wealth, promote social well-being, and restore the environment," as well as pushing for reforms in both economic and political systems. Much of this social entrepreneurship has taken the form of citizens' groups – which now number two million in the U.S.[14]

Socially Responsible Investment

The idea of investing your money in accordance with your values is not new – it has been practiced for hundreds of years, and is rooted in Jewish, Christian and Islamic traditions.[15] There has been a fifty-fold increase in socially responsible investment (SRI) over the past 25 years! The funds that manage "socially responsible investing" now account for $2.3 trillion of the $24 trillion U.S. investment marketplace.[16] Their share of total investment is increasing, growing 40% faster than all professionally managed investment assets in the U.S.[17] This movement has gotten the attention of the corporate world; over 70% of CEOs surveyed by the World Economic Forum believe that mainstream investors will have an increased interest in corporate citizenship issues.[18]

Socially responsible investment takes three main forms. First, it can involve utilizing positive and/or negative screens of investment portfolios or mutual funds: for example, excluding companies involved in war production, or including companies with a strong environmental record. Second, socially responsible investment can involve shareholder advocacy – that is, taking active roles as owners to transform the behavior of one's company, through dialoguing with management, and filing and advocating for shareholder resolutions. A third form of SRI is community investment, which directs capital to traditionally underserved communities. Community investing institutions finance or guarantee loans for housing, small business creation, education, or international community development.[19] The simplest way to practice community investment is to bank with a socially responsible bank or credit union.

Live Your Power: Insights from the Workshop Participants

The participants listened attentively and politely to my presentation on socially responsible consumption, work, entrepreneurship, and investment. Then one said, politely and with suppressed irritation, "Yes, this is all good, but when are we going to talk about the really alternative, radical options?" At this point, the discussion expanded to include movements not to consume, especially freeganism.

It also expanded from the individualistic-orientation of my presentation to a discussion of community economies. Based on my notes, the session transcript, and my subsequent Internet research, I summarize each of these areas of discussion below.

What Is Freeganism?

A number of the workshop participants discussed their experiences living as "freegans." The freegan lifestyle involves minimizing one's participation in the monetary economy, because of distress over the unethical practices which permeate its institutions. Strategies shared were dumpster-diving, free boxes and stores, couch surfing, squatting, sharing, and swapping.

One participant became engaged in the search for better ways to consume when he watched the movie "Affluenza" as a child. "I don't buy much... I live off of free boxes and people's cast-offs, and the garbage, and the waste stream economy. I've been living off of less than $7,000 a year for the past fourteen years." He emphasized (as did our Community Economies panel, see Ch. 8) that the monetary economy was actually only one of the other possible economies we can engage in for our sustenance: "there's the gift economy, there's the barter economy, there's the waste-stream economy, there's the equal exchange and hospitality economy, there's the economy of just being good to each other as human beings, and actually separating what our needs are from our desires." He noted that some families survive in these other ways because they have to – and others, because they choose to, such as middle class youth whose parents taught them to dumpster-dive. He also mentioned the Catholic Worker movement as a source of information about alternative ways of getting resources and surviving. "Learning to look and actually perceive what's out there... getting away from looking at fancy packaging... is really important. It takes a little training, but once you start seeing this other world, there's so much bounty there."

These comments were echoed by a second participant, who was active in New York City's vibrant freegan community. He had spent about $500 over the past year. Pointing to his clothes, backpack, and pad of writing paper, he explained that he had gotten all of it for free.

> I've probably dumpstered a couple thousand pounds of food in the last year from grocery stores and other outlets. I've been a part of communal houses that have supported dozens of people on entirely reclaimed waste food. Good stuff. Clean stuff. They just run down the aisle, they put it all in a bag, they seal it up in the store, and they just place it in the dumpster. It's a lot of fun because, it's like, what do we do with forty pounds of asparagus? Alright, let's figure this out. That's a big part of it.

He noted that dumpstering is technically illegal, but this law is generally not enforced; he had dumpstered "literally thousands of times in my life, and I've been stopped for it twice," both in the South.

This participant discussed the diverse communities which were growing up around freeganism, especially in New York City, which included youth, "crusty punks," Jewish moms from the Upper East Side, and dads from Brooklyn: "There's meet-ups, there's trash tours, people coming together to exchange stuff or to explore trash together… th[ese] communities are starting to break ground in becoming more accessible, and I think that's a really crucial step. I encourage people to set up events in their own towns."

When asked how he obtained housing, this participant said that his preferred method of obtaining housing was squatting:

> Preferably I squat, which is to live in an abandoned or otherwise unused piece of property, generally without the permission of the property "owner," which is great. I've lived in some absolutely phenomenal spots, like unbelievable real homes with furniture and great vibes, and really a wonderful place to come home to. I've also lived in some rat hole, but it is what you make it.

A number of the younger participants said they also participated in the "couch-surfing" community. Organized through the internet (www.CouchSurfing.com), with the motto, "Participate in Creating a Better World, One Couch At A Time," this free accommodation swap travel service has 400,000 members world-wide.

A college student commented on a simple system that her college used to facilitate the free exchange of goods among students, "easing people into a freegan lifestyle." Every dorm hall had a simple box, with words on it, like "free stuff" or "take some of this stuff." Students deposited what they didn't need, and looked through it for what they might be able to use. There was also a sewing machine available in their wellness center for altering the recycled clothes. At the end of the year, instead of throwing things away, students put them in the boxes, and then take what is left to nearby thrift stores.

Others mentioned free stores – full-time spaces where people can come and donate goods, as well as get things which they need. Some free stores have dual purposes, such as coffee shops, or selling literature and records.

Freecycling was mentioned as another way of getting what you need free; it is organized via the web, (www.freecycle.org); under the motto "changing the world, one gift at a time." Currently, the network includes "4,249 groups with 4,486,000 members across the globe. It's a grassroots and entirely nonprofit movement of people who are giving (and getting) stuff for free in their own towns. It's all about reuse and keeping good stuff out of landfills." Others mentioned Craig's List.

As one young man summarized, "For essentials, consume green if you can, but consume nothing if possible."

Changing Ones Relationship to Goods and Services, and to Others: Developing Community Economies[20]

A theme which emerged in the rich discussion during the workshop was how these new ways of participating in the economy transformed one's relationship to things and to other people, from competitive consumerism to cooperation and sharing. A related theme was our need to develop community, and the ways in which community economic institutions can both build community and fill our material needs ethically and efficiently.

The self-identified freegans noted how freeganism changed their relationships to material goods   from competitive consumerism "grabbing and hoarding" to sharing.

> In a community of people like I run with, an amazing thing happens. When almost all of your goods are not really paid for, like for instance these pants, this backpack, this notebook, these were all free from trash, for instance, what happens is, in your community of friends, "Hey, you're cold. Do you want this sweater? Here, take this sweater." No questions asked. Or, "Hey, do you want this ipod?" Crazy surreal things that materialistic people would not be able to get their head around become completely natural. It's because, easy in, easy out, you can just flow materials and goods pretty much on a completely different level without this self-consciousness and hoarding instinct.

A college student spoke of dumpster divers who would donate what they found to community kitchens, and suggested that it could be a way for service-oriented groups to help feed homeless people. Being less materialistic allows more sharing, and sharing can help create community. She notes that life was very communal in her college; it was easy to do a free box, there was communal eating.

She worried about maintaining a sense of community after she graduated; in so many neighborhoods, people don't know one another.

Conversely, community can support ethical and simple consumption. A woman spoke of a housing cooperative she lives in, with sixteen members, which costs $400 a month, per person. They buy bulk organic, via a food cooperative in the city; support local organic food; and have the benefit of living in a supportive community. She had found this community via www.IntentionalCommunities.org.

Another participant talked about her community in Willimantic, Connecticut, in which people pay $10 per month to collectively rent a space which is used as a member-run coffeehouse and social justice center. The space, called Wrench in the Works, includes a lending library, is used for "workshops, meetings, performances, or just hanging out with a cup of fair-trade coffee or tea." (www.wrenchintheworks.org). Members also meet up monthly, bringing and exchanging their unneeded stuff. Willimantic also started a local currency, "Thread City Bucks," which essentially facilitates a local barter system.

Another innovative community which one participant brought up, and which I then researched on-line, is Ganas on Staten Island, New York (www.Ganas.org). Founded in 1979 by a group of six, it now includes 75 members living in eight, mostly adjacent houses, who eat together five nights a week in their main dining room. About one-third of the members work in one of Gana's four stores, called Every Thing Goes: Thrift and Vintage, which sell recycled clothes, books, art, and furniture, much of it donated. Another third work in gardening, maintenance, housekeeping, meal preparation, administration of Ganas.; and a third work outside the community and pay their expenses. The workshop participant said that they sell very good quality stuff for good prices.

One recent college graduate spoke of a community garden that she and some other students started in an industrial area one mile from their college. They went to 200 houses in the area, knocked on the doors, and offered people land to farm in the summer. Ten households responded to this face-to-face contact, and joined the project. The land was private property. The students used government funds to get it, and to pay student interns to work there over the summer.

We discussed other strategies to build community economies. Suggestions included going to a publicly designated safe space, library, café, or open park. Some mentioned having free events in parks, with food, to get people in the neighborhood together to converse over meals. Here, you can bring up ideas of buying clubs, food co-ops, community spaces and gardens. The group City Repair in Portland started with this type of conversation. They took an empty lot and built a glass tea house on it out of old windows. This attracted lots of attention, and they used the exercise to challenge zoning laws. They also did a community mapping exercise, getting neighbors together to discuss how they shop; they found they were driving five to ten miles on average to get things which they could get within a five block radius. "It's actually just starting a consciousness of building community and finding out who your neighbors are, rebuilding that neighborhood community feel, and that creates public spaces so that people can come together and meet each other."[21]

A final type of community economic institution was described by a participant from Florence, Italy: solidarity buying groups. These are small groups of families who get together weekly or bi-weekly, "and buy and sell things which they need everyday, from groceries to toilet paper, to whatever." They locate local farmers and companies to buy from, and divide up the work of taking the orders and obtaining the merchandise: "Like I will be a reference for the groceries, and another person will collect the orders for something else, and then when we meet there's a little market." Key to the buying group is getting to know the producers; visiting them, and forming relationships with them. Money is exchanged – it's not freecycling or freeganism – but there is no profit made by the group. Most food is organic, and there is a strong focus on recycling and minimizing waste.[22]

The Italian participant had very interesting observations about the way in which the solidarity buying groups were growing. It is crucial, he noted, that the groups not get too big – because if they do, the people don't know one another any more, they start delegating tasks, and the whole thing collapses. So when a group gets to a certain size, over twenty or thirty families, it always splits, and produces another group. In one year, the number of solidarity buying groups in Florence grew from two to fifteen. Furthermore, now they have started a process of intergroup ordering – groups ordering together things which come from further, and connecting to the groups who know the local producers in that area, "for instance oranges that come from Sicily, that are not produced in our area." Thus, the solidarity buying groups are communicating with one another, with the idea of creating "solidarity economy districts," that are about the size of a province.

Conclusion

The discussion which transpired during the workshop was a testament to the originality and diversity of solidarity economy initiatives which are springing up across the country and abroad. Wherever you live, and whatever you do, there are surely a wealth of ways for you to live your power in ways that will help people and planet – you only have to look around you, on the web, or inside, to your own creativity and yearning.

References

Bornstein, David. (2004). *How to Change the World: Social Entrepreneurs and the Power of New Ideas.* New York: Oxford University Press.

Business in the Community. (2004, March). "A Survey of Leading CEOs by World Economic Forum's Global Corporate Citizenship Initiative (GCCI) in partnership with the International Business Leaders Forum (IBLF)." *The Business in the Community Research Review.* www.bitc.org.uk.

Co-op American. (2000, September, 18). Fundraising letter.

Everett, Melissa. (1991). *Making a Living While Making a Difference.* Gabriola Island, BC, Canada: New Society Publishers.

Hickie, Jane, Ellen Komar, and Steven Tomlinson. (2005). "Aligning CSR with Power: Two Pragmatic Strategies for Transformational Change." Center for Responsible Business Working Paper Series. University of California, Berkeley. http://repositories.cdlib.org/cgi/viewcontent.cgi?article=1027&context=crb

Macy, Joanna and Molly Brown. (1998). *Coming Back to Life: Practices to Reconnect Our Lives, Our World.* Gabriola Island, BC, Canada: New Society Publishers.

Matthaei, Julie and Barbara Brandt. (2007), "The Transformative Moment," in Richard Westra et al, *Political Economy and Global Capitalism: The 21st Century, Present and Future.* London: Anthem Press.

Matthaei, Julie and Barbara Brandt. (2007). "The Transformative Moment for Activists," on www.TransformationCentral.org, publications.

National Consumers League News. (2006, May 31). "Survey: American Consumers' Definition of the Socially Responsible Company Runs Counter to Established Beliefs." http://www.nclnet.org/news/2006/csr_05312006.htm

Ray, Paul H. and Sherry Ruth Anderson. (2000). *The Cultural Creatives: How 50 Million People are Changing the World.* New York: Three Rivers Press.

Social Investment Forum. (2003, December). *2003 Report on Socially Responsible Investing Trends in the United States.* Washington: SIF.

www.cityrepair.org
www.communityinvest.org
www.CoopAmerica.org
www.fairtradefederation.com

www.livingeconomies.org
www.seikatsuclub.coop/english
www.socialinvest.org/resources/sriguide/srifacts.cfm
www.whitedog.com

Notes

[1] For a more detailed description of the emergence of this new consciousness, see Julie Matthaei and Barbara Brandt. (2007). "The Transformative Moment," in Richard Westra et al, *Political Economy and Global Capitalism: The 21st Century, Present and Future.* London: Anthem Press., and "The Transformative Moment for Activists," on www.TransformationCentral.org, publications.

[2] Paul H. Ray and Sherry Ruth Anderson. (2000). *The Cultural Creatives: How 50 Million People are Changing the World.* New York: Three Rivers Press.

[3] Joanna Macy and Molly Brown. (1998). *Coming Back to Life: Practices to Reconnect Our Lives, Our World.* Gabriola Island, BC, Canada: New Society Publishers.

[4] Melissa Everett. (1999). *Making a Living While Making a Difference.* Gabriola Island, BC, Canada: New Society Publishers.

[5] *National Consumers League News.* (2006, May 31). "Survey: American Consumers' Definition of the Socially Responsible Company Runs Counter to Established Beliefs." http://www.nclnet.org/news/2006/csr_05312006.htm

[6] Co-op American. (2000, September 18). Fundraising Letter.

[7] Hickie, Jane, Ellen Komar, and Steven Tomlinson. (2005). "Aligning CSR with Power: Two Pragmatic Strategies for Transformational Change." Center for Responsible Business Working Paper Series. University of California, Berkeley. http://repositories.cdlib.org/cgi/viewcontent.cgi?article=1027&context=crb

[8] Fair Trade Federation website, www.fairtradefederation.com. For more on Fair Trade, see "Buyer Be Fair," an excellent documentary.

[9] New York: Penguin, 1992.

[10] "*National Consumers League News.* (2006).

[11] Everett (1999), Ch. 1.

[12] www.whitedog.com.

[13] www.livingeconomies.org. Editors' note: See Ann Bartz' piece in Ch. 12 for more on BALLE.

[14] David Bornstein. (2004). *How to Change the World: Social Entrepreneurs and the Power of New Ideas.* New York: Oxford University Press.

[15] Social Investment Forum. (2003, December). *2003 Report on Socially Responsible Investing Trends in the United States.* Washington: SIF, p. 5.

[16] SRI was $40 billion in 1984. www.socialinvest.org/resources/sriguide/srifacts.cfm

[17] Hickie, Jane, Ellen Komar, and Steven Tomlinson. (2005); see also www.CoopAmerica.org.

[18] Business in the Community. (2004, March). "A Survey of Leading CEOs by World Economic Forum's Global Corporate Citizenship Initiative (GCCI) in partnership with

the International Business Leaders Forum (IBLF)." *The Business in the Community Research Review.* www.bitc.org.uk.

[19] www.socialinvest.org/resources/sriguide/srifacts.cfm; www.coopamerica.org/socialinvesting; www.communityinvest.org.

[20] Editor's Note: See also Chapter 8 of this volume for more on building community economies.

[21] For more information, see www.cityrepair.org.

[22] This story reminded me of the Seikatsu consumer cooperatives in Japan; started in 1965 by women seeking poison-free, organic milk, who formed a buying club, there are now 600 cooperatives, with 22 million members, about 1 of every 6 Japanese! www.seikatsuclub.coop/english.

22
Household Economic Justice Strategies

John Parker

> *John Parker is a resource on issues related to community economic development, entrepreneurship, and cross-cultural leadership. Currently, he is director of Good Work (www.good work.org), a community-based organization with a focus on economic empowerment and enterprise development. John serves on the boards of the Beloved Community Center of Greensboro, stone circles (www.stonecircles.org), and Clarence E. Lightner Leadership Endowment Fund (www.lightne rfund.org). Other areas of work experience include community development finance, applied cultural anthropology, and ethnographic research. He and his wife, Easter Maynard, and their two children, Lila and James, live in Raleigh, North Carolina. John can be reached at johnp@goodwork.org.*

The purpose of this article is to give you a brief sketch on how to initiate and explore economic justice strategies at the household level.

If we advocate for social, economic, environmental, and political justice, an underemphasized underpinning for our success is that we must encourage everyday people to develop practices and strategies to nurture justice at home. In particular, the household is a wonderful environment to experiment with economic justice strategies. Economics is about money and our relationship to it, so it's important to dialogue in our households about our feelings, thoughts, and beliefs about money and economics before we explore and experiment. There are many questions and activities that stimulate rich discussions. For example:

- What is the amount of monthly income that flows into the household and where does it come from?
- What are the average monthly expenses?
- What are the household assets and debts?
- Calculate your household net worth.
- What is your economic biography? Did you grow up poor, working class, middle class, or owning class? How do you live now?

- What environmental characteristics encourage economic security and progress?
- Do you know the workers and owners of the businesses where you shop?
- Create some individual and household economic goals.
- What is progress?
- What is success?

Below are areas of study and action. Develop economic justice strategies. Start at home.

- *Socially Responsible Investing, Shareholder Activism, and Community Investing.* Encourage socially responsible businesses and financial institutions, and greater access to capital for the everyday people moving your money to support community development financial institutions, good work, and companies that are making a difference in their industry and the world. The Social Investment Forum site: www.socialinvest.org

- *Debt.* Got debt? Reduce it. Get rid of it. Be an advocate against debt, predatory lending and predatory business practices. A helpful resource for predatory lending opponents is the Center for Responsible Lending (www.responsiblelending.org). If you or someone you know needs help, contact the National Foundation for Credit Counseling and find a member agency nearby: www.nfcc.org or 1-800-388-2227.

- *Responsible Consumption.* Co-op America has developed a good site to research corporate abuse and scandals, find responsible products and services that grow the green economy, and join activist campaigns against particular companies or for specific industry reforms. Co-op America's Responsible Shopping site: www.coopamerica.org/programs/rs/

- *Economic Justice Issues.* The Center for Economic and Social Justice (www.cesj.org) explains economic justice this way: "Economic justice, which touches the individual person as well as the social order, encompasses the moral principles which guide us in designing our economic institutions. These institutions determine how each person earns a living, enters into contracts, exchanges goods and services with others and otherwise produces an independent material foundation for his or her economic sustenance. The ultimate purpose of economic justice is to free each person to engage creatively in the unlimited work beyond economics, that of the mind and the spirit." United for a Fair Economy (UFE), a national, independent, nonpartisan, nonprofit organization, is a premier resource for everyday activists, equipping them with tools and knowledge to strengthen work for greater equality. UFE raises awareness that concentrated wealth and power undermine the economy, corrupt democracy, deepen the racial divide, and tear communities apart. United for a Fair Economy's site: www.faireconomy.org

- *Giving and Philanthropy.* Everyone can share their time, talents, and resources to strengthen or encourage what is good and has potential for improvement, or can increase the quality of life of others. Design strategic giving plans. Align your values and interests, and where you take action. Discover how to develop cooperative giving strategies with other people. Read more and find links to other resources: en.wikipedia.org/wiki/Philanthropy

- *Social Entrepreneurship.* According to Wikipedia, a social entrepreneur is someone who recognizes a social problem and uses entrepreneurial principles to organize, create, and manage a venture to make social change. Whereas business entrepreneurs typically measure performance in profit and return, social entrepreneurs assess their success in terms of the impact they have on society. While social entrepreneurs often work through nonprofits and citizen groups, many work in the private and governmental sectors. Read more and find links to other resources: en.wikipedia.org/wiki/Social_entrepreneurship

- *Local Economies and Living Locally.* Buying from locally owned businesses recycles resources within local and regional economies, improving the quality of life of local and regional communities, and encouraging additional local investment, resource control, employment, and business. Locate local networks of businesses committed to sustainability and discover their organizing principles through the BALLE (Business Alliance for Local Living Economies) network (www.living economies.org). Identify green enterprises, simple living resources, and links to other resources at Co-op America's site: www.coopamerica.org

- *Food*: *Why Locally-Grown Food?* According to Local Harvest, "People worldwide are rediscovering the benefits of buying local food. It is fresher than anything in the supermarket and that means it is tastier and more nutritious. It is also good for your local economy. Buying directly from family farmers helps them stay in business." Find local food at: www.localharvest.org

At the US Social Forum we had approximately a dozen people, young and old, including a father-daughter team, friends bringing friends, and a married couple, participate in our workshop from all over the United States, from New York, San Francisco, Atlanta, and Louisville, Kentucky. After significant introductions where each participant shared who they are, where they spend their time for paid work (if appropriate), where they volunteer and contribute their time, talents, and resources in the community, we discussed the examples of economic practices described in Ethan Miller's article, "Strategies for Building New Economies From the Bottom-Up and the Inside-Out" (www.geo.coop/files/Solidarity EconomicsEthanMiller.pdf). Afterwards we discussed the principles of Asset Based Community Development, where development and organizing is based on:

- identifying and mobilizing individual, associational, institutional, physical, and economic assets, strengths, and gifts;

- an inside-out approach where initial organizing and investment of time, talent, and resources occurs first in order to develop local leadership and achieve local understanding and control, and to not develop dependency on outside leadership; and

- relationships that are built, strengthened, restored, and renewed within networks, connections, and social capital among people, associations, organizations, and institutions.

More information on Asset Based Community Development and related resources can be found at the Asset Based Community Development Institute at the Institute for Policy Research at Northwestern University: www.sesp.northwestern.edu/abcd/.

In assessing what the participants gained from their participation, most of them identified strategies to employ in their homes and with their closest relationships, through family, friends, and co-workers, to engage in more ways to share their time, talent, insight, and resources with others. There was a strong emphasis on renewing relationships to create authentic community and true accountability as well as openness and transparency. The proposed actions included, but moved beyond, mainstream economic goals (increasing income and assets, and reducing debt) to incorporate examining new volunteer activities, building new networks, community organizing, renewing their spiritual practice, and being more deliberate, mindful, and intentional. Since we agreed to confidentiality, I will not go forward with any intimate detail of people's personal situations or plans.

From a spiritual perspective, the more we explore these questions and areas of study and action, the more we begin to understand where our economic behaviors are in alignment with our values and beliefs, or not. Over time it's easier to move into dialogue and practice around the "economics of enough" - discovering where we live in abundance, putting limits and boundaries on our lifestyle, expenses, labor, etc. It may be uncomfortable or emotional at times to find a sense of consensus and mutual understanding about economics, particularly with housemates or family. However uncomfortable it may be when the rubber meets the road, I believe we can all create justice in the world by striving to live out Gandhi's quote, "We must be the change we wish to see in the world."

On a personal note, in order to be the change we wish to see, I believe each of us must develop an open mind and heart, spirit of goodwill, and wild imagination. We also need to motivate others to better understand the forces that impact their lives, create goals based on their values and beliefs, and take action to become more self-reliant. Finally, we must encourage everyone to be good stewards and share their time, talent, insight, and resources in ways that develop transformative relationships and create opportunities for building inclusive, restorative, sustainable, and creative communities.

23
Spirituality and Economic Transformation

Julie Matthaei, David Korten, and Nichola Torbett

Moderator's Introduction
Julie Matthaei

I organized this panel because I believe that spirituality has a key role to play in the transformation of our economy into a sphere characterized by mutual respect, solidarity, and justice. I will first speak about my research in this area, followed by David Korten of the Positive Futures Network and *Yes! Magazine*, and Nichola Torbett of the Network of Spiritual Progressives.

Spirituality and the Transformative Moment
Julie Matthaei

> *Julie Matthaei has been active in anti-war, feminist, ecology, lesbian/gay, and anti-racist movements in the U.S. since she went to college at Stanford in 1969, where she first learned to meditate and lived in a Gandhian commune called Columbae. She has been teaching economics at Wellesley College for 30 years, and begins each of her classes with a short meditation. Julie began actively educating herself about spirituality over the past ten years: by joining a monthly spiritual philosophy class with Ellen Tadd (1997-2001); participating in conferences on education and spirituality at Wellesley (1998) and the University of Massachusetts at Amherst (2000); and attending two national Science and Consciousness conferences (2000 and 2001). Her research and forthcoming book with Barbara Brandt, The Transformative Moment, sees healing the "spiritual/material split" as a core component of progressive personal and social change. Julie was a member of the Working Group for the US Social Forum, which planned the caucuses and sessions which are documented in this book, and is currently a member of the US-Solidarity Economy Network Coordinating Committee. She lives with her husband Germai*

Medhanie, her daughter Ella, and her three cats in Cornerstone Cohousing in Cambridge, Massachusetts.

In this talk, I will briefly present a theoretical framework which I have developed with Barbara Brandt, and then use it to help elucidate the crucial role of spirituality in the process of progressive and liberatory economic transformation in the contemporary U.S.

I define spirituality as having a sense of what your place is in the whole; a sense of your connection to the life process; a sense of your larger purpose and your life meaning. Spirituality gives us awareness of the values that guide our actions – and is at the core of all religions.

The Hierarchical Polarization Paradigm: A Brief Introduction

Like Riane Eisler, Barbara and I believe that it is helpful to take a long historical view of our current economy in order to understand its possibilities for transformation. Eisler calls the reigning paradigm the "Dominator Model."[1] Barbara and I call it the Hierarchical Polarization Paradigm.[2] This paradigm has been characteristic of the last five thousand years of human history, although there have been indigenous communities who have escaped it, and whom we can learn from.[3]

The Hierarchical Polarization Paradigm divides people into distinct and unequal categories; for instance: men and women, colonizers and colonized, whites and Blacks, heterosexuals and homosexuals. It also creates a "man"/nature division; we humans are taught to conceptualize ourselves as separate, distinct from, and superior to nature, even though we are really part of the natural ecosystem. This paradigm teaches us to divide up and hierarchize our very selves – e.g. to create a hierarchical polarization between our minds and our bodies, and between the material and spiritual aspects of ourselves and our lives.

The Hierarchical Polarization Paradigm produces and reproduces itself through a variety of processes. First of all, categories are created. Then, through ascription—usually based on parentage, or physical features—people are assigned to one or the other of these categories. Also, these categories are completely polarized: for example, men are supposed to be the opposite of women, and whites and Blacks to be distinct and different. And, of course, hierarchy is created between the groups; one group is put above the other. The hierarchy is maintained through violence—both overt violence and institutionalized violence. Colonization was an overt violent form, whereby white Europeans dominated many other peoples with physical violence, and with the threat of violence. Violence by the oppressing group sows the seeds of violence among the oppressed, who tend to respond to it violently, continuing the cycle of violence.

The various hierarchical polarizations which comprise the paradigm are legitimized through rationalization, reinforced through stigmatization, and made "natural" through institutionalization. Religious doctrine has been the main source of rationalizations for race, gender and other hierarchical polarizations: God created people this way, and it is a sin to deviate from these categories. So while religions have the potential of being wonderful and liberatory, most, even in their current forms, serve to reproduce the Hierarchical Polarization Paradigm – for example, by providing reasons why women should be obedient to men, or why homosexuals are abominations. Through our socialization, by parents, schools, and religious institutions, we all internalize them, and end up policing ourselves into the polarized categories and into social inequality – even when we are in the oppressed categories. To further cement the hierarchical polarizations, there is stigmatization: anybody who doesn't play along with the rules is stigmatized severely – teased, humiliated, shamed, or attacked. Finally, the hierarchical polarizations – and the inevitability of human inequality – are built into social concepts (even the language, such as stewardess or chairman), practices, and institutions.

The Hierarchical Polarization, Religion, and Capitalist Development

Spirituality has been terribly distorted by this Hierarchical Polarization Paradigm, institutionalized into mutually exclusive and antagonistic religions which insist that their god is the only God, their religion the only truth. In this way, traditional religions have divided us and made us hate one another. For example, Christian religious intolerance fueled the crusades, the Inquisition, and the witch-hunts, which killed millions of people. It is telling that we do not yet have a word in English to express adequately the depth of discrimination, hatred, and desire to dominate, forcibly convert, or kill proponents of another religion which is still commonplace in our country and the world. This distorted form of spirituality, while bringing members of the same religion together, destroys any overarching sense of our interconnectedness, and ignores and violates the spiritual values and ethics of love and tolerance which most religions articulate.

Capitalist development has rapidly and radically transformed the place of religion and spirituality in our lives, especially in our economic lives. In traditional societies, spiritual belief in the form of religion was considered dominant over everyday, economic life. For example, the Christian Bible viewed usury as sinful, and thus money-lending was left to Jews in medieval Europe (a fact which then fueled anti-Semitism). With capitalism, science developed and began to displace the rule of religion, at least in the economic realm. Religious values were supposed to be cultivated by homemakers in the private sphere, and celebrated in church on Sundays. In the second half of the nineteenth century, science went even further; unable to find scientific evidence of God using Newtonian physics, intellectuals proclaimed that He was dead.[4]

While U.S. capitalist market relations emerged out of a deeply Christian country, they were based on science, not religion, and have increasingly been able to free themselves from the restriction of religious values. Key to this liberation was gender polarization among the dominant European American population. The capitalist economy developed as a ruthless competition between free white male providers, constructed as "bread-winners."[5] This term captures the essence of their economic roles – they competed with each other for money. Women, on the other hand, were supposed to marry and engage in homemaking for their husbands and children. Husband-providers, under the heavy responsibility of providing for their wives and children (or else not be real men!), were pressured to focus on financial gain in the economy – to the exclusion of other values, including religious ones. In this way, economic "man" was defined as a materialistic, narrowly self-interested, competitive being. Thus, in this capitalist structure, the effect of their work did not matter – it was immaterial whether they were making nerve gas or curing AIDS; what mattered was whether they were making money. "Success" was measured by this sole metric. Spiritual values did not apply to this masculine "dog eat dog" world; it governed the separate, feminine sphere of the home and personal life, and reigned in churches on Sunday.

In the early twentieth century, a second kind of narrow materialistic competitive self-interest emerged, which Barbara and I call "competitive consumerism." In their striving for continual profits and growth, firms found they needed to work to expand consumer needs. They did this through product innovation, through marketing and advertising, and through branding and planned obsolescence. They connected consuming with status—the need to keep up with the Jones's. Competitive consumerism and bread-winning reinforce and fuel one another, since consuming more than others marks you as a winner in bread-winning, and bread-winning buys you the wealth of new commodities which firms have made available.

Together, bread-winning and competitive consumerism came to define economic behavior in the 20th century United States. While our economy is usually thought of as secular, ruled over by objective science, it is actually imbued with values and assumption about a person's proper place in the whole. As David Loy has noted, and we have shown above, it is actually characterized by a "Religion of the Market."[6] A good person is hard working and earns lots of money; a person who does not work hard is lazy and sinful. The road to fulfillment, to being saved, is through consumption. Television is the church, and Madison Avenue the preacher who propagates this religion. Any of you who are parents realize the virtual impossibility of freeing your children from this religion-of-the-market programming.

The Transformative Processes and the Rise of a New Spirituality

Over the past two centuries, a variety of social movements – labor, civil rights, feminist, gay/lesbian, and disability – have been struggling against the hierarchical polarities which oppress them. While these movements have usually organized in isolation from one another, Barbara and I have found that they all are characterized by seven distinct transformative processes.

Through the first process, *questioning/envisioning*, an oppressed group, such as Blacks or women, begins to question and challenge their oppression and boldly envisions a better way of life, such as through Martin Luther King's famous "I Have a Dream" speech. The questioning/envisioning process is the spark which puts all of the other six processes in motion; however, the one which usually comes into focus next is the *equal opportunity* process.

The religion of the market – and its creed of equal opportunity to compete for more money – has, ironically, been a key force behind Civil Rights and feminist organizing. When the economy emerged as the sphere offering equal opportunity, only white men were allowed into the competition. By the nineteenth century, both Blacks and women had begun to organize based on the principles of equal rights and opportunity against their economic subordination, and these movements had second waves in the twentieth century which successfully defined and discredited race and gender discrimination in the economy. These were extremely significant victories, which undermined the Hierarchical Polarization Paradigm's claim that the sexes and races were naturally different and unequal.

On the other hand, the transformative power of this *equal opportunity* process was limited by the fact that the movements which embodied it accepted the basic rules of the economic game – that is, that the game would be characterized by narrowly materialistic self-interested competition, in the form of bread-winning and competitive consumerism. In other words, Blacks and white women have had to act like white men to succeed. The anti-spiritual value system of capitalism – the religion of the market – went unchallenged by equal opportunity movements; indeed, these movements extended its reach. Further, while a few women and people of color, most of them with class privilege, have been able to make it "to the top," the average economic position of Blacks has deteriorated,[7] and almost one third (31%) of those living in single-mother families live in poverty.[8] Those who do make it to the top are inevitably those who are willing to put winning the competition above everything else; anyone who actively cares for children, or about the true well-being of their employers' workers or consumers, will have difficulty.

The limitations of the equal opportunity process have contributed to the emergence of the *valuing-the-devalued* process. Individuals and groups that are striving for equal opportunity have realized that they do not want to give up their values and culture and become like white men; women have realized that they value child-rearing and unpaid work at home. The *integrative* process forms a bridge between the previous two processes: it comes out of the healthy desire to combine what has been polarized, be it the races (multiculturalism), or paid work and family. The next process, the *discernment* process, emerges when participants in social movements begin to realize that social values, practices, and institutions need to be restructured for true liberation to be achieved: for example, feminists realize that jobs must be made compatible with family life, and that firms and workers must be oriented around caring as well as financial balance.

Whereas the first five processes usually take place in single-issue, isolated movements, based on identity politics – i.e. shared membership in the oppressed group – the last two processes begin to bring people and movements together across differences, around a shared value system, which can be seen as a new spirituality. In the *combining* process, people who are multiply oppressed identify and challenge oppressive practices operating within movements they are active in. Black women critique racist practices within the feminist movement, women workers decry sexism within the labor movement, et cetera. Also, as movements have begun to realize that they have common goals – such as a shared rejection of the religion of the market and the organization of production around profits – their efforts to work in coalition force them to work together on the hierarchical polarities which divide them. In this way, the combining process starts to create solidarity across hierarchical polarities – white feminists who are anti-racist; male workers who are pro-feminist; feminist organizations like the National Organization for Women (NOW) which have anti-racism, anti-poverty, and pro-gay policies; and participants in the globalization-from-below movement who support the struggles of women, indigenous peoples, workers, lesbians/gays, and poor countries. In this way, the combining process starts to break down the divisions and hierarchies which have kept us and our movements separated from one another, creating the possibility of what Martin Luther King called "the beloved community."[9]

The final process which we have identified – the *unifying / diversifying / globalizing* process – builds on the previous processes to construct a new kind of consciousness, grounded in a commitment to combat all forms of oppression, and thus, to stand in solidarity with all who are oppressed. It is also grounded in an understanding that the Hierarchical Polarization Paradigm itself – and the economic and social institutions built upon it – is the problem, and has to be transcended. Nevertheless, in contrast to the Hierarchical Polarization Paradigm's "either/or" standpoint, the diversifying/unifying/globalizing process sees change in a "both/and" way, as epitomized by the Zapatista saying, "un solo no, un million de si" – "One no (to neoliberal economics), a million yeses." We have a million alternative institutions, from worker cooperatives to socially responsible firms, from buy-local movements to fair trade organizing to self-provisioning. We value, even cherish, the cultural diversity among us — but we want to unify within our diversity, based on common values that we are beginning to develop and that are exemplified in the social forum and solidarity economy movement. We all want economic democracy. We all want economic justice. We all want political democracies. We all want sustainability.

What is emerging, then, from these seven transformative processes is a new type of spirituality, a spirituality which is freed from the hierarchy and intolerance which have distorted religions. This spirituality is also emerging from the multifaith movement, which is discovering, as Matthew Fox puts it, that the various religions all tap into the same ground water, the same body of spiritual values. It is emerging as well from quantum physics and the science and consciousness movement, which have discovered, and scientifically proven, how truly interconnected and "nonlocal" we all are, including the healing power of prayer.[10] This new spirituality of solidarity and inclusion, in its many diverse forms – some religious, some not – is at the core of the emerging new post-materialist, post-hierarchical, post-polarization paradigm.

Barbara Brandt and I call the present "the Transformative Moment," because it has the potential to transcend the Hierarchical Polarization Paradigm which has ruled our lives in the West for millennia. In this present, transformative moment, we stand on the shoulders of generations of activists who have taught us about the problems and the mis-teachings of the Hierarchical Polarization Paradigm, and have begun the process of dismantling it. We have learned about the many different forms of oppression created by this paradigm. We have learned that, far from being secular, the reigning paradigm promotes a religion, the religion of the market, which is built into our economic institutions – a religion which we need to actively reject. Replacing it with a new spirituality of solidarity and inclusion is the core principle behind the construction of a new, solidarity economy, in all its beautiful diversity.[11] We have also learned to value the diversity of forms which social activism takes – and that no one of us alone, or no one movement, can fully embody the transformative spirit. And we have learned that spirituality is at its best when it embraces and learns from, rather than rejects, other forms of spiritual practice.

We are in a very exciting time. We have the possibility to do terrible things to one another and to our dear planet which could send our society back to the dark ages – and we have the possibility to move humankind to a much higher level of existence. I hope you each will do the best you can to help co-create this new future.

From Empire to Earth Community

David Korten

> *David Korten is co-founder and board chair of the Positive Fu-*
> *tures Network, which publishes YES! magazine, founder and*
> *president of the People-Centered Development Forum, a found-*
> *ing associate of the International Forum on Globalization, a*
> *board member of the Business Alliance for Local Living*
> *Economies (BALLE), and a member of the Social Ventures Net-*
> *work and of the Club of Rome. He is the author of The Great*
> *Turning: From Empire to Earth Community, the international*
> *best-seller When Corporations Rule the World, The Post-*
> *Corporate World: Life after Capitalism, and Globalizing Civil*
> *Society. Korten holds MBA and Ph.D. degrees from the Stan-*
> *ford Business School, has thirty years experience as a develop-*
> *ment professional in Asia, Africa, and Latin America and has*
> *served as a Harvard Business School professor, a captain in the*
> *US Air Force, a Ford Foundation Project Specialist, and re-*
> *gional adviser on development management to the US Agency*
> *for International Development.*

I believe that a spiritual awakening is an essential foundation of the work at hand. In my book, *The Great Turning: From Empire to Earth Community* (2006), I apply the historical frame Riane Eilser presented in *The Chalice and the Blade* (1987). According to this frame, some five thousand years ago, we humans moved from the egalitarian and gender-balanced communities of most early hu-man societies to the dominator hierarchy of Empire that prevails to this day. Or-ganization by domination creates an inevitable and often violent competition for the few positions at the top, and leads to a fundamental spiritual alienation from human and Earth community. We now need to navigate a change of course to re-store the partnership relations of Earth Community – a course that depends on a reawakening to our inherent spiritual nature.

I am becoming aware that virtually every progressive leader I know is working from a spiritual place. And yet we never talk about it. It is time to come out of the closet on that issue, because it is so foundational to our work. Indeed, I be-lieve that sharing our spiritual stories needs to become central to our work. Empire must maintain our alienation to maintain its hold. This in turn depends on holding us in a cultural trance that keeps us divided, one against another, by clouding our ability to see ourselves as manifestations of a unitary spiritual consciousness. This trance is maintained by fabricating false stories to answer many of the defining questions of our lives:

a) What is prosperity and how is it achieved?
b) What is security and how is it achieved?
c) How do we find meaning in life?

The prosperity stories constantly communicated through the media and through the economics courses of our universities convey the core idea that money is the measure of wealth and prosperity depends on basing decision-making on maximizing returns to money. How does this relate to the Empire? Well, when we focus on money, we define our relationships by money rather than by our innate spiritual connection. When we make decisions based on maximizing returns to money, it means that we are maximizing returns to people who already have money in proportion to the amount of money they have – inexorably increasing inequality. We get completely *bamboozled*.

I have MBA and PhD. Degrees from Stanford Business School, served on the faculty of the Harvard Business School, and taken a lot of economics, accounting, finance and business courses. In the course of all this, I never learned what money really is. It was only long after severing my relationships with academia that I learned that money is only an accounting chit. Even our language obscures the reality. The terms wealth, resources, assets, capital make no distinction between money, which is an abstraction that has no existence except in our minds, and the real wealth of human, social, and natural capital on which our lives and well-being depend.

Money is the most successful con game humans have ever devised. It gives those with the power to create and allocate money license to concentrate the ownership of wealth in their own hands virtually without limit. The majority, who find their lives and assets diminished by this scam, they have no idea of the source of their impoverishment, and so are virtually powerless to respond in any way other than to play the game as the money barons chose to define it. Part of waking up is coming to understand money and, in particular, learning to distinguish between financial wealth, which is just a number, and the real wealth of living capital that is essential to our survival and well-being.

Empire Creation Stories

Our most important meaning stories are the creation stories by which we define what it means to be human, the nature of the cosmos, and our place in the larger scheme of creation. I assume you are all familiar with the debate centered on two competing creation stories: the imperial religion story of patriarchist Creationism, and the imperial science story of materialist Evolutionism. The apparent conflict between them notwithstanding, both alienate us from one another and Earth and affirm the necessity and righteousness of inequality and a dominator hierarchy.

According to patriarchist Creationism, a distant God created heaven and earth, and gave man dominion over them in return for faithful obedience. He rewards the righteous with wealth and power, and commissions them to rule over the slothful sinners whom he condemns to poverty and misery. Surrounded and polluted by evil and unworthy of salvation except by divine grace, we humans can only hope for salvation in the afterlife in return for belief and obedience in this life to God the father and to those who rule in his name.

According to materialist Evolutionism, the universe is best understood as a mechanical clockwork that was set in motion at the beginning of time and is gradually running down to a heat death as its spring unwinds and entropy increases. Only the material is real. Life is nothing more than an accidental outcome of material complexity; consciousness and free will are illusions. Life has evolved through genetic mutation and a competitive struggle in which the fit survive and the unfit perish. Theories of Darwinian competition, selfish genes, and economic man tell us it is our human nature to be individualistic competitors and profligate consumers. Competition for wealth and power is the natural order and victory is proof of superior worth.

Although seemingly in deep conflict, both the patriarchist Creationism story and materialist Evolutionism story alienate us from our sense of connection to Earth and to Earthly community, deny our human capacity to form caring, cooperative communities grounded in a sense of mutual respect and responsibility, and affirm dominator hierarchy as the natural order. Together these stories share major responsibility for the spiritual crisis that now threatens the very survival of our species.

In stark contrast to Empire meaning stories that give us a choice between a dead and meaningless universe and a universe ruled by a distant and jealous patriarch, the Earth Community Meaning story celebrates the integral spiritual intelligence from which all being manifests. It proclaims that, far from being a deadly competition for survival, life is a fundamentally cooperative enterprise in which the species that survive and prosper are those that find their place of service in Creation's epic creative search for unrealized possibility. Far from being lost souls in a dead or evil universe, we humans are participants in the greatest of all creative adventures.

Earth Community Creation Stories

My initial exposure to the deep significance of our Creation stories came in the fall of 1999. The Washington State and Seattle Council of Churches hosted a conference in Seattle just before the historic demonstration against the World Trade Organization. Marcus Borg and I were two of the plenary speakers. Marcus is a well-known Christian writer who issued the following challenge: 'Tell me your image of God, and I will tell you your politics.' He observed that the Christian Bible has two sets of metaphors for God. One evokes an anthropomorphic image God. The other evokes a spirit image. They each lead to very different politics. The anthropomorphic God sets up a hierarchy of righteousness. This God is proclaimed to be all-knowing and the maker of all decisions, which translates into a belief that people who have power and wealth must be more righteous than the poor and powerless, as they are clearly those most favored by God.

The other image of God is that of universal spirit manifest in the whole of Creation. Actually I find the term God awkward in this context, because it is almost impossible to say God without invoking the image of the anthropomorphic God. I prefer to speak in terms of integral consciousness, integral spirit, or spirituality, which to my mind creates a bridge between religion and the findings of science. Science has some powerful data that gives us enormous insights into what actually happened in the creation process and how it evolved. The problem is with the ideology of science. The whole idea that only the material is real and the whole wondrous process of life and creation can be explained solely by material mechanism or by random chance is ludicrous. This proposition has not been, nor can it ever be, proven by formal scientific method. It is nothing more than an assumption of classic scientific method. To confuse an assumption with fact is to lapse into ideology and is highly unscientific.

Break it down and we have three primary choices of Creation story. One says there is no intelligence, no consciousness in creation. A second says "yes, there is intelligent consciousness, but it is out there in a far place." A third says that conscious intelligence is integral to the all of Creation, the ground from which all else manifests. I think of Creation as a process by which a profound integral consciousness seeks to know itself and its possibilities through a constant process of becoming toward ever greater complexity and potential. So if one wants to see the face of God, look into the face of any human, cat, or grain of sand. All are manifestations of the eternal spirit. Within this story there is simply no place to pit my God against your God, and no need to devote one's life to trying to figure out what the big guy wants by pouring over the text of a very old book. Once we recognize the interconnectedness of all reality and the process of continuous recreation toward ever great complexity and potential, we can recognize that far from being the end product of Creation, we humans, and every other being, are participants in a co-creative process.

I think of humans as Creation's most daring experiment in reflective consciousness. It is our responsibility to use that capacity in serving Creation's continued unfolding. We thus confront the question, "How do we use this capacity to explore our own higher potentials as human beings? How do we move beyond the terribly destructive dynamics that we have embedded in our institutions and cultures for 5,000 years?"

We are experiencing a phenomenal shift in our human context that creates an extraordinary moment of opportunity to free ourselves from the self-inflicted dysfunctions of Empire. We face the imperative to change or risk self-destruction at the same moment we have acquired the technological capability to connect every human on the planet into the seamless web of cooperation and communication, thereby creating the potential to act as a species to choose our future with conscious collective intent. We must now use that capability to reconstruct our institutions and our cultures around a new image of human possibility.

Creating a New Bottom Line
Nichola Torbett

Nichola Torbett, the Director of National Programs for the Network of Spiritual Progressives (NSP), has been writing and thinking about the intersection of love, meaning, and politics for almost twenty years. Before laying down her corporate fishing rod to follow the NSP to California, she worked as a professional writer and editor in Minnesota. She was inspired to join this movement by having helped coordinate Representative Dennis Kucinich's presidential campaign in 2004, an experience that convinced her that 1) so many Americans want a more compassionate culture, and 2) many of those Americans are afraid to stand up for that "unrealistic" desire in the absence of evidence that there are many others who want the same thing. She views the Network of Spiritual Progressives as a powerful way for Americans to demonstrate to each other that they are interested in more than looking out for themselves and that they want a world based on compassion. Nichola has degrees from the University of Toledo and Indiana University at Bloomington. She has read widely in cultural studies, theology, and psychology and brings the insights from that reading to her organizing efforts.

I am Nichola Torbett, and I am the director of National Programs for the Network of Spiritual Progressives (NSP). We are an interfaith organization also open to people who have not found home in an organized religion, but share in a lot of what has been said here–that essentially there is more to life than accumulating material wealth and that material wealth accumulation isn't our highest purpose on our planet.

The mission of our organization is really to bring about what we call "the new bottom line." According to the old bottom line, every institution and social practice is to be judged efficient based on the effect it has on money and the power you need to protect it. We see this bottom line applied in our foreign policy, we see it in our domestic policy, and it's everywhere. The new bottom line that we are about says that those institutions and social practices should be judged efficient not only based on money and power, but also based on the effect they have on us. In particular, they must be judged by their effect upon our human ability and our human desire to be loving and caring and kind and generous and compassionate, to be connected to the Earth, and to be able to experience awe and wonder and radical amazement at all there is. We realize that changing to this new bottom line is a tall order.   But the good news is that there is incredible energy behind making such a change – as evidenced by the people here, and by the huge amount of work that is coming out right now about the "great turning" and this exact project.

Economic Transformation and Spiritual Awakening

I want to say a few words about spiritual awakening.   I agree completely with David, that what is going to make this transformation happen is a broad spiritual awakening.   Does that mean that we need to get everybody in a church, synagogue or mosque? No! The spiritual awakening we need is an awakening to our interdependence, to the fact that we are all interconnected, and that we cannot attend to the well-being of one person without also attending to the well-being of all people connected to that person. It just doesn't work. And likewise we cannot attend to the well-being of the United States without also caring about the well-being of all the peoples on the planet. The fact that we have not been doing that is at the very root of the terrorist problem, and we are not solving it by committing more violence. In fact, we are making it worse.

The way I think about economic transformation is a little different from the way we have talked about it during a lot of the sessions at this conference. We often speak in terms of class warfare–that eventually the working class is going to rise up and overthrow the ruling class.   The assumption behind this analysis is that people of privilege are never going to give up their privilege voluntarily. That is an assumption that in many cases has some historical truth to it. It also is an assumption that we at NSP do not entirely accept.   The reason we do not buy it in the Network of Spiritual Progressives is that we have evidence that people are deeply alienated by a culture of greed and materialism even as they participate in it. Most people respond more strongly to messages about their spiritual needs than about their economic needs precisely because they are suffering so deeply from the spiritual deadness of our culture.   In fact, we have seen that evidence in this country in some unfortunate ways. The Right has done a much better job at tapping into peoples' need to feel like their lives have some higher meaning, that they can be a part of something of purpose and indeed, by connecting them patriotically to the United States, and to the notion that the United States is a force for good in the world. They have done a better job at responding to peoples' need for relationships with their "family values" campaign. Although we all know that there is a lot of hypocrisy in that messaging; the Left has not yet figured out how to do messaging around spiritual needs at all.

So I want to talk just a little bit about the spiritual needs. There is a real hunger among Americans to have a life that means something. This need was established, for example, in research done at the Institute for Labor and Mental Health which looked at workplace stress. Researchers went into the study with the assumption that most of the workplace stress among working people would be about not making enough money. What they found instead is that people did care about not making enough money, but they cared about not making enough money because they didn't feel adequately compensated for a life that had no meaning. It felt like the purpose of their life was really to make money for somebody else or to climb up the systems of power and inequality. They were deeply dissatisfied with what felt like a wasted life, and their desire for more money was about a compensation for that. I think this is actually very good news. We can use this dissatisfaction to organize for an alternative to our current culture of greed and materialism.

One of the most exciting things that I have been learning about at the US Social Forum is the solidarity economy movement that is emerging finally in the United States. One of the insights shared at the NSP conference which we held before the Forum was that solidarity is a resource: it is something that is available to us, because people are so hungry to be working in collaboration with other human beings. We hunger for solidarity because we live in a system which deprives us of meaningful human contact and collaboration. Told that we need to devote our highest energy to accumulating money and power, we have lost our ability to genuinely connect with other human beings, to see people not as resources but as embodiments of the sacred. In fact, we use this term human resources as if people are no more than what they can do on the job. Similarly, the whole immigration debate – it drives me crazy – is actually cast in those terms: it is all about our need for labor – as if these are not human beings we are talking about, human beings with families, relationships and needs for meaning and mutual recognition of their humanity.

So we have lost that ability to really connect with other human beings. Many of us go through a day feeling like we are never really seen for who we are; we are only seen for what we can do for other people. This is as true for people who work at home as it is for people who are in a work place – I see you in terms of what can you do for me. Likewise, we treat the Earth as a collection of natural resources that are there for our use. This has had a huge emotional effect on us: we can no longer access our deep connections to other people or to the Earth.

Many of us are hungry for a sense of a sort of magic that the world used to have when we were kids. Remember that? The feelings have been dulled or flattened as we have gotten older, as if there is no magic any more. Much of this flattening is the very effect of focusing only on what you can see and experience with your senses, and on believing that that is all that is real. Our current social and economic system, then, makes us lose touch with the magic of the world, and there is a lot of suffering around that.

This deep sense of alienation, emptiness, and spiritual dissatisfaction creates an opportunity to organize, and that's what the Network for Spiritual Progressives is trying to do. We are bringing people together first of all to talk about the ways in which their lives are not satisfying. We are bringing people together from across the class spectrum. This includes bringing together people of privilege so that they can finally talk about the ways in which they are disappointed. They thought they got into the system, and made it, and that this was really going to "do it" for them, and it did not. So we are trying to organize all these different sectors. Our challenge is to build a movement that addresses people's spiritual hunger – and by that I mean the hunger for connection, for being recognized as an embodiment of the sacred, for having a meaning and a purpose in their lives. If we can build that kind of movement, then there is incredible potential to draw in huge numbers of people and to mobilize them for peace, for economic justice, for social justice, for all the causes that we are talking about at this Forum.

Implicit in this organizing is a whole new idea of what wealth means. Wealth is not just about money, but also about our relationships, about our connections to the Earth, about the meaning in our lives. This view of wealth creates such a different view of economic transformation, that it can be difficult for us to convince people that we are for real. It is particularly difficult to convince people who are currently economically disadvantaged that this new view of wealth is not just a way to make the wealthy feel better about having privilege.

The Global Marshall Plan

NSP has a concrete program, the Global Marshall Plan, that demonstrates our commitment to fundamental economic transformation. It is a part of what we are calling our strategy of generosity. We are trying to shift how Americans think about security, to show them that true security is not obtained by trying to dominate and control the rest of the world, as the U.S. has done and continues to try to do. Instead, security is obtained by working in solidarity with the rest of the world, through generosity. I'll say a little about what I mean by generosity in a minute, because I know that the word has some negative connotations.

Concretely, our Global Marshall Plan proposes that we commit 1 or 2% of our GDP every year for the next 20 years, and lead the other G8 nations to do the same, in order to eliminate global poverty once and for all, and heal the global environment. Those are two critical priorities. There are several components to how the plan would eliminate poverty, including revising treaty agreements so that it is not just a matter of giving money to poor countries while keeping the same unjust systems in place. Likewise we want to set the program up in such a way that it can't be used as one more savvy way of opening new markets for US interests. So we need to approach this development aid in way which is transparent. It has to be administered by a global nongovernmental organization that will be made up of people with a proven commitment to the common good over any allegiance to any organization or government. Currently, we are working with about fifty organizations around the world, who independently have proposed something called Global Marshall Plan, to figure out some of these details about how we would actually implement it. Such a plan needs to be offered in spirit of humility, with apologies, and in the spirit of reparations for the damages that we have done through 200 years of colonization and industrialization.

This Global Marshall Plan needs to be offered in a way that is not just another savvy way of approaching our own self-interest. There is a kind of a paradox there, because it is in our interest to act in this way: it is the best way to increase security not only for us, but for everyone on the planet. But it can't be about that. It has to be a genuine expression of caring and concern for the rest of the world. So we are looking at ways that we can make sure that is in place. And because we are one of the few spiritual organizations participating in this Global Marshall Plan process, we feel that our role in the process is to make sure it does uphold these values. The spirit of humility with which we need to approach this project also means that we recognize that we have a lot to learn from other cultures in the world; cultures that we have considered "undeveloped." Indeed, we need to learn some of those other spiritual traditions, some of the ways of conceptualizing the world, as exemplified by the indigenous sections of the Forum.

When I tell people about the Global Marshall Plan as a way to eliminate poverty, people often say to me, "That's great, but what about the poverty here in the U.S.?" I want to emphasize that the U.S. is part of the globe, and so it will be included in the Global Marshall Plan. Thus, it would mean reparations for minorities in the U.S.; rebuilding our inner cities; taking care of our impoverished rural areas; building infrastructure; creating jobs. All of that is included in the domestic part of the plan.

Compassionate Organizing

I want to move on to discuss a few other components of our movement. One is that we need to include some serious anti-racist organizing. That's a huge replication of the problem. It is insufficient to redistribute economic resources if we do not work to get rid of the racial hierarchies. I have been really impressed by the work that is being done by United to End Racism. What I like about their approach is that it is universally compassionate, and it recognizes the ways in which racism hurts everyone. I think that the NSP will be working much closer with them going forward. Likewise, we need anti-classist organizing, because there are all these false assumptions about poor people, about people deserving to be poor. We have to work on the ways in which we have all internalized those ideas.

The most important thing I want to say about this movement is that it needs to be universally compassionate. We must get past this tendency to create "others," even when the others are supposedly the bad guys. We need to be able to look at the driver of a Hummer in the next lane and see the pain on that face. A friend of mine who lives in D.C. told me a story about the night after the Iraq war started. She had been doing all this work to stop the war. She and her partner went into a restaurant, sat down, and noticed that there were secret service agents all around. They saw Donald Rumsfeld sitting at a table: he looked haggard and ill. We have to recognize that the people we would like to blame for the situation we are in are also victims of the system that created the situation. They are not the root of it. They are involved in it – as are many of us – in ways we need to understand.

It is important, then, that the policies and plans which we propose and concretely support involve compassion for everyone. For example, universal healthcare is a wonderful idea. It is something we support, and it has to cover everyone. Candidates keep proposing slightly better healthcare plans, such as a plan which would cover all children. This would be a great thing to have, and I would certainly not come out against it, but it will never generate the kind of movement we need to bring it into being unless it covers everyone. Why not? Because if there is any chance that my redneck Uncle Bill feels like he is not going to be covered, he will never support it.

Everyone has to be included in the circle of care. Everybody's well-being has to be taken into account in the policies we propose. This is why the solidarity economy is so exciting to me – it is a way to start conceptualizing programs that are win-wins for everyone. The Network of Spiritual Progressives looks forward to participating fully with efforts to organize the solidarity economy and to bringing a recognition of our deep spiritual needs to that work.

References

Amott, Teresa, and Julie Matthaei. (1996). *Race, Gender and Work* Boston: South End Press.

Conrad, Cecilia, et. al. (Eds.). (2005). *African Americans in the U.S. Economy.* Lanham: Rowman & Littlefield.

Dossey, Larry. (1999). *Reinventing Medicine.* New York: HarperCollins.;

Eisler, Riane. (1987). *The Chalice & The Blade.* New York: HarperCollins.

Korten, David C. (2006). *The Great Turning: From Empire to Earth Community.* San Francisco: Berrett-Koehler Publishers and Bloomfield: Kumarian Press.

Korten, David C. (1995, 2001). *When Corporations Rule the World.* Bloomfield: Kumarian Press and San Francisco: Berrett-Koehler Publishers.

Matthaei, Julie. (1982). *An Economic History of Women in America.* New York: Schocken Books.

Matthaei, Julie, and Barbara Brandt. (2007). "The Transformative Moment" in Westra, Richard et al (Ed.). Political Economy and Global Capitalism: The 21st Century, Present, and Future. London: Anthem.

Targ, Russell and Jane Katra. (1998). *Miracles of Mind.* Novato: New World Library.

Notes

[1] Riane Eisler. (1987). *The Chalice and the Blade: Our History, Our Future.* San Francisco: Harper & Row.

[2] See Julie Matthaei and Barbara Brandt. (2007). "The Transformative Moment," in Richard Westra et al (Ed.). *Political Economy and Global Capitalism: The 21st Century, Present and Future.* London: Anthem Press for a fuller discussion of the Hierarchical Polarization Paradigm.

[3] See, for example, the work of Hawaiian lawyer and activist Poka Laenui (a.k.a. Hayden Burgess), e.g. http://www.opihi.com/sovereignty/economic.txt

[4] The famous April 8th, 1966, Time Magazine cover asking "Is God Dead?" marked this shift.

[5] See Julie Matthaei. (1982). *An Economic History of Women in America.* New York: Schocken Books; and Teresa Amott and Julie Matthaei. (1996). *Race, Gender and Work.* Boston: South End Press for a more detailed discussion of this history.

[6] The American Academy of Religion, 65/2
http://www.colorado.edu/economics/morey/4999Ethics/Loy.pdf

[7] Cecilia Conrad, et. al. (Eds.). (2005) *African Americans in the U.S. Economy* Lanham: Rowman & Littlefield.

[8] U.S. Census Bureau, Current Population Reports, 2006.

[9] Scott King, C. (2004. January 22). "Building the Beloved Community." http://www.hum.wa.gov/Diversity/coretta%20scott%20king.html

[10] Larry Dossey. (1999). *Reinventing Medicine.* New York: HarperCollins; Russell Targ and Jane Katra. (1998). *Miracles of Mind.* Novato: New World Library.
[11] Editors' Note: See Michael Lewis and Dan Swinney in this volume, who argue that solidarity values form the core of the solidarity economy.

SECTION VIII:

THE BIRTH
OF THE
U.S.
SOLIDARITY
ECONOMY
NETWORK

24
Solidarity Economy Caucus I: Defining the Solidarity Economy
Wednesday, June 27, 2007

Jenna Allard

> *Jenna Allard works for Guramylay: Growing the Green Econ-*
> *omy, and is part of the coordinating committee for the U.S.*
> *Solidarity Economy Network. She graduated from Wellesley*
> *College with a B.A. in Political Science and Peace and Justice*
> *Studies. She was excited to be part of the first U.S. Social Fo-*
> *rum, and spent most of her time there behind the single eye of a*
> *camera lens, recording workshops in the solidarity economy*
> *track and the caucuses. She has been passionate about studying*
> *and experiencing the solidarity economy ever since she traveled*
> *to Brazil and visited a small women's handicraft cooperative in*
> *an informal community on the outskirts of Rio de Janeiro.*

Author's Note: This caucus was convened by the Solidarity Economy Working
Group for USSF 2007, for the day before workshops started. Participants from a
variety of progressive organizations were invited to attend. This caucus focused
on familiarizing the participants with the solidarity economy framework through
conceptualizations and international examples, and on developing a common
language. I filmed the caucus for Guramylay: Growing the Green Economy, and
I used these tapes to create this summary of the proceedings.

Introductions

Emily Kawano, Executive Director of the Center for Popular Economics (CPE), and Ethan Miller, from Grassroots Economic Organizing (GEO), introduce the commencement of the caucus, as members of the Solidarity Economy Working Group for USSF 2007, who put together the Social and Solidarity Economy track of workshops and organized the caucus meetings. Emily states the reason for the first caucus meeting: to discuss both the social and the solidarity economy. She sees the meeting as an opportunity to bring people together at a forum they would already be attending, and to create the basis for exchange of knowledge and practice. She wants to both put forward the solidarity economy framework in the U.S. and promote experiments all around the country, inspired by practices from all over the world. All kinds of alternative economic initiatives can fit under the solidarity economy umbrella. But because the term is not yet in general use in the United States, one of the first tasks will be to set out definitions, and to start a conversation about it while it is in the process of being forged.

> *Emily Kawano: We see this as just a great opportunity to bring together people who are going to be here anyway to talk about, explore, debate, engage, and exchange experiences in how to move this idea forward, how to move this framework forward. We see this as an incredible opportunity to help to bring together, and to support, and to strengthen all these amazing initiatives, practices, and experiments that are going on, from cooperatives to local currency to community-supported agriculture to various kinds of community organizing to green technology..."*

Ethan goes over the agenda, and wants to think of the first meeting as a time to get to know the participants, and to lay some basic groundwork for long-term organizing. He hopes that this meeting will help develop a shared base around the concept of the solidarity economy, and will allow us to learn more about what kind of solidarity economy organizing is being done in the rest of the world. Then the conversation will turn to what building a solidarity economy in the U.S. that connects and strengthens economic alternatives would really look like. There will be a discussion that focuses on the specific challenges and opportunities of growing the solidarity economy in the U.S.

International Experience

Dan Swinney, Executive Director of the Center for Labor and Community Research (CLCR), introduces speakers from Canada and South America. He discusses how all the participants represent a broad range of practice, and he wants everyone to benefit from the richness of meaning and experience in the room. He also invites the participants to not shrink from disagreeing and bringing forth their experience to challenge the impressions of others.

Mike Lewis's Presentation

Mike Lewis, Executive Director of the Centre for Community Enterprise in Canada, proposes to talk primarily about the conceptual terrain. The Center for Community Enterprise is structured as a for-profit company that functions under a trust, giving its profits to a nonprofit organization, therefore having a self-financing basis for its social change agenda. In Canada, the growth of the community economic development movement has resulted in social and solidarity economy organizations that involve many sectors, are territorial, and contain stake-holders from many sectors. Still, in the Canadian context, outside of Quebec, the language of the social and solidarity economy is still not common currency. His presentation will map conceptual terrain, not only to locate current modes of social/solidarity economy organizing, but also to explore the implications of our current definitions on how we think, strategize, and act.

He introduces the first diagram that emerged out of practice and conceptualization in Europe (see p. 33). It includes three systems with three different logics: the private system, which is profit-oriented; the public system, which is planned; and the self-help system, which is based on reciprocity and service. These three systems are distinguished by their separate logics, even though the boundaries between them are permeable. What distinguishes the social economy from other non-profit initiatives, here, is that they are interacting with the market.

Mike Lewis: I think of solidarity, not just as a concept, but as a resource. I think of, for instance, a place like Villa El Salvador in Lima, a shanty town of 350,000 people, where there are no property taxes so the municipal government completely marginalizes them. Solidarity in that context is an economic resource. It's a social resource, it's a cultural resource and ultimately, I would suggest that it's also a moral resource.

There are several questions that emerge from this model. First of all, how permeable are the boundaries between the systems? The intention and consciousness of an initiative becomes an important way of qualifying and categorizing it. Also, if an initiative is owned socially and cooperatively by the community, is it automatically part of the social economy? Finally, if these initiatives see themselves as part of the third system and work primarily within that sector, how does this impact strategy and organizing?

He then presents a second diagram where the solidarity economy is conceptualized as a cross-cutting approach (see p. 39). This cluster of shared values needs to contend across all sectors. At the heart of this approach is a conception of our shared work as radically re-inserting social values into economic life. This approach is concerned with transforming the way markets operate.

Although we may feel comfortable in the third system, can we make the fundamental and radical changes we need to deal with the major cross-cutting crises of our time – namely, climate change, peak oil, food security and sovereignty, water quality and access, deepening poverty and inequality? Thinking about the solidarity economy as a cross-cutting approach has very real implications for how we organize.

He then turns to his own reflections on the word "solidarity." He thinks of solidarity not just as a concept, but as a resource, economically, socially, culturally, and morally. These crises are going to force us to re-localize our economies. Solidarity teaches us of the need to re-learn how to live at the household level and the societal level. In the solidarity economy movement, we are also learning that social justice and ecological justice are two sides of the same coin, and that resistance activity and constructive activity are also two sides of the same coin. We have to bring all these movements to work together.

He then presents the third diagram, inspired by Yvon Poirier's work in Canada, which represents that we are not that far along to implementing our vision and social agenda (see p. 43). This map, however, can inform strategy, and shows us that this "blessed unrest" is happening all over the world.

Nedda Angulo Villareal's Presentation

Nedda Angulo Villareal, from the Grupo Red de Economia Solidaria del Peru (Solidarity Economy Network of Peru), and a member of the Intercontinental Network to Promote the Social Solidarity Economy (RIPESS) board, focuses her presentation on the solidarity economy in the Latin American context. She notes that the term "solidarity economy" is very much in use there, whereas the term "social economy" has a long history in Western Europe.

Nedda: The solidarity economy is not a proposal; it is a reality. The solidarity economy is a different way of creating economies that is allowing certain segments of the population to survive. We are talking about a certain concrete experience of resistance...and of being included, and of having recognized rights. Its characteristics are producing goods for the market, and producing welfare services. But there is another dimension when we are talking about the solidarity economy, and that is the theoretical contribution of the solidarity economy. Because analyzing these experiences and processes gives them the status of theory, we are thus contributing in the ideological war against neoliberalism.

In Latin America the solidarity economy is trying to respond to the social necessities for cooperation. The solidarity economy has to respond to the aftermath of structural adjustment, as well as to build on and support indigenous forms of economic activity. The solidarity economy attempts to support people who are excluded from the labor market and who need social services that are not covered by the state. This results in the production of goods for the market, and welfare services for the community. This movement was spurred by the introduction of neoliberal policies in Latin America.

In Latin America, 40% of the population lives in poverty. This fact calls for the solidarity economy to address different priorities; it needs to produce welfare services for the survival of the poor, and to produce material wealth in order that it may be distributed equitably. Not all solidarity economy enterprises, therefore, have collective ownership of the means of production. Still, the solidarity economy is contributing to the democratization of the economy, forcing the state to recognize these marginalized, small-scale producers.

In Latin America, the solidarity economy is not a proposal; it is a reality. It is allowing certain segments of the population to survive, and is leading to the recognition of the rights of these peoples. Another dimension of the solidarity economy is the theoretical analysis of this experience, to give it the status of theory, and to contribute to the ideological war against neoliberalism. A third dimension of the solidarity is its project – meaning reality, theory, and organization. We have to aspire to new economic order where the person is the center. It is a political challenge, to find how people can control the tools to reproduce their lives. The challenge is not only to make a solidarity economy, but also a solidarity culture. We need to share our experiences and to offer each other feedback, because we are fighting against a system that is globally applied.

Solidarity is a resource, and a factor to reduce the cost of transactions. This resource is valuable in capitalism, but solidarity is also a resource to construct another economic order in which the person is the center.

When we think of the three sector approach, how do we know which is really the first sector? Jean-Louis Laville, a French social and solidarity economy researcher, writes about this. These three different ways of organizing economies have always existed, and the market-driven sector has always been part of the economy. It is in the interest of capitalism, however, to make other parts of the economy invisible. Therefore, the solidarity economy is not a system, because it is intertwined in all different types of economic activity.

International Experience: Discussion

In the initial reactions to the presentations, discussions focused on whether the concept of the solidarity economy required the idea of placing restrictions on private wealth accumulation, and, more broadly, how we should think about profits in the solidarity economy. The discussion then turned to whether the solidarity economy should talk about capitalism as a system, and, more generally, what language would most effectively convey the principles of the solidarity economy, and build the movement.

Nada Khader, Executive Director of WEASPAC foundation, began the conversation by asking if the principles of the solidarity economy require that there be limits placed on personal wealth. Dan asserts that part of the solidarity approach, which will contend in all sectors, is a public sector that can create just regulation. Jessica Gordon Nembhard, Professor of African American Studies at the University of Maryland and member of Grassroots Economic Organizing and the Democracy Collaborative, also agrees that there should be limits placed on personal monetary wealth, but adds that the solidarity economy broadens the conception of wealth to include non-traditional, non-monetary forms, so that wealth can truly be an unlimited resource. Limiting monetary wealth, in the short-term, is important, but broadening the conception of wealth should be our main project in the solidarity economy.

Jessica Gordon Nembhard: I agree that no one should possess more than a certain amount of wealth, but one thing that I like about the solidarity economy is that it broadens our notion of wealth, so that wealth is no longer a limited resource. Rather, it is an unlimited resource because we are creating all kinds of non-traditional wealth and value. In the short term I think it is imperative that we figure out how to regulate and redistribute great wealth, but I think our main focus should be on the many possibilities for wealth and prosperity through the solidarity economy.

Matt Hancock, from the Center for Labor and Community Research, points out that the solidarity economy must not only focus on levels of personal wealth accumulation, but also on the means of accumulation. Increasingly, wealth is being produced through financial speculation, which does not produce anything useful, and is in fact a destructive force in the economy. He believes this speculative accumulation needs to be restricted first and foremost.

David Schweickart, professor of philosophy at Loyola University in Chicago, then points out that accumulation of profits also occurs within solidarity economy enterprises, and wonders why no one is using the word "capitalism" – is it an ideological or a tactical decision? Emily picks up on this point, noting that inequalities occur as a result of the way the economy is structured, and that we need to think about ways of restructuring the economy so that it doesn't generate inequality in the first place, rather than just redistributing income more efficiently via the public sector. She thinks that most people at the caucus are comfortable with using the word capitalism critically, but using that word might not be as effective outside very progressive circles. Nada agrees that critique of capitalism might not be popular outside of progressive circles, because most Americans associate it with political democracy, even though it is really more like fascism. She would really like to see the U.S. Solidarity Economy movement try to consciously raise awareness on this point.

Dan argues against using the word capitalism for tactical reasons. He works with many types of economic and political actors, and feels it is useful to be system neutral. He wants the language of the movement to be as inclusive as possible, so that we can get as many people as possible in the discussion, to talk about real values and connections. Mike also discusses how the language we use affects the coalitions we form. In Latin America, and in the first RIPESS meetings, for instance, the solidarity economy was conceptualized as a person-centered economy, but that can at times be a focus that comes at the expense of thinking about solidarity between people and their environment.

Ethan conceptualizes the solidarity economy as a way of thinking about economic alternatives that doesn't open up an "either, or" binary. It is not about creating "the" second big model, but about linking together practices in a connective process, which is much the way that capitalism emerged historically. He wants to open up discussions about the multiple meanings of capitalism, and change the way we view it, rather than creating another binary model. Matt continued discussing the way the conversation could be broad and inclusive by advocating a framing that focused on using values as a yardstick. Capitalism, particularly parasitic and speculative capitalism, cannot measure up to these values. Yet one of modern capitalism's greatest triumphs has been to move the systems discussion into the background, and to use more seemingly benign code words like "free markets." Erica Swinney, an organizer for Greenaction, also echoed the idea of creating space and broadening the conversation by talking about how to shift the hegemony of the American dream, which currently means success in the first system, and instead create space in the mind of the average American to experiment and to create alternative dreams. This systems-level discussion should be accessible to average Americans.

Ethan Miller: I like the way the solidarity economy is a way of thinking about economic alternatives that doesn't necessarily have to put us into that "either- or" binary. Partially because, in my mind, the solidarity isn't about creating "the second big model" that's going to be the alternative to capitalism. It is so much more about linking together practices, and this bottom-up connective process of linking things together across all different sectors, which seems to me more like the way that capitalism emerged historically.

Emily plays devil's advocate by discussing how it important it is to explicitly take a stand against neoliberal capitalism, especially since there is a global movement already standing in opposition to neoliberal capitalistic globalization. Neoliberal capitalism is not a vague term, but instead describes a very specific economic system. It's not just that we need better values in this system, but it is the system itself, which strives for profit maximization at all costs, that causes so much damage. When you have a neoliberal ideology that believes that markets are the only answer, and either tries to shrink, or doesn't even recognize other sectors, then it's a war where you have to name your enemy. There can be no accommodation. Capitalism is malleable and survives many crises. If we don't fight it head-on, it will subsume us.

Nancy Neamtan, President and Executive Director of the *Chantier de l'Économie Sociale* (Working Group on the Social Economy) in Quebec, argues that we can be against a market economy, in which markets are the only solution, and still be for an economy with a market. Fundamentally, capitalism is about giving control to the people who have capital. It is not that we don't want to control capital, in fact we do, but we insist in our movement that there be a primacy of people over capital, and that there be democratic control of capital. If this happens, capitalism is dead. Focusing on acquiring and using capital in a way that is not destructive to communities is not directly anti-capitalist, but can be very subversive. David argues that it is much easier to talk about capitalism now, without the "specter of the Soviet Union." Still, we have to work with the dialectic, and hold the contradiction in our minds that we both have to talk about capitalism, and can not talk about capitalism.

Janelle Cornwell, from the Community Economies Collective, talks about how capitalism is often equated with entrepreneurship, and how understanding that capitalism is just one system among many – despite the large amount of money, power, and resources currently backing it – can help everyone build their own economic definitions and visions, as opposed to trying to define the economy into just one vision. Nada talks about how the solidarity economy is based on a motivating that is radically different from that of capitalism: meeting the genuine needs of human beings. Although everyone has their own vision, we can offer a set of solidarity economy principles, primary among which is the idea that local people control local resources.

Matt wraps up the discussion by reminding us that if we openly oppose neoliberalism, we may acquire some tactical allies that do not actually share our values. He gives the example of the National Association of Manufacturers, where smaller member companies are rebelling against neoliberalism for reactionary, protectionist, and often racist reasons. In regards to profit maximization, he thinks the important question is the constituency for whom profits are being maximized – passive shareholders or worker-owners. He also believes that we need to distinguish between the financial market, driven by a speculative short-term mentality, and the market for ownership.

International Experience: Concluding Remarks

Dan concludes the discussion on defining the language of the solidarity economy by reminding us all of the objective in building the solidarity economy movement: to gather together the fragments of a global movement that is seeking fundamental economic transformation, sustainable development, and radical economic and political democracy. In order to do this, we need a program that articulates our transformative vision, but also highlights the practical component of what we do. We have to be guided by theoretical analysis and critical thinking, and this movement has to look at the systems issue. At the same time, it is useful to have ambiguity in our language in order to gather a broader coalition for a very clear purpose. We can be system-neutral, and use the useful language of "high road, low road" to distinguish between practices. He also summarizes the main issues brought up in the discussion, from questions about language and engaging in systems discussions, to the scale of enterprises and points of intervention.

Challenges for the Solidarity Economy

Emily opens up the discussion on the some of the conceptual and political challenges of building the solidarity economy. First of all, solidarity economy organizing could potentially reinforce neoliberalism. In neoliberalism, the private sector is constantly trying to expand while simultaneously shrinking the public sector. The social and solidarity economy could potentially be asked to fill the gap left by the withdrawing state. In the long term, she also does not want the movement to become self-satisfied and lose its transformative agenda. She gives the historical examples of the labor movement and the cooperative movement. This is where she sees a positive role for critical discussion within the movement. At the other end of the spectrum, how do we respond to critics on the left who see our whole movement as too reformist? How do we balance our transformative agenda with openness to making alliances and embracing some needed reforms?

Jessica offers some more interpersonal and organizational challenges, concerning race, class, and gender, for the solidarity economy movement. First of all, she wants to know how we not only break through the perception that the movement is primarily white, intellectual, upper-middle class, and male, but also actively organize so that we can bring more people to the table. Part of this challenge is being aware of economic realities, and realizing that some people do not have the "movement space" to participate. Sometimes solutions can be as simple as paying people for their time and travel. Secondly, we need to deal with the power issue – if people do not feel they will have some control, and that their input will be meaningful, they will not participate. We need to make our organizations as non-hierarchical as possible, because simply being small-scale does not guarantee equal power sharing. The movement needs to proactively construct democratic mechanisms that minimize the unintentional spill-overs of power dynamics within the wider society.

Challenges for the Solidarity Economy: Discussion

Much of the discussion hinged on balancing theory and practice at the grassroots level. Melissa Hoover, the Executive Director of the U.S. Federation of Worker Co-ops, for instance, believes that because her own organization is so deeply engaged in practice most of the time, the rare discussions they do have about theory are rich and fruitful. She believes that if this movement honored people's practice, it could achieve system neutrality and flip the power dynamic. She is not anti-theory, but rather pro-practice.

Melissa Hoover: We often don't get a chance to talk about these theoretical, more abstract issues, because we are actually doing the work. When we do have those discussions, they are grounded in our practice, so they are really fruitful, and they are inspiring... I think we can achieve system-neutrality in our discussions in a fairly effortless way, and also flip the power dynamic, if we concentrate on, or at least honor, people's practice, and put that first in our discussions.

Jessica adds to Melissa's point by asserting that we can prioritize practice and bring more people into the movement by connecting with activists who are already doing solidarity economy organizing on the ground but do not have the time or terminology to make the connection to our movement. We need to show them, she says, that, "what they do is what we mean," so that people can see themselves in the solidarity economy. She noted that in the civil rights movement, economics had deliberately been taken off the table because they were viewed as too divisive, but that people are acknowledging more and more that now is the time to talk economics.

Others also reaffirmed the importance of practice guided by theory for keeping the movement true to its long-term goals. Matt spoke of how the labor movement in the United States used to be guided by a very particular theory of social transformation, and how, in his trips to the Emilia Romagna region of Italy, the grassroots level organizers of the labor movement were deeply engaged in theory, and were put in a position to shape theory regardless of their formal education level.

Nancy offers her perspective on the labor and cooperative movement, noting that as those in the cooperative movement focused their vision on creating more and more co-ops, they committed themselves to succeeding in the capitalist world, and compromised on their broader social vision. In Quebec, she is creating alliances of solidarity economy organizations based not on structure, but on vision and values. All types of actors, from cooperatives, to non-profits, to territorial organizations and networks, to social movements, are engaged in the process of critiquing and building the movement. So far, this strategy has worked for the past ten years to keep the movement's social vision.

Nancy Neantam: Basically we are going against the principles of the International Cooperative Alliance, which says that your first alliance is based upon your cooperative structure, not on your values, not on your vision, not on a vision of social transformation, but on the fact that you belong to a cooperative independently of what it is doing. Our organization had success – as I said it has been ten years and we will judge it in fifty years – by bringing together networks of cooperative organizations, networks of non-profit organizations that are working within the economy, of territorial organizations that are working on revitalizing local communities, and social movements. Bringing unions to check us out on working conditions, the environmental movement to check us out on how we are producing the goods and services within our enterprises, the women's movement to talk about gender issues, the community movement, and so on, right into our structures, so that the debate and the checks and balances are integrated right into the structure of what our organization is and does.

Dan offers another vision of what went wrong in the labor movement, arguing that the movement was led by people with an anti-capitalist vision, but when they had success, they focused on that success and gave up their intellectual debate and their systems critique to focus on practical issues. He feels that we need to continue to foster discussion on systems and on our long-term goals, especially among the grassroots organizers in the movement.

Erica reaffirms the need for movement space. As a grassroots-level environmental justice organizer, she is constantly doing work on the ground, but wants to have the opportunity to step back and look at how to solve these problems structurally and economically, and how to set priorities. Jorge Osuna, Leadership Development Coordinator from the Environmental Health Coalition, echoes the idea that he would like more help and support in connecting local issues to global economic practices, but also reports that his low-income constituents are already starting to make the connection, in a general way, between neoliberal policies and the local destruction of their communities.

Dan notes that not only do we need to integrate more systems analysis into our organizing work, but we also need to be prepared to occupy a more mainstream position in the economy, and not be content to be small and marginalized non-profits, with salary-levels that are so low that they almost guarantee white middle class leadership. He also notes that our position within the economy can be part of our development strategy. Part of the reason why Mondragon is a successful cooperative is because they chose to work in manufacturing, which is a high-value-added area of work, and an area where we also have an opportunity to solve many environmental problems.

To close the discussion, Nada offered two resources for anti-racist training: the People's Institute for Survival and Beyond's (www.pisab.org) "Undoing Racism" workshop, and United for a Fair Economy's (www.faireconomy.org) "Closing the Racial Wealth Divide" workshop.

Concluding Remarks

Julie Matthaei, professor of economics at Wellesley College and Co-Director of Guramylay: Growing the Green Economy, thanks everyone for coming to the caucus. The next caucus, which will take place after the last workshop session on Saturday, will be focused on trying to create ongoing links between all these practices and initiatives, especially within the U.S. She invites everyone to read "Solidarity Economy Organization in the U.S. Context: A Think-Paper Towards First Steps" to get an idea of what these connections might look like, and what benefits they might have. She asks if anyone wants to participate in a working group that will meet before the next caucus, and then closes the first caucus meeting, thanking people for their participation.

25
Solidarity Economy Caucus II: The Role of a Solidarity Economy Network
Saturday, June 30, 2007

Jenna Allard

> *Jenna Allard works for Guramylay: Growing the Green Economy, and is part of the coordinating committee for the U.S. Solidarity Economy Network.. She graduated from Wellesley College with a B.A. in Political Science and Peace and Justice Studies. She was excited to be part of the first U.S. Social Forum, and spent most of her time there behind the single eye of a camera lens, recording workshops in the solidarity economy track and the caucuses. She has been passionate about studying and experiencing the solidarity economy ever since she traveled to Brazil and visited a small women's handicraft cooperative in an informal community on the outskirts of Rio de Janeiro.*

Author's Note: This caucus was convened by the Solidarity Economy Working Group for USSF 2007, immediately after the last workshop of the Forum. Invited participants, and others who had become interested in the solidarity economy during the workshops, attended and discussed the potential role and form of a U.S. network. At the end of this meeting, the caucus voted to create the U.S. Solidarity Economy Network (U.S. SEN) . I filmed the caucus for Guramylay: Growing the Green Economy, and I used these tapes to create this summary of the proceedings.

Insights from the Solidarity Economy Workshops at the USSF

Julie Matthaei summarizes the proceedings of the first caucus, discussing how the participants listened to insights from international solidarity economy activists, engaged in a discussion about the language we should use to build the movement, and then talked about some challenges of building the movement in the United States. After introductions, Melissa Hoover opens up a discussion about what was learned from the track of solidarity economy workshops that had gone on over the last three days, so that we can use these insights in our organizing.

Melissa starts off the discussion by talking about how participant questions in her workshop on worker cooperatives, "Another Workplace is Possible," spurred her to think about how to include non-workers in the co-op movement. The solidarity economy is not just about changing how institutions network and link up; it is also about how these institutions conceive of their constituents. Dan Swinney refers her back again to Mike Lewis's graphical representation of the solidarity economy, which shows the need for the solidarity economy to contend in all sectors of the economy, not only in the private, for-profit sector, but also in the public and social sectors. This allows solidarity economy initiatives to truly permeate society.

Julie, as a member of the working group which had been planning the track for months, was delighted to see that the sessions were well-attended, and included many participants who attended more than one workshop in the track and thus were able to bring insights from other workshops to the discussion. Carl Davidson, editor of Solidarityeconomy.net and co-chair of Chicagoans Against War & Injustice, was glad that the track and the tent allowed people to really start learning about the concept of the solidarity economy, and hopes that the term can start to become well-known in the U.S., as it is well-known throughout the rest of the world. Heidi Garret-Peltier, a Center for Popular Economics staff economist, commented on how convenient it was to have the track organized so that she could concretely direct participants who had questions about economic alternatives to relevant workshops.

> Carl Davidson: In Chicago, when I would talk about my website, www.solidarityeconomy.net, people would say, "What's that?" Here, as a result of the track we had, and the tent, people might have different definitions of the solidarity economy, but everybody would say, "That's cool!" It's a concept whose time has come, and I know the solidarity economy is well-known around the world, but it was sort of a "coming-out" party for us here in the U.S.

Heather Schoonover, a policy analyst at the Institute for Agriculture and Trade Policy (IATP), saw that participants were constantly asking how to work towards systems change at the very personal level, even in workshops outside of the Solidarity Economy track. For her, this highlighted the importance of always bringing our systems-level discussions down to the very personal level. John Parker, Director of Good Work, also heard this hunger for personal and practical solutions among USSF attendees at his workshop, "Household Economic Justice Strategies." Ethan Miller's article, "Solidarity Economics: Strategies for Building New Economies from the Bottom-Up and the Inside-Out,"[1] worked well to provide a framework to people who were not very economically literate. It opened up their minds to think about how to be creative about their economic possibilities. We need to keep in mind how to do popular education with people who are not interested in reading about radical economic ideas and organizing, but do want to live them out. How do we develop oral and picture-based materials that can include these people in the movement?

John Parker: I work with a lot of lower-income people; many of them are not literate in general. My challenges, when I do my empowerment and radicalizing popular education with people who are actually not interested in reading handouts, and not interested in reading books, but are interested in living it out, is how do you talk about this orally, and use pictures and stories, in a way that really grabs people? They're not interested in studying more about it; they're interested in getting into it. I think this is one of the challenges of making the solidarity economy accessible to people from a variety of educational backgrounds.

Emily Kawano reinforced the fact that the solidarity economy movement is still embryonic in the United States, and, as such, there is not a lot of jargon associated with it. Ethan Miller echoed this thought, noting that not many organizations currently self-identify as solidarity economy enterprises. He also talks about a project trying to create a directory of organizations and initiatives with transformative social missions, the Data Commons Project, which could in the future be a great resource for people looking to become involved in the solidarity economy at the household level.

Jessica Gordon Nembhard also found that the workshops did a great job of getting the word out to people that were interested in economic transformation, but thought that, at times, the workshops still seemed a little jargon-y. She thinks we need to continue to think about conducting training so that we can both develop a common language and also tailor our message based on the types of conferences we are presenting at. Stewart Burns, historian and Director of the Center for Community Engagement at Williams College, discussed the possible connections of solidarity economy language with the language of the economic human rights movements, and thinks that the solidarity economy is a particularly good answer to how people will be able to exercise their right to work.
Carl talked about the unique and inspiring demographics of the U.S. Social Forum – 10,000 to 15,000 attendees who were overwhelmingly young, multi-racial, and engaged in community-based, radical politics. These people are the engine for change in the U.S., and we need to figure out how to engage with them. Ra

Chaka, from the African American Alliance for Peace and Justice in Chicago, Illinois, was also surprised to see so many youth at the Forum. In the workshops, he saw powerful and small-scale solutions challenging the system, and he wants to see these ideas more widely disseminated and copied. People were starting to discuss economic and structural roots to their community problems, and economics were also at the forefront of many of the solutions that they discussed. Germai Medhanie, Co-Director of Guramylay: Growing the Green Economy, was also impressed by the youthful participants in his workshop, "Immigrants, Globalization, and Organizing for Rights, Solidarity, and Economic Justice," who were able to eloquently connect the processes of immigration with the processes of globalization. He thinks that immigrants are an important group to reach out to in the solidarity economy, and he was glad that they were included in the solidarity track.

Report Back from the Working Group

Dan applauded the hard work of the core members of the Solidarity Economy Working Group for USSF 2007. Putting together the caucuses and the track was an experiment, and the organizers are very pleased with the initial response and attendance. The Working Group met after the first caucus meeting to plan for this caucus meeting, and to talk about how to move forward after the US Social Forum, building on the relationships and momentum we have created together.

> *Dan Swinney: There's a broad range of opinion; there's a broad range of discussion; there's a broad range of experience; but there really is a deep desire to unite around what we call the solidarity economy. We felt there was a mandate, and that we should see if that was really the case: that what we ought to do is move towards creating a formal national network that would be a very big tent, in the sense that we represent a very diverse range of experiences and projects. It would be a place that we would have extensive exchange of practice, and it would provide the basis for mutual support.*

Moving forward, they do feel there is a mandate to move towards creating a formal solidarity economy network, that would be a big tent, with an extensive exchange of practice and mutual support. Its purpose would be transformation and system change, and it would have a place for critical thinking and critical exchange. It would be a place to discuss practice and policy; a place to talk about big issues, under a relatively simple mission statement.

Our objective would be towards creating a non-profit organization with a board that would reflect the movement's values and diversity. The network would seek funding, and manage internal and external communications. Dan proposes a small working group chaired by Emily Kawano that could work through initial organizational issues and then get back to the membership. This discussion could possibly culminate in a conference next year. This U.S. Solidarity Economy Network could be a springboard for participation in the international conversation about the solidarity economy, through the Intercontinental Network for the Promotion of the Social Solidarity Economy (RIPESS) and the North American Network for the Solidarity Economy (NANSE). Dan proposes that during this caucus, we discuss this proposal and decide whether to launch this network or not.

Tom Pierson: Strategic planning is something that a lot of non-profits and community organizations involved will be doing, and it would be helpful if we were able to participate in some way in informing how the solidarity economy can fit into strategic planning, either as a fee-for-service, or by finding funding to specifically do that. I think that we need to work with the longer-term visions of these organizations. We can't just meet them at their urgent needs, we need to meet them in their long term planning stages.

Brainstorming on Ways to Grow the Solidarity Economy Movement in the U.S

A list of some suggestions from the participants:

- o Develop a clear set of principles that defines succinctly our vision for the solidarity economy
- o Translate key documents on the topic of the solidarity economy
- o Develop educational materials that are targeted to activists that work on specific issues, and explain how the solidarity economy relates to their area of organizing
- o Put together a speaker's bureau
- o Publish articles about the Solidarity Economy in progressive magazines
- o Write op-eds, strategize about a targeted media communications campaign
- o Publish this track of workshops at the U.S. Social Forum as a book
- o Start a weekly radio program at a progressive outlet, like Pacifica Radio
- o Produce a documentary about international examples of the solidarity economy

- o   Send statements of principles to potential allied organizations for outreach
- o   Start a Solidarity Economy persona on social networking sites, like Facebook and Myspace
- o   Disseminate information about the solidarity economy to members of food cooperatives

> *Ethan Miller: When we talk about the idea of the solidarity economy as an idea that connects together all these different practices, it is easier for certain types of people, who tend to be working in support organizations that are helping these sorts of initiatives, or perhaps people with a more academic orientation, to get excited about this. My question is: if we are trying to build a network that really is based in social movements, and really is based in practice, what does that look like? What does it look like for social movements participating in the network to feel like, amidst all their priorities of immediate day-to-day struggle, participation in the network, and what could become an abstract discussion, is still meaningful?*

The Vision of the Solidarity Economy in the U.S.

One participant asks for clarification on the vision of the solidarity economy, and what it would concretely look like when implemented. Emily answers this by reiterating that the solidarity economy is a framework grounded in principles such as cooperation, mutuality, sustainability, equality, democracy, and the idea of valuing people over profits. Many practices support these principles and values, but they look very different from the mainstream capitalist economy. These practices may satisfy some parts of the visions but not others, and so, as in the Canadian case, the solidarity economy in the U.S. want to bring social movements into dialogue.

Erica Swinney adds that the solidarity economy can ultimately replace neoliberal capitalism. The vision is creating economic practices outside of capitalism that can at some point become the dominant framework. Julie also adds that, like the Social Forum movement, the solidarity economy brings together many progressive causes while still respecting their diversity and their local solutions.

Principles of the Solidarity Economy in the U.S.

Nina Gregg, the U.S. Representative for the Charter of Human Responsibilities Project, notes that describing practices and enumerating principles are both important and distinct ways of communicating about the solidarity economy. She wants to know more about the principles of the movement, and the process for defining and developing them.

Melissa builds on the point by talking about how helpful it can be to examine and borrow from the values statements of other international organizations doing the same work. A succinct statement of principles could be a great outreach tool to send to potential allied organizations in the United States and to start to build our network. Dan reaffirms the idea that there are other organizations, like NANSE, that have already gone through an extensive process of developing principles. The benefit of being last is that we can make lots of lateral exchanges, and we can study international experiences to see how we can apply them in the U.S.

In response to a question by David Korten, Dan also gives a brief definition of high road business practices, and explains how that terminology can be helpful in building the solidarity economy movement. He notes that when activists talk about the perniciousness of corporations, they are generally talking about publicly traded companies, as opposed to the eight million privately-held businesses that now depend on a public partnership to survive. High road business practices are characterized by a long-term view of the company, community, and sector, transparent and participative structures, and local ownership. Ambiguity can be useful as the movement is growing. As an organizer, Dan works with businesses that might not initially consider themselves as part of the solidarity economy, and part of his role is to make that transformation happen over time.

The Role of a Solidarity Economy Network in the U.S

Stewart Burns recognizes that diversity and localization are at the heart of the solidarity economy movement, but he believes that we cannot lose sight of the fact that we need some element of coordination to keep the movement together. We can't lose our commonality. He wants us to discuss in more detail what types of decisions a network might make.

Stewart Burns: Obviously decentralization and diversity are at the heart of all that we are doing and envisioning, but I do have a concern that without some element of coordination – which might be a dirty word for some of us in this room – and without some understanding of the kinds of decisions we need to make as a whole movement, and how those decisions are going to be made, we might become so decentralized and so diverse that the centrifugal force might pull us into ether-space, and we would lose our commonality. This is what Ella Baker did with the civil rights movement in creating SNCC. There was all this great activity going on at the grassroots, but she had the idea that there needed to be some sort of coordinating structure to really make that movement cohere.

Heather talks about a possible need for the Network to set some sort of criteria for membership. Citing the growth of the "going green" movement, she sees a whole continuum of companies that are engaging in high road practices because they have some sort of social mission, to those who do it for the publicity, to those who are even misleading in their representation of their practices. How do we ensure that membership in a solidarity economy network means something substantive?

Membership

Nina poses the question of why someone would want to be a member. Do they want to spread the word about the practices, or do they need something, like technical support? Ethan builds on this question by asking what would motivate members of social movements who are engaged in day-to-struggles to participate in a movement that can at times be more abstract and long-term. The idea of connecting practices may motivate people with academic inclinations, or those who work in support and technical assistance organizations, but what would motivate other members to join?

Chilo Villarreal: In Latin America, there is a network of academics who are researching the solidarity economy, and they are systemizing what we are doing. When we are doing our work at the grassroots, we don't have the time or the skills to do that, so we are close to people in the universities.

Chilo Villarreal, a member of the Rural Coalition, shares her experience building Solidarity Economy networks in Mexico. Initially, representatives from several regional organizations in the Mexico City area began meeting each month. After one year, they decided to put together a national meeting. Each organization invited ten other organizations to participate with them. After a few years, after analyzing the needs of the members, they began to have regional training workshops, called diplomados.

Mike Lewis talks about how the solidarity economy movement in Canada was initially built around community economic development. After a few years, they put a working group together with the main goal of learning from their practice, scaling up practice, and mobilizing for policy initiatives. They have also become a network of networks. They have had regional workshops on policy issues, which they used to build national policy forums, and they have an annual conference with an attendance of about 700 people from all over the country. At this point, he feels that the organization is becoming a bit too staff-led, and they have to re-focus on how to re-involve members.

Julie Matthaei: I was in Nairobi at the World Social Forum in January 2007, and I went to all the solidarity economy events. One of the things they were saying was that there was a lot of difficulty communicating because in Latin America there is not a lot of web access, and in Europe there are a lot of different languages. I was sitting there thinking, most people in the United States speak English, and have access to the internet. We have this incredible resource for connecting.

Charges to the Solidarity Economy Network Working Group

o   Move the yearly conference geographically so that it can spark and sustain local grassroots activism in many different communities
o   Take agency in the initial governance process to make the initial plenary less messy
o   Create structures that break down natural hierarchies; avoid being "pale, male, and stale"
o   Consciously make educational materials accessible to people from all educational backgrounds
o   Maintain the breadth and diversity of the working group, so that they can effectively build the network

Potential Roles for the Solidarity Economy Network

o   Provide technical support for grassroots organizations
o   Facilitate creative, imaginative processes for organizations to build in constructive processes to oppose and replace neoliberalism
o   Develop graduate-level degrees in the solidarity economy, and generally involve academics in researching and promoting the solidarity economy
o   Gather information for mapping solidarity economy initiatives
o   Provide a place for members to list their organizational affiliations, the practices that they engage in that are part of the solidarity economy, and what resources they need
o   Advocate for policy initiatives

The Creation of the Solidarity Economy Network

Ethan brings the participants back to the proposal of creating a network. Dan advocates for giving a lot of agency for the working group to make major decisions. After a brief discussion about who will be involved in the working group, and whether they have the breadth to carry the organization forward, the members of the Solidarity Economy Working Group for the US Social Forum who will serve on the Solidarity Economy Network Working Group are named: Emily Kawano, Julie Matthaei, Michael Menser, Ethan Miller, Jessica Gordon Nembhard, and Dan Swinney. Mike Lewis and Yvon Poirier from Canada agree to provide continuing guidance and support without being formally involved. Mike Lewis talks about how building the U.S. network is also part of the process of building regional networks like NANSE. Emily echoes the need to be patient with the breadth and growth of the movement, mentioning that the Solidarity Economy Working Group had tried to do outreach, but it is part of an educational process, and a process of relationship-building. We shouldn't be disappointed if our new network can't be what we aspire to be right away.

Tom Pierson, Executive Director of North American Students of Cooperation (NASCO) proposes an amendment that the working group be able to start the governance process, so that the initial plenaries can go more smoothly. After being asked if there were additional amendments, the participants voted unanimously to start the network! Afterwards, they got together to pose for a group photograph to commemorate the historic occasion (see next page)!

U.S. SEN Founding Caucus Meeting, U.S. Social Forum
June 30th, 2007, Atlanta, Georgia

Top Row (Left to Right): Yvon Poirier, Stewart Burns, Helen Scharber, Nada Khader, Ra Chaka, Matt Riddle, Tom Masterson, Tom Pierson, Ethan Miller, Jenna Allard, Whit Forrester, Dan Swinney, Evan Mulligan, Erica Swinney, Carl Davidson, Jim Tarbell.

Bottom Row (Left to Right): Mike Lewis, Nedda Angulo Villareal, Nina Gregg, Doug Gamble, Julie Matthaei, Germai Medhanie, Emily Kawano, Melissa Hoover, Miss Muffy, Heather Schoonover, Shannon Tracy, Heidi Garrett-Peltier.

Not Pictured: Michael Albert, Anita Dancs, Omar Freilla, Jessica Gordon Nembhard, David Korten, Fred Matthaei, Nancy Neantam, John Parker, Hector Saez, Nichola Torbett, Chilo Villarreal, Tom Wetzel.

Notes

[1] Ethan Miller's "Solidarity Economics: Strategies for Building New Economies from the Bottom-Up and the Inside-Out," is available at http://www.populareconomics.org/ussen/webfm_send/12

26
The Emerging Solidarity Economy: Some Common Themes

Solidarity Economy Working Group for USSF 2007

The Solidarity Economy constitutes an alternative economic model to neoliberal capitalism, one which is grounded on solidarity and cooperation, rather than the pursuit of narrow, individual self-interest, and that promotes economic democracy, alternative models of local economic governance, equity and sustainability rather than the unfettered rule of the market.

While noncapitalist, cooperative forms of economic organization have always existed, solidarity economy is a recent and evolving concept and practice, which is being defined from the bottom/up: The term "solidarity economy" emerged about 10 years ago, and solidarity economy organizations and networks now exist in Latin America, most European countries, Africa, Asia, and Canada. While the U.S. has many solidarity economy practices, institutions, and networks, the term itself is not well known in the US. As of yet, we do not have either a framework that unites them conceptually as an overall system, or an overarching network of solidarity economy organizations.

Solidarity economy involves three overlapping but distinct types of solidarity:

– Values-based solidarity: solidarity with people, movement groups, NGO's, worker cooperatives and other businesses who share economic justice values – e.g. Fair Trade, ethical consumption, and socially responsible investment practices
– Anti-oppression solidarity: solidarity with oppressed countries or with oppressed groups of people, especially the poor, women, indigenous peoples, people of color, gay/lesbian/bisexual/transgendered peoples, and workers
– Vision-based solidarity: solidarity among people, economic organizations, and social movements based on shared visions for local and global economic development that are economically, socially, and environmentally restorative, and shared advocacy of transformative institutions and policies such as Bolivia's People's Trade Agreement, participatory budgeting and labor-based investment funds

Solidarity economy involves two levels of solidarity:

– Micro-solidarity: egalitarian and participatory economic behavior by individuals, workers, and producers, such as by an individual who is an ethical consumer, worker, or investor, or by a worker co-op, fair trade business, or progressive union

– Macro-solidarity: the development of networks aimed at supporting and growing the solidarity economy among individuals and institutions. This involves networks of organizations involved in micro-solidarity, such as the Fair Trade Federation, SAS (Students Against Sweatshops), and national, regional, and international networks of solidarity economy organizations such as RIPESS (The Intercontinental Network for the Promotion of the Social Solidarity Economy), and NANSE (North American Network for the Solidarity Economy). A key aspect of macro-solidarity is organized activity by these networks, in coalition with other progressive groups, aimed at transforming the state and global institutions so as to make them supportive to the growth of the solidarity economy.

Reform and Revolution:

Solidarity economy involves both transforming current economic institutions, and growing alternatives to them. Solidarity economy values, practices and institutions currently coexist with neoliberal capitalist ones in all sectors of the economy. The ultimate vision is 1) to grow these values, practices and institutions through conscious activity designed to transform civil society, the market, and the state, and 2) to link these solidarity economy activities in a network of mutual support, such that they transform neoliberal capitalism into a just, democratic, and sustainable economic paradigm and system.

Solidarity economy involves a continuum of forms of relations of production, and different solidarity economy networks link various subsets of these:

– From landless workers to family farmers to agricultural cooperatives
– From self-employed entrepreneurs and local small-scale businesses, to high road businesses and corporations, to worker-owned cooperatives and collectives and community businesses
– Indigenous, collectivist forms of production

Solidarity economy involves a range of social sectors and focuses:
– The Canadian social economy involves cooperatives and non-profit enterprises in many sectors, which are often supported by government programs obtained through the mobilization of social movements, especially in the Quebec province
– The Brazilian solidarity economy relies heavily on unions, landless worker organizing, and the creation of cooperatives among those living in informal settlements
– The European platform for ethical and solidarity-based initiatives focuses on anti-materialism and ethical consumption
– NANSE (The North American Network for the Solidarity Economy) is committed to organizing against the neoliberal vision on all levels and in all sectors

Solidarity economy simultaneously promotes unity and diversity:

– Unity around shared values of equality (especially gender, race, and economic equality), participatory democracy, cooperation, sustainability, community
– Diversity is not only accepted but valued, encouraged, and celebrated, including diversity of culture, of conceptual frameworks, of ways of structuring economic institutions, of priorities, and of ways of movement building

To Read More about the Solidarity Economy:

The Intercontinental Network for the Promotion of the Social Solidarity Economy website: http://www.ripess.net /en/

The Alliance 21 website:
http://www. alliance21.org/2003/sommaire_en.php3

The Workgroup on Solidarity Socio-Economy website:
http://www.socioeco.org/en/index.php

The Canadian Social Economy Hub website:
http://www.socialeconomynetwork.ca/hub/

Brazilian Forum of Solidarity Economy, article Brazil's solidarity economy movement:
http://www.fbes.org.br/docs/BrazilianSolidarityEconomyMovement.pdf
See also www.geo.coop and www.transformationcentral.org.

27
Solidarity Economy
Organization in the U.S. Context:
A Think-Paper Towards First Steps

Solidarity Economy Working Group for USSF 2007

"Solidarity Economy" is a framework for connecting alternative economic practices and institutions which are grounded in solidarity and cooperation, rather than the pursuit of narrow, individual self-interest, and that promote economic democracy, alternative models of local economic governance, equity and social and economic sustainability rather than the unfettered rule of the market. By linking diverse transformative economic efforts together as parts of a common movement on a scale from the local to the global, the solidarity economy approach creates a shared space of debate, exchange and collective growth for its participants and works to strengthen and develop grassroots alternatives through networking and mutual support.

The Solidarity Economy Working Group for the U.S. Social Forum 2007 has convened these caucus meetings for the purposes of developing a stronger shared language—that of the "solidarity economy"—for the development of economic alternatives in the U.S., linking with current international efforts to build alternatives to neoliberal globalization, and building toward sustainable, long-term organizational structures for the creation and promotion of these alternatives.

Our thinking in the realm of solidarity economy organizing can be guided, in part, by the following questions:

1) What forms of economic solidarity already exist in our midst?
2) How do we identify them? How are they distinguished from other initiatives?
3) What do these initiatives need to be strengthened and supported?
4) How do we foster the *conditions of emergence* for more such initiatives?
5) How do we work to connect these initiatives together in webs of mutual support and recognition?

The following document presents some possible directions in which solidarity economy organizing in the U.S. context might go. It is meant as a starting point for further discussion, elaboration and planning. We suggest first an overview of possible strategies, then briefly outline a possible structure through which such strategies might be implemented.

Some Possible Strategies for Solidarity Economy Organizing in the U.S.

1. Developing a shared definition of the solidarity economy. Defining, through dialogue and constructive debate, a collective understanding of the values and visions that constitute a solidarity economy movement in the U.S. context.

2. Mapping the existing solidarity economy. Taking inventory of existing initiatives, practices and visions in the U.S. and abroad with the aim of identifying allies and increasing the visibility and viability of diverse elements of the solidarity economy. The Data Commons Project, currently working to build a collaborative database of such initiatives in the U.S., can provide the technical and organizational base for such an effort (see http://dcp.usworker.coop).

3. Networking across diverse sectors in the U.S. Fostering a shared "movement" identity, building cross-sector relationships and facilitating mutual support among diverse organizations and initiatives that are engaged in solidarity economy and economic justice work.

4. Popular education and publicity for a solidarity economy. This might involve: the creation of clear and accessible educational materials; the development and practice of participatory workshops for community and church groups, schools, activist organizations, businesses, business organizations, labor unions, etc.; and the development of media strategies to "mainstream" the solidarity economy into a larger sphere of public consciousness.

5. Public policy development and advocacy. Developing a strong public voice for the solidarity economy vision of economic and social development in the U.S. and abroad, along with collaborative efforts to develop and implement public policies in support of this vision.

6. Strengthening existing U.S. and international solidarity economy initiatives and supporting the creation of new ones. Investigating and developing ways to build collaborative support systems for solidarity economy development. These could include such initiatives as solidarity development loan funds, movement-wide cooperative insurance and pension systems, solidarity exchange/commerce tools (such as an online "marketplace," cross-sector barter exchanges, and a "Solidarity Made" marketing label/certification), and development resources and technical support.

7. Developing stronger relationships with global solidarity economy networks and organizations. Facilitating increased interchange between solidarity economy organizers in the U.S. and others around the world.

A Draft Vision of a U.S. Solidarity Economy Network

Rationale: In Latin America, Europe, Canada, Africa and Asia, solidarity economy organizing has taken the form of local, regional, national and international networks that link together diverse economic justice initiatives. The Brazilian Solidarity Economy Forum, for example, brings together twelve national networks and membership organizations with twenty-one regional Solidarity Forums and thousands of cooperative enterprises to build mutual support systems, facilitate exchanges, create solidarity enterprise incubator programs and shape public policy. Many such regional and national networks are convened globally through the Intercontinental Network for the Promotion of the Social Solidarity Economy (RIPESS). In North America (Mexico, Canada, the US and the Caribbean) organizations have come together under the banner of the North American Network on the Solidarity Economy (NANSE)

The creation of a national-scale network in the United States would be a powerful step in the direction of: a) developing a stronger and more unified progressive vision for economic alternatives based on the values of the solidarity economy; b) building deeper shared identities and mutual-support relationships between existing U.S.-based efforts to create such alternatives; and c) joining and learning from international efforts to build viable and powerful alternatives. The following is a first-draft sketch of what such a U.S. network might look like:

The **mission** of the U.S. Solidarity Economy Network would be to connect a diverse array of individuals, organizations, businesses and projects in the shared work of building and strengthening regional, national and international movements for a solidarity economy. Through publications, a website and mailing list, and face-to-face gatherings, the network would facilitate: ongoing communication and dialog relating to the development of solidarity economy ideas, values and practices; the sharing of experiences, models and skills; and the creation of collaborative, movement-building projects between network members.

Network **membership** could be open to any organization, business or individual who shares the mission of the network and actively works to promote values, visions and practices that are resonant with the solidarity economy idea (without necessarily using the term "solidarity economy"). Members could be distinguished through a set of categories:

Solidarity Economy Initiatives. Organizations, businesses, and groups working to directly implement specific solidarity-based structures and principles in their operation.

Solidarity Economy Networks and Associations. Organizations which network, convene, or coordinate multiple solidarity economy initiatives and/or support organizations. The U.S. Federation of Worker Cooperatives is an example.

Support Organizations. Organizations that provide direct or indirect support (through research, funding, technical assistance, media, or other avenues) to solidarity economy initiatives and/or to general efforts to develop a solidarity economy.

Allied Organizations. Organizations whose work may not involve the direct creation of economic alternatives, but is crucial nonetheless to the success of such efforts and to our shared work of creating economic justice.

Individuals. Individuals who seek to support and participate in the building of a solidarity economy.

The network could be coordinated by a national Coordinating Committee of ten to twenty people, elected by the network membership. An initial ad-hoc Coordinating Committee might be necessary until the network solidified its structure and capacity to engage in such voting. Organizations in the network membership would select two delegates to participate in network decision-making processes. Votes could be weighted based on membership categories.

Developing the resources and structure with which to support at least one paid staff person for the network might be a high priority. Identifying sources of initial financial support from foundations and other donors may be a crucial first step in the overall organizing process. Another possible source of revenue might be through a sliding-scale membership dues payment from network members.

Appendix A

Workshops & Events at the U.S. Social Forum

Building and Strengthening Economic Alternatives & the Social/Solidarity Economy

---

Solidarity Economy Tent
Located next to the Civic Center

SPONSORING GROUPS: Guramylay: Growing the Green Economy, the Center for Popular Economics, Grassroots Economic Organizing, the U.S. Federation of Worker Cooperatives, the Center for Labor and Community Research, the Democracy Collaborative, Institute for Agriculture and Trade Policy, Groupe Economie Solidaire Quebec, Canadian Community Economic Development Network, the Union for Radical Political Economics, SweatFree Communities, STITCH, U.S./Labor Education in Americas Project, and *Dollars & Sense* magazine.

Schedule of Organized Tent Activities:

All Day: listings of workshops on "Economic Alternatives and the Social/Solidarity Economy," literature on economic alternatives that are being constructed in the US and abroad, and on the emerging Solidarity Economy networks; literature tables of groups active in economic transformation

Thurs., Fri, and Sat. at 9 am: Introduction to the Solidarity Economy

Wed, Thurs, Fri, and Sat. after the evening plenary (about 9:30 pm): Political Song Circle, open to all musicians, singers, and listeners and led by Ray Korona, singer-songwriter

Fri. at 5 pm: open discussion, "Using the Web for Economic and Social Transformation"

Sat. at 5 pm: open discussion, "Changing the World Through Political Song," led by Ray Korona, singer-songwriter

Workshops Organized by the Solidarity Economy Working Group

2265. Why We Need Another World: Introduction To Neoliberalism

Heidi Garrett-Peltier
Matt Riddle
Helen Scharber (Center for Popular Economics)

Why do we need 'another world'? If you have a gut level feeling that something is wrong with the global economic system, but feel a need to understand more of the nitty gritty of how it works—who are the big players; what is the ideology & policies; who are the winners and the losers; how do race, ethnicity, gender play out—this is the workshop for you.

2267. The Sky as a Common Resource: Fighting Global Warming by Asserting Equal Rights to our Atmosphere

Matt Riddle
Sirisha Naidu (Center for Popular Economics)
Little Village Environmental Justice Organization

This workshop will use a combination of participatory exercises, discussion and presentation to explore the twin challenges of global warming and inequality, how the neoliberal economic system contributes to both, and how the use of a 'Sky Trust' can reduce greenhouse gas emissions while also helping to achieve a more fair distribution of the Earth's wealth. A Sky Trust would assert the shared nature of our atmospheric resource by forcing anyone who emits carbon into the atmosphere to pay into a trust fund that would then be distributed evenly to all people.

2287. Why Promote an Economic Human Rights Framework?

Poor People's Economic Human Rights Campaign
U.S. Human Rights Network
Center for Popular Economics

This workshop will explore the ways in which the framework of economic human rights can be used to build a social movement to end poverty and build a solidarity economy. We will use both presentations and participatory methods to define Economic Human

Rights and briefly review how neoliberalism has undermined them; look at ways that the poor in the U.S. are uniting across color lines with students, social workers, religious leaders and others to win Economic Human Rights for all; and focus on how to move from protest & survival to creating a new world.

3228. Building a Solidarity Economy From Real World Practices

Manos Unidas
Center for Popular Economics
Grassroots Economic Organizing

This collaborative workshop will combine theater, art and economic analysis to create an active visual representation and experience of a Social/Solidarity Economy.

2005. Participatory Budgeting I: Community Control Over Public Money

Gianpaolo Baiocchi (University of Massachusetts)
Juscha Robinson (Liberty Tree Foundation)

This session will be an introduction to participatory budgeting and how it has been applied in Latin America and North America. Participatory budgeting is a process in which city residents directly decide how part of a municipal or public budget is spent.

2040. Participatory Budgeting II

Gianpaolo Baiocchi (University of Massachusetts)
Juscha Robinson (Liberty Tree Foundation)

3024. There is an Alternative: Economic Democracy

David Schweickart (Solidarityeconomy.net)
Michael Albert, Z Magazine

Another world is possible? We keep repeating these words, but what exactly would that world look like? More specifically, what might be its underlying economic structure?
David Schweikart and Michael Albert will propose two contrasting models of Economic Democracy. David Schweikart will discuss market socialism featuring worker-self-management of enterprises and social control of investment. Michael Albert will describe participatory economics, or ParEcon, a classless economic alternative to both

capitalism and what Albert calls coordinatorism (including market and centrally planned socialism).

2380. Alternatives in Action: Economic Democracy in Emilia Romagna, Italy

Matt Hancock (Center for Labor and Community Research)

Workshop participants will learn about the main features of the "Emilian Model" of development in the Emila-Romagna region of Italy, one of the most significant examples of an Economic Democracy in a developed, industrialized society. The workshop presents a positive and sustainable alternative to neoliberalism, based on economic democracy, sustainability and a commitment to local development in the context of international development.

2367. High Road – Low Road

Dan Swinney and Matt Hancock (Center for Labor and Community Research)
Erica Swinney (GreenAction)

Our local development strategy in Chicago is to "lead the race to the top in global high performance/high value-added manufacturing" with a social high road partnership of labor, business, government, community, and educational institutions. Sharing work and ideas that are informed by 25 years in the trenches of community and economic development in Chicago as well as best international practices such as Mondragon in Spain and the Emilia Romagna model in Northern Italy, we hope to contribute to the international discussion that seeks a competitive alternative to neoliberalism.

2143. Solidarity Economy in Canada

Nancy Neamtan (Groupe d'économie solidaire du Québec - GESQ)
Michael Lewis (Center for Community Enterprise)
Ethel Coté (Économie Solidaire Ontario)

Social economy has a long history in Canada. From the start of the 20th century to today, cooperatives have played a strong role for workers and farmers to organize their lives. In the last 25 years, many new initiatives have sprung up all over Canada. In particular, this renewal has been very strong in Quebec province. Networks and national organizations are also very active. The objective of the workshops is to share information and experience about the Social and Solidarity Economy (SSE) with US counterparts to strengthen solidarity economy as part of the alternative globalization movement.

2142. Solidarity Economy As a Strategy for Changing the Economy

Michael Lewis (B.C.-Alberta Research Alliance on the Social Economy)
Nedda Angulo Villareal (Grupo Red de Economía Solidaria del Perú - GRESP)
Éthel Côté (Canadian Community Economy Development Network - CCEDNet)

The Social and Solidarity Economy (SSE) sector has gained strength in the last years, at the national, continental and international level, as a fundamental approach in building an alternate globalization. The workshop will focus on both the conceptual aspects and networking strategies in building this other world.

3390. Beyond Reform or Revolution: Economic Transformation in the U.S.: A Roundtable Discussion

Julie Matthaei (Union for Radical Political Economics)
Kevin Danaher (Global Exchange)
Juliet Schor (Center for a New American Dream)
Emily Kawano (Center for Popular Economics)
Dan Swinney (Center for Labor and Community Research)

The roundtable discussion session will have a two-fold focus: 1) to identify actually existing transformative economic values, practices and institutions such as worker coops, socially responsible economic decision-making, green enterprises, and the like, and 2) to discuss ways to work together across our organizations to support movement towards more fully egalitarian and democratic economic forms which are free of race, gender, sexuality, disability, environmental, and international domination and exploitation. Sponsored by Guramylay: Growing the Green Economy

2428. Live Your Power: Socially Responsible Consumption, Work, and Investment

Dennis Brutus (Graduation Pledge and TIAA-CREF Campaign)
Juliet Schor (Center for a New American Dream)
Victoria Cepidia-Mojaro (United Students Against Sweatshops)
Denise Hamler (Coop America)
John Parker (U.S. Federation of Worker Coops)
Moderator: Julie Matthaei (Guramylay: Growing the Green Economy)

A key way to transform and transcend unsustainable and oppressive economic institutions in the U.S. is to live our power -- by expressing liberatory, sustainable values in our everyday economic actions and choices. This session is about how we Americans are rejecting materialistic, competitive conditioning and are learning how to use our economic power to express just and sustainable values in every aspect of our daily economic lives, from consumption and investment decisions to work choices to socially responsible citizenship. Sponsored by Guramylay: Growing the Green Economy

3660. Feminist Economic Transformation

Julie Matthaei (International Association for Feminist Economics)
Hiywete Solomon and Alexis Frank (Guramylay and Transformation Central)
Kristin Rowe-Finkbeiner (Mom's Rising)
Heidi Hartmann (Institute for Women's Policy Research)
Kristin Sampson (Gender and Trade Network)

If we are to build another world, we must engage in feminist transformation: the deconstruction of gender polarization and domination, which are continually produced and reproduced by our current economic values, practices and institutions. Women continue to be oppressed at home and discriminated against in labor markets. Caring labor, crucial to our survival and well-being, is devalued by markets, public policy makers, and mainstream culture, creating a crisis in care. Women and men struggle to find ways to find time to do unpaid, as well as paid, work. In this session, feminist activists will discuss the ways their organizations are working towards women's economic empowerment and feminist economic transformation, sharing their successes and the challenges they are facing. Sponsored by the International Association for Feminist Economics.

3379. Growing Transformative Businesses

David Korten (Business Alliance for Local Living Economies)
Jessica Gordon Nembhard (Grassroots Economic Organizing, Democracy Collaborative)
Melissa Hoover (U.S. Federation of Worker Cooperatives)
Kevin Danaher (Global Exchange)
Karen Werner (Community Economies)
Moderator: Germazion Medhanie (Guramylay: Growing the Green Economy)

Key to economic transformation is the restructuring of business, from profit-centered transnational corporations which concentrate wealth and threaten human well-being and the health of the planet, to transformative businesses which take on the crucial work of redressing these imbalances. In this workshop, leaders in the movement to create businesses which are green, socially responsible, and/or worker- or community-owned will share their wisdom and experiences. They will discuss the growth of transformative businesses in the U.S., and successful strategies to encourage this growth, and will provide information about how to create transformative businesses for existing or would-be entrepreneurs, communities, and worker collectives.

2262. Re-creating the New city: Worker Ownership in an African American Context

Jessica Gordon Nembhard (Democracy Collaborative and Grassroots Economic Organizing)
Ajowa Nzinga Ifateyo (U.S. Federation of Worker Cooperatives and Grassroots Economic Organizing)

This will be an interactive workshop to introduce participants to the concept of democratic community-based economic development and ways that worker owned businesses contribute to their community and to community economic development. Discussion will focus on needs of marginalized communities and explore the history of African American worker cooperatives and community owned businesses. Participants will be tasked with identifying needs in their communities and designing the elements of a "new city."

2435. You Are What You Eat

Heather Schoonover (Institute for Agriculture and Trade Policy)
Helen Scharber (Center for Popular Economics)

We live in a world where farmers struggle to make a living producing crops for export while struggling to feed themselves and their communities; where farms get larger and larger while rural communities get smaller and smaller; where the long-term productive capacity of the environment is sacrificed for short-term gains; where the most affordable foods are the worst for our health; and where the decisions of a few powerful players increasingly determine the playing field for everyone else. This workshop will examine the many impacts of the industrialized food system and will explore positive alternatives from both the grassroots and policy arenas.

3561. Global vs Local: What's Our Vision For the Future Economy?

Sally Kohn (Center for Community Change)

Is a global, trade-dependent economy the best hope for ending poverty and creating opportunity worldwide? Are local, sustainable economies the best hope for economic equity and justice? Or does it not even matter what we think --- globalization unstoppable and the best we can hope is to tame it? This interactive conversation will feature two advocates on either side of the global/local economy debate, making their cases for what the progressive economic agenda should be. We'll then break up into small groups to discuss the pros and cons of globalization and localization and develop ideas for what the progressive solution might be.

3483. Another Workplace is Possible: Co-ops and Democracy in the Workplace

Melissa Hoover (U.S. Federation of Worker Cooperatives)

Looking for an alternative to corporate capitalism that works? Interested in the real everyday ways that economic democracy can support real political democracy and social change? This introductory workshop, for those new to worker cooperatives or curious about their basic functioning, will explain the worker-ownership and democratic workplace model that has inspired workers from Argentina and Venezuela to Italy and Spain, and is now a growing movement in the U.S. We'll answer some practical questions, make some connections to broader movements for social and economic justice, and talk about challenges and strategy facing worker cooperatives in the U.S.

3024. There Is An Alternative: Economic Democracy

Tim Huet (Association of Arizmendi Cooperatives)
Jessica Gordon Nembhard (Eastern Conference for Workplace Democracy and Grassroots Economic Organizing Newsletter)

This workshop provides an interactive discussion (both within and among participants and presenters) about economic democracy, showcasing one of the most democratic of economic organization types, the worker-owned cooperative. We provide a short introduction to the range of worker cooperatives from collectives to manager-run cooperatives, from as small as three worker-owners to thousands; and address the history and potential of worker cooperatives to assist folks who have been disenfranchised and shut out of the ownership culture.

3485. Spirituality and Economic Transformation

Michael Lerner and/or Nicola Torbett (Network of Spiritual Progressives)
David Korten (Positive Futures Network)
Julie Matthaei (Guramylay: Growing the Green Economy)

The U.S. economy is built on the myth that the search for money and power through consumerism and careerism can bring well-being and fulfillment. The spiritual emptiness of this narrow self-interested materialism, along with the anti-religious/anti-spiritual bias of the left, has helped feed the rise of the Religious Right in the U.S., and various forms of religious fundamentalism all over the world. This workshop will focus on the important role that spiritual healing and spirituality-based activism plays in progressive economic transformation.

2793. Building Community Economies Any Time Any Place

Community Economies Collective

We will share our experiences developing worker owned cooperatives, such as Collective Copies and creating complementary currencies, including the North Quabbin Time Bank in the deindustrialized towns of Orange and Athol, Massachusetts. We will put this work into a broader context about community economies, which we see as spaces of ethical decision making. We highlight an economy of trust through honor-system based exchanges at small farm stands in Western Massachusetts and cooperative decision making around economic surplus. Our aim is to make visible a broader spectrum of what economic development and interdependence can look like.

3999. Bolivia: Free Trade vs Sovereignty

Tom Loudon (Alliance for Responsible Trade)

Bolivia is in the midst of profound transformations in this historic moment. Come join us for a session where we learn around strategic changes occurring in Bolivia as the country shifts from a system of domination to one of sovereignty. As an alternative to the 'free trade' model, the Bolivian government is promoting 'A Peoples Trade Agreement' based on a radically different set of values and principles. We will explore how successful experiences and lessons learned from Bolivia can inform our struggle in the U.S. Context.

3996. The North and the South united against the FTAA and 'Free Trade': the experience of the Hemispheric Social Alliance

Tom Loudon (Alliance for Responsible Trade)

The HSA is a space in which social movements throughout the Hemisphere; North, Central and South America and the Caribbean come together to resist the imposition of the neoliberal model on our countries and peoples. From the outset, the HSA wanted to promote a vision of the world we would like to see as well mounting resistance to the policies and structures we oppose. Now that the FTAA has been thwarted by social movements and governments from the South who are creating, 'in real time,' alternatives to the old model, the HSA is redefining and re-envisioning how we can best contribute to the deepening and expansion of these new models. Come hear from, dialogue and strategize with sisters and brothers from Bolivia, Argentina, Brazil, Costa Rica, El Salvador, Mexico, Canada and other countries in the Hemisphere about the principles and values which guide this movement, the current continental struggles, and ways we can work together to forge a broader based movement.

2738. Katrina and Co-operative Solutions

Cornelius Blanding (Federation of Southern Cooperatives)

On Monday, August 29, 2005, Hurricane Katrina slammed into the Gulf Coast Region upsetting the lives and livelihoods of thousands of people including Federation/LAF member farmers, families and surrounding rural communities - as well as devastating the urban communities of New Orleans, Gulf Port and Biloxi. The impact of the effects of this hurricane was massive at all levels. In the workshop we will discuss cooperative solutions for a rural recovery and rural disaster preparedness in the community and through government policy changes. The panel will include cooperative development experts from the Federation staff; farmers and fishermen impacted by Katrina.

3377. Immigrants, Globalization and Organizing for Rights, Solidarity, and Economic Justice

Germai Medhanie, Guramylay: Growing the Green Economy
John Jairo Lugo, Unidad Latina en Accion

This panel will focus on issues of immigrant issues and organizing. Germai Medhanie will discuss his experience as an Eritrean immigrant, including the global conditions causing Eritrean immigration to the U.S.; the depoliticization of many first generation Eritrean and Ethiopian immigrants; the use of recent African immigrants as token Blacks in the labor market; and the need for African immigrants to build solidarity with African Americans and other people of color. John Jairo Lugo, a Columbian immigrant, will discuss his organizing work with Unidad Latina en Accion in New Haven, Connecticut.

4106. U.S. Inequality and What We Can Do About It

Tom Masterson, Union for Radical Political Economy, Levy Institute, CPE
Suresh Naidu, Center for Popular Economics
Geert Dhondt, Center for Popular Economics

The panel will address economic inequality in the US from three perspectives: measurement, policy and collective action. We will present alternative measures of inequality and discuss their differences. We will present policy proposals that directly address economic inequality. And we will discuss the role of collective action in addressing economic inequality.

3711. U.S. Changing the Federal Budget from the Grassroots Up: Facts and Strategies for Justice

Anita Dancs, National Priorities Project, Center for Popular Economics
Keisha Carter, Women's Action for a New Direction (WAND)

This workshop will provide an overview of the federal budget, how it impacts local communities and what activists can do. Atlanta has a child poverty rate of 58.8%! Yet the Iraq War costs Atlanta taxpayers 1/3 of a million dollars a day every day since the war began. This is an example of the upside down priorities this workshop will address. We'll provide: Cost figures on the war for your state, congressional district, local communities, and what else it could buy; Preventive national security strategies that are more effective and less costly than Pentagon spending; Proven coalition-building actions to strengthen a movement and hold elected officials accountable; Specific legislation that would significantly change how we spend our tax dollars.

2791. Household Economic Justice Strategies

John Parker (Good Work)
johnp@goodwork.org

Our workshop on household economic justice strategies provides space to tell stories, discuss, and map the various strategies and practices households can take to create an alternative solidarity economy that builds relationships and strengthens community. The strategies that will be presented for discussion include organizing around asset-based community development, household and workplace democracy processes, economic justice organizing that builds solidarity and community across differences, community development financial institutions, community investing & socially responsible investments; debt & debt reduction; social change giving and community-based philanthropy; lifestyle changes that move a household toward greater simplicity, environmental stewardship, and sustainability; just consumerism and buying local; self-employment, enterprise development, cooperatives, and social entrepreneurship; organizing around meaningful work and good jobs; and spiritual practices for reflection, learning, renewal, and sustainability.

Allied Events

1678. Race, Property and the Commons
POCLAD and The Alliance for Democracy
Jan Edwards

3525. Community Land Trusts As An Anti-Gentrification Tool
San Francisco Community Land Trust
Tom Wetzel

1721. Big Box Retailer Organizing & International Day of Action
Big Box Collaborative
Trina Tocco

1833. Globalization At the Crossroads
Environmental Health Coalition
Jorge Osuna

1842. Navigating the Great Turning: From Empire to Earth Community
YES! Magazine
Fran Korten

2151. Food Sovereignty: Building Sustainable Futures for Farmers Globally - 4 - Food Sovereignty Perspectives on Biofuels
Grassroots International
NikhilAziz

2430. Creating Jobs and Keeping Jobs: Women's Perspectives on alternatives for sustainable livelihoods
Center of Concern
Kristin Sampson

2563. Creating the Local Green Economy: Success Stories from the Grassroots
Global Exchange

2738. A Model for Rural Disaster Response: Katrina and Cooperative Solutions
Federation of Southern Cooperatives/Land Assistance
Cornelius Blanding

2806. California's 'Global Warming Solutions Act' and Blue-Green Alliances - Which Way Forward?
URPE - Union for Radical Political Economics
Dave Shukla

3003. Promoting Black Environmental Thought and Action
AfroEco
Rose Brewer

3011. Permaculture's Role In Addressing Our Environmental and Social Crisis
Earth Activist Training
Eileen Rose

3757. Community Benefits Agreements: Accessing Community Power to Impact Development
Georgia Stand-Up
Melissa Conrad

3821. Building Local Living Economies As an Alternative to Globalization
Business Alliance for Local Living Economies BALLE

3863. Beyond Neoliberalism: Alternatives from Latin America and Beyond
50 Years Is Enough Network
Ruth Castel-Branco

3960. Using Methods of Green Building to Develop Affordable Housing
WE ACT, Greenproofing, West Harlem Group Assistance
Laurel MeiTurbin

4033. Taking on Global Warming starts w/ the US - Building a Movement from the Ground Up
Labor/Community Strategy Center
Tammy Luu

4089. Doing It For Ourselves: Local Solutions to Build National Power for Climate Justice
EJ & Climate Change Init, Ella Baker Cntr, GAIA
Alli Chagi-Starr

1606. Taking Back the Land
Max Rameau
Center for Pan-African Development

2717. Saving Black Owned Land
Federation of Southern Cooperatives/Land Assistance
Cornelius Blanding

1597. Food Sovereignty Action Gathering
Stephen Bartlett
Agricultural Missions Inc. (AMI)

4053. Banana Transformation! Farmer-Ownership in a Global Marketplace
Isaac Grody-Patinkin
Oké USA

4048. Living Wage Campaigns: Building the Movement for Economic Justice
ACORN
Jen Kern

3926. Building Solidarity From Below: Grassroots Labor Activism Today
Labor Notes
Mark Brenner

3299. Right to the City: Building a National Movement Against Displacement and Gentrification
Tenants and Workers United
Alicia Schwartz

3256. Whose City? Our City!: Blacks and Latinos Fighting Gentrification in Miami
Workers Center
Joseph Phelan

3097. A War Economy or an Economy for Peace?
Kate Zaidan

2756. High School Students: Make your School Sweatfree!
Liana Foxvog
SweatFree Communities

2642. Fair Trade Means Another World is Here!
Global Exchange and United Students for Fair Trade

2369. Introduction to Economics of Liberation
Nada Khader
Proutist Universal, WESPAC Foundation

1675. Tools For Change: the Women's Self-Reliance Program
Rose (Mirabai) Lord
Global Coalition for Peace (GCFP)

2285. The Revolution Will Not Be Funded: Beyond the Non-Profit Industrial Complex, Part I
Left Turn & INCITE!
Max Uhlenbeck

3950. Overcoming Financial Oppression: Rebuilding Community Via Collective Ownership
OneTorch Inc.
Pamela Jolly

2097. Food Sovereignty: Land and 'People' (Life Communities) in Harmony and Abundance
Agricultural Missions, Inc. (AMI)
Stephen Bartlett

2147. Food Sovereignty: Building Sustainable Futures for Farmers Globally - 1 - Fixing the Broken Food System
Grassroots International
NikhilAziz

2149. Food Sovereignty: Building Sustainable Futures for Farmers Globally - 3 - The 2007 U.S. Farm Bill
Grassroots International
NikhilAziz

4002. Food Justice Nourishes All Movements
Community Services Unlimited Inc.
Neelam Sharma

3011. Radical Sustainability and Regenerative Activism
Earth Activist Training
Eileen Rose

2629. Health Care Re-Imagined
Northeast Radical Herbalism Network
Jacoby Ballard

3707. Another Politics Is Possible: Living the Vision from Below and to the Left
Sista ii Sista, Immokolee Workers, Refugio
Eric Tang

4124. Unembedding Neoliberalism: Learning from Latin America
Global-Local Links Project and Yes! Magazine
GraceSloan

3800. We Are Not For Sale
World March of Women
DianeMatte

2675. International Campaign Against Coca-Cola
India Resource Center
Amit Srivastava

4057. Hopes and Dreams, Esperanzas y Sueños / Street Vendors and their Youth / Inter-generational Organizing
Esperanza del Barrio/Sueños Del Barrio
Rafael Samanez

1757. The Coalition of Immokalee Workers: Fighting for Fair Food
Coalition of Immokalee Workers
JuliaPerkins

2597. Migrant's Rights & Corporate Globalization
Chicago Jobs With Justice
Jerry Mead-Lucero

3558. Approaches To Organizing On Trade
Grassroots Global Justice
JonathanKissamue

1998. Community Organizing To Build Worker Power: Bridging The Gaps
Chicago Jobs With Justice
CarlosFernand

2409. Sweatshops & Sweatshops In the Fields: What Can You Do About It?
International Labor Rights Fund
Beth Myers, STITCH (immigration and women)
Trina Tocco, International Labor Rights Fund (garments)
Charity Ryerson, USLEAP (bananas & cut flowers)
Liana Foxvog, SweatFree Communities (local government policies)

2635. Using Your University To Support International Worker Organizing

United Students Against Sweatshops
ZackKnorr

2954. Coalitions That Work: Jobs With Justice Model of Uniting Community, Faith, Student and Labor
Jobs With Justice – National
FranTobin

4045. Service Workers Rising: Building Power for Service Workers at Home and Globally
UNITE HERE
Abbie Illenberger

3926. Building Solidarity from Below: Grassroots Labor Activism Today
Labor Notes
Mark Brenner

2588. Creating Jobs and Keeping Jobs: Women's Perspectives On Alternatives For Sustainable Livelihoods
Sociologists for Women in Society
Marina Karides

2133. Day 1: "Raising Awareness of the State of the World"
Share The World's Resources (STWR)
Rajesh Makwana

2135. Day 2: "Envisioning a Better World"
Share The World's Resources (STWR)
Rajesh Makwana

2136. Day 3: "Strategies for creating a better world"
Share The World's Resources (STWR)
Rajesh Makwana

2537. Tools for Organizers in the Global Economy: Education to Build Worker Power
Solidarity Center and UC Berkeley Labor Center
Cathy Feingold

Appendix B

Annotated Bibliography:
Some Sources for More Information
About the Solidarity Economy

Jenna Allard

Articles

Miller, Ethan. "Solidarity Economics: Strategies for Building New Economies from the Bottom-Up and the Inside-Out"
http://www.geo.coop/SolidarityEconomicsEthanMiller.htm
> *A tool to place solidarity economy initiatives into a "whole economy" context and to facilitate discussion regarding possible areas for relationship-building and strategic intervention*

Reintjes, Carol. "What is a Solidarity Economy?"
http://www.zmag.org/carolase.htm
> *An outline of the Solidarity Economy issues discussed at the World Social Forum 2003.*

Reyes, Alma Cecilia and Jorge Santiago Santiago. "Solidarity Economy", an excerpt from the book, "Si Uno Come, Que Coman Todos, Economia Solidaria", translated by Chris Treter
http://www.globalexchange.org/countries/americas/mexico/ppp/desmi.html
> *A description of the solidarity economy, and how it contrasts with the neoliberal economy, as well as list of fundamental elements and principles of the solidarity economy.*

Manish Verma. "What is the Solidarity Economy?"
http://www.awid.org/go.php?stid=811
> *A personal investigation of the solidarity economy as an example of an economy where "money is not God"*

Documents

Brazilian Forum of Solidarity Economy. "The Management and Organization Experience of the Solidarity Economy Movement in Brazil"
http://www.fbes.org.br/docs/Brazilian_Solidarity_Economy_Movement.pdf
A case study of the actors and organizational strategies of the solidarity economy movement in Brazil.

Latin American Confederation of Cooperatives and Worker's Associations. "Solidarity Economics: An alternative for development, equity, social justice, and peace in Colombia"
http://www.zmag.org/content/VisionStrategy/colacot-solidarityecon.cfm
A vision statement of how the solidarity economy differs from the neoliberal model of development, and can be used to bring peace, equity, and justice to Columbia.

European Conference on Awareness-Raising and Development education for North-South Solidarity, Brussels, 2005. "Solidarity Economy and Fair Trade"
http://www.dgci.be/documents/en/topics/european_conference_public_aware ness/solidarity_economy_fairtrade.pdf
A pamphlet on the possibilities for North-South solidarity through solidarity finance, sustainable tourism, and fair trade.

Third International Meeting on the Globalization of Solidarity, Dakar, 2005. "Solidarity Socioeconomy as an Integral New System: Global Vision"
http://www.transformationcentral.org/solidarity/solidaritydocuments/dakar05 vision.pdf
Various short essays about the solidarity economy, in English and Spanish, as well as an annex of different terms relating to the solidarity economy.

Networks

U.S. Solidarity Economy Network (U.S. SEN)
http://www.ussen.org

Alliance for a Responsible, Plural, and United World (Alliance 21)
http://www.alliance21.org/2003/sommaire_en.php3

Intercontinental Network for the Promotion of the Social Solidarity Economy
(RIPESS)
http://www.ripess.net/en/default.htm

Collections of Articles

Workgroup on Socio-Solidarity Economy Documents Page
http://www.socioeco.org/en/documents.php

B.C.- Alberta Social Economy Research Alliance (BALTA)
http://auspace.athabascau.ca:8080/dspace/handle/2149/457

Grassroots Economic Organizing (GEO)
http://www.geo.coop/

Index

D

E

F